MODERN MORAL PHILOSOPHY IN THE NINETEENTH CENTURY

Stephen Darwall is a moral philosopher who has played a central role in contemporary debates around the foundation of ethics. This book is a sequel to his earlier volume *Modern Moral Philosophy: From Grotius to Kant*, and like its predecessor it explores the history of the period through its key ethical thinkers. Fichte, Hegel, Marx, Kierkegaard, and Nietzsche – the founding members of the "continental" tradition – are masterfully examined as they are brought into vivid conversation with both analytic philosophy and the mainstream Anglophone philosophical tradition. The author addresses topics that include the utilitarianism of Bentham and Mill; the anti-naturalism of Sidgwick and the British idealists; and Nietzsche's late century critique of morality. He reveals that all these canonical thinkers – just like their precursors and successors – were wrestling with fundamental and enduring modern ethical problems, even when they claimed otherwise or were presenting their views in new and challenging terms.

STEPHEN DARWALL is the Andrew Downey Orrick Professor of Philosophy at Yale. He is the author of *The Second-Person Standpoint* (2006), in fundamental ethical theory, and *Modern Moral Philosophy: From Grotius to Kant* (2023), in the history of ethics.

MODERN MORAL PHILOSOPHY IN THE NINETEENTH CENTURY

STEPHEN DARWALL
Yale University

CAMBRIDGE
UNIVERSITY PRESS

CAMBRIDGE
UNIVERSITY PRESS

Shaftesbury Road, Cambridge CB2 8EA, United Kingdom

One Liberty Plaza, 20th Floor, New York, NY 10006, USA

477 Williamstown Road, Port Melbourne, VIC 3207, Australia

314–321, 3rd Floor, Plot 3, Splendor Forum, Jasola District Centre,
New Delhi – 110025, India

103 Penang Road, #05–06/07, Visioncrest Commercial, Singapore 238467

Cambridge University Press is part of Cambridge University Press & Assessment,
a department of the University of Cambridge.

We share the University's mission to contribute to society through the pursuit of
education, learning and research at the highest international levels of excellence.

www.cambridge.org
Information on this title: www.cambridge.org/9781009543873

DOI: 10.1017/9781009543835

When citing this work, please include a reference to the DOI 10.1017/9781009543835

First published 2025

Printed in Great Britain by CPI Group (UK) Ltd, Croydon CR0 4YY

A catalogue record for this publication is available from the British Library

Library of Congress Cataloging-in-Publication data
NAMES: Darwall, Stephen L., 1946– author
TITLE: Modern moral philosophy in the nineteenth century / Stephen Darwall,
Yale University, Connecticut.
DESCRIPTION: 1. | Cambridge, United Kingdom ; New York, NY : Cambridge University
Press, 2025. | Includes bibliographical references and index.
IDENTIFIERS: LCCN 2025014887 | ISBN 9781009543873 hardback | ISBN 9781009543866
paperback | ISBN 9781009543835 ebook
SUBJECTS: LCSH: Ethics – History – 19th century
CLASSIFICATION: LCC BJ1012 .D324 2025
LC record available at https://lccn.loc.gov/2025014887

ISBN 978-1-009-54387-3 Hardback

For the many teachers, colleagues, and students from whom I have learned so much

Contents

Preface

This is the second of three projected volumes on modern moral philosophy in the West.[1] The first was *Modern Moral Philosophy: From Grotius to Kant* (Darwall 2023a), and the third will be *Modern Moral Philosophy in the Twentieth Century*. All three are framed by the challenge Elizabeth Anscombe famously issued in "Modern Moral Philosophy" that Western ethical philosophers' focus on deontic *morality* during this period has been substantially misplaced (Anscombe 1958). (More on this in the Introduction.)

In this volume, I am much more out of my depth than I was in Darwall (2023a). I had been thinking about most of the figures I wrote about there for about forty years. Not so with the philosophers we encounter here, except for Bentham and Mill. I owe to Karsten Harries my initial exposure to post-Kantian "continental" philosophy. In my sophomore year at Yale, he taught a wonderful course on existentialism, which began with Kierkegaard's *Either/Or* before going on to Heidegger's *Being and Time* and Sartre's *Being and Nothingness*. I still have the books for that course, although I am embarrassed by my annotations.

As I mentioned in the preface to Darwall (2023a), I agreed over twenty years ago to write what Cambridge and I then thought would be one volume on the history of modern ethics. Painfully aware of my ignorance of various periods and important figures, especially post-Kantian continental thinkers, I undertook to fill in some of the gaps. Allow me to quote from the preface to Darwall (2023a) concerning what ensued:

> I began to study Fichte and Hegel and came upon Allen Wood's *Hegel's Ethical Thought*. There I found Wood's chapter on Fichte and its section "Fichte's theory of recognition." I read this with something approaching ecstatic endorsement, with a resounding "yes!" as

[1] I should say, "now projected," since the first sentence of the preface of the first volume spoke of two volumes, rather than three!

> Nietzsche might put it (Wood 1990: 77–93; Nietzsche 2007: 377). Encountering for the first time Fichte's idea that it takes a "summons" (*Aufforderung*) from another person to gain practical consciousness of our own freedom, and that this reciprocal awareness of summoned and summoner alike can ground fundamental principles of a theory of equal right, it felt as if the scales had fallen from my eyes (Fichte 2000: 35–83).
>
> I came face-to-face with an idea that, as I allowed it to penetrate my thought fully over the weeks and months to come, seemed to me to provide the missing piece necessary to adequately ground morality, something I had been searching for perhaps my entire philosophical life.
>
> I pretty much put aside my historical project and devoted myself to the ideas developed in *The Second Person Standpoint* and subsequent essays (Darwall 2006, 2013a, 2013b).
> (Darwall 2023a: xii).

In the early 2010s, I returned to doing history of philosophy with work on Grotius, Pufendorf, Kant, Smith, and other figures, hoping to build momentum for my long-ago promised history. It is in this volume that I lay out the results of my interrupted work on nineteenth-century philosophy, beginning with the figure Johann Gottlieb Fichte, whose *Foundations of Natural Right* set me on my systematic philosophical path so many years ago.

Although I had read around in Fichte, Hegel, Marx, Kierkegaard, Nietzsche, and the British idealists, what I found when I read them thoroughly, in relation both to their historical context and to contemporary philosophical debates, was a wealth of philosophical riches. Naturally, second-personal themes seemed almost to jump off the page of many of the nineteenth-century figures I discuss here, as they did with philosophers like Grotius, Pufendorf, Reid, and Smith, discussed in Darwall (2023a). In this volume, we encounter them most obviously in Fichte – seeing, as well, important differences in the way recognition functions in Fichte's view and the way it does in Hegel's – but also in Mill and T. H. Green. Green's conception of the common good includes, for example, "as participators of the good, all who have dealings with each other and who can communicate as 'I' and 'Thou'" (Green 2003: §209).

A running theme is the relation that different nineteenth-century philosophers have to "Anscombe's Challenge," which I will discuss at the beginning of the Introduction to follow. As we learn from Mill, this actually connects to the second-personal aspect of deontic morality. Mill says that "we do not call anything wrong unless we mean to imply that a person ought to be punished for doing it . . . [for example], by the reproaches of his own conscience" (Mill 2002: 5.14). Punishment, conceived as a form of accountability, rather than as penalty or sanction, and conscientious reproach are second-personal in their nature (Darwall 2006, 2013i).

As I note in the preface to Darwall (2023a):

> Since I have "a horse in the race," readers will want to keep my philosophical biases in mind. I can only hope that my having something at stake as a philosopher makes for a more philosophically engaged (and engaging) historical account. My biases may make me sensitive to things others might not see, though perhaps I am just looking through "second-personal glasses" that distort my reading of texts and obscure important historical context. I hope my fellow historians of ethics, and you, dear reader, will keep me honest. Recalling the old Russian proverb that Reagan loved to quote to Gorbachev – "Trust, but verify" – I hope you will ignore the first and pursue the second (xiii).

Acknowledgments

I should begin with my debt to Paul Guyer, Gary Hatfield, and the late Terry Moore of Cambridge University Press, for the original invitation to write a history of early modern ethics. As readers of the preface to Darwall (2023a) will know, that was well over twenty years ago, and they, and, more recently, Hilary Gaskin of Cambridge, have been extraordinarily patient as I took a detour to work out the second-personal framework laid out in Darwall (2006, 2013a, and 2013b). I am very grateful to all of them for their forbearance.

I dedicate this book to the teachers, colleagues, and students from whom I have learned so much about nineteenth-century ethical philosophy. This begins with Karsten Harries, who taught the course on existentialism at Yale that I mentioned in the Preface. When I was an undergraduate, Allen Wood was a graduate student at Yale, and though I didn't know him then, he was a grader in one or two of my courses, not, I think, in Harries's course. My debt to Wood is mostly to his writings, and to conversations with him through the years. Yale was a center of study of continental philosophy during my years as an undergraduate, so although I was mainly attracted to analytical approaches, I have always had an appreciation for phenomenology. That has only grown.

In Darwall (2023a), I expressed my appreciation to Jerry Schneewind, who was one of my teachers at the University of Pittsburgh. I thanked him for a seminar he gave on Hobbes, Hume, and Kant, and for all of the marvelous work he did subsequently on early modern moral philosophy, including pretty much all the figures I discuss in that book. What Schneewind was primarily working on during the period I was at Pittsburgh, however, was his great work, *Sidgwick's Ethics and Victorian Ethical Philosophy* (Schneewind 1977). It was partly engaging with Schneewind that led to my first paper on Sidgwick – "Pleasure as Ultimate Good in Sidgwick's Ethics" (Darwall 1974) – and to thinking about Sidgwick ever since.

During my years at the University of North Carolina (UNC) at Chapel Hill, I was exposed to David Falk's wide knowledge about the history of ethics, including nineteenth-century figures. I recall doing a reading course with an undergraduate there on Hegel's *Philosophy of Right* and supervising Jeannette Falk's MA thesis on Bradley. During my later years at UNC, Jerry Postema was a close colleague from whom I learned a lot on Bentham.

At Michigan, Frithjof Bergmann's work on Nietzsche and other continental figures helped to keep them salient for me during a period when Jerry Schneewind jokingly referred to me as an "analytic thug." I worked there with Nadeem Hussain and Gabriel Zamosc-Regueros on dissertations on Nietzsche. Happily, Michelle Kosch arrived as an assistant professor at Michigan just after I had discovered Fichte through Wood's writings, and a seminar she gave on Fichte's *The System of Ethics* was especially eye-opening for me. Her *Fichte's Ethics* and *Freedom and Reason in Kant, Schelling, and Kierkegaard* are among the best books that exist on their respective topics. I have learned an enormous amount from her.

Returning to Yale in 2008 brought me back to a department that both cherishes the history of philosophy and its relation to contemporary debates, and that has always valued philosophical "pluralism," at a time when I was especially open to it. The arrival of Paul Franks, who became a valued interlocutor, brought us an expert on Fichte. Moreover, Karsten Harries remained a strong presence in the department, as he had been when I was an undergraduate, until his retirement a few years ago. I also worked with Dylan Vollans on his dissertation on Nietzsche. Most recently, after I had written a draft of the chapters in Part II, I gave a seminar on Marx, Kierkegaard, and Nietzsche that was extremely helpful in formulating my ideas. I am grateful to the students in that seminar for their insights. Since I began teaching at Yale, I have found it an unparalleled environment to do philosophically engaged history of philosophy. It has been wonderful also to work with Jacob McNulty, who joined the faculty recently. His knowledge of nineteenth- and twentieth-century continental thinkers, most relevantly here, Hegel, has been a godsend. Even more recently, we have been joined by Robert Gooding-Williams, who in addition to being a preeminent scholar of Black political thought, is a specialist on Nietzsche. Even those whose publications seem ahistorical often have serious historical interests, such as Shelly Kagan's in Sidgwick. And it is also wonderful to be around such excellent systematic philosophers. Without Yale and those who have been there over the years, this book would not exist.

There are also many colleagues outside the departments where I have been employed from whom I have learned an enormous amount, for example, in addition to Wood, Robert Pippin, Robert Brandom, Frederick Neuhouser, and Terry Pinkard on Fichte and Hegel. David Brink's work on Mill, Sidgwick, and Green has always been especially informative, and I have benefitted enormously from philosophical conversations with him over the years. David Phillips's work on Sidgwick has also been very helpful, as have our conversations.

I am especially indebted to John Rawls. Although Rawls is mostly known for his systematic work, he had a thorough grasp of the history of ethics that informed his philosophical theories, as is shown both by the footnotes to *A Theory of Justice* and *Political Liberalism* and by his volumes *Lectures on the History of Moral Philosophy* and *Lectures on the History of Political Philosophy* (Rawls 2000, 2007). Rawls has always been a model for me of the importance of the history of ethics for systematic ethical philosophy, and vice versa.

Peddling my second-personal ideas through Europe, I have increasingly come into contact with continental versions of related ideas, for example, in Habermas, Levinas, and Apel, which have their roots in Fichte and Hegel. Exchange with European philosophers working on nineteenth-century figures, like Sebastian Rödl on Fichte, has been both illuminating and inspiring. I am thankful, too, to all the European departments that hosted me as I worked on this book.

I am also grateful for all of the supporting infrastructure, institutional, personal, and physical, that has supported my work, some in perhaps unexpected ways. Most obvious are excellent libraries, especially at the University of Michigan and at Yale, and through them, access to the increasingly vast collections of nineteenth-century philosophical materials online.

I am especially appreciative for research support from various sources. Yale University provided a Triennial Leave, which, added to a National Endowment for the Humanities fellowship and a fellowship from the John Simon Guggenheim Memorial Foundation, made it possible for me to devote the 2023–2024 academic year to working on this and the companion volume, *Modern Moral Philosophy in the Twentieth Century*, yet to come. Also, a grant from Yale's A. Whitney Griswold Faculty Fund helped with copy editing and indexing.

There are also many other, less obvious, sources of support. Ever since I read Bertrand Russell's *Autobiography* while in graduate school, and his account there of his long philosophical walks both alone and with G. E. Moore, I have become a peripatetic philosopher. Almost every original idea I have ever had alone has occurred while I was on the move: running, walking, swimming, cycling, or driving. I am grateful therefore to the Payne Whitney Gymnasium Practice Pool at Yale and the pool at the Hampshire Regional YMCA in Northampton, Massachusetts, where I live with my wife Laura. I am thankful also for the highways and byways I have frequented during the writing of this book: to the streets I walk in New Haven and Northampton, especially through the meadows by the Oxbow of the Connecticut River – where Jonathan Edwards had his philosophical thoughts more than 250 years ago. And to I-91, which runs from Northampton to New Haven and back.

Of course, many good ideas have come in conversation with those to whom I dedicate this book. In addition to academic colleagues and students, I am grateful to friends, like Andrew Ford and Frank Marotta, who have shown interest in my philosophical scholarship and helped me to see new angles, as has of course been true with all the philosophers I have discussed the book with over the past several years.

I am indebted, again, to Hilary Gaskin at Cambridge University Press, and to two anonymous reviewers for their helpful comments.

Molly Montgomery copy edited and did the index for this book, as she did for Darwall (2023) and Darwall (2024). I would not want to contemplate writing books without her. Her judgment is flawless, and her friendship is dear to me.

Closer to home, many conversations with my son, Will Darwall, have greatly deepened my grasp of Marx. Will was also helpful in presenting and discussing Marx in the seminar mentioned earlier. My other son, Julian Darwall, is a constant source of support: philosophical, intellectual, and emotional. I could not be more grateful to my sons. My debt to Laura Radwell is inestimable. She was willing, first, to live with, then to embrace and more fully to engage with, my obsession for philosophical work. Without her love and support, life would be a much less joyful thing.

Introduction

Anscombe's Challenge

As in the first volume, my attention here will be devoted mainly, though hardly entirely, to ethical philosophers' attempts to come to grips with deontic morality understood in the terms of Anscombe's critique. Sometimes, these will be defenses and theoretical accounts, as with, for example, the nineteenth-century utilitarians – whether empiricist, like Bentham and Mill, or "philosophical intuitionist," like Henry Sidgwick – or the moral theories of British idealists like T. H. Green and F. H. Bradley. But unlike mainstream seventeenth- and eighteenth-century moral philosophy – for instance, the modern natural lawyers, Grotius, Pufendorf, Hobbes, Locke, and Cumberland, the British rationalists, and Kant – the ethical philosophy of the nineteenth century is more often concerned to criticize deontic morality or to put it in its place. Examples here are Hegel, Marx, Kierkegaard, and, of course, Nietzsche.

It will help to set out briefly the main lines of Anscombe's critique (summarizing the opening pages of Darwall 2023a: 2–3). Anscombe's most basic problem with modern ethical philosophy was that it is, as she put it, "*moral* philosophy." It concerns, even if not exclusively, what it calls *morality*: a set of putatively universal deontic or "juridical" norms of right and wrong that purport to *obligate* all normal human adults, indeed, all *moral agents*, as it terms beings who have the capacity to respond to obligation. Anscombe called this a "law conception" of ethics (Anscombe 1958: 5) since it posits a moral law of right and wrong, what Grotius and his followers called "natural law" (5).

The individuals who populate modern moral philosophy are *moral agents* or persons. "Person" is, Locke says, "a Forensick Term" that "belongs only to intelligent Agents capable of a Law" (Locke 1975: 346). To be "capable of a Law," in Locke's sense, someone must have the capacity to guide themselves by the moral law, which binds them simply as one moral agent among others. For many, maybe most, modern moral philosophers, it is not enough that they be able to comply with the law from whatever motive, say, fear of "external sanctions." They must have be able to be moved by what Mill calls the "internal sanction" of conscience (Mill 2002: III.6). They must be capable of knowing what morality requires and acting as required, for that very reason.

However, Anscombe thought it obvious that no practical law of any kind can exist without a lawgiver. So there can be a moral law only if it has a legislator whose jurisdiction transcends any posited earthly realm, even, indeed, that of the international law (*jus gentium*) that Grotius himself helped to originate in the early modern period.[1] Anscombe concluded that there can be such a thing as morality only if it is legislated by God.

The idea that morality binds only because it is divinely legislated has certainly been represented in modern moral philosophy, for example, in seventeenth-century natural lawyers like Pufendorf and Locke. But it has been a decidedly minority view. Certainly this was true in the nineteenth century. Most moral philosophers then, as now, were content to employ the essentially juridical concept of morality without grounding it in divine legislation. And many denied that morality is even the kind of thing that *could* be legislated, even by God. It is not some existing thing that was made actual by creation or legislation. It is an essentially normative deontic structure. Anscombe thought that this left modern deontic concepts with no "discernible content except a certain compelling ['psychological'] force" (Anscombe 1958: 18).

In Darwall (2023a), I called this "Anscombe's Challenge," which Anscombe posed to much of the ethical philosophy in the West since the early seventeenth century. I think that Anscombe was unquestionably right that a central feature of "modern moral philosophy" has been its fundamentally deontic or juridical character, though I am more sanguine than she that her challenge can be met. Modern moral philosophers have indeed been concerned to articulate, understand, defend, and attempt to ground *morality* with its distinctively obligating normativity, and many of their attempts are promising.

Even modern critics of the idea of morality – most prominently, Nietzsche, but also more qualified critics like Bernard Williams – have focused on the deontic features that Anscombe identifies. In seeking to overturn or at least rein in deontic morality they have implicitly accepted

[1] Grotius's *De jure belli at pacis* (*The Rights of War and Peace*) was published in 1625 (Grotius 2005).

her point that it has been a, if not the, central focus of modern ethical thought (Williams 1985: 1–4, 174–196; Nietzsche 2007).

The nineteenth-century figures we shall consider in this volume are either defenders or critics of deontic morality. Nietzsche, of course, is an unmitigated critic. But Kierkegaard and Marx are mitigated critics in different ways. And so is Hegel, perhaps, though more modestly. On the other side, the nineteenth-century utilitarians are mostly solid defenders. Mill begins *Utilitarianism* by decrying "the little progress which has been made . . . respecting the criterion of right and wrong" (Mill 2002: I.1). This makes clear that Mill's aim in *Utilitarianism* is to defend the principle of utility as a deontic "criterion of right and wrong." It also reflects Bentham's agenda-setting influence since he did much to shift utilitarianism's focus from assessment of motive and character to concern with the rightness and wrongness of acts.

Ancient versus Modern

Anscombe's challenge is one marker of a difference between modern moral philosophy and the ethical philosophy of the ancient Greeks and their followers, including the classical natural law tradition of Aquinas. A second, as Sidgwick pointed out, is that where the ancients were generally eudaimonists or, in Sidgwick's terms, egoists, modern moral philosophers, including many nineteenth-century figures, like Sidgwick, were not. As he put it memorably: "In Greek moral philosophy generally, but one regulative and governing faculty is recognised under the name of Reason . . . ; in the modern ethical view, when it has worked itself clear, there are found to be two, – Universal Reason and Egoistic Reason, or Conscience and Self-love" (Sidgwick 1964 : 198). This is a contrast within what philosophers these days call "normativity" or the force of normative reasons or oughts.

This is connected to the central aspiration of deontic morality: to provide moral agents *reasons* intrinsic to morality – rather than eudaimonist considerations of self-interest – for complying with moral duties. Thus although Mill calls the normative reason to be moral an "internal sanction," it is clear he is denying the eudaimonist position that any reason to comply with morality must be a consideration of the good of doing so:

> The internal sanction of duty, whatever our standard of duty may be, is one and the same – a feeling in our own mind; a pain, more or less intense, attendant on violation of duty, which in properly cultivated moral natures

> rises, in the more serious cases, into shrinking from it as an impossibility. This feeling, when disinterested, and connecting itself with the pure idea of duty, and not with some particular form of it, or with any of the merely accessory circumstances, is the essence of Conscience. (Mill 2002: III.6)

Mill is but one example of a nineteenth-century philosopher who aims to argue the fact that an action is morally wrong is reason *in itself* not to do it. As we shall see, Kierkegaard is another, although he is a mitigated critic of morality even so.

"Continental" and "Analytic" Canons

A third theme running through this book concerns figures who look forward to what will be called "continental" and "analytic" philosophy in the twentieth century. Both schools proudly claim most modern philosophers up through Kant as ancestors, but the lines then divide. Post-Kantian German idealists, like Fichte and Hegel, and later, Kierkegaard and Nietzsche, pursue a phenomenological approach that is formulated in more explicitly phenomenological terms in twentieth-century thinkers like Husserl and Heidegger. Among the ethical philosophers we will be considering, Bentham, Mill, and Sidgwick pursue philosophical approaches that would come to be called analytical.

As it happens, Bentham, Mill, and Sidgwick are all theorists of deontic morality. This is most explicit in Bentham and Mill. Sidgwick turns out to be more equivocal. On the one hand, he cites the "quasi-jural" character of modern morality and a major difference between ancient and modern ethical thought. According to "the Greek schools" of ethics, Sidgwick says:

> right action is commonly regarded as only a species of the Good . . . Their speculations can scarcely be understood by us unless with a certain effort we throw the quasi-jural notions of modern ethics aside, and ask (as they did) not "What is Duty and what is its ground?" but "Which of the objects that men think good is truly Good or the Highest Good?" (Sidgwick 1962: 105–106).

On the other hand, his "Axiom of Rational Benevolence," which comprises, along with the "Axiom of Prudence," Sidgwick's "dualism of practical reason," is formulated entirely in nondeontic terms.

Rawls calls Sidgwick's *Methods of Ethics*, "the first truly academic work in moral philosophy" (Sidgwick 1981: 2). By this, Rawls means that Sidgwick's careful way of laying out different ethical theories or "methods" so that their costs and benefits can be assessed for pedagogical, as well as for systematic adjudicatory, purposes, arguably originated with him. Sidgwick's project, moreover, is generally taken up by self-styled academic philosophers more than continental ones. In Darwall (in press), I will be arguing that G. E. Moore's *Principia Ethica* (1903), which has been looked to as the founding work of analytic metaethics, began a divide between Moore's analytic followers and the continental ethical philosophy Moore so decisively rejects.

Sidgwick's analytic instincts are most apparent in his claim that all ethical judgments contain "the fundamental notion represented by the word ought" (Sidgwick 1962: 25). This is analytic philosophy par excellence. Moore credits Sidgwick with seeing that all ethical concepts must share a common basic notion, though Moore identifies it with good rather than ought (Moore 1993a: 69). Sidgwick did not, however, pursue a *program* of analytic philosophy in the way that Moore would.[2] Still, Moorean analytic metaethics undeniably descends from Sidgwick.

Another signal feature of Sidgwick's and other proto-analytic philosophizing that we will encounter in this volume is the aim of articulating *normative* ethical theories and fundamental "principles," not in their eighteenth-century sense as springs of action, but as standards or "criteria" of right and wrong. The aim of articulating normative moral *theories* is a hallmark of proto-analytic modern moral philosophy in the nineteenth century.

Modern Freedom and Individuality

A fourth theme is that defenders and detractors of deontic morality alike seek to lay out and justify distinctively modern forms of individuality and freedom. This is true of thinkers as diverse as Mill, Fichte, Kierkegaard, Bradley, and Nietzsche. Thus Mill says that "the free development of individuality is one of the leading essentials of well-being" (Mill 1977: 224). A central aspect of Fichte's critique of Kant is that for all of his concern with respect for persons as ends-in-themselves, he overlooks their individuality. Thus Fichte says that Kant cannot "understand by pure apperception the consciousness of our individuality or confuse one with the other." The latter is "necessarily accompanied by another consciousness, that of a Thou and is only possible on this condition."[3] Fichte's

[2] See, however, Hurka's arguments that little in Moore was really an analytical advance over Sidgwick (Hurka 2003, 2014).

[3] Quoted by Wood 2016: 86.

famous argument that a (second-personal) summons commits summoner and summoned alike to a fundamental principle of natural right is likewise connected to a form of individuality for which, as Fichte sees it, Kant's theories cannot account.

Nietzsche is another clear case of a defender of what he calls the "sovereign individual," but his defense is part of his critique of deontic morality. Nietzsche's autonomous individuals transcend the deontic moral ideas of their culture and attempt to realize an ethical conception that is "beyond good and evil." They create themselves as "autonomous, supra-ethical individual[s]" (Nietzsche 2007: 37). We find a similar idea in Kierkegaard, though, quite differently from Nietzsche, it is tied there to religious faith.

In the nineteenth century, ideals of individuality go together with conceptions of "subjective freedom," which is, Hegel says, "the pivotal and focal point in the difference between *antiquity* and the *modern* age" (Hegel 1991: 151). Freedom, in Hegel's subjective sense, is quite different than the freedom that is realized by practical reason, as in Kant. The latter is something that moral agents all actualize in the *same* way, following universal laws of pure practical reason. Subjective freedom, by contrast, is something we each realize in *our own* way, pursuing our own chosen paths. This is an aspect of the ancient/modern contrast that does not "work itself clear," to use Sidgwick's phrase, until the nineteenth century (Sidgwick 1964: 198). To be sure, a keystone of Kant's ethics is respect for one another's right to pursue our own ends. But Kant does not proclaim the *value* or good of our doing so in a way that nineteenth-century thinkers like Kierkegaard, Nietzsche, Mill, and the British idealists do. This turns out to be an important difference between Bradley and Green and those thinkers that Terence Irwin calls "Aristotelian Naturalists," with whom they otherwise share ideas.[4]

Social Freedom

One of Marx's great contributions to the history of ethics is his insight that many of our most important and intractable problems do not concern how we treat one another individually but how political, economic, and social structures in which we participate affect us, and that these are within collective human control. This is at the center of Marx's thought, for

[4] See Darwall 2023a for a discussion of the contrast between Irwin's conception of the history of ethics and the one I am providing in these volumes (Darwall 2023a: xlii–xliii).

example, in his rich account of the various forms of alienation to which human beings are subject in a capitalist political order in *Economic and Philosophic Manuscripts*, and also in his theory of exploitation in *Capital*. Although Marx is not himself a proponent of the idea of distributive justice because he thought that it was tied to capitalist political-economic orders, it became a staple of the moral and political philosophy of progressive thinkers in the late nineteenth and twentieth centuries (Fleischacker 2004). It is connected to the role that Mill gives social and political practices in his theory of justice and rights, and it is front and center in Rawls's signature claim that "justice is the first virtue of social institutions" (Rawls 1971: 3). When Nozick attacks Rawlsian "patterned principles," as he calls them in *Anarchy, State, and Utopia*, it is for thinking that justice can consist in structural features rather than properties of interactions between individuals (Nozick 1974: 156–159).

Marx, too, is the source of the idea that there is a distinctive kind of structural, social freedom or "liberation" that contrasts with various forms of social oppression, whether they are political-economic, like capitalism, or orders of oppressive gender or racial relations in patriarchy and white supremacy. The opposites of the latter are liberation from oppressive orders of these (structural) forms. Marx's insight also shows up in versions of non-ideal theory in the late twentieth century, like that of Charles Mills, that focus on resisting and overcoming structural racial oppression here and now rather than attempting to take steps toward some ideally just society (Mills 2005).

Social Activism and Moral Theory

Finally, an especially notable feature of nineteenth-century ethical philosophy is the connection many philosophers make between theory and practice. This is perhaps clearest with Marx, who in his *Theses on Feuerbach* famously says that "philosophers have only interpreted the world, in various ways; the point, however, is to change it" (Marx 1978b: 145). For Marx, one might say, adapting Kant's well-known phrase: "theory without practice is empty, practice without theory is blind."[5] Marx also put his money where his mouth was, working for radical social change, informed by theory, throughout his working life.

Marx is far from the only nineteenth-century philosopher who ties together philosophical theorizing with social and political activism. The

[5] A saying of William Sloane Coffin, who was chaplain at Yale during my time there as an undergraduate in the late 1960s.

utilitarianism of Bentham and Mill is tied closely to social and political reform. From Bentham's circle of "philosophical radicals" to the early Mill's activism against the Corn Laws to the mature Mill and Harriet Taylor's *The Subjection of Women* and feminist activism that it called for, the connection between theory and practice is a central feature of nineteenth-century moral and political philosophy. Indeed, this utilitarian line can be extended to Sidgwick since he was a strong promoter of women's educational rights at Cambridge.

The point is not that nineteenth-century ethical thought had practical effects that were lacking among that of earlier, say, eighteenth-century, thinkers. Kant's doctrine of the equal dignity of all persons and Grotius and Locke on natural rights obviously had enormous practical upshots. The difference was that Marx, Bentham, Mill, and Sidgwick were all themselves socially and politically active not just in disseminating their philosophical ideas but in attempting to put them into practice. And influence went in the other direction as well. As we shall see in Chapters 7 and 8, Bentham's deepest argument for the principle of utility is that it is uniquely suitable for free informed political debate, much like Rawls's arguments in *Political Liberalism*, and the most promising interpretation of Mill's utilitarianism is a rule or practice version that reckons the rightness and wrongness of acts in terms of the effects of social practices that hold people accountable for performing them.

Finally, a perhaps unexpected instance is the British idealist T. H. Green. Green's idealism calls for a social order in which participants share a common mutually accountable life whose benefits they can share. Green himself practiced what he preached in his work with the Liberal Party. Of course, not all nineteenth-century moral philosophers were activists. Obviously, Kierkegaard and Nietzsche were not.

PART I

Post-Kantian German Idealism

Viewed from our contemporary perspective, Western moral philosophy after Kant can seem to have two quite different trajectories. One, beginning with Johann Gottlieb Fichte (1762–1814) and Georg Wilhelm Friedrich Hegel (1770–1831), leads to what is frequently called "continental" philosophy. The other, running through figures like Jeremy Bentham (1748–1832), John Stuart Mill (1806–1873), and Henry Sidgwick (1838–1900), begins a tradition that is often termed "analytic" ethics. Although both traditions claim Kant as a predecessor, they diverge after him. Among Kant's successors, it was the proto-continentals, Fichte and Hegel, who worked most explicitly within Kant's framework of the critical philosophy and who began to develop what will be seen more clearly as a phenomenological approach in the twentieth century. But both also departed from Kant in significant ways. Each developed important ethical ideas of their own and bequeathed new ways of framing philosophical issues to later continental thinkers.

Although he is less well known than Hegel, Fichte may have been the more original and fertile moral philosopher. Allen Wood calls him "the most influential single figure on the entire tradition of continental European philosophy in the last two centuries" (Wood 2016: ix). Fichte's focus on the conditions, structures, and dialectical development of consciousness, and his contrast between alienating abstraction and harmonizing actuality, anticipate Hegel's better-known development of these themes. And there are further new developments in Fichte leading in the directions of other later figures, from Kierkegaard, Nietzsche, and Marx, to de Beauvoir and Sartre (Wood 2016).

For his part, Hegel's influence on later continental writers was massive (see, e.g., Rosen 1999). It was mainly through Hegel, indeed, that Fichte's dialectical treatment of consciousness came to structure later continental phenomenology. And it was also largely in response to Hegel that subsequent continental philosophical critics as diverse as Kierkegaard, Nietzsche, and Marx developed their ideas. Hegel was, as well, the main source for the British idealists Bradley and Green. And so was he also, through them, a major target of G. E. Moore's critique of idealism, which played such an important role in the development of analytic philosophy in the twentieth century, including analytic ethics and metaethics, and the creation of an analytic/continental divide.[1] Even Moore's own ethical philosophy bore Hegel's imprint in Moore's "principle of organic unities," which states that the value of a whole need not equal the sum of the values of its parts (Moore 1993a: 78–80).

[1] See chapter 1 of Darwall (unpublished), *Modern Moral Philosophy in the Twentieth Century.*

CHAPTER 1

Fichte

We begin with Fichte. It is Kant who stands most clearly behind Fichte's method of "transcendental philosophy." It was in response to his thought that Fichte's *Foundations of Natural Right* (1796) and *System of Ethics* (1798) were composed. Fichte's first exposure to Kant's works made him an "immediate and ardent convert" to the critical philosophy (Wood 2016: 6). In 1791, Fichte traveled to Königsberg to meet Kant, a meeting that evidently left Kant unimpressed. Undeterred, Fichte remained in Königsberg long enough to compose a short work, *Attempt at a Critique of All Revelation*, which Fichte presented to Kant a month later. The book sufficiently impressed Kant that he recommended it to his own publisher, and it became Fichte's first publication the following year.

What Fichte found most inspiring in Kant's critical philosophy was its Copernican focus on the transcendental conditions of conscious thought, its doctrine of the autonomy of reason, and, most especially, its fundamental commitment to freedom of the will (Wood 2016: 6). Like Kant's, Fichte's ethics are very much an ethics of freedom or autonomy, which, also like Kant's, are situated in a systematic critical or transcendental philosophy. The "fundamental motivation of Fichte's entire philosophy," Wood plausibly claims, "is moral and political" (29). Fichte tried to work out his overall *Foundations of Transcendental Philosophy* (*Wissenschaftslehre*) at various points in the 1790s in difficult and incomplete works. Happily, as Allen Wood and Michelle Kosch have shown, we need not delve into these to comprehend what is most significant in Fichte's moral and political thought (Wood 2016; Kosch 2018).

Kant's influence on Fichte's moral and political philosophy was profound, even beyond its transcendental philosophical setting. Kosch argues, indeed, that during much of the nineteenth century, philosophers primarily got their understanding of Kant's ethics from their reading of Fichte's (Kosch 2021). However, neither Fichte's *System of Ethics* nor his

Foundations of Natural Right could have been informed by close study of Kant's later ethical writings. *The Metaphysics of Morals*, which contained Kant's *Doctrines of Right* and *Virtue*, only appeared in 1797, after Fichte's *Foundations of Natural Right* (1796). And although Fichte's *System of Ethics* (1798) was published (just) after *The Metaphysics of Morals*, Fichte's earlier *Lectures on the Scholar's Vocation* (1794) already contained many of the *System*'s main ideas (Kosch 2018: 5).

Kant's and Fichte's philosophies of right are especially close in form and content. Both works treat the philosophy of right as a separate subject that is independent of ethical philosophy, and both ground their theories in a fundamental right of freedom from interference. Hegel makes a well-known remark in his *Philosophy of Right* that "the right of *subjective freedom*, is the pivotal and focal point in the difference between *antiquity* and the *modern* age" (Hegel 1991: 151). Fichte's *Foundations of Right* is, like Kant's and Hegel's treatises of right, a thoroughly modern text in this sense. Together they established freedom as a, if not *the*, central concept of modern political and legal philosophy. Thus we see, right at the outset, the importance of freedom in modern moral philosophy in Anscombe's sense.

We shall begin, however, with Fichte's ethics. As we shall see, Fichte's ethics of autonomy or, as he usually prefers to say, "self-sufficiency" or "independence," departs from Kant's in several important ways. The most important structurally is that whereas autonomy is at the heart of grounding what Kant takes to be the fundamentally *formal* character of the moral law – the will's capacity to be "a law to itself (independently of any property of the objects of volition)" (Kant 1996a: 4:440; 1996b: 5:27–29) – Fichte holds, against "all of the authors who have treated ethics merely formally," that self-sufficiency or independence is a "material" kind of freedom. As Kosch puts it, "autonomy is," for Fichte, "a constitutive end of rational agency" (Fichte 2005: 140; Kosch 2018: 2). This means, Kosch argues, that for Fichte, morality's fundamental principle is a "material" rather than a "formal principle" in Kant's sense (Kosch 2018: 6). It sets autonomous self-determination as a fundamental moral end, a "determinate," "infinite goal," as Fichte puts it (Fichte 2005: 68, 142, 158).[1] Fichte himself advertised this "material" aspect of his view when he wrote in 1794 that he would be

[1] Fichte 2005: 142 uses "determinate goal," in a way that contrasts with the "infinite goal" of absolute self-sufficiency. A "determinate goal" is a more proximate goal that a moral agent sets from their current deliberative situation as a next "step" on the "path" of an "infinite series" of steps leading to the "infinite goal." He also says (158), though, that this "infinite goal" is also "determinate" (presumably, metaphysically if not epistemically).

advancing a "new [theory] of morality, the principles of which are material as well as formal" (Fichte 1988: 135).[2]

A signal feature of Kant's ethics is his doctrine that rational beings are ends in themselves together with his second formulation of the Categorical Imperative, which dictates that they must always be treated as ends and never as means. It is clear that this sense of "end" is significantly different from the idea of a final end state or goal as it features in Fichte's "principle of morality," even though the "infinite goal" at which Fichte says we are to aim is itself constituted by the free self-determination of rational beings. Given the way Kant interprets what it is to treat rational beings or "rational nature" as an end, he seems on firm ground in holding that the Formula of Humanity is no less a formal principle than is the Formula of Universal Law.

As we shall see, Fichte explicitly discusses this Kantian idea and distinguishes his own view from it, though he nevertheless says that their views are consistent (Fichte 2005: 244). When Kant says that rational beings are ends in themselves, and are therefore "called *persons*," he claims that they have a kind of choice-*constraining* value that "limits all choice" (Kant 1996a: 4:428), not that their autonomous rational action helps constitute a goal or end state that moral action should bring about or promote. But that is precisely what Fichte holds: We should relate to both others and ourselves in ways that tend to bring about the goal of the independence of all rational beings and, therefore, the self-sufficiency of reason itself. All rational beings are, he says, "tools of the moral law" and of the "infinite goal" that it sets (Fichte 2005: 288).

A second important departure from Kant is that whereas Kant's ethics are grounded in pure practical reason and practical laws that are, in effect, laws of the nature of perfectly rational beings, Fichte's ethics have no such ideal basis. What Fichte calls the "pure drive" aims at absolute independence, but it can dictate actions only when it is synthetically united with our "natural drive" as individual embodied natural beings. Only the "ethical drive" that emerges from this synthesis can prescribe specific courses of action and, even then, not by attempting, as in Kant, to emulate what one would do with pure practical reason. Any such purity exists only from a transcendental perspective. The principle of morality rather counsels "a series [of actions], through the continuation of which" the absolute independence of "the I" can (infinitely) be approached (Fichte 2005: 142). Fichte's ethics are thus not fundamentally "from nowhere" but from the

[2] On this, see Breazeale and Zöller's introduction to *The System of Ethics* (Fichte 2005: xiii).

embodied empirical perspective in which individual moral agents are actually situated here and now. They are in this respect a nonideal rather than ideal theory.[3]

It is also important for Fichte that moral agents are *specific individuals* who relate *to other individuals*. It is at this point that Fichte introduces an idea whose full philosophical significance will only begin to be appreciated with the discourse ethics of Karl-Otto Apel and Habermas and the writings on moral accountability and obligation by Strawson and his followers in the late twentieth and early twenty-first centuries (Strawson 1968; Watson 1987; Apel 1988; Habermas 1990a; Wallace 1994; Darwall 2006). Consciousness of ourselves as free individual agents can be achieved, Fichte argues, only with a "summons" (*Aufforderung*) to free action from other rational individuals. The summons places summoner and summoned alike into a "participant" or "second-person" standpoint of relationship *to* one another (Strawson 1968; Fichte 2000; Darwall 2006). This puts *inter*subjectivity at the center of Fichte's ethics and philosophy of right.

This is most obvious in the *Foundations of Right*, in which Fichte's summons argument plays an essential role in grounding his fundamental "rule" or "formula" of right. But essentially intersubjective reasoning and deliberation also plays an important role in Fichte's ethics, for example, in his account of our duties to one another and the essentially communicative character of shared moral reasoning. As Wood puts it, "although Fichtean ethics is," as we shall see, "a first-person conception in its *motivation*" – grounding its "principle of morality" in the perspective of an "I" – "at a very fundamental level it is second-person in the application of the moral principle" (Wood 2016: 207).

"The most striking demonstration of the incompleteness of Kant's critical philosophy," Fichte wrote, "is that Kant has never provided an explanation of . . . how I come to assume that there are rational beings outside of me" (Fichte 1992: 303). This is a lacuna in Kant's theoretical and practical philosophy, both in his account of the presuppositions of experience of a natural world that includes rational beings and in his recounting of the necessary conditions of moral agency and interagency. Moreover, although a form of self-awareness – the transcendental unity of apperception – is essential to Kant's critique of pure reason, this is not, Fichte stresses, an awareness of ourselves as individual thinkers. Kant

[3] In something like the sense involved in our contemporary distinction between "ideal" and "nonideal" forms of political theory in Rawls 1971 and Mills 2005.

cannot "understand by pure apperception the consciousness of our individuality, or confuse one with the other," Fichte writes. The latter is "necessarily accompanied by another consciousness, that of a Thou, and is possible only on this condition."[4]

Kant's ethics plainly presuppose such an awareness on the practical side. It is impossible for agents to apply the Universal Law Formulation of the Categorical Imperative in their own practical reasoning unless they can be aware of their own deliberative maxims. They have to be able to ask themselves, "What reason am I considering acting on?" To this, Fichte replies, "No Thou, no I; no I, no Thou" (Fichte 1982: 172–173). The only way we can come by an awareness of ourselves as deliberating agents is through a summons that includes reciprocal *recognition* (*Anerkennung*) of one another as free rational agents.

Self-Sufficiency or Independence: The I and the Not-I

At the outset of Fichte's *System*, however, there is no Thou or I/Thou to be found. The grounding of the "principle of morality" in Part I is entirely within an unmodified first-person perspective. But this is not the standpoint of some *individual* agent in particular. For that, according to Fichte, second-personal recognition must already be in place. It is the perspective of what Fichte simply calls "the I." The project of the "Deduction" in *System*'s Part I is to establish morality's fundamental principle from how "we are required to think of ourselves" as an occupant of the first-person (I) perspective of moral agency (Fichte 2005: 22).

To occupy a first-person practical perspective, the I must posit itself (as an I) in opposition to a Not-I that "resists" it. The Not-I is simply anything that is "given" in deliberative thought that the I can think about or reflect on, including aspects of itself and its own mental states (36).[5] By definition, the I is active, and what it posits in opposition (the Not-I) is passive in relation to it. The I's conscious thought is "grounded" in "pure activity" (17). But such activity is, necessarily, with respect to something the I can think about, the Not-I, and actual *practical* activity consists in the I's affecting the Not-I causally. "Without causality upon a Not-I there is therefore no I at all." Moreover, "such causality is not a contingent feature of the I, but belongs to it essentially" (90).

[4] Quoted by Wood 2016: 86.
[5] References to *The System* will be simply to page numbers of Fichte 2005, except when necessary.

It is crucial to Fichte that consciousness (the I) is not simply active; it is *self*-active or self-determining. Moreover, "the essential character of the I, through which it distinguishes itself from everything outside of it [the Not-I], consists in a tendency to self-activity *for self-activity's sake*" (34, emphasis added). This "tendency" or "compulsion" (*Zunötigung*), Fichte says, is the "*moral* or *ethical* nature of human beings as such" (19). And ethics, as he defines it, is "the *theory of our consciousness* of our moral nature in general and of our specific duties in particular" (21).

Although the I's self-activity can have causal effects on the Not-I, its activity is not itself governed by causal laws. Fichte contrasts the I's tendency to spontaneous self-determining practical thought with that of a steel spring that has a tendency and "striving to push back against what presses upon it" (32). The spring is like the I in that the ground of its striving does not lie in the compressing body though its striving activity requires something compressing it. Thus far, the I and a spring are alike. Just as the spring's action requires a compressing "not-spring," so "a rational being cannot determine itself to engage in an actual act of willing unless it stands in reciprocal interaction with something outside of itself" (32). But the spring is not free in the way Fichte holds a conscious will necessarily is. Moreover, the freedom that the spring lacks and conscious wills have does not consist merely in indeterminacy, in "blind chance" that defies formulation in causal laws. If the spring's activity were random and utterly unpredictable, that would not mean that the "spring . . . *determines itself*" to press back in the way that conscious wills can determine themselves to act (38).

Steel springs, but also nonhuman animals, lack "consciousness" in Fichte's distinctive sense, which includes the capacity for reflective agency. Even if other beings are conscious in the ordinary sense of having sense experience, feelings, and felt drives, they lack the ability to step back from these and consider what to do in light of them. The conscious I, as Fichte understands it, is defined by its tendency to reflectively step back from what he calls its "natural drives" and ask what Korsgaard calls "the normative question": "What should I do?" (Korsgaard 1996a: 7–48). Fichte's claim is that this normative perspective is essential to the I. He also puts this point by saying that we are "to determine ourselves consciously, purely and simply through concepts, indeed, in accordance with the concept of absolute self-activity" (Fichte 2005: 52). As Kosch observes, "Fichte defines rational agency as the disposition to form intentions spontaneously on the basis of concepts of ends" (Kosch 2018: 8).

Despite Fichte's departures from Kant's language, this places us in a terrain made familiar by Kant's discussion in the *Groundwork* of the distinctive capacity of rational agents to act for what we call *their reasons* (Kantian maxims) – on what Kant calls a "conception of law" or "law of freedom" (Kant 1996a: 4:412; 1996b: 5:69). Also relevant is Kant's distinction at the outset of *Groundwork III* between a "*negative* definition" of freedom as being undetermined by "alien causes" and a "*positive* concept of freedom" that is instantiated when rational agents determine themselves autonomously by the moral law (4:446–447). Although Kant held that the validity of the moral law and freedom understood as autonomy entail one another, he ended up holding that we know our freedom only because we know that we are morally bound (as a "fact of reason") and infer our freedom from this fact (1996b: 5:30–31).

Fichte's position is more in the spirit of Kant's position in *Groundwork III*. Rational beings are self-active in their nature and have autonomy or self-sufficiency as their "constitutive end" (Kosch 2018: 2). Because it posits itself as self-active, a rational I must posit itself as free. This is not so much a presupposition that an I is committed to having as an I. Rather its being as an I is partly constituted by practical thinking on this assumption. And this essential aspect of self-positing brings commitment to the moral law as a "law of freedom" in its train. "When you think of yourself as free, you are required to think your freedom under a law" (Fichte 2005: 55).

What the "Principle of Morality," which it is the project of Part I to deduce, requires is that any rational being, any I, "ought to determine its freedom in accordance with the concept of self-sufficiency, absolutely and without exception" (60). Actually, what Fichte calls the "principle of morality" is not this moral or ethical normative claim itself, but the *philosophical* claim that a thought with this normative content is "the necessary thought of the intellect" (60). Fichte says, moreover, that a crucial point on which this philosophical claim itself depends – that "a rational being, *considered as such*, is absolute and self-sufficient" – is not something he has attempted to prove; neither "can it be proven." "It is," he says, "simply up to each rational being to find himself in this manner and grant the same" (52–53).

As will become clear in the next section, Fichte intends the "ought" in the principle of morality to be understood in a distinctively deontic sense. Recall that for Kant, any normative practical proposition expressible by "ought," "duty," "obligation," and other deontic terms – propositions that are on the command/law side of Suárez's distinction between law and counsel – must be addressed to *finite* rational beings. Kant contrasts these with propositions concerning what it would be (practically) good or bad to do that characterize the deliberations of beings who have no motivational source other than pure practical reason. Imperatives "say that to do or to omit something would be good, but they say it to a will that does not always do something just because it is represented to it that it would be good to do that thing" (Kant 1996a: 4:413). Strictly speaking, the moral law, indeed anything that can be characterized as a prescriptive law in Suárez's sense, does not arise within pure practical reason itself.[6]

As we shall see in the next section, Fichte actually agrees that imperatives, oughts, and the deontic enter from the perspective of an embodied I who is naturally situated in an empirical context. But, quite unlike Kant, he does not contrast this with a realm of pure reason and purely rational beings. The I is always necessarily embodied in nature, indeed, in specific individual rational beings, indeed, in individuals who can reason and act together in specific societies and groups. Moreover, what such beings ought to do, in their specific individual contexts, is not what they *would* do if purely rational, or even what they would do if they were able most closely to approximate that. It is rather what steps are called for, here and now, for someone who is on a *collective* path that approaches – as closely as possible for human beings (in the fullness of time) – to fully reason-guided, self-sufficient, collective action.

Pure Drive, Natural Drive, and Ethical Drive

Having deduced the "principle of morality" in *System*'s Part I, Fichte turns in Part II to a "deduction of the reality and applicability of the principle of morality" (Fichte 2005: 65). It is here that we see both how concepts of deontic morality enter into practical thought – for Fichte, as for Kant, from the perspective of embodied empirical practical reason – but also how Fichte departs radically from Kant in holding that pure practical reason, or, as he puts it, the "pure drive" of the I (a "pure will"), can never be "actual," but only a "mere idea" (141). According to Fichte, the I can determine itself only through a synthesis with the "natural drive" in an embodied individual, but social, natural being – not through an actualization or realization of the abstract idea of the pure will.

What the "principle of morality" dictates, again, is self-determination in accordance with the "concept of self-sufficiency, absolutely and without

[6] On the significance of Suárez's distinction between "law" and "counsel" for modern moral philosophy, see Darwall 2023a: 17–25.

exception" (60). But the I cannot determine itself or act except within the sensible natural world. "I cannot originally determine myself by means of free ideal activity" but only as "a determinate object" in the natural world (208). That "I *ought* to do something means," Fichte says, that "I ought to produce the thing in question outside of me" (68). There must be "something in the sensible world *upon which* I . . . have to act" (68). This natural "stuff" is the Not-I; and it includes not just physical bodies outside the boundaries of our own but also our own physical and mental states insofar as we can reflect upon and affect these through deliberative practical thought.

For Fichte, rational agency consists in forming intentions on the basis of concepts of ends (Kosch 2018: 8). But "a *concept of an end*," Fichte tells us, is "a *model* or *pre-figuration* of something outside of us" in the natural world (Fichte 2005: 72). The point is one that philosophers now put in terms of "direction of fit." Whereas beliefs attempt to "model" or "fit" the world as it actually is, desires and intentions provide a model for the world to fit. Fichte concludes that all actions aim at end states in the natural world.

We shall see that this thought plays a role in Fichte's derivation and defense of the idea that what the principle of morality (ultimately) directs us toward is an agent-neutral state of the world that all rational beings can have as a *common* end. This is a profound departure from Kant (see Kosch 2018). Kant also holds that morality and categorical imperatives are possible only if there is an "objective end." But, for Kant, as we have already noted, this end is not an agent-neutral state of the world that actions might bring about or promote; it is the dignity of rational beings as ends *in themselves* as "limit[ing] all choice" (Kant 1996a: 4:428). For Kant, the dignity of persons grounds agent- and patient-relative restrictions, "common laws" that demand that agents treat each and every rational being as ends in themselves (4:443, 438).

Fichte holds, moreover, not only that a rational I can act only on, or thereby bring about, states of the natural world, but also that it can do so only by mobilizing natural "drives" or forms of motivation it finds within itself already. Although it can be guided by the *idea* of a "pure will" (Kant's pure practical reason), it cannot *actualize* itself as such. It can only actualize itself in the natural sensible world. This means, Fichte holds, that the I must be subject to a "natural drive," like any empirical being capable of natural activity. "I never actually do anything nor can I ever do anything that is not demanded by the natural drive because the latter exhausts the entire sphere of my possible acting" (Fichte 2005: 141). Fichte puts this memorably: "I cannot will anything other than what nature would also will, if it could will" (141).

Other natural beings lack will, which is free in its nature. Other natural beings do not, however, operate by causal mechanisms. They are, like us, self-organizing beings whose activity is the result of nonmechanical, teleological drives that aim at meeting their biological needs and the completion of self-organizing processes. What they lack is the I's defining capacity to step back from and reflect on these. So they can neither reflectively shape their natural drives nor choose, including whether and when, to act in light of them. This is a familiar theme in modern moral philosophy in, for example, Cudworth and Locke. In Fichte's hands, however, it informs a dialectical phenomenology that Fichte bequeaths to Hegel and many who follow in his path.

I, like any natural being, am "an organized product of nature," a self-preserving natural whole, "every possible part" of which "strives to unite other determinate parts with itself," and whose self-preservation consists in a "reciprocal interaction" between this striving and the striving's "causality" (117). Any natural being's "drive for self-preservation" is "directed" not "toward mere existence as such," but "toward a determinate existence": "to be and to remain what it is" as a self-organizing whole (117). "This is how things stand with me [the I] as well. There is in me a drive, one that has arisen through nature and that relates itself to natural objects in order to unite them with my own being" (118). Moreover, the drive often takes a proto-conscious form, as it does in other beings who, though they lack self-consciousness ("consciousness" in Fichte's distinctive sense), nonetheless have feelings and sensory awareness. I naturally seek to "unite" natural objects with my own being not in the way that "food and drink are absorbed through digestion, but to relate them as such to my natural needs, to bring them into a certain relationship with me" (118).

The I is thus subject to "natural" drives that limit the field of possible actions. Natural drives necessarily are directed toward objects and, when subjected to reflection, give rise to desires and ultimately inform willed actions. Although we usually experience desires as responses to their objects, whose features we generally take as justifying or rationalizing them, Fichte maintains, somewhat like Hobbes, that this picture gets things backward.[7] Suppose, Fichte asks us to imagine,

> my drive is directed toward object X. Is it perhaps the case that the stimulation or the attraction originates in X, takes hold of my nature and determines my drive accordingly? By no means. The drive originates

[7] For Hobbes, see Chapter 2. For the idea that desires are focused on and can be justified by features of, their objects, see Darwall 1983: 37–42, Pettit and Smith 1990, Scanlon 1998: 37.

> entirely from my own nature, through which what is supposed to exist for me is already determined in advance (118).

It is our own natural drives that determine their objects, and we view these objects as attractive in their light.

When the I first reflects on a drive, the drive presents itself as a "longing": "something – we know not what" seems to be "missing" (119). When, in a second mental act, the I reflects on this longing, it necessarily makes the indeterminate longing more determinate in the form of a desire for some specific object or objects (some X). In addition to being more determinate, desires differ also from longings, Fichte says, because the freedom that is implicit in all self-reflection is "already manifest in" them (121).

On reflection, natural drives present themselves as desires for determinate objects. But the "pure drive" of the reflecting I itself has no determinate object; it is a "*drive for freedom, simply for freedom's sake*" (132). "The reflecting subject," Fichte says, "stands higher than what it reflects upon: the former rises above and includes within itself the latter" (125). "Higher" here does not yet have a normative sense; it simply indicates the logical scope of reflection. Whenever we reflect on something, even some aspect of ourselves, it is from a presupposed position outside the scope of, and, in that sense, "higher" than, what we are reflecting on.

However, Fichte also holds that a (self-)conscious agent, a practical I deliberating about what to do, must regard the reflective standpoint as *normatively* higher than any provided by its natural drives as well. Unlike any natural drive that "is *contingent* to the I itself," "the pure drive is essential to the I; it is grounded in I-hood as such" (135). It is "present in all rational beings, and whatever follows from it is valid for all rational beings" (135). The pure drive is therefore, he says, a normatively "higher drive" than any natural drive. And here Fichte uses the vocabulary of *deontic* normativity. The pure drive "demands that I, as an empirical, temporal being, elevate myself above nature" and "determine myself utterly independently of the impetus of nature" (135). As Kant says about the law of pure practical reason, Fichte says that the pure drive "fills me with respect, summons my self-respect, and determines my dignity as something elevated above all nature" (135).

Just at this point, however, Fichte's thought takes a distinctively un-Kantian turn. Fichte holds, again, that it is impossible to do anything "that is not demanded by the natural drive"; "the latter exhausts the entire sphere of my possible acting" (141). This leaves us with something like a "contradiction" (142). We cannot will anything that is not the object of our natural drive, and our natural drives, having nothing of the pure will's freedom within them, are incapable of free choice by themselves. Fichte's "synthetic method" enters here (100):

> How can this contradiction be resolved? According to the laws of synthesis, this is accomplished as follows: the matter or content of the action must, in one and the same instance of acting, be simultaneously suitable to both the pure drive and the natural drive, so are they united in the actuality of acting (142).

Reflective deliberative thought unites the pure and natural drive. The I chooses an action on the basis of grounds or reasons "valid for all rational beings" that, while not simply consequences of the motive force of given, unreflective natural drives are nonetheless informed by our natural drives as these are shaped by (potentially infinite) reflection in the limit (135).

Fichte's idea is not, however, like Kant's, that what a finite (natural) rational being should do is what they *would* do if they were ideally (purely) rational.[8] Pure rationality is less a standard or direct guide to our conduct than a "final end." The "[goal] of ridding ourselves of our dependence upon nature" is one that "necessarily lies in infinity" and can never "be achieved" (142). The way the pure and natural drives are unified is by identifying policies and actions, here and now, that lie "in a series [of actions], through the continuation of which the I would have to become independent" (142). In this respect, again, Fichte's is a nonideal rather than an ideal theory.

Although it is not obvious at this point in Part II, it becomes clear in the *System*'s Part III that the I's final end is not the individual agent's *own* self-sufficiency or independence but that of all rational agents, indeed, as they are organized in rational community with one another. Fichte thinks, after all, that self-awareness as an individual I is only possible in the company of other rational beings and then only through a second-personal summons. In Part II, however, this element of Fichte's thought has not been brought into the argument. What we have so far is that the I unifies its natural and pure drives in deliberative thought by choosing determinate actions called for by reflectively informed natural drives.

Fichte follows Kant, though, in holding that the standpoint of pure reflection (Kant's pure practical reason) presents its practical directives in distinctively deontic, juridical terms.[9] When deliberative thought stemming

[8] In this way it also differs from ideal deliberation views like Richard Brandt's (Brandt 1979).

[9] On this aspect of Kant's view, see Darwall 2023a: 325–334.

from the pure drive aiming at fully independent self-sufficient action as a final end is synthetically united with natural drives in a determinate natural deliberative context, this yields what Fichte calls "the *ethical* drive" (144). Unlike the pure drive whose end is the infinite goal of absolute independence, the ethical drive is "directed toward determinate actions" that lie "in the series" of policies and actions the continuation of which will approach the I's absolute independence in the limit. Fichte says that the "ethical drive makes itself known as respect; and obeying or not obeying this drive provokes approval" (145). It "commands categorically;" "whatever it demands, it demands as necessary" (145).

As is true also with Kant, it is not obvious what, at this point in Fichte's *System*, is supposed to ground this deontic normative element. When the ethical drive conflicts with recalcitrant natural drives, what justifies the thought that not only do agents have most reason to act in accordance with their ethical drive, indeed, not only that they necessarily have most reason, but that this is what reason *demands*? It is, of course, uncontroversially true that so acting is a requirement of reason in the truistic sense that acting otherwise *cannot* accord with practical reason. But what is demanded by practical reason in this constitutive sense says nothing about whether acting otherwise violates distinctively deontic normative demands that are on the law/command side of Suárez's distinction between law and counsel. What grounds this distinctively deontic normative thought?

I argue (in Darwall 2023a) that writers like Pufendorf and the British rationalists follow Suárez in tying moral law to accountability conceptually. As Wood notes, however, moral accountability plays no significant role in Fichte's ethics, even less indeed than in Kant's (Wood 2016: 73–74). Fichte's account of freedom is not one of accountable moral agency. It is more like Spinoza's, as Wood also points out. Unlike philosophers who hold that the very idea of moral obligation requires that all agents subject to it have the capacity to hold themselves accountable in their own autonomous reasoning, "Spinoza and Fichte agree," Wood says, "in seeing humanity as divided into two contrasting groups: a small group of those who truly act, and are free, and a much larger group who are passive, victims of their own erroneous view of the world and consequent slavishness of mind" (74). The latter, Fichte says, "do not in fact really will," but "always allow themselves to be pushed around and driven by a blind propensity." He concludes, indeed, that "such persons do not possess any consciousness, properly speaking" (Fichte 2005: 131). Even so, Fichte was a strong proponent of republican democracy and public education (2013).

In Kant's moral psychology, respect functions as a feeling through which finite rational agents hold themselves accountable for complying with "commands of reason" (Kant 1996a: 4413). Fichte uses similar language: the higher drive "fills me with respect, summons my self-respect, and determines my dignity as something elevated above all nature" (Fichte 2005: 135). But rather than holding me to account when I give in to lower drives, respect registers "disdain for all enjoyment" and renders enjoyment "contemptible" (135).[10]

Formal Conditions of the Morality of Actions

Part III of the *System* lays out Fichte's normative ethical theory. Section I, with which we shall be concerned next, focuses on the "formal" conditions of moral action, by which Fichte means the conditions necessary for an action to have what Kant calls "moral worth" or to manifest "good will" (149). Section II, by contrast, concerns, at a very general level, the "material content of the moral law," or, as we might put it, what, in general, makes right acts right (Fichte 2005: 196; Ross 2002). In Section III, Fichte lays out more specifically what he takes our moral duties to be.

Before we examine Fichte's views on the formal conditions of morally good action, it will be helpful to note some things Fichte says in the course of Section I that clarify his picture of reflective deliberate choice. "A free being," he says, "determines itself only through and only in accordance with concepts" (Fichte 2005: 170). Choice, therefore, "presupposes a concept of that choice, of what is chosen thereby" (170). Suppose a choice is between A, B, and C. "If the free being in question chooses . . . C, then can it prefer C for no reason and without any ground – that is, without any intelligible ground in a concept?" (170). "Absolutely not," Fichte replies, "since in that case the choice would not occur through freedom but through blind chance . . . There simply must be something in C that makes it stand out. Let us call this something X" (170).

The I's deliberate choices are guided by its reflectively shaped desires. In our example, then, the I will necessarily regard its choice of C as grounded in some property of C, X, that it sees as its reasons for choosing C. But this raises a further question, Fichte notes: "why is the choice in question decided precisely by X, and not some possible non-X?" (170). "The reason for this can only lie in a universal rule that the rational being already possesses" (170).

10 On the difference between contempt and moral blame (in which recognition respect for persons is implicit), see Darwall 2018b.

This recalls Kant's well-known statement that though "everything in nature works in accordance with laws[, o]nly a rational being has the capacity to act *in accordance with the representation* of laws" (Kant 1996a: 4:412). Only rational agents can act for their own reasons, and something can be *someone's reason* for doing or choosing something only if they regard it as a *normative* reason *for* them so to choose (Darwall 1983: 28–29). Further, something can be a normative reason for some particular person only if it would be a reason also for any rational agent in their circumstances.

In our example, therefore, the I must regard X, its reason for choosing C, as grounded in a "universal rule" for all rational beings, what Kant calls a "practical law." What exactly would such a "universal rule" or "practical law" say? A constraint on any universal rule the I could appeal to in justifying choice is that it must relate appropriately to the I's natural drive. Moreover, Fichte says that the universal rule must not only apply to any rational being, but be "already possesse[d]" by them (Fichte 2005: 170). This entails that any eligible rule or principle must somehow be internal to an I's natural motivations in something like the way "internalists" like Bernard Williams would later come to identify (Williams 1981b). What might such universal rules, valid for any rational being, include?

Although natural drives aim at, and give rise to desires for, various specific objects like food, drink, and warmth, what these all have in common, Fichte holds, is the agent's own pleasure. The natural drive, he says, "aims only at enjoyment and has pleasure as its incentive" (Fichte 2005: 171).[11] It follows, Fichte thinks, that "since the only drive that occurs within [the I's] consciousness at this point is the natural drive," the only universal rule that could provide the I's reason or function as its "maxim" at this "point" of reflection is the principle of "prudence" (154, 171). "One must choose that which promises the greatest pleasure, in terms both of intension and of extension – in short . . . the maxim of his own happiness" (171). What reflective deliberation yields at this juncture, therefore, is something like hedonistic egoism or a hedonistic version of Butler's "principle of self-love" (Butler 2017). "At this level," Fichte says, "the human being becomes an intelligent animal" (Fichte 2005: 171). It has consciousness of a kind, but not yet that of the full rationality or independence to which the self-actualizing I can aspire. Its free will is like the

[11] This ignores Butlerian arguments that the specific objects desires aim at are distinct from the agent's own pleasure. Against Fichte, Butler would urge that agents' pleasures are themselves explained by their desires for specific objects (other than their own pleasurable mental states).

sort that Cudworth called "animal free will" (Cudworth ~1670) with rational prudence being "nothing other than intelligent choice between several satisfactions of a natural drive" (Fichte 2005: 154; see Darwall 2023a: 138).

So long as "a human being continues to occupy this point of reflection," prudence is "the only maxim that is possible for him" (Fichte 2005: 172). "Human beings" are not, however, condemned to be only "intelligent animals." They "*ought*" to raise themselves "to a higher level of reflection" beyond this self-centered one. Because they can do so, they are "to blame" for the "unworthy [egoistic] maxim that flows from [their] failure to raise [themselves] to a higher level of reflection" (172).

Fichte's thought here is not unlike the line that Hutcheson pursued (and that Sidgwick will pursue) in arguing that from an individual's own point of view, egoistic prudence is uniquely recommended, and that nothing from within that perspective can lead to a more impartial point of view beyond it (though ultimately nothing recommends the partial over an impartial perspective) (Sidgwick 1962; Hutcheson 2002). According to Fichte, however, actual individual human beings necessarily already do have – in actuality, though not at this stage in Fichte's dialectical phenomenology – the capacity to view themselves as "one person among others," in Thomas Nagel's phrase (Nagel 1970). Indeed, Fichte will argue, they can have a conception of themselves as individual free agents only if they have been summoned and thereby related to second-personally by other individuals. But at this dialectical juncture, this standpoint is not available:

> There is something incomprehensible here, and it cannot be otherwise, since we are now standing at the boundary of all comprehensibility: namely, the doctrine of freedom as it applies to the empirical subject. So long as I do not yet occupy a higher standpoint of reflection, then this standpoint does not yet exist for me, and hence I cannot have a concept of what I am supposed to do before I actually do it. Yet it nevertheless remains the case that this is what I absolutely ought to do. That is to say, when judged from the perspective of another person, one who is acquainted with the higher standpoint of reflection, the act in question is something I ought to do . . . Once I have attained this standpoint I will no longer excuse myself by appealing to my own incapacity, but will blame myself for not having done what I ought to have done much sooner (Fichte 2005: 172).

Although Fichte's remarks suggest a temporal perspectival ordering, his point here is dialectical. As we will see in Section II, Fichte thinks that at any point at which an actual human being can engage in practical reasoning as an individual they must already have been summoned by other rational agents in ways that necessarily put them in this "higher standpoint of reflection."

With these points in hand, we can turn now to Fichte's discussion of the "formal conditions for the morality of our actions" (149). It becomes immediately clear in Section I of Part III that Fichte means *deontic* morality, that is, morality in the distinctively modern sense with which we have mostly been concerned. Already in the last paragraph of *System*'s Part II, indeed, before he has even begun Part III, Fichte announces what will be Section I's major result, namely, that "the formal condition for the morality of our actions is" "*always act in accordance with your best conviction concerning your duty*," which Fichte has already identified with "conscience" (a "higher feeling" that demands "respect" 139–140, 148, 148–149).

We should bear in mind that Fichte's discussion of the formal conditions of moral action in Section I occurs *before* the passages concerning the impossibility of gaining the "higher standpoint of reflection" that Fichte holds is necessary for any practical reasoning going beyond prudence, like moral reasoning. By Fichte's own declaration, therefore, the distinctively deontic terms in which he sets the question of the formal conditions of the morality of actions have not yet been properly grounded. Neither, indeed, can they even be properly understood from within the I's deliberation at the "point of reflection" that Fichte's dialectical phenomenology has so far revealed.

At this point, we do best to ignore this, however, and consider Fichte's discussion of formally moral action in its own (deontic moral) terms. Since Fichte begins by saying that "formal morality" is also called "good will," his distinction between the "formal" and "material conditions of the morality of our actions" might seem simply to repeat Kant's distinction between acts that accord with duty and actions that are also done "from duty" and therefore have what Kant calls "moral worth" (Kant 1996a: 4:398; Fichte 2005: 149). This would make formally moral action the same as actions manifesting goodness of will in the Kantian sense, namely that they are the result of morally good motives. By contrast, material morality would not (except in special cases) be a matter of motive at all. It would simply consist in the agent's doing the right thing, what duty requires, in confronting the situation.

The point can be put most clearly with a distinction W. D. Ross makes between *acts* and *actions*. Ross reserves 'act' to refer to an alternative for voluntary choice, considered independently of motive. And he uses 'action' to refer to the whole consisting of a chosen act together with the reason or motive for which it was chosen. When it comes to moral assessment, Ross says, "we should . . . talk of a right act but not of a right action, of a morally good action, but not of a morally good act" (Ross 2002: 7). This is a helpful distinction, one that it would be useful for moral philosophers to establish as general usage. Using Ross's coinage, we can say that on this initial Kantian reading, there can be materially moral acts (but not actions) and formally moral actions (but not acts).

This way of reading Fichte gives him a clean and relatively straightforward view: Material morality consists in an *act*'s according with moral duty, and formal morality consists in an *action*'s being done from the motive of duty. But this risks significantly oversimplifying Fichte's position. Someone might accord (materially) with their duty and their action might be motivated by their (correct) belief that this is so without them being sufficiently conscientious in *forming* their belief. Their action might not have resulted from what Fichte calls their "best conviction concerning [their] duty" (Fichte 2005: 148). In Section I, Fichte develops a wonderfully subtle view about *conscientious* moral *conviction* and its essential role in formally moral action.

Although on any plausible reading, Fichte holds that formally moral action must accord with agents' own beliefs about their duty, he is vividly aware of the fallibility of moral belief. And not just about specific cases. "Just as I can err in my judgment of an individual case, so can I also err . . . in my conviction concerning my convictions as a whole" (156). The conscientious person must take this into account. And when they do, they "must either take a chance and act" on their best conviction or conclude that they are "not permitted to act at all" (156).

"For dutiful conduct to be possible at all," however, the latter possibility must be rejected. Further, if that is so, he says, there must then be some "absolute criterion" that the agent can apply *subjectively* without having to worry about the possibility of massive moral error. Indeed, Fichte says that duty requires us to make that assumption. We must presuppose that "there is something present in the power of cognition" "without which there could be no duty," and "it is a duty to regard it as such" (156–157).

The "criterion" Fichte has in mind is the "feeling of certainty" that comes with a "calm" settled conviction that is achieved in what Rawls will later call "reflective equilibrium," when an agent resolves their doubts upon fully informed reflection (159). It is only if the agent can calmly "accep[t] the risk of not being able to alter either his manner of acting or the principles in accordance with which he is acting in this manner" that their ensuing action is formally moral (160). A conscientiously formed "best conviction" is one the agent is prepared to be "stuck with . . . for all eternity, with no possibility of ever altering this conviction" (148, 166).

Fichte says not only that conscientious conviction is essential to morally *good* action, but also that pursuing reflective deliberation to this conclusion is itself morally *required*: "conscience is a consciousness that is itself a duty" (164).[12] Fichte adds, moreover, that everyone is not only "supposed to convince himself of what his duty is," but also that everyone is always "in every case able to do this." To this, he gives a Kantian gloss: "This is, so to speak, the constitutive law of all morals: that one give a law to oneself" (164).

I argue (in Darwall 2023a) that Kant's derivation of freedom as autonomy from the consciousness of the moral law (the "fact of reason") in the *Critique of Practical Reason* implicitly relies on the conceptual connection between moral obligation and accountability (Darwall 2023a: 324–333). If that can be assumed, I claim, Kant can safely suppose that in seeing themselves as obligated by the moral law, moral agents must presuppose that they necessarily have all that is necessary to knowingly act *from* it just by virtue of the fact that they are thus obligated. Otherwise, it would be unintelligible to hold them morally accountable. This returns us to the question we decided to ignore in considering Fichte's discussion of formal morality in Section I. What can underwrite the deontic moral language and concepts of Suárezian law in Fichte's framework? To attempt to answer that question, we must turn to Part III's Section II.

"The Material Content of the Moral Law"

The topic to which Section II is primarily addressed is the moral law's "material content." Using Ross's helpful distinction between acts and actions, whereas formal morality is a property of *actions*, material morality, for Fichte, is a feature of *acts*. Formal morality concerns the whole action: not just the "what" (the chosen act) but also the "how" (by what process and with what motive it was chosen). This Rossian distinction is implicit, indeed, in Fichte's titles for Sections I and II. Section I concerns "formal conditions for the morality of our actions" (Fichte 2005: 149). And Section II discusses "the material content of the moral law" or "our duties" (196). It is concerned with what – which acts, in which circumstances – duty requires. To use another Rossian phrase, it is concerned with "what makes right acts right" (and wrong acts wrong) (Ross 2002). In Fichte's

[12] Here Fichte quotes Kant 2018: 203.

terminology, this is what makes our acts "legal" in the sense that they accord with moral, not positive, law (Fichte 2005: 148).[13]

Fichte's account of formal morality, as we have just seen, is more complex than a theory only of morally good motivation. Conscientiously forming firm and stable convictions on the basis of duly diligent reflection is not simply morally good. Rather, "conscience is a consciousness that is itself a duty" (164). But if that is so, part of the content of the moral law follows directly from that. Part of what we are morally required to do is to undertake due conscientious reflection and to act on our "best conviction" (148).

But since our "best conviction" is itself "concerning our duty," conscientiousness cannot be the moral law's whole material content. The deliberative issue to which conscientious reflection is itself addressed is the substantive "material" question of what moral duty requires of us considered independently of how we best form a conviction on that very question. Although Fichte says that we should form and act only on our "best conviction concerning [our] duty," that cannot supply the moral law's whole "material content" (148). When Fichte says that the "feeling of certainty" is "the sole sure criterion of true conviction," he means not that our best conscientious convictions are necessarily *materially* true or correct (159–160). He means that this is a criterion for having formed our best conviction.[14]

We can put the point this way: conscientious deliberation addresses the first-order question of what morality requires of the agent in the deliberative situation confronting them. In addition to this first-order question, however, a second-order question arises: have I fulfilled my moral duty in deliberating about this first-order question? Fichte holds that morality requires conscientious conviction so that provides part of the content of the moral law. But it cannot provide the whole content since it cannot provide the answer to the first-order question to which deliberative moral reflection is itself addressed. Fichte generally reserves "material content," indeed, for this first-order deontic question.

At the most general level, the material content of the moral law follows directly from Fichte's "principle of morality" if we fully take account of the complexities introduced by the dialectical interaction of the pure, natural, and ethical drives. The "principle of morality" says, again, that the I "ought to determine its freedom in accordance with the concept of self-sufficiency, absolutely and without exception" (60). Absolute independence or self-

[13] On this, see Kosch 2018: 128–129. [14] On this, see Kosch 2018: 134–136.

sufficiency is the end at which the pure drive aims. In this respect, Fichte's theory of the moral law's material content – his normative theory of moral right and wrong – is a teleological rather than deontological theory (Frankena 1963: 13; Rawls 1971: 24). It begins with an independent account of an end that moral action is to promote or achieve and grounds its theory of morally right and wrong acts in that.[15]

Typically, teleological theories are also consequentialist: they hold that what makes acts morally right or wrong has to do with consequences for promoting the end that their teleological character sets. The classic cases are desire-satisfaction or hedonistic forms of utilitarianism grounded in the intrinsic (nonmoral) goodness of satisfaction or pleasure. Teleology supplies the end, and consequentialist structure sets the relation between promoting it and acts' deontic properties. Hedonistic act-utilitarianism reckons right and wrong by acts' consequences for overall net pleasure. Hedonistic rule-consequentialism reckons right and wrong by the consequences for overall pleasure of a (socially embodied) rule requiring a given act. And so on.

Fichte's theory is less straightforward. Most importantly, the end the principle of morality dictates, and at which the pure drive aims, on the one hand, and action it recommends as promoting it, on the other, are not fully independent in the way that those of hedonistic utilitarianism are. Its final end itself consists in self-sufficient *actions*, consisting in agents acting for good reasons, not anything that actions might bring about as independent effects, like pleasure. Moreover, since Fichte holds that conscientiousness provides a further substantive moral requirement – that moral agents have this second-order duty in addition to their first-order ones – this complicates things even further beyond the usual teleological, consequentialist framework. "The ethical drive," Fichte says, "demands *freedom* – for the sake of *freedom*" (Fichte 2005: 145). Conscientious action itself realizes a form of self-sufficiency or freedom and does not just aim to bring it about.

The principle of morality and the pure drive set the final end of independence or self-sufficiency. But agents must unify pure and natural drives to yield the ethical drive, which dictates specific acts to be taken in agents' deliberative context, here and now, by considering which acts lie "in a series [of actions], through [a potentially infinite] continuation of which the I" would "become independent" (142). And morality dictates also *how* this end is to be approached, namely, only through conscientious

[15] This element is emphasized by Kosch 2018.

actions that themselves realize a form of freedom here and now. As Fichte puts it, "I am supposed to act *freely* in order to *become free*" (145).

Fichte formulates the question of the moral law's material content as follows: "which actions lie in that series of actions that approaches [the end of] absolute self-sufficiency" in the limit (199–200). Fichte has been considering this question up to this point as if from the perspective of an individual rational agent who is "supposed to act *freely* in order to *become free*" *themselves* (145). And we have noted that the "point of reflection" reached by the end of Section I is an egocentric one from which the only conceivable grounds of choice are those of egoistic hedonism. In Section II, however, Fichte is eager to leave this dialectical perspective behind. To do that, he has to show how the I can achieve the impartial "higher standpoint" on which properly moral reflection itself depends.

Individuality and the "Summons"

This is the point in Fichte's *System of Ethics* where his well-known claim in *The Foundations of Natural Right* enters: that the self-consciousness in which consciousness "properly speaking" consists can come about only *interpersonally* through a "summons" addressed second-personally from one rational being to another (131). Before we consider how this arises in the *System*, though, we should note a substantial dialectical tension that surfaces already in reflective deliberation as we have so far analyzed it *intrapersonally*. According to Fichte, the sole principle or "universal rule" available to a fully reflective, deliberating agent is that of egoistic hedonism (153–154, see also 170). "One must choose that which promises the greatest pleasure, in terms both of intension and extension – in short . . . his own happiness" (171). But this is an end state, *quite* unlike that set by the pure drive, that is, in principle anyway, *entirely* independent of whether the agent's own actions are self-sufficient or not. It obviously could be the case that an agent is likelier to maximize their own satisfactions if they do not attempt to do so deliberately as the result of rational reflection. And it is at least conceivable that independent, reasoned choice might play relatively little role within the end state of maximal satisfaction itself.[16] If this were so, it *would* yield a conflict between the end the pure drive aims at and that the ethical drive directs us to take action toward, on the one hand, and

[16] Of course, empirical details regarding our natural drives might show that either of these possible phenomena are not the case.

what reflective deliberation itself delivers by the point of reflection that is reached at the end of Part I, on the other.

Even before he has reached a "higher" point of refection in Part II, however, Fichte lays out six kinds of duties – three duties of the body and three of the intellect – which cut against the egocentric hedonist principle of Part I, and which he believes he already has resources to establish. Concerning the body, there are "three material commands of ethics" (205). First, "our body . . . absolutely may not become an object of enjoyment for enjoyment's sake." Second, "the body ought to be cultivated in a manner . . . suitable for all the possible ends of freedom." And third, any enjoyment that "cannot be related" to cultivating the body suitably for freedom "is impermissible and contrary to the law" (205). Similarly, he sets out three duties of the intellect having an analogous structure. "Negative: never subordinate your theoretical reason as such . . . Positive: cultivate your power of cognition" as much as you can. And "Limitative: . . . refer all of your reflecting to your duty" (207).

Even these duties can only be interpreted egocentrically at this point, however. After listing them, Fichte turns straightway to the task of gaining a higher reflective perspective than that offered by any individual's own. For Fichte, properly conscious activity always involves some form of self-reflection. Thus, desire results from reflection on a longing that becomes focused thereby on a determinate object of desire. And prudential reasoning results from reflection on desires and satisfactions (hence pleasure) at different times. It achieves a higher, more inclusive, scope of reflection than any involved in particular desires and pleasures themselves.

Can any such self-reflection give one an awareness of one's own free activity, however? This would seem to be impossible. In being thought *of* by oneself, any such free activity immediately becomes perforce an object of thought and therefore no longer freely active itself.[17] Of course the reflection is itself freely active, but it is not what is being thought about.

Suppose you freely and independently consider some deliberative question, say, whether to continue reading beyond the next paragraph. Now reflect on your consideration of that question. Your deliberative consideration has now become fixed; it is no longer actively reflectively open. Of course, your reflective thinking about your considering is itself free activity. But once you reflect on and think about that, then *it* is no longer freely

[17] For different treatments of Fichte's summons argument concerning individuality and self-consciousness, see, in addition to Wood 2016 and Kosch 2018, Neuhouser 1990, and McNulty 2016.

active. And so on. It would seem that no further iteration can successfully give you a reflective awareness of your own free activity.

In Section I, Fichte writes, he had established that "I find myself as a natural drive" (208). Moreover, "it is obvious that I have to reflect in order to find this, and thus that I have to be an intellect" (208). We cannot be conscious "of this reflection as it occurs," but only through a "new act of reflection" (208). Both reflective acts must "be ascribed to the *freely acting* I" (209). However, my own reflection cannot supply awareness of my own free activity by itself since any such reflection immediately fixes what it is reflecting on as object in thought. Somehow "I must *find* myself *to be free;* I must be given to myself as free" (208), but I cannot through my own reflection.

The only solution to this reflective dilemma, Fichte argues, is a "summons" addressed to oneself *as a free agent* by "an actual being outside of myself" (209). Such a summons, he says, "communicate[s] to me a concept: namely, the concept of an action that is demanded [of me]" (209). It is crucial that the demand is addressed to one *as a free agent.* To understand the concept of an action that is demanded of one, one must have a concept of oneself as a free agent. The demanded act is not simply to be causally produced; it is to be *freely chosen.* As Fichte puts it in *The Foundations of Natural Right*, where the summons argument is more explicitly developed, the summoned agent's activity "is by no means to be determined and necessitated by the summons in the way that . . . an effect is determined and necessitated by its cause; rather the rational being is to determine itself in consequence of the summons" (2000: 35). The only way an agent (an I) can determine itself, of course, is by acting on a ground or reason that it accepts as such. It follows that the summons must attempt to give the summoned agent some reason for acting such that in acting on it they can freely determine themselves.

Fichte also says that "the summons to engage in free self-activity is what we call upbringing [*Erziehung*]" (2005: 38). And Wood notes that "*Aufforderung*" has a broad meaning that includes invitations and requests as well as demands (Wood: 2016: 92). What is common to all of these is the attempt to give the summoned agent a reason for acting through second-personal address in a way that differs from simply pointing to already existing reasons or getting them to see that such a reason exists in some other way. Invitations, requests, and demands all create reasons for acting that would not have existed otherwise and thereby attempt to engage the summoned agent in a kind of *interpersonal* deliberation or reasoning that is concluded by the summoned agent's free self-determination (de Kenessey 2017).

Consider, for example, the address of a putatively legitimate demand from another person, say, to remove one's foot from on top of theirs (Darwall 2006: 5–10). Such a demand is addressed to one as a free agent and purports to give one a distinctive reason for removing one's foot that differs from any that cannot be given in some other (non-second-personal) way. It summons one to choose freely to remove one's foot for a distinctive reason, namely, that this has been justifiably demanded of one. Such a reason exists only if the demand is legitimate, and that is so only if the other indeed has the authority to address the demand to one in this way.

Compare this reason with the fact that being on the other's foot is causing them pain, which could be relieved by simply removing one's foot. And compare the way in which a legitimately demanding summons gives one a reason with the way one might appreciate a reason to relieve someone's pain through a compassionate desire that they be pain free, where such a desire is caused by empathic experience of their manifest pain (Batson and Shaw 1991; Darwall 2002).[18] One becomes aware, in both cases, of a reason to remove one's foot. But there are three important differences between these two cases. The most obvious is simply that the reasons involved are different, independent reasons. There would be a reason to remove one's foot consisting in the pain one is causing whether or not the other had a claim to one's not causing them that pain. Second, the reason consisting in the other's pain would exist whether or not one was aware of it through the empathically induced desire that the other be pain free. Through the desire, one becomes aware of a reason that exists already independently. But this is not so in the case of the demanding summons. The reason that a legitimate demand distinctively purports to give is not independent of the summons and what the summons presupposes, namely, the other's authority to summon and one's capacity freely to act on their summons. Because the reason conceptually implicates the (second-personal) authority to give it to another through second-personal address, I call it a "second-personal reason" (Darwall 2006). Any summons purports to give the summoned agent a second-personal reason for acting.

There is a third difference between the two cases that follows from the second. A compassionate desire focuses the desiring agent on a state of the world, the other's pain, and the reason for removing one's foot that it represents. A legitimate demand, on the other hand, is *addressed to one as a free agent* in a way that neither the other's pain nor the normative reason that consists in it is. The summons focuses the summoned agent on the fact

[18] See also Adam Lerner (unpublished), "Empathy as Evidence."

that the demand summons *them* to *choose to act for this (second-personal) reason*. Once a summoned agent deliberates about whether to do so, they must reason on the assumption that they *can* do so, that they can freely decide to act on a summons-based legitimate demand (Darwall 2006).

The same (second-personal) structure is revealed in other *Aufforderungen*.[19] When one person makes a *request* of another, they purport to give the person of whom they make it a reason to act that is independent of any reasons that might otherwise exist, and they ask the person freely to comply *because they have requested this of them*. Similarly, when one person *invites* another to do something, they give the invitee a reason to do it beyond any that existed independently of the invitation, and, as well, they invite the invitee to do it (freely) *for the reason that they have been so invited*. And the same thing is true of upbringing as Fichte conceives of it. A parent or teacher summons a child to act and thereby purports to give the child a summons-based reason so to act, calling upon the child to decide to do so for this very reason.

To see the point, compare four different cases. In the first, a child's attention is somehow drawn to pain they are causing to another, which they thereby empathically appreciate and grasp as a reason to stop. In a second, the child's attention is somehow so drawn by their parents, without the child knowing that their parents have directed their attention. In a third, a parent directs (summons) the child to attend to the pain they are causing in the hope that this will elicit an empathic desire to stop. In a fourth, a parent demands, or even just asks, that the child stop causing the pain.

No summons is involved in either of the first two cases, in both of which the child comes to appreciate reasons to stop causing pain that are entirely independent of any summons or second-personal address. In both the third and fourth cases, by contrast, a summons is involved that gives the child a reason for acting that would not have otherwise existed. There is, however, an interesting difference between the summonses involved in the third and fourth cases and, therefore, between the summons-based reasons they create. The fourth case is like the summons-based case in our initial contrast between the two cases we considered earlier. The parents' demand gives the child a reason to stop causing pain to the other that consists not simply in the badness of the pain they are causing but rather in a legitimate demand to stop causing it, and it summons the child freely to choose to act for this reason and, therefore, to deliberate about whether to do so on the assumption that they *can* so choose, regardless of whether they are

[19] Wood argues that Fichte's "summons" is "the concept of a *ground* or *reason* for doing something" (Wood: 2016: 92). I hope it is clear in what follows why this is mistaken.

empathically engaged by the other's pain and compassionately desire that they be free of it.

This, however, is not true of the third case. In the third case, the parent does indeed demand that the child *attend* to the other's pain and thereby purports to give a demand-based reason so *to attend*, independently of whether the child might see any already existing reason so to attend. But since the demand is simply to attend to the pain and not directly to stop causing it, the child is not thereby given any summons-based reason to stop causing the pain that is independent of reasons not to cause pain deriving from the badness of pain. To the contrary, in the third case, the parent hopes that the child will appreciate the badness of the other's pain empathically so that they will be moved to act for that reason and not any reason deriving from their summons.

The general point, then, is that any summons engages the summoned *interpersonally* in a way that gives them an awareness of the free agency of both summoner and summoned. It puts both into an interpersonal deliberative space in which they take a "second-person standpoint" on one another and themselves (Darwall 2006). As Strawson puts it, it places them in a "participant" perspective of relating *to* one another (Strawson 1968).[20]

Fichte makes this idea do real philosophical work in his *Foundations of Natural Right*, where he argues that reciprocal recognition of one another as individual agents through a summons commits summoner and summoned alike to what he there calls the "formula" or "rule of right": "limit your freedom so that the other alongside you can also be free" (Fichte 2000: 10, 82). As we shall see, however, Fichte holds that the philosophy of right and ethics are independent philosophical domains, and questions arise concerning the specific ethical implications of claims of right in the distinctive "legal" sense with which Fichte is concerned in his *Foundations of Natural Right*.

What Fichte is mostly concerned with when he introduces his summons argument in the *System* is to show that that the I's self-sufficient activity includes "posit[ing] itself" as "an individual," and that this is possible only through a second-personal summons from another. Any summons necessarily places summoner and summoned in an *interindividual* deliberative space within which each relates to the other (and to themselves relating to

[20] Cf. the discussion of Pufendorf on the perspective of a free accountable agent who has been addressed a putatively legitimate demand (God's command) and the comparison with Hobbes's agent viewing alternatives from the perspective of desire in Darwall 2023b: 82–86.

the other) *as* particular individuals. It therefore gives both parties a practical awareness of themselves as particular individuals in interindividual relation.[21] And it gives each an awareness of themselves as *free* individuals relating to other free individuals.

Consciousness of "individuality" is, Fichte says, "a condition of I-hood," and this consciousness of individuality comes, again, only through reciprocal recognition with other free individuals (2005: 206–207). So, in parallel with his similar argument in *Foundations*, Fichte declares here that "My I-hood, along with my self-sufficiency in general, is conditioned by the freedom of the other" (210). Therefore, "it follows," Fichte says, "that my *drive to self-sufficiency* absolutely cannot aim at annihilating the *condition of its own possibility*, that is, the freedom of the other" (210). Fichte says further that "this limitation of the drive [for self-sufficiency] therefore contains within itself an absolute prohibition against disturbing the freedom of the other, a command to consider the other as self-sufficient, and absolutely not to use him as a means for my own ends" (210).

Universal Self-Sufficiency as a Common End and Common Moral Culture

Owing to this prohibition, "there are certain points beyond which I should not proceed with my freedom," certain "*ought-not*[*s*]," owing "to the presence of other free beings" (214). This suggests a framework of deontological restrictions or "side constraints" that prohibit certain acts that treat others as means, however worthy the end might be (Nozick 1974: 28–33). And indeed, there are aspects of Fichte's ethics that tend in this direction, for example, an "absolute prohibition . . . against lying" or even "leading another person into error" (Kosch 2018: 270). But Fichte's ethics are decidedly not the kind of deontology one normally associates with absolute prohibitions and side constraints (Kosch 2018). Its fundamental structure is teleological, setting the I's self-sufficiency as a final end. The "material content" of its prescriptions must be reckoned by which actions lie in that series of actions "the continuation of which" "approaches [the end of] absolute self-sufficiency" in the limit (Fichte 2005: 146, 199–200).

That Fichte's ethics take this fundamentally teleological structure, despite its "absolute prohibitions" and seeming foundation in something like the Kantian idea that persons must always be treated as ends and never as

[21] On the summons's role in relation to individuality, see esp. Neuhouser 1990.

means, becomes evident straightaway in his treatment of "a contradiction of the drive to self-sufficiency – and hence of the moral law – with itself" (218). From an egocentric perspective, as we earlier noted, the moral law apparently requires me to "subordinate everything that limits me" in achieving *my own* self-sufficiency as a final end (218–219). But once I recognize that I am simply one among many individual agents, I see that I am not permitted to "subordinate to my own end [even that of my own self-sufficiency] some of those things that certainly do limit me," namely, other individual agents (219).

The "only way" this contradiction can be resolved, Fichte argues, is "to presuppose that all free beings necessarily share the same end," so that "the liberation of one would at the same time be the liberation of all" (219). It is only if all individuals can be assumed rationally to share the *common end* of the self-sufficiency of each and every person that morality can escape contradiction. Therefore, what morality must require is that each plays their respective roles so that that *together* all can bring about their common independence.

It is important to keep in mind that what Fichte means by this end is "a *model* or *pre-figuration* for something outside of us," a state of affairs in the natural world (72). It is thus quite unlike Kant's idea that rational beings are "objective ends" in themselves. The common independence of each and all is rather, for Fichte, a *goal* or end *state* that individual agents are to act in common to achieve rather than anything from which deontological constraints can follow directly. And both end state and the actions to be taken on the path leading to it involve shared common actions and practical reasoning.

The fact that an end for Fichte is a model of a possible state of the world thus plays an important role in his argument. There is a sense in which agent-relative theories like rational egoism and deontological moral theories give every agent the same end, namely, their own happiness or interest or compliance with deontological constraints *themselves*. In Fichte's sense, however, rational egoism and deontology actual give the agents to whom they apply *different* ends since the states of the world for which their ends are models are different. Under rational egoism, my end is realized by the state of the world in which my interest is actualized, and yours is realized by the state in which yours is. Similarly, deontology requires me to keep my promises and you to keep yours, and these are realized by different states of the world. The only way in which rational agents can ultimately have the same end in Fichte's sense is if the end is agent-neutral rather than agent-relative since states of the world are not agent-relative; they are agent-neutral.

Although it may be clear enough how Kant's idea that persons are ends in themselves who possess an inviolable dignity can yield side constraints against their use, this may not seem to be possible on a view with a teleological structure like Fichte's. But even forms of hedonistic utilitarianism, like rule utilitarianism, can ground absolute side constraints in principle, if, for example, embodying such constraints in social practice would maximize overall net pleasure. Given the significance of coordinated common action for Fichte, a consequentialist structure that is even friendlier to Fichte's ethics might be likelier to be some form of "cooperative" consequentialism like that proposed by Donald Regan, as Kosch has pointed out (Regan 1980; Kosch 2018: 94–99). Fichte's final end is, quite unlike that of utilitarianism, one in which self-sufficient action must be realized *in common*. This seems far likelier to yield the kind of demanding constraints Fichte has in mind since aggregative trade-offs are not permitted. Actions favoring one person's self-sufficiency at the cost of others' are not permitted since they could be no part of the common final end.

Fichte emphasizes that "it is for I-hood as such a contingent fact that *I*," the occupant of the first-person standpoint, am the particular individual I happen to be (Fichte 2005: 220). The pure "drive for self-sufficiency is supposed to be a drive of I-hood, essentially as such" and "not the self-sufficiency" of any particular individual (220). "Our ultimate goal" is therefore "the self-sufficiency of all reason as such," as realized in each and every embodied rational agent. "It is necessarily a matter of utter indifference to me whether I present this drive or it is instead presented" in other individuals (220). Moreover, "there is no such . . . self-sufficiency except by means of the formal freedom of all individuals" (221).

Just as freedom enters in two different places in Fichte's earlier formulation of the moral law – to act *freely* in order to bring about ("for the sake of") *freedom* – so also does the current formulation end up requiring *common, coordinated activity* in two different places, both in the end state to be realized, and in the actions that bring about or "approach" that end state in the limit. The final end is the common independence of all persons, and it is to be realized by steps that themselves involve coordinated activity in common.

This finds two distinct expressions in Fichte's thought. One is familiar from the social contract tradition in political philosophy, most especially in Kant's argument that individuals in a state of nature would be obligated to establish a civil condition in which there are shared public institutions for administering justice. Even with the best will in the world and a punctilious respect for others' rights, individuals may find themselves in irresolvable conflict if they lack commonly accepted judicial procedures. The I's self-sufficiency thus requires public civil order or organized states. "Agreement concerning how human beings are permitted to influence one another – i.e., agreement concerning *their communal* rights in the sensible world – is called the *state contract*; and the community that has achieved such agreement is the state. It is an absolute duty of conscience to unite with others in a state" (226). There is also a second way in which *shared interpersonal* reasoning plays a role on the path to the I's self-sufficiency. Recall that when Fichte earlier says that we are to act "freely" for the sake of approaching full freedom (self-sufficiency) in the limit, he identifies the former free action with *conscientious* conduct here and now (145). Acting on one's firm, carefully formed, and stable "best conviction" is not just the "formal condition" of morally good action; it is also morally required (148). So long as only one's own particular egocentric perspective is in play at the "point of reflection" in Section I, this can apparently be realized by achieving reflective equilibrium *intrapersonally*. Once we see, however, that we are simply one particular individual among others, this is no longer possible:

> At this point, however, the following additional question arises: which use of freedom violates the moral law, and who is able to be the judge who passes universally valid judgments on this question? If *the other person* claims to have acted according to his best conviction, and if *I* act differently in the same situation, then according to *his* conviction *I* am acting immorally, just as *he* is acting immorally according to *mine* (221).

Here we face the problem of moral epistemic disagreement. Once we take seriously that we are just one individual among others, we realize both that we have, in principle, no better access to what morality demands of us than do others, but also that there are moral demands of action placed on each of us precisely because we are one individual among others.

Ultimately, both of these bring into play essentially *interpersonal* reflective reasoning and the achieving of an *interpersonal reflective equilibrium*: "reciprocal interaction of everyone with everyone for the purpose of producing communally shared practical convictions" (224). A "communal end" can only be achieved with shared interpersonal reasoning in which we attempt to "convince" one another, but also leave ourselves open, reciprocally, to being convinced. It is important for Fichte, nevertheless, that individuals retain a sphere of freedom in which they cannot rightfully be constrained by others. Even if we may permissibly attempt to convince others not to act in ways we think unwise, we may not, within this sphere, restrain "the other's physical behavior" (222). As we shall see in the next section, however, Fichte argues in *The Foundations of Natural Right* that what most deeply underlies rights of individual freedom is the form of intersubjective engagement and reasoning he calls the "summons."

Fichte calls the shared communal conversation that joint conscientiousness requires an "ethical commonwealth" or "church" (224). "Everyone," he says, "is supposed to be a member of the church" (224). This idea of a shared public ethical or moral conversation and culture plays a large role in the moral and political philosophy that follows Fichte, from Hegel's critique of the abstractness of Kant's ethics to Rawls's idea of public reason. I shall argue in Chapter 7 that it is in the background of Bentham's derivation of the principle of utility.

Section III of *System*'s Part III is concerned with the "doctrine of duties in the proper sense of the term" (243). Fichte begins with a discussion of how his theory of duties relates to Kant's at the most basic level, revealing again that his theory is teleologically oriented around a final end state or goal, in a way that Kant's is not. "Kant has asserted that *every human being is himself an end*, and this assertion has received universal assent" (244). Fichte says that "this Kantian proposition is compatible with mine," implying that while his and Kant's fundamental ideas are different, they can nevertheless yield the same dictates, at least in principle (244).

For Kant, the idea that each individual person is an end in themselves who must always be treated as such is put forward not as a goal of action, but as the expression of a kind of value persons have, dignity, that is a direct source of (agent-relative) constraints that "limi[t] all choice" (Kant 1996a: 4:428). Fichte, however, declares that individuals are all "mere tool[s] of the moral law" (Fichte 2005: 244). What the moral law demands of each and every individual is coordinated conscientious conduct aiming to approach, in the limit, the final goal of self-sufficient reason, realized in the fully self-sufficient shared practical reasoning and action of all individuals. In one sense, each individual is simply an instrument to accomplishing this essentially shared objective. In another, however, "everyone is an end" since this objective is itself realized only in the shared free reasoning of each and every agent (245).

Although Fichte says that each individual being a "tool" of the moral law is consistent with the Kantian idea of each as ends in themselves, he draws different lessons for specific moral duties than Kant does. Kant holds that our own moral perfection is an imperfect duty we owe to ourselves, although we have no such analogous duty to perfect others (Kant 1996c: 6:446). For Fichte, however, it is "egotism" to be concerned to perfect oneself and not others. Indeed, Fichte denies that any genuine duties to self actually exist. No duty really has oneself as end in the Kantian sense. Even when I am "the immediate object" of a duty, such as the duty to perfect myself, that does not mean that I am the duty's end. "I am and remain a means for a final end outside of myself" (Fichte 2005: 246). For that reason, Fichte declines "to call such duties 'duties to ourselves'" (246). They are rather, he says, "*mediate*" and "*conditioned*" duties: "'mediate' or 'indirect', because they have as their object the means for all our efficacious acting" (246). And "conditioned" because they are demanded as a condition of what morality otherwise demands: "the realization through me of the dominion of reason outside of me" (246).

Four Distinctions in Duty: Particular versus Universal, Conditioned versus Unconditioned

Each individual is a "tool of the moral law," so each has "conditioned" duties to maintain themselves in good working order since reason's self-sufficiency can be realized through them only on this condition. Under this heading, Fichte includes both a "negative" duty not to endanger self-preservation and a "positive" duty to do everything necessary to further it (250). Finally, since we are "commanded to live" as a "necessary condition for . . . carrying out the [moral] law," suicide is "absolutely contrary to duty" (252). However, we are not "permitted, for the sake of life, to do anything that violates duty," since "life itself is an end only for the sake of duty," only because it is necessary to comply with the moral law (258).

There can be "conditioned" duties only if there are also "unconditioned" ones. The latter are the duties, compliance with which "conditioned" duties are conditioned on. These consist in the rest of what moral philosophers generally include under moral duties other than duties to the self. Like Kant, Fichte includes duties to promote others' well-being and familiar prohibitions on harm, lying, deception, and other violations of trust, promise, and contract (e.g., 272). But unlike Kant, he adds a duty to further the perfection of others to the duty to perfect oneself, which Kant counts as a duty to self and Fichte a conditioned duty.

Fichte makes a further distinction between "universal" and "particular" duties that is especially relevant to the duty to further others' perfection. The occasion for the distinction is the problem of *coordination*. The moral law requires each to "to do all [they] can to further reason's self-sufficiency" (246). But if each "responds to this command" *individually* without coordinating responses with others then "many different things will happen in many different ways, and some things will not happen at all" (247). This is where interpersonal, shared reasoning enters most explicitly into Fichte's account of moral duty.

It is often necessary that individuals organize themselves and coordinate their activities to approach or advance morality's final end. Many issues simply cannot be addressed individually because doing any good requires more than any individual can muster by themselves. And there are other things people can do *something* about individually, say, to help feed the hungry, but genuinely effective action requires people organizing themselves to respond to the need more comprehensively. In many cases, effective pursuit of the moral law's final end requires a division of labor with different groups working on different problems.

Coordinated arrangements of these kinds "can arise only by means of agreement, through the union of several different individuals for the end of such a distribution [of responsibility]" (247). It takes the kind of "*mutually expressed*" common knowledge that Hume includes under "convention" in his account of justice as an "artificial virtue" (Hume 1978: 490). Therefore, each "has a duty to bring about a union of this sort" (Fichte 2005: 247).

The most general such union within any given territory is a state, through which individuals can decide in common how to distribute moral responsibilities at the most general level. But Fichte also has in mind local political communities as well as more informal social groups that operate within, but also under the authority of, the state. "Such an arrangement," Fichte says, "involves the *establishment of different estates* [*Stände*]" to whom different social and political tasks can be "delegated" (247). Some such "estates" are political ("estates of the realm") constituted by different political offices and roles, where others are social and economic, comprising different professions and trades. Different estates have distinctive tasks in discharging moral duties that require different forms of coordination. Everyone has a "duty to work for the establishment" of the estates that are necessary to work *together* to approximate and bring about morality's final end: the realization of reason's self-sufficiency in each and every individual self-sufficiently acting *together*.

Once estates have been established, everyone has a duty "to select a specific estate for [themselves]" (247). And in choosing an estate, one "thereby selects the particular manner in which [they] will assume responsibility for furthering the self-sufficiency of reason" (247). The estate-specific responsibilities individuals thereby assume is one thing Fichte means by "vocation."[22] "Particular"

[22] He also speaks more generally of the "vocation of man" (Fichte 1987).

responsibilities are thus "delegated" from more inclusive political and social collectivities to less inclusive estates, and ultimately within those estates to individuals who occupy different offices and roles within them. In this way, each individual ends up playing their role in the collective enterprise of furthering morality's final end together.

This collective, distributed feature of our moral tasks sets up a second contrast between moral duties, which cuts across Fichte's first contrast between conditioned and unconditioned duties. Duties that are collectively "delegated" to different estates and, then, to different offices or roles within these "in particular," Fichte calls "particular duties." "What can be delegated," he says, "is a *particular* duty of the individual to whom it is transferred" (247). Any duty that "cannot be delegated is a *universal* duty" because it falls on all individuals equally.

Although Fichte's category of "particular duties" may seem to conflict with the Kantian idea that all duties are grounded in universal moral law, it need not. Something that is a particular duty in Fichte's sense, because it involves delegation to some particular estate or role, will still be covered by a categorical imperative having universal form in Kant's sense, namely, one requiring any individual who happens to belong to the relevant estate or to occupy the relevant office within it to comply with the relevant Fichtean particular duty.

This leaves Fichte with "two ways of dividing duties" – conditioned versus unconditioned and particular versus universal – that cut across one another (247). There are thus both "*universal* and *particular conditioned* duties" and "*universal* and *particular absolute* [unconditioned] duties." It is also important to keep in mind that what Fichte means by "conditioned duties" is different from what is normally meant by "conditio*nal* duties," that is, duties that arise only under specific conditions. Fichte's "conditional duties" arise in every actual – indeed, Fichte thinks, any imaginable – condition since they concern maintaining in good working order the requisites of any actual individual's being a "tool of the moral law." "Conditioned duties" are all, therefore, unconditional in the usual sense.

Universal conditioned duties include, again, duties of self-preservation and prohibition of suicide. By contrast, *particular conditioned duties* are those whose "object" is our "empirical selves, insofar as we belong to this or that particular estate" (259). These include "cultivat[ing] one's mind and body in the particular ways that will make them of use to the estate to which one has dedicated oneself" (261).

Universal unconditioned duties include the duty to promote others' well-being or happiness and prohibitions on murder, fraud, and theft. And *particular unconditioned duties* include all "delegated" duties, not concerning our own "empirical selves," that attach to different offices and roles within estates, including the "natural estate" of the family (247, 259, 310). Of particular interest is Fichte's treatment of the duty to further others' perfection or morality – the subject, again, of a disagreement with Kant. Fichte treats these as particular duties tied to socially organized *educational* estates, to the "duties of the scholar" and other "moral teachers of the people." Fichte calls this socially organized educational structure the "church" (327–330).

"Morality," Fichte says, "develops itself freely and by means of purely rational education in the context of social intercourse and solely from the human heart" (330). As Wood emphasizes, Fichte further develops this theme in his 1794 *Lectures on the Scholars' Vocation*, where he characterizes the "social drive" in every individual as "aim[ing] at *interaction, reciprocal* influence, *mutual* give and take, *mutual* passivity and activity. It does not aim at mere causality, at the sort of mere activity to which the other person would have to be related merely passively" (Fichte 1988: 158). This is further evidence for Wood's claim that "although Fichtean ethics is a first-person conception in its *motivation*, at a very fundamental level it is second-person in the application of the moral principle" (Wood 2016: 207).

Philosophy of Right, the Summons, Recognition, and Deontic Normativity

The more foundational Part I of Fichte's *Foundations of Natural Right* was published in 1796, just before Kant's *Doctrine of Right* appeared in 1797.[23] There are profound similarities between Fichte's and Kant's works. Both treat the philosophy of right as a separate philosophical subject that is independent of moral philosophy. And both consider matters of fundamental right to concern reciprocal relations of freedom. However, there are also deep differences in the ways Fichte and Kant respectively ground natural right that, I shall argue, give Fichte a more promising view. The role Fichte gives to the summons in the foundations of natural right can provide resources for an account that is superior to Kant's explication of right in terms of justified coercion.

For Kant, "right and authorization to use coercion . . . mean one and the same thing" (Kant 1996c: 6:232). Although Fichte recognizes a "right of coercion," he holds that its justification is downstream from any analysis of

[23] This section draws closely from Darwall 2013g and Darwall 2014c.

the concept of right itself (Fichte 2000: 83, 88–92). For Fichte, justified coercion requires a "common" and "reciprocal willing" of all persons as a postulated "community," which reciprocal willing acknowledges a common (second-personal) standing that any summons presupposes and from which the normative force of natural right derives (83, 92). Thus, whereas Kant takes a right against someone to consist in justification to coerce them, Fichte takes it to be something that is recognized or acknowledged in free compliance with it.[24] I shall argue that Fichte's is a superior view of relations of right.

Before we begin, note how similarly Fichte and Kant situate natural right in relation to the maintenance of "external freedom" of beings who live alongside one another and who are capable of what Fichte calls "inner freedom" and Kant calls "internal" "law-giving" or "choice" (Kant 1996a: 6:214; Fichte 2000: 10): "The concept of right is the concept of the necessary relation of free beings to one another" (Fichte 2000: 9); "Right is therefore the sum of the conditions under which the choice of one can be united with the choice of another in accordance with a universal law of freedom" (Kant 1996c: 6:230).

And here is what they respectively say about the "rule," "formula," or "law of right": "The rule of right, 'limit your freedom through the concept of the freedom of all other persons with whom you come in contact'" (Fichte 2000: 10); "The formula of right – limit your freedom so that the other alongside you can also be free" (Fichte 2000: 82); "The universal law of right, so act externally that the free use of your choice can coexist with the freedom of everyone in accordance with a universal law" (Kant 1996c: 6:231).

It is common ground between Fichte and Kant that relating to others in a rightful way involves forbearing interference in and respecting others' "spheres" of freedom. Where the two diverge is in the way they respectively ground relations of right and what they take the right to be one's own master within this sphere ultimately to amount to.

Throughout, it is important that the fundamental right with which Fichte and Kant are concerned – the "rule" or "law" of right – is at least partly a "claim right" in Hohfeld's sense (Hohfeld 1923). Unlike a mere Hohfeldian "privilege" or "liberty" (permission), such as Hobbes's right of nature, it is something others *violate* if they interfere with one's freedom of action (see, e.g., Fichte 2000: 101).

[24] Kant agrees that property rights can only be made determinate and conclusive in a civil, rightful condition that requires the united will of all.

Fichte and Kant both hold that there is a fundamental right to freedom of action within one's own sphere. This entails both a privilege of action within that sphere and a claim right that others not interfere by going outside their sphere and intruding into one's own. Any such interference or intrusion is a violation of fundamental right. Kant is somewhat clearer on the fundamental right's including both the requisite privilege and claim right, but Fichte is committed to this also.

Kant's "Universal Principle of Right" is an explicit statement of the privilege: "Any action is *right* if it can coexist with everyone's freedom in accordance with a universal law" (Kant 1996c: 6:230). In other words, any action within one's sphere of freedom that is consistent with others' equal spheres does not wrong them. But Kant also makes clear that he is concerned with "the concept of right, insofar as it is related to an obligation corresponding to it," (6:230) that is, with rights that entail correlative (directed) *obligations*, hence with claim rights. Since the fundamental right of freedom is held against all persons, the correlative obligation not to interfere is owed by each person to every other.

"Now," Fichte says, "in the doctrine of right there is no talk of moral obligation" (Fichte 2000: 11). But this seems mainly to do with his view that any rights against others within communities must be derived from a person's "free, arbitrary decision to live in community with others" and not from some fundamental moral obligation to do so (11). I will return to this later when we consider the role of the summons in Fichte's grounding of natural right since even this seems inconsistent with fundamental aspects of his summons argument. We can set this aside for now, however, since even if there are no rights against particular others within one's community absent a "free, arbitrary decision to live with" them, we are interested in what Fichte is committed to when the right to freedom against others in fact holds. And it is hard to see how Fichte can avoid the conclusion that his fundamental right to freedom is a claim right if he is to think, as he clearly does, that it is something that others *violate* when they interfere with one's freedom of action.

When Kant says that "right and authorization to use coercion ... mean one and the same thing," this amounts to an analysis of a claim right (Kant 1996c: 6:232). The right we each have that others not interfere with or "hinder" our freedom consists in our having justification to coerce them not to, to "hinder" their "hindrance," as Kant puts it (6:231).

Kant derives this right in two stages.[25] He argues, first, that the Universal Principle of Right follows from fundamental features of the "concept of

[25] For an excellent discussion, see Ripstein 2009. For a discussion of Ripstein, see Darwall 2013h.

right," which he sums up in the formula, "Right is therefore the sum of the conditions under which the choice of one can be united with the choice of another in accordance with a universal law of freedom" (6:230). From this the Universal Principle of Right follows more or less directly: an "action is *right* if it can coexist with everyone's freedom in accordance with a universal law" (6:230).

Actions that "hinder" others' freedom, however, are not covered by this privilege. And Kant argues, second, that just as "resistance that counteracts the hindering of an effect promotes this effect and is consistent with it," so also must "*hindering of a hindrance to freedom*" be "consistent with freedom in accordance with universal laws" (6:231). It follows that the hindering of hindrances to freedom is rightful also. They are covered by the fundamental privilege that is the Universal Principle of Right. But if that is so, then Kant evidently regards it as following from his definition of a (claim) right as justification to coerce that each person has a claim right that others not hinder their freedom since they can rightfully hinder the others' hindrance. Kant concludes: "Hence there is connected with right by the principle of contradiction an authorization to coerce someone who infringes upon it" (6:231). The fundamental claim right as a normative proposition follows from the concept of a claim right taken together with the Universal Principle of Right, which follows from the very idea of rightful relations between free persons.

But now note two consequences of Kant's analysis and derivation of the fundamental claim right to noninterference. The first is that no correlative *relational obligation* of others to respect the claim right follows. Of course, Kant believes that everyone is prohibited by the "universal law of right," not to mention by the categorical imperative, from violating the right to noninterference. But this is not a relational obligation *to* the right holder that is entailed by and correlative to the claim right they hold (Hohfeld 1923). Taken in itself, all the claim right can involve, for Kant, is a justification to force others not to interfere with the right holder.

As Feinberg has shown, however, claim rights consist in the (second-personal) authority to claim or demand of the obligee (the person against whom the right is held and who is therefore obligated *to* the right holder) that to which the right holder has the right, as well as the authority to hold them accountable for providing it (Feinberg 1980; Darwall 2006a: 18, 2013a). Nothing like this can possibly follow from the claim right to noninterference as Kant analyzes and derives it.

The second consequence follows from the first. When someone stands on their right to noninterference and refuses to consent to its infringement, we ordinarily take it that they are, inter alia, asserting or implying that a distinctive *reason* exists for another *not to interfere*, namely, *that it would violate their right*. But again, no such reason follows from the claim right to noninterference as Kant analyzes and derives it. All that follows is that those against whom the right holder has the right will not be wronged and cannot rightfully complain if the right holder uses force to "hinder their hindrance." There may of course be reasons related to their right, or at least to their taking themselves to have it, that will come into play, for example, that any attempt at interference will be resisted forcefully and indeed rightfully. But the fact of the right will itself provide no reason against interference. The point is not that Kant has no way of generating a reason not to interfere with people's freedom. Both the categorical imperative and the universal law of right supply this. The problem is that neither of these follows from the fact that people have a claim right not to be interfered with and, consequently, that we are obligated *to them* not to do so.[26]

By contrast, Fichte's derivation of natural right provides materials to resist these two consequences of Kant's doctrine of right. It can, consequently, yield a more adequate account of fundamental claim rights. I should emphasize that Fichte himself would not have agreed with this claim. Fichte resists talk of obligation in the philosophy of right, draws a sharp line between morality and right, and derives claim rights against particular others within the agent's community from the other's free "arbitrary" decision to live in community with the agent, "not through

[26] At least, this does not follow in the sense we normally have in mind when we speak of obligations. In the sense Kant uses 'obligation' (*Verbindlichkeit*), however, it might be argued to follow in the following way. As I argue in Darwall 2023a, Kant distinguishes between moral or practical "necessity," on the one hand, and what he calls "necessitation," on the other (Kant 1996c: 6: 222). The former is a thoroughly normative fact whereas the latter is ultimately *psychological*: an imperfect rational being's determining themselves to do what the law objectively required. Strictly speaking, then, only beings for whom compliance with the objective law is "subjectively contingent" can be under obligation (1996a: 4: 413). "Obligation involves not merely practical necessity (such as a law in general asserts) but also *necessitation*" (1996c: 6:223). Although all rational agents, including "holy beings," are under the practical law, only imperfect rational agents are under obligations or "imperatives"; and they determine or "constrain" themselves to follow the law through addressing reasons' commands to themselves and following them. This means that obligation is ultimately a psychological phenomenon for Kant. Moreover, Kant distinguishes between "internal" and "external constraint." We imperfect rational agents act *ethically* through *self-constraint* when we give ourselves commands of reason and follow them. By contrast, the philosophy of right is concerned with *external* constraint of action, both by others and, in a civil condition, by the state. Rights for Kant involve authorization to constrain others' conduct. But that implies that they can "necessitate," and, in that sense, "obligate" others' not to violate their rights, by hindering their hindrance. On Kant's use of 'obligation,' therefore, claim rights do imply correlative obligations to right holders. I hope it is obvious, however, how Kant's ultimately psychological sense of 'obligation' expresses something different from the distinctive normative items we normally take obligations to be.

any obligation" (Fichte 2000: 15). Nevertheless, Fichte's strategy is clearly to "deduc[e]" the concept of right as a "condition of self-consciousness" and thereby to show that it is "an original concept of pure reason" (9). And there is no question that he takes a reciprocally recognizing, and thus a second-personal, summons from a free rational being to the agent (as a free rational being) to be necessary for self-consciousness. My claim would be that the best philosophical interpretation of Fichte's thesis that fundamental claim rights can be grounded in a presupposed summons a priori entails a presupposition of equal basic second-personal authority that can ground the second-personal nature of fundamental claim rights and the second-personal reasons for acting to which they give rise (Darwall 2006, 2013b).

Consider, first, how Fichte argues for the necessity of a summons for self-consciousness as a free agent.[27] "In acting," Fichte says, "the rational being does not become conscious of its acting; for *it itself* is *its acting* and nothing else" (Fichte 2000: 4). The agent is conscious of its "*object*," "of what emerges for it in this acting" (4–5), not of itself as a self-determining will. Fichte's idea, as I interpret it, is that the first-person perspective of unsummoned agency is focused on various states of the world that the agent can bring about by their actions as ends, the relative desirability of these ends, what it would take to bring them about, their costs and benefits, and so on. The objects of unsummoned practical thought are the alternative actions before the agent, and the practical question is, "Which to choose?"

The agent's focus is, as it were, outward, on the objects before them, not inward on their own agency. For an unsummoned agent, thoughts of their own free agency can have practical relevance only insofar as they relate to the objects before the agent – for example, the choiceworthiness of bringing about some state of the world, what it would take to do that, and so on. Any attempt to focus on one's own free agency as such risks a futile attempt to observe one's own agency.

For a subject to gain self-consciousness of themselves as a free agent, the "object" of the subject's consciousness must be "synthetically unified" with the "subject's efficacy." The object of consciousness must be "nothing other than the subject's efficacy" itself so that "the two are the same" (31). Fichte's transcendental claim is that this can be achieved only *second*-personally, by a "summons" from one rational agent to another "calling upon it to resolve to exercise its efficacy" (31). The summons is to the other *as a free agent,* so in being aware of it, the other is aware of themselves as thus regarded. So far,

[27] In what follows, I draw from Darwall 2006 and 2014c.

however, this might be no different from a *third*-personal, observer's awareness. That the other sees one as an agent, or even that they so see themselves, is but another aspect of the way things are anyhow.

What makes all the difference is that a summons addresses the agent *second*-personally; therefore, in responding to it the agent perforce relates to the other relating to them as an agent. They operate within a second-personal relationship in which each reciprocally recognizes the other as a "you" to whom the first is a "you" in return. The presuppositions of intelligible second-personal deliberative thought simply require that the agent *deliberate under the assumption* that both are free agents. This gives them a practical awareness of their agency that is irreducible to any consciousness they have of themselves as part of a causal order. *They simultaneously "posit" themselves and the other as free and rational agents within their own deliberation*, from the practical point of view (9). They grasp themselves "in this identity of acting and being acted upon" (23, see also 40).

The most perspicuous interpretation of Fichte's idea, again, is in terms of second-personal reasons. *A summons is any address of second-personal reasons to another agent.* Since it addresses the other *as agent*, a summons necessarily involves the giving of reasons. "The rational being's activity is by no means to be determined and necessitated by the summons in the way that . . . an effect is determined and necessitated by its cause; rather, the rational being is to determine itself in consequence of the summons" (35). A summons, whether a claim, demand, or request, attempts to give another agent reasons by which they can freely determine themselves, reasons that are grounded in a presupposed authority to summon the agent to act in some way, even if only to figure out for themselves what to do. And not just any normative reason for acting, but, as we have seen, a reason whose very existence is tied conceptually to the authority to address it second-personally in this way.

The address of any second-personal reason arguably presupposes a shared reciprocal authority of summoner and summoned to address such reasons to one another as well as a shared capacity to recognize this authority and freely determine themselves by reasons that derive from its exercise (Darwall 2006). Any summons that purports to give an addressed agent a second-personal reason for acting, even just to make up their own mind and act, presupposes the capacity of addresser and addressee to freely determine themselves by reasons that are grounded in a shared second-personal authority it simultaneously presupposes. Fichte's own position is, however, equivocal here. On the one hand, he says things that seem to deny this possibility. But other things he says seem to require it.

For Fichte, the "concept of right," again, "is the concept of the necessary relation of free beings to one another" (Fichte 2000: 9). The "*complete object* of the concept of right [is]. . . *a community of free beings as such*" (10). In a community of right each recognizes others' right of "external freedom" through "inner freedom" (10). Fichte denies that there is any obligation *of right* to enter into a community of right.[28] Since "the thought and task of such a community is arbitrary," the concept of a community of right is only "technical-practical." The most it entails is that "*if* someone wanted to establish" "a community among free beings," it would have to be done "in accordance with the concept of right" (10, emphasis added). This would clearly seem to rule out the line of thought I am suggesting.[29]

Fichte allows that "it has indeed been shown that, if a rational being is to come to self-consciousness – and hence if it is to become a rational being" this can only be done through reciprocally recognizing, second-personal rational influence that itself involves recognizing the other's sphere of external freedom through internal freedom. "But that," he says, "even after self-consciousness has been posited, rational beings must continue to influence the subject of self-consciousness in a rational manner, is not thereby posited" (81). The "enduring existence" of a community of free beings related by right is thus an "arbitrary," rationally optional "postulate" that an agent may or may not adopt "of his own free choice" (81). Although there may be "an obligation to will this" "within the sphere of morality," "in a theory of natural right" all that can be said is that *if* an agent wills to be a member of a community of free beings, then the agent is bound to them by relations of right (81).

On this "voluntarist" interpretation, it takes an individual's voluntary participation in a "reciprocal declaration" to be obligated to another by the principle of right (15). Each obliges the other and themselves by an actual reciprocal recognition (44). Moreover, both the recognition and the obligation it gives rise to are reciprocally conditional. "This manner of treatment is conditioned by the first's treatment of the other; and the first's treatment of the other is conditioned by the other's treatment and knowledge of the first" (42).

Nonetheless, there are reasons for thinking that Fichte cannot hold to a voluntaristic interpretation if he is to maintain that the conditions for self-awareness are sufficient to validate the principle of right. Fichte's official

28 As we have seen, however, he does think we are *morally* obligated to enter political communities and estates.

29 For relevant discussion, see Ware 2010 and McNulty 2016.

position, again, is that it is only a voluntary "reciprocal declaration" of recognition with a specific individual that obligates the agent to recognize that individual's sphere of freedom and to limit their own. However, even here, Fichte says that although one cannot complain that another does one an injury in refusing recognition, the "doctrine of right" nonetheless warrants the claim that the other "must then remove himself from all human community" (12). This suggests, first, that Fichte believes that the only way an individual can avoid the obligations of the principle of right is to avoid other people altogether. But, second, it is not clear why this should be so on voluntarist assumptions. Why might there not arise various *communities* of right, that is, associations within which individuals are obligated by the principle of right, with no obligations of right to outsiders? It is hard to see how a voluntarist interpretation can avoid this consequence.

Other things Fichte says fit no better with a voluntarist interpretation. First, Fichte asserts that agents demand continued recognition of themselves and their freedom "for all the future" when they reciprocally recognize one another (48). But again, why should this be so on a voluntarist interpretation? It would seem that individuals would be as free voluntarily to obligate one another for a limited temporal period as to do so indefinitely. Of course, if, as I have been suggesting, reciprocally recognizing individuals are committed to the claims rational persons have *as such* to address second-personal reasons, not as a matter of voluntary agreement but as a presupposition of their intelligibly addressing claims to one another second-personally at all, then such a demand would be expected.

Fichte also frequently says that reciprocally recognizing agents recognize one another *as* rational beings, and that they are thereby committed to treating one another *as* rational beings or "persons" (e.g., 42, 43). But these claims presuppose that there are ways of mistreating rational beings *as such* and, therefore, that failing to recognize a rational being is not simply forbearing to make a voluntary commitment one is free not to make. They presuppose that rational being is itself a normative standing, that there are ways of respecting or mistreating them just by their nature as rational beings capable of reciprocal recognition (second-personally competent), and that, therefore, one is not free not to recognize and respect them. Again, this makes perfect sense on a "presuppositional" interpretation, but not on a voluntarist one.

Finally, the most significant problem with the voluntarist interpretation is that, unless we assume background relations of right and an obligation to keep voluntarily made commitments, a voluntarist interpretation is powerless to explain how reciprocal recognition can give rise to any obligation to respect spheres of freedom in the first place. This is the problem that, as I argue in Darwall 2023, besets Pufendorf's and Hobbes's forms of voluntarism as well: any normative power, like the authority to bind oneself by contracts and agreements, or even God's authority to bind us by promulgating natural law, must assume that such authority is itself independent of the obligations that are created by its exercise (Cudworth 1996: I.ii.3). And that, it seems, can be so only if conditional obligations to comply independently exist. Further, it must be presupposed that both those exercising the authority and those obligated by its exercise are already obligated not to use coercion and force, and thereby violate these obligations, in ways their authority permits them to do, were they to lack the requisite authority.

Fichte clearly assumes that individuals have warranted claims against each other if they violate the other's sphere of freedom once reciprocal recognition has transpired. If I have conformed to the law we both committed ourselves to in reciprocally recognizing one another, and my co-respondent subsequently violates that law, then I am in a position to charge them with a violation of my right:

> I ... appeal to a *law* that is valid for us both, and apply that law to the present case. I thus posit myself as *judge*, i.e. as his superior... But, insofar as I appeal to that common law in my opposition to him, I invite him to be a judge along with me; and I demand that in this case he must find my action against him consistent and must approve of it, compelled by the laws of thought. (47)

But what gives any "law" we voluntarily commit ourselves to normative force? The fact that we committed ourselves to it, as if adopting it together? Unless we assume that we each already have the normative standing to obligate ourselves through our reciprocal commitments, no reciprocal willing can yield any obligating law.

Fichte says that once someone has (arbitrarily, reciprocally) willed to live in community with others – has accepted this "hypothetical" "postulate" – they "must also necessarily will the law," "thus the law has hypothetical validity" (81–82). Fichte's terming the concept of right a "technical-practical" concept encourages us to read him as saying that since relations of right are necessary to any community of free beings, any agent who wills the latter must will the former, as Kant says about hypothetical imperatives, "insofar as reason has decisive influence on his actions" (Kant 1996a: 4:417). The problem is that this just assumes that rational agents *can* impose obligations on themselves. But this they cannot do without the requisite authority, and that authority cannot *itself* be explained by its being necessary to something they arbitrarily will. From the fact that relations of right are necessary to something I will nothing can possibly follow that could actually make me subject to them. And if we assume that you and I have the authority or power to obligate ourselves by our reciprocal willing, then we unavoidably assume that we stand in relations of right already.

We give Fichte a more promising view if we interpret him as saying that whenever you and I enter into a reciprocally recognizing, second-personal relation of summoned and summoner, we are committed thereby to assuming that we each have the standing as beings who are capable of rational second personality to be sources of second-personal reasons for one another. In seeking treatment from one another as rational second persons, we do not *endow* one another with this dignity or standing; we presuppose that we each independently have it. Interpreting Fichte in this way builds basic second-personal authority into the transcendental second-personal condition of self-consciousness in a way that allows us validly to deduce the concept of right. And it can account, moreover, for the relational, second-personal aspects of fundamental claim rights, and the second-personal reasons for acting to which these give rise, in a way that Kant's theory cannot.

What has been implicit in Fichte's argument here is the distinctive interpersonal attitude (and expressive action) he calls "recognition" (*Anerkennung*). It is through *Anerkennung* that we reciprocally *recognize* one another as free individual agents and implicitly commit ourselves to respecting the natural rights that are grounded in our reciprocal authority, which we must presuppose, to summon one another to comply with them. "The concept of individuality is," Fichte says, a "*reciprocal concept*," which "can exist in a rational being only if it is posited as *completed* by another rational being" (Fichte 2000: 45). Thus, "this concept is never *mine*," Fichte concludes. "It is a shared concept within which two consciousnesses are united into one" (45).

Wood persuasively proposes that the shared concept "necessary for individuality is that of recognition." *Anerkennung* involves, he says, "expressive action, an *admission* on both sides, and one which is shared" (Wood 2016: 262). Wood adds that the reciprocal recognition "gives rise to a . . . norm," the rule of right, thereby reading Fichte as a voluntarist. I have suggested that it is more promising to interpret Fichte as holding that reciprocal recognition commits both parties to the rule of right as a necessary presupposition. This would make its validity a transcendental condition for the very possibility of free individual agents.

Wood also emphasizes that the rule of right to which reciprocal recognition is tied is a "distinctive norm, which is *different from any ethical norm*" (262). This is undoubtedly Fichte's view. I have been arguing, however, that maintaining it risks depriving the right of its distinctive deontic normativity. In conclusion, I would like to suggest that blurring Fichte's distinction between moral philosophy and philosophy of right, or at least, blurring his way of drawing it, can help give Fichte an account of the distinctively deontic normativity to which his moral philosophy aspires, but which has so far proven elusive with the materials implicit in the I's first-person perspective alone.

Wood insightfully remarks that though Fichte's ethics are "second-person in the application of the moral principle," Fichte intends it as "a first-person conception in its *motivation*" (207). This is no doubt the way Fichte intends to be read. Taking note, however, of how any (reciprocally recognizing) perspective from which we can summon and make putatively legitimate demands of one another already puts a summoner into a second-personal space of mutual accountability can point us toward a plausible source of deontic normativity itself (Darwall 2006). Through the recognition that is already implicit in any summons, summoner and summoned alike are committed to their mutual accountability and obligations to one another as a transcendental condition of the very possibility of free individuals. Both are placed thereby into a deontic normative conceptual framework of shared obligation and mutual accountability.

This takes us back to the Grotian idea that the law and right of nature are grounded in the capacity of rational *sociable* persons to recognize their common competence and authority to make reasoned claims and demands against one another and to live with one another on terms that respect this common standing (see Darwall 2023a: 36–38). My suggestion here is that Fichte provides us with more materials to envision how such an idea might be worked out.

CHAPTER 2

Hegel

The other philosopher writing in Kant's wake who figures prominently in the origins of "continental" philosophy is, of course, Hegel. Although, as Wood stresses, many of the seeds of Hegel's thought were planted by Fichte, Hegel's works ultimately had far greater direct impact (Wood 2016: ix).[1] Hegel was not, however, an ethical or moral philosopher like Fichte. Irwin plausibly claims, indeed, that Hegel actually denies that moral philosophy is "a distinct discipline" (Irwin 2009: 182).[2] For this reason, I am devoting more attention to Fichte's ethics and philosophy of right than I will to Hegel's. But Hegel had a massive influence on the history of ethics even so, including on "modern moral philosophy." Partly this was as a critic, not just of moral philosophy, but also of the modern conception of morality itself. Hegel argues that what he and other moderns call "morality" (*Moralität*) is a formal abstraction that is incapable of "truth" or "reality." Moral philosophers who focus on oughts and obligation mistake, in his view, an abstract moment of practical thought for something realizable; they fasten on a desiccated abstraction rather than the "living good" that is embodied in actual modern (liberal) customs and institutions, what Hegel calls "ethical life" (*Sittlichkeit*) (Hegel 1991: 189).

Hegel's critique of morality begins a tradition that runs through Marx, Kierkegaard, and Nietzsche in the nineteenth century and through Anscombe and Bernard Williams toward the end of the twentieth. Despite this, many of the same philosophical ideas that we have seen to be central to modern moral philosophy also play an important role in Hegel's thought, even, indeed, in his critique of morality. Hegel is especially clear about what he takes to be fundamental differences

[1] According to Google Books Ngram Viewer, there were more references to Hegel than to Fichte in English-language books in every year after 1850. By the twentieth century, Hegel was referred to three times more than Fichte, and in the most recent year surveyed, 2019, Hegel was referred to more than seven times more than Fichte (https://tinyurl.com/m7tzjb7u).

[2] For a careful and helpful discussion of this issue, see Wood 1999: 8–10.

between ancient and modern ethical thought and that his sympathies are with the moderns rather than the ancients. Here it is important to bear in mind that Hegel's conception of "ethical life" is put forward as part of a philosophy of *right*, in contrast to any eudaimonist conception of the good.

At the foundation of Hegel's philosophy of right is a distinctive kind of freedom, which Hegel calls "subjective freedom," the right to which, he says, is "the pivotal and focal point in the difference between *antiquity* and the *modern* age" (151). In grounding the philosophy of right in freedom, Hegel self-consciously follows Kant and Fichte. Hegel's "subjective freedom" is a close cousin of Kant's "autonomy" and Fichte's "conscience." As we shall see, distinctively modern conceptions of freedom, as well as modern moral philosophy's companion idea of accountability, are governing presuppositions of Hegel's thought, including, remarkably, his account of the transition from *Moralität* to *Sittlichkeit*.

At the same time, Hegel opposes his thought to "all reflective philosophy, as in that of Kant" in which "freedom is nothing other than this formal self-activity" (49). Purely reflective practical thought can never advance beyond the formal abstractions of morality. Moreover, it leaves those who reason from its abstract "moral point of view" alienated from modern life and unable to find themselves "at home" in it. Actual participation in the shared customs and practices that constitute modern "ethical life," on the other hand, makes possible a "reconciliation" consisting in "the unity of objective freedom . . . and subjective freedom" (186, 276).

Hegel was thus a critic of morality and of its alienating role in lived modern experience. He was arguably the first philosopher, indeed, for whom modernity was itself a philosophical problem (Habermas 1990b: 23–44, Pippin 1997: 19). Hegel was the first to see that the juridical idea of alienation, so central to modern conceptions of property and contract, is deeply connected to alienation as a modern psychosocial complaint. What Hegel proposes in response is itself a distinctively modern solution, one that is possible only through a dialectical process that gives "abstract right" and morality specific content and brings them alive within modern institutions and practices in which participants can be "at home" and reconciled with themselves.[3]

There are elements of Fichte's thought that, as we saw, also drive him in this direction. For Fichte, the I can realize freedom only within a shared

[3] On the significance and role of reconciliation in Hegel's social philosophy, see Hardimon 1992 and 1994.

interpersonal social space in which individuals *recognize* one another. *Anerkennung* plays a leading role in Hegel's thought too. The "struggle for recognition" is as critical to Hegel's account of the emergence of free self-consciousness as recognition by other free agents is to Fichte's (Hegel 1977: 111–119, 1991: 87). However, there is a fundamental difference between Hegel's and Fichte's accounts of reciprocal recognition that significantly affects their respective philosophies of right. Whereas, for Fichte, recognition is tied to an essentially second-personal "summons" (*Aufforderung*) that can ground the right in presuppositions of intelligible practical claim making, the form that recognition takes in Hegel's thought requires neither a Fichtean summons nor acknowledgment through it of any putatively legitimate practical claim.[4]

The process with which Hegel is most fundamentally concerned is *identification* and identity formation, both when the will identifies itself with something external as its property and when it sees its identity as free confirmed by others' recognition. The role of recognition in this latter process is primarily *epistemic*, confirming one's "practical identity" in something like Korsgaard's sense (Korsgaard 1996a: 101). It is true that recognition of both Fichte's and Hegel's kinds implicitly attributes authority. But whereas the authority that is acknowledged in a Fichtean summons is the practical authority of a "self-originating source of valid claims," as Rawls puts it, in practical reasoning, the form implicated in Hegel's "struggle for recognition" is ultimately epistemic, the authority to *see* a successful opponent as someone who is willing to risk death to preserve freedom, and therefore, one whose identity is that of a free being (Rawls 1980: 546). An important upshot is that although Fichte has available a plausible grounding of the juridical aspects of a philosophy of right in the presuppositions of second-personal summoning that is necessary for self-consciousness, it remains an open question what within recognition as Hegel conceives it can ground the distinctively modern, juridical aspects of right that Hegel hopes to retain within ethical life.

Toward a Philosophy of Right

We shall return to this question later when we examine Hegel's discussion of the struggle for recognition in *Phenomenology of Spirit*. Mostly, however, we shall be concerned with Hegel's mature statement of his practical philosophy in *Elements of the Philosophy of Right*, published fourteen

[4] On this point, see Stern 2021.

years after *Phenomenology*, in 1821. What Hegel means by "philosophy of right" is much broader than what Kant and Fichte pursued under that heading. For Hegel, the "*philosophical science of right*" comprises "Morality" and "Ethical Life" in addition to "Abstract Right" (Hegel 1991: 25, 62), whereas Kant and Fichte restrict their philosophies of right to this last category. Hegel regards his three "subdivisions" of philosophy of right, moreover, less as divisions of a common subject or discipline than as successive developments of the concept of right in the direction of its "actualization" or "actuality." Philosophy of right's "subject-matter," he says, "is the *Idea of right*," that is, "the concept of right and its actualization" (25).

Philosophy, as Hegel understands it, "has to do with Ideas" rather than "*mere concepts*" (25). We can hardly plumb the depths of Hegel's dialectical logic here, but his contrast is between "abstract," "one-sided," and un-"develop[ed]" concepts, on the one hand, and fully developed Ideas having "truth" and "actuality," on the other (25, 26).[5] Transcendental philosophers, like Kant and Fichte, reason with mere concepts and can never get beyond abstractions. Philosophy's true task, for Hegel, is "immanent" rather than transcendent. It starts with reflection on actual human practice and custom and seeks rational development within them. It seeks to comprehend "present and . . . actual" custom and practice "so that the content which is already rational in [it] may also gain a rational form and thereby appear justified to free thinking" (11, 20).

"The *truth* concerning *right*," is "*as old*," Hegel says, as "*public laws*" and "*public morality*" (11). Ancient Greek custom and law is thus a riper source for ethical reflection than ancient philosophical (eudaimonist) theory. Of course, Hegel thinks that modern laws and practices are even better sources since they manifest the Idea of right as a more developed concept, as actualizing human *freedom*. According to Hegel's dialectical logic, "the concept, in science, develops out of itself and is merely an *immanent* progression and production of its own determinations" (59). The concept's "moving principle," "which not only dissolves particularizations of the universal, but also produces them, is what I call dialectic," Hegel writes (60). The "basis of right," as a developed concept or Idea, is the "*realm of spirit*," more precisely, the realm of "the *will*" and its freedom, so that "the system of right is the realm of actualized freedom" (35).

We shall turn presently to Hegel's analysis of the will as having three distinct "moments" and their relation to philosophy of right's three

[5] But see McNulty 2023.

subdivisions – Abstract Right, Morality, and Ethical Life – which Hegel lays out in *Elements*' introduction. First, however, we should note a distinction Hegel makes in the preface between "laws of nature" and "laws of right" since this can help us appreciate his fundamental opposition to transcendental "reflective" philosophical approaches, like Kant's and Fichte's, and his own contrasting "immanent" method.

"Laws of nature are simply there and are valid as they stand," Hegel says. "The measure of these laws is external to us, and our cognition adds nothing to them" (13). "Laws of right," by contrast, "are something *laid down*, something *derived from* human beings" (13). Moreover, unlike the laws of nature, "the human being . . . claims to have within himself the measure of what is right" (13). This clearly recalls and may be intended to recall, Kant's distinction between "laws of nature" and "laws of freedom" (Kant 1996a: 4:387). According to Kant's doctrine of autonomy and self-legislation, it is an a priori truth, confirmed by Kant's "reflective" transcendental method, that all moral agents must have "within [themselves] the measure of what is right," as Hegel puts it. But there is a crucial difference between Kant's "laws of freedom" and Hegel's "laws of right," even though Hegel says that "the system of right is the realm of actualized freedom" (Hegel 1991: 35).

For Hegel, we initially get to know laws of right, not through our own reflective activity, as deliverances of our own reason, but, like "laws of nature," "simply as they are," as given to us in positive law and custom. Laws of right are "laid down" all right, but not through internal self-legislation; they are implicitly legislated, rather, within public practices and institutions. Hegel does think that not just any given positive law or custom counts as "valid" or actually "binding." "In laws of right, . . . the thing is not valid because it exists" (13). But the distinction between mere custom and valid law must itself be rooted in actual practice. Validly "binding" duties must always be at least implicit in existing law and custom (191–192). And whether a law is valid or binding is, for Hegel, a different question than any concerning "how the world *ought* to be" (23, emphasis added).[6]

Modern moral philosophers generally take their subject to be concerned with oughts and obligations almost by definition. Sidgwick says in *The Methods of Ethics* that all ethical judgments contain "the fundamental

[6] See also Hegel's remark that normative critiques expressed with "'ought' have [no] place within the interests of philosophical science" (Hegel 1975a: §6, quoted in Wood 1999: 9). Also: "The true ideal is not what ought to be actual but what is actual, and the only actuality" (quoted in Wood 1999: 12).

notion represented by the word 'ought'" (Sidgwick 1962: 25). The distinctive character of oughtness or normativity, moreover, has often been held to be the source of the most fundamental problems of metaethical or metanormative theorizing. Arguably, it is what drives Moore's well-known open-question argument for the unanalyzability of good in *Principia Ethica*, published in 1903, which fueled so much of the analytic metaethics that followed (Frankena 1942: 102; Moore 1993a; Darwall, Gibbard, and Railton 1997: 4–6). In addition, we have seen how the distinctive deontic normative idea of obligation and, I argue, its connection to accountability, lie at the core of modern moral philosophy, more narrowly conceived (Darwall 2006, 2023a).

In Hegel's view, however, this focus has misled modern moral philosophers, though for reasons different than those lying behind Anscombe's critique in "Modern Moral Philosophy" (Anscombe 1958).[7] Any philosophy that attempts to "*issue instructions* on how the world ought to be" or assumes any "obligation to construct *a state as it ought to be*" indulges in abstractions that lack genuine content (Hegel 1991: 21, 23). And any such philosophy would be powerless to bring its abstract conceptions to life, in any case. Philosophical normative critique is both empty and impotent. As Hegel famously puts it: "When philosophy paints its grey in grey, a shape of life has grown old, and it cannot be rejuvenated, but only recognized, by the grey in grey of philosophy; the owl of Minerva begins its flight only with the onset of dusk" (23). Philosophy's proper task is therefore "the *comprehension of the present and the actual*, not the setting up of a *world beyond*" (20). Its comprehension and critique must be immanent, not transcendent. Philosophy must bring out what "is already rational" in current practice and thereby demonstrate how the "actual is rational" and the "rational is actual" (11, 20). By "actual," again, Hegel means not simply *existing* practices, but those aspects of them that develop and "actualize" the Ideas they essentially involve – in the case of rightful practices, "objective freedom." A philosophy of right must therefore show how current law and custom have developed dialectically and actualized the concept of right in actualizing freedom.

By Hegel's own lights, however, nothing in *Elements of the Philosophy of Right* that precedes Part 3 on "Ethical Life" can yet be immanent in this sense. Both the introduction's discussion of "speculative method" and Hegel's three-moment analysis of the will, as well as Parts 1 and 2, on Abstract Right and Morality, proceed at a transcendental conceptual level,

[7] For discussion of "Anscombe's Challenge" see Darwall 2023a: 1–4.

not by reflecting on going institutions and practices. Hegel's central claim, after all, is that without realization in actual practice, abstract right and morality remain abstract formal concepts.

This will turn out to have important consequences, since, for example, Hegel represents Abstract Right as essentially including a "commandment of right" – "*be a person and respect others as persons*" (69). This certainly seems to be something like a Kantian categorical imperative that could also be expressed with an "ought." Its similarity to Kant's Formula of Humanity is striking.

As is the case with Kant's formula, however, the philosophical question arises, what can ground the normative claim that one ought to treat others with respect as persons? And in addition to this broadly metanormative question, there is also a more narrowly meta*moral* question connected to morality's deontic character: What can ground the deontic normative claim that conduct violating the "commandment of right" is morally wrong and contrary to our moral duty (see Darwall 2023a: 325–333)?

Hegel will want to resist these questions. Since they essentially involve ought and obligation, they are not properly philosophically posed in the sense in which he is interested. He can, however, recognize related questions, namely, whether laws and customs that give these abstract propositions definite content are "valid" and "binding," as he puts it, in modern law and customary morality.

Despite this, modern philosophers' questions of normativity and obligation will nonetheless remain, even if they are read out of Hegel's philosophical canon. From their point of view, any question of "duty" and "valid" "binding[ness]" (to use Hegel's preferred terms) that can be settled from within actual law and practice will remain a "positive" rather than a "normative" question in the sense employed by legal positivism (see, e.g., Hart 2012). (Hegel, indeed, calls his philosophy of right a "positive science of right" (Hegel 1991: 26, 28, 244).) To modern metaethicists and metamoral theorists there will always seem to be a further normative question, however, and hence a further philosophical question about what could ground an answer to Hegel's positive question, whether we call these "philosophical" or not.

Three Moments of the Will and Three Subdivisions of the Right

We can turn now to Hegel's three-moment analysis of the will. The context in *Elements'* introduction is Hegel's framing remark that the "precise location and point of departure" of right "is the *will*" (35). This is evidently a conceptual claim. The right, in the sense in which Hegel (like other modern philosophers) intends, concerns voluntary conduct by definition. Moreover, Hegel takes it as given that "freedom" is "as much a basic determination of the will as weight is a basic determination of bodies" (35). This can likewise be taken as a conceptual claim or even as a stipulative definition. Any substantive philosophical question can be posed in terms of whether anything satisfies or "actualizes" this conceptual definition.

Hegel's first moment "(α)" is familiar from Fichte's reflective analysis of "the I." Hegel defines it as follows:

> The will contains (α) the element of *pure indeterminacy* or of the "I"'s pure reflection into itself, in which every limitation, every content, whether present immediately through nature, through needs, desires, and drives, or given and determined in some other way, is dissolved; this is the limitless infinity of *absolute abstraction* or *universality*, the pure thinking of oneself (37).

Like Fichte, Hegel takes it that the will intrinsically involves the self-reflective capacity to step back and reflect, in principle, from anything about which one can think – including states of oneself like desires – and deliberate about what to do. In so deliberating, one necessarily suspends (as Locke would put it) the motivating force of given desires. From this perspective, one "free[s] [oneself] from everything" and "renounce[s] all ends" (38). Though one can take into account the fact that one has whatever ends one has, in considering whether to pursue them, one adopts a perspective from which their motivating force is suspended. Of course, one may not be successful, and the force of given desires and ends may affect one's self-reflective practical thought despite one's best efforts.

Hegel's point is essentially the same as Fichte on the I and the not-I. Anything given and not posited by the I is part of the not-I, including unconscious motivations that mask themselves as part of the I's own self-positing practical thought. Hegel is loath to put this in terms of a presupposed transcendental I or Kantian "transcendental unity of practical apperception." But, at this point anyway, it is hard to see why he should resist such formulations since he is now proceeding at a conceptual level that leaves metaphysical questions of actuality and truth to one side. Hegel seems just to be assuming, like many other modern moral philosophers, that any agent that could intelligibly be subject to standards of right must have the self-reflective capacities involved in the will's moment (α). This is frequently taken for granted on the grounds that the right necessarily has to do with accountability (Darwall 2006, 2023a). I shall be arguing that something like this assumption plays a central role in Hegel's thought.

Hegel characterizes (α) as *absolute abstraction* or *universality* and *pure indeterminacy* (Hegel 1991: 37). By contrast, the will's second moment (β) "is the transition from undifferentiated indeterminacy to *differentiation*, *determination*, and the *positing* of a determinacy as a content and object . . . Through this positing of itself as something *determinate*, *'I'* steps into existence [*Dasein*] in general." (β) is "the absolute moment of the *finitude* or *particularization* of the 'I'" (39). Having abstracted from all determinate content in (α), the will "cancels" this indeterminacy upon settling on a particular practical alternative. In so doing, Hegel says, it "posits itself" in a committed particular way (41). It commits itself to a practical identity and identifies itself in the world.

Hegel emphasizes what he takes to be an important difference with Fichte. Whereas, as Hegel reads him, Fichte takes "the abstract '*I*' *for itself* [(α)] to be *the truth*" and "*positive*" in itself, and maintains that "the *negative*" "is therefore something added in" a particular volition in (β), Hegel holds that *both* (α) and (β) involve an abstracting negation and cancellation of their respective alternatives, which nonetheless remain contained within them (40). "Just as the particular is in general contained within the universal, so in consequence is this second moment [(β)] already contained within the first [(α)]" (39). Hegel believes that Fichte mistook an abstract moment of the will [(α)] for something positive, "true," and "concrete" in itself (40–41).

Recall now Hegel's claim that "freedom is just as much a basic determination of the will as weight [or mass] is a basic determination of bodies" (35). (α) and (β) are both abstract moments; so both are incapable of "constitut[ing] the concept or substantiality of the will" (41). Neither can constitute the will's freedom. That can be accomplished only by the will's third stage, (λ), which achieves "the unity of both these moments [(α) and (β)] – *particularity* reflected *into itself* and thereby restored to *universality*" (41). Only if (α) and (β) are unified in (λ) is the particularity of (β) "reconciled" with the universality of (α) and the will's "substantiality," the "freedom of the will," constituted.

"What is properly called the will," (λ), "contains both the preceding moments [(α) and (β)]." But whereas (α) and (β) are abstract moments of thought, (λ) is a concrete whole in which these are unified. Abstractly, in (α), "I" is "with itself" from an "[un]determined," "universal" point of view (42). When, in (β), "I" "determines itself," it "posits itself as an other and ceases to be universal" (42). The I's perspective in (α) is that of *an* (hence universal) undetermined, uncommitted agent facing a specific kind of practical situation. In (β), it is that of a *particular* agent who has committed themselves with a particular intention or decision. Only in "the third moment," (λ), in which (α) and (β) are unified, is "'I' *with* itself [as 'universal'] *in* its limitation, in this other [as particular determination]" (42, emphasis added). The will "determines itself" in some particular way in (λ), as it does in (β). But unlike in (β), in (λ), will "does not cease to hold fast to the universal"(42).

Unlike the "abstract" and "one-sided" moments (α) and (β), in which pure universality and indeterminacy are opposed by pure determinacy and particularity, (λ) achieves a reconciliation of universality and particularity and of indeterminacy and determinacy (42). In concrete free choice, "we are not one-sidedly within ourselves" (as in [α]); neither do we pass out of the "universal" selves we are *with* by some particular arbitrary choice (as in [β]). Rather, in (λ) we "willingly limit ourselves with reference to an other, even while knowing ourselves in this limitation as ourselves" (42). We see the limitation of concrete choice not just as an other, but as something in and through which we recognize and understand ourselves and our identity.

As an analogy, Hegel cites choices that express friendship and love. Action for a friend's sake involves self-limiting particular determination (from the perspectives of [α] and [β]), but because friends willingly *identify* with one another and their plight, action for friends' sake is not viewed as mere limitation. To the contrary, because friends value one another and see relating to each other as part of their own identity, they view action for their friends' sake as expressing and realizing their own identity as well. Wholeheartedly embraced limitations such as these are experienced less as limiting the self than as opportunities for self-actualization and realization of freedom.

We can put Hegel's point in terms of a distinction between blind arbitrary choice on the one hand, mere "plumping," and choices that express what an agent values or cares about (Watson 1975; Ullmann-Margalit and Morgenbesser 1977; Frankfurt 1998). Blind choice is consistent with moment (β), but it can leave an agent with a practical path they are not identified with and that seems alien to them. What they have chosen may lack any capacity to speak to them as a chooser (that is, from the perspective they occupied in [α]). When we view what we value and care about as choosers, by contrast, things we value and care about seem to be the very paradigm of things we take ourselves as choosers to have normative reason to pursue. Choices that express our values, unlike arbitrary or capricious ones, seem to reconcile the deliberative (unlimited) perspective and the committed one of particular limitation. We actualize and, Hegel says, "[know] ourselves in this limitation as ourselves" (Hegel 1991: 42).[8] We see loving actions for friends' sakes, for example, as revealing who we really are – our practical identity or "deep selves" (Wolf 1987; Korsgaard 1996a).

Now ultimately, Hegel's aim will be to show that it is only in "Ethical Life" that "right" and "freedom" can be realized and made concrete as "Ideas." His three-moment analysis of the will is intended to set up this point. (α) and (β) are but abstract, one-sided moments of practical thought and are therefore incapable of making freedom and right complete and concrete. They involve an irresolvable "contradiction between subjectivity [(α)] and objectivity [(β)]," as well as between universality and particularity (Hegel 1991: 57), and indeterminacy and determinacy (Hegel 1991: 57). Any putative philosophy of right that employs only these moments of will, as Hegel will argue that "Abstract Right" and "Morality" do, is incapable of capturing the right as a "realm of actualized freedom" (35).

(λ) provides the concept of will necessary to realize concrete freedom. (λ) "cancel[s] the contradiction between subjectivity and objectivity and ... translate[s the will's] ends from their subjective determination into an objective one, while at the same time remaining *with itself* in this objectivity" (57). In not simply "picking" ends, but choosing them as expressions of our values, we see our ends as things to care about, as things that are valuable and give us normative reasons.

Having given his three-moment analysis of the will and signaled (λ)'s relation to realizing concrete freedom, Hegel gives the closest thing to a definition of right that he provides in *Elements*: "*Right* is any existence [*Dasein*] in general which is the *existence* of the *free will.* Right is therefore in general freedom, as an Idea" (58). By "Idea" here, Hegel clearly means a developed, actualized concept, not just any "mere concept" (25, 87).

Hegel immediately contrasts his view of the relation of freedom and right with Kant's as contained in Kant's definition of right in his *Rechtslehre*. Hegel quotes the "essential element": "the *limitation* of my freedom or *arbitrary will* in such a way that it may coexist with the arbitrary will of everyone else in accordance with a universal law" (Hegel 1991: 58; cf. Kant 1996c: 6:230). "Freedom" in Kant's definition is what Kant calls

[8] As Wood points out, Hegel's ethics are perhaps best viewed as an ethics of self-actualization rather than as a teleological or deontological theory (Wood 1999: 37).

"external freedom," by which Kant means our freedom, once having chosen to do something, actually to do it. So, by Hegel's lights, it involves the will in its second abstract moment (β), in its "negative determination" of "limitation" in the "arbitrary will[ing]" of actions in the "external world" (Hegel 1991: 43, 58). The "positive [element] – the universal law or so-called 'law of reason'" – Kant holds, according to Hegel, to be implicit in the formally universal point of view involved in (α).

The elements of the will in play in Kant's definition of right are both abstract and therefore incapable of concretely actualizing freedom as Hegel understands it in his "definition" of right as "freedom, as Idea" (58). The only moment of the will that can is (λ), which, unifying (α) and (β), can choose actions that, though they respect "limitations" on external conduct, nonetheless are "rational" and realize the agent's practical identity because they give the agent's values and cares an external public expression (58). As Hegel says about friendship, we "willingly limit ourselves with reference to an other, even while knowing ourselves in this limitation as ourselves" (42). Such actions reconcile us to a world from which the abstract concepts of will and right alienate us.

Having presented his three-moment analysis of the will and his "definition" of the right as the actualized "*existence* of the *free will*," Hegel completes *Elements*' introduction with a statement of the three parts of philosophy of right – Abstract Right, Morality, and Ethical Life – which he will then discuss in Parts I, II, and III, respectively (58, 62–64). Hegel says that these follow from three "stages in the development of the Idea of the will," but "stages" here seems to mean something different from the will's three moments: (α), (β), and (λ), though these are closely related (62). For example, the first stage, (A), which is the concept of will implicated in "abstract or formal right," is "that of *personality* and its *existence* is an immediate external thing." It has externalized itself in its actual chosen acts, whatever these might be, in the space of Kantian "external freedom" (62). But though this is still an abstract concept of will in the way that (α) is, and so incapable of actualizing freedom as a developed concept or Idea, as (λ) can, it is nonetheless not identical with (α). (A) is better thought of as (α) "reflected" into (β) by an actual action as an embodied "thing" in the "external world" (62).

Similarly, (B), the stage of the will that Hegel holds to be involved in Morality is "the will reflected from its external existence . . . *into itself*," which is less like (β) taken in itself (the will's particular externalization) than (β) reflected back into (λ) (62). Hegel's contrast between Morality and Abstract Right is like Fichte and Kant's between ethics and philosophy of right in their restricted sense of the philosophy of rights and law. Like Fichte and Kant, Hegel takes Abstract Right to concern what is enforceable by justified coercion. Also like Kant, Hegel takes Morality to concern the aspect of will that is precisely not externally coercible: the will taken in itself (as "subjective"), but which, nonetheless, externalizes itself by taking action in the external world.

Finally, "the unity and truth of these two abstract moments" is simply (λ), through which the will as actualized freedom "exists no less as *actuality* and *necessity* than as *subjective* will" (62). Thus are the Ideas of Good, Right, and Freedom realized simultaneously "in the internally *reflected will* and in the *external world*" through the public common practices and institutions that Hegel calls "ethical life" (62).

Abstract Right

The sphere of Abstract Right is that of *external* rightful conduct, that is, "legality" in Kant and Fichte's sense of actions that accord with right regardless of the agent's motive or "subjective will" (Kant 1996b: 5:71; Fichte 2005: 148). It is the sphere of rights, which Kant holds to consist in what can rightfully be coerced (Kant 1996c: 6:232). Although Abstract Right concerns external behavior, it is crucial for Hegel (as it is for Kant and Fichte) that right (in this restricted sense) concerns external *conduct* – that is, the willed behavior of a self-reflective I. Accordingly, capacities for both of the two abstract moments of the will – (α) and (β) – must be in play. The beings to whom Abstract Right applies must be capable of self-reflective "formal universality" – deliberating about what to do from a perspective that abstracts from the particularity of given desires or inclinations (α). But they must also be capable of adopting particular ends, committing themselves to external conduct, from this perspective – of giving their wills particularity (β) (Hegel 1991: 67).

Hegel collects both abstract moments under the concept of "personality." *Persons* are essentially "self-conscious" (that is, formally universal in their self-reflection) beings who are considered in their particularity or determinacy as "*this* person," having a "completely determined . . . inner arbitrary will" that they gave an "immediate external existence" (67–68). Abstract Right concerns the particularity of persons as it affects other persons in their particularity (70).

Hegel distinguishes between persons and the broader category of "subjects," by which he means conscious "living" beings, whether self-conscious or not (68). All subjects have a point of view on the external world and behave in ways that reflect their subjectivity. "A person," Hegel says, is "a subject which is aware of this subjectivity" (68). When persons act, they externalize their practical self-awareness in a way that gives their personality an external existence. Their personality "give[s] itself reality" (70). Questions of Abstract Right necessarily arise for persons because the external world also contains other persons. Abstract Right concerns how persons may rightfully conduct themselves in a world of other persons.

Other persons are not, moreover, simply other inhabitants of the sphere of Abstract Right. It is critical to Hegel, too, that the realm of Abstract Right is a *common* sphere in which a person "relates himself to *another person*" (70). This relational element is clearest in Hegel's account of property, which he ties *both* to the externalization of self that is involved in persons' property-claiming conduct and to the relating to others that any such property-claiming conduct necessarily involves. In Abstract Right, Hegel says, "it is only as owners of property" that persons "have existence [*Dasein*] for each other" (70).

The three concepts of Abstract Right, personality, and property constitute a mutually entailing circle for Hegel. "Personality . . . constitutes the concept" and "basis" of "abstract and hence *formal* right" (69). And persons acquire property simply by exercising their personality when, in the company of other persons, they exert their wills in the external world. The fundamental "commandment of right is therefore" simply: "*be a person and respect others as persons,*" that is, to respect them "as owners of property"(69, 70).

What it is to respect persons, and hence to comply with the commandment of right, consequently, is to respect their capacity to acquire and transfer property by exercising their wills. Hegel stresses on these grounds that Abstract Right fundamentally concerns not persons' "interests" or "welfare," but simply their particularity, which they realize through exercising their wills on anything external – on the Not-I, in Fichte's terms – in the company of others (69). "*Personality* alone confers a right to *things*," and so "personal right is a right of things" (71). This is "the right of *personality* as *such*" (71). In this way, again, Hegel's concepts of personality, Abstract Right, and property mutually entail one another.

But how exactly, according to Hegel, does the exercise of the will with respect to "things" enable persons to acquire property in them? What Hegel calls the "rational aspect of property" consists in the metaphysical fact of "the superseding of mere subjectivity" through exercising the will in the external "objective realm of actions" in some particular way (73, 149). Even in taking a walk, a person makes the external path on which they have embarked their own, and anyone stepping in their way is attempting to possess their property. In Hegel's capacious sense, property includes all external conduct and, therefore, freedom.

Hegel's claim that persons acquire property through exercising their wills can be interpreted as an uncontroversial metaphysical thesis, as following directly from his analysis of the will. Thus, Hegel says of the doctrine of first possession, "that a thing belongs to the person *who happens to be the first* to take possession of it," that it is "immediately self-evident," indeed, "superfluous" (81).

However, Hegel is also advancing his claims about property and first possession as propositions of right. It is part of the latter that "a second party cannot take possession of what is already the property of someone else" (81). Of course, in a purely nonnormative metaphysical sense, a second party *can* do this, as any successful theft proves. The thief externalizes their subjective will in the objective realm no less than the original possessor does. For the doctrine of first possession to not simply be thus falsifiable (metaphysically), we must understand it to mean that a second party cannot *rightfully* take what another has already rightfully possessed, *and* that rightful possession itself derives from the exercise of the will on something that is not already rightfully possessed.

The capacities to acquire and transfer property, as we ordinarily understand them, are not nonnormative metaphysical capacities; they are normative powers (what Pufendorf calls "moral powers" [Pufendorf 1934: 18; 2009: 229]). We take it that what one acquires or transfers are not primarily particular external things that constitute the property, but distinctive *rights* over those things, including rights to exclude others from their use. Hegel's analysis of the will can explain how when someone exerts their will on something external, they thereby create a new metaphysical relation to it. And we can even stipulate a metaphysical difference between the relation created by a first exercise of the will on something and any brought about by subsequent exercisings of other wills. But neither of these can explain, by themselves, how any *rights* have been thereby created or violated. It remains unclear how Hegel's metaphysical analysis of the will, or even any related thesis of his dialectical logic, could underwrite his claims about personality and property as matters of Abstract Right.

Kant stresses in his "deduction" of "original acquisition" in the *Rechtslehre* that he considers property to be not just a "relation of a person to objects," but a "relation of a person to persons" (Kant 1996c: 6:268). Kant holds the relation to be a normative one consisting in the fact that others "are *bound*, with regard to the use of the thing, by the *will* of the first person," though only so far as the first person's will was itself consistent with the Universal Principle of Right (6:268). In Kant's view, as in the commonsense view, to acquire property in something is to acquire rights with respect to it that obligate others.

As we saw, Kant understands rights in terms of authorized coercion (6:232). This means that property rights for Kant consist in the normative power to coercively prevent others from attempting to impede one's use of what one owns – the authority to "hinde[r]" their "hindrance" (6:231). Such a normative power, however, involves a Hohfeldian privilege and an immunity. It enables one to use coercion against the hinderer without wronging them and makes one immune to others' attempts to appropriate what one owns (Hohfeld 1923). As we noted, however, acquired privileges and immunities are impotent by themselves to explain any proprietary claim rights that entail correlative obligations against whom the rights are held. This is an essential feature of property as we ordinarily understand it. When one acquires a property right in something, one is entitled to expect that others will respect that right and, equivalently, that they are obligated to do so.

Now Hegel agrees with Kant that property is fundamentally a relation not just to the thing owned but to other persons. "A person, in distinguishing himself from himself, relates himself to *another person*"; and "it is only as owners of property that [they] have existence [*Dasein*] for each other" (Hegel 1991: 70). Hegel also agrees with Kant that right authorizes coercion. "Abstract right," he says, "is a *coercive right*" (121). We will return to this second point of agreement later since it plays an important role in Hegel's account of the transition from Abstract Right to Morality. But we will focus first on the way relation to others enters into Hegel's account of property no less than it does into Kant's.

Especially noteworthy is the role Hegel gives to *recognition*. It is essential to my acquisition of property that others are able to "recognize" my voluntary relating to it. In *manifestly* externalizing my will, I make it the case that my will can "be recognized by others" (81). "My inner act of will which says that something is mine must also become recognizable by others" (81). Others might recognize that the metaphysical relation between my subjective will and the objective thing I will to possess obtains without thereby recognizing that thing as my property in any normative sense, that I own it rightfully and that others are obligated to respect that. Any recognition that can constitute *respect* for personality, as the commandment of right requires, however, must acknowledge not just the metaphysical relation but a normative relation that is ultimately grounded in a presupposed normative status of persons as a matter of right. It must presuppose an essentially normative recognition of persons.

Reciprocal recognition is central also to Hegel's treatment of *contract*, which, like Kant, Hegel treats as issuing from a "common will" (Hegel 1991: 103; Kant 1996c: 6:273). "Contract," Hegel says, "presupposes that the contracting parties *recognize* each other as persons and owners of property" (Hegel 1991: 103). Here again, it is crucial that the relevant recognition is not merely metaphysical but normative. It is part of the very idea of contract that what the contracting parties offer is something they own as a matter of right since only if that is true can they transfer any right by the contract. The capacity to contract is thus like the capacity to acquire property, a normative rather than a metaphysical power.

Two people can enter into a contract only if they understand one another as having this normative power; and they can exercise the power only through relating to one another in a way that reciprocally recognizes each other as having it. When Hegel says, therefore, that contract presupposes that the contracting parties reciprocally recognize one another as "persons and owners of property," we might put this more perspicuously by saying the parties must recognize each other as having the normative power to own and transfer property and, even more fundamentally, as having the normative authority or status as persons that grounds these normative powers. This brings contractual rights more clearly under the commandment of right's requirement to "respect persons."

We have seen how Fichte can fruitfully be interpreted as grounding his philosophy of right in a shared fundamental (second-personal) authority or status that is presupposed by a summons and that is, he argues, necessary to give persons a deliberative awareness of themselves as free agents. Similar ideas are involved in Grotius and Pufendorf, and in a different form in Smith on justice and Reid on "social operations of the mind" (see Darwall 2023a). In addition to its centrality to Hegel's views on property and contract, reciprocal recognition also plays an essential role in his theory of the development of self-consciousness in *Phenomenology*. Despite the superficial similarity of this phenomenological project to Fichte's, however, recognition ends up functioning quite differently in Hegel's thought than it does in Fichte's. As we shall see, recognition for Hegel is less a second-personal engagement that acknowledges a shared fundamental authority to make practical claims that can ground normative powers than a mutual confirmation of a shared practical identity as beings who value their metaphysical freedom.

To conclude this section on Abstract Right, we move to Hegel's account of the transition from Abstract Right to Morality, which occurs because of contradictions to which Abstract Right is susceptible in the rectification of wrongs. Note, first, a move Hegel makes concerning the relation of right to coercion that is similar to Kant's. "Abstract right is," Hegel says, "a coercive right, because a wrong committed against it is a force directed against the *existence* [*Dasein*] of my freedom in an *external* thing [*Sache*]" (Hegel 1991: 121). Wrongs all involve coercion, which is the denial, or "hindrance," to use Kant's term, of freedom by definition. Equivalently, for Hegel, wrongs all involve forceful takings of another's property. Kant thinks, again, that the right authorizes coercion in response to unauthorized coercion – the "hindering of a hindrance to freedom" (Kant 1996c: 6:231). Hegel broadly agrees with this, but he also believes that it is the source of contradictions that are unresolvable within Abstract Right as an abstract conceptual structure.

The category of wrong that Hegel calls "crime" is the intentional violation of right, hence any attempt to "cancel" the free exercise of another's particular subjective will. There is a sense, Hegel thinks, in which any such attempted (wrongful) cancellation is itself a "nullity," in that any such coercive infringement immediately calls for its own "nullification" by a coercive response as a kind of metaphysical completion. Since the will has existence only if it is free, willed unfreedom calls for its own cancellation or nullification through a coercive response. This is what is metaphysically required by the dialectical development of the concept of wrong or crime itself (Hegel 1991: 121–130).

So far conceived, however, there may be no *recognizable* difference between the subjective will of the first coercer and that of the second attempting to respond to it. Both involve coercive force directed by one subjective will against another. According to Hegel's metaphysics, an *unjustified* use of coercion requires completion by the coercion it calls for. But what makes it the case that any particular use of coercion *is* unjustified rather than a justified response to some earlier coercion or threat of it? "What is at first sight objectionable about retribution is that it looks like something immoral, like revenge, and may thus be interpreted as a personal matter" (129). If there is no publicly recognizable difference between a "punitive" and an "avenging justice" – that is, the valid meting out of justice and personal retaliation – then there is nothing to stop indefinite cycles of coercion and violence (130–131).

Partly, Hegel's point is a familiar theme of modern social contract theories, from Locke through Kant. Without either "magistrates" or public "laws," "punishment always takes the form of revenge," or, at least, there is no publicly recognizable way of determining that that is not the case (130). Abstract Right as an abstract conceptual structure is impotent to actualize in a publicly recognizable order even the specific rights of persons it commands all persons to respect. But Hegel also has in mind a further point about the moral psychology of accountability that we noted in connection with Kant's coercion-centered account of right. The fact that an action would invite a coercive response has no intrinsic connection to the fact that it would violate a right and therefore be wrong; these facts should function quite differently the practical reasoning of a would-be rights violator.

We ordinarily take it to be part of the very idea of rights that they provide, in themselves, weighty reasons for acting. So long, however, as the will is only subjective, willing its own particular expression, as in Abstract Right, the conceptual resources are simply lacking to enable it to recognize any reasons except those grounded in its own particularity. To put it in the terms of Bernard Williams's "internal" and "external reasons," considerations of right and wrong can only appear as "external reasons," and therefore not in a form that agents can act on without alienation (Williams 1981b).

"Punitive" – in contrast with "avenging" – justice requires a subjective will that "also wills the universal as such" (Hegel 1991: 131). This is a conceptual requirement not of Abstract Right but "of *morality*" (131). From the moral point of view, we will for ourselves only what we would will universally. From that perspective, what we would otherwise see as personal retaliation we can see as what we ourselves will universally. Within Morality, therefore, we can view acting rightly as something we ourselves have (moral) reason to do.

The contradictions that are created within Abstract Right can be resolved, or, at least mitigated, therefore, by Morality, the concept that, Hegel says, "has emerged in the course of this movement itself" (131). Morality marks a development in the concept of the will in that we can now make a distinction between the "universal will" and the "individual will" (131). Thus, coercive nullification of a previous nullification that crime involves within Abstract Right, leads "through punishment ... to affirmation, i.e., to *morality*" (132). As we shall see, Hegel thinks that the problems that emerge within Abstract Right cannot wholly be resolved within Morality, since reasoning from the moral point of view *individually* will not solve issues of specification of content and disagreement that can only be resolved by the collective reasoning involved in common public practices and institutions of Ethical Life.

The element within Abstract Right that leads Hegel to Morality is the right's conceptual relation to accountability and what we can demand of one another. It is a conceptual feature of claim rights that they are what right holders have the authority to claim and what those against whom the rights are held are obligated to respect and so are thereby accountable for respecting. As Pufendorf points out, we can only intelligibly hold someone accountable if we presuppose that they can take up an interpersonally impartial perspective from which they can accept the demands we implicitly make of them as giving them sufficient reasons for acting and thereby hold themselves accountable.[9] As we shall see in the next section, the conceptual connection of obligation to accountability is, moreover, both central to Morality as Hegel understands it and essential to his dialectical transition from Morality to Ethical Life.

Morality

"The moral point of view," Hegel says, "is the point of view of the will in so far as the latter is *infinite* not only *in itself* but also *for itself*" (135). Recall the basic contrast between Hegel's first two moments of the will. (α) is "infinite," "subjective," and "universal," whereas (β) is "finite," "objective," and "particular." In (α), the agent steps back from any given content to a perspective that, while "subjective," is nonetheless "universal" and "infinite." The agent deliberates, as if from nowhere, about some specific external, objective situation that confronts them. When they make up their mind what to do and form an intention, in (β), the upshot is "objective," "finite," and "particular." They give their will a particular expression in the external, objective world as the particular finite agent they are.

Insofar as any decision of a self-conscious agent involves (α), it implicates a perspective that is infinite "in itself." What is distinctive about willing from the moral point of view is that it makes a universal and infinite form of the will also the will's object; it is infinite "for itself." When, Hegel says, "the will has universality, or itself as infinite form, as its content, object [*Gegenstand*], and end, it is free not only *in itself*, but also *for itself*" (52). The moral point of view, as Hegel is thinking of it, is the perspective the will adopts when it is "reflected ... *into itself*" from "its external existence," as it is conceived in its full particularity in Abstract Right

[9] I call this "Pufendorf's Point" in Darwall 2006: 249. See also Darwall 2023a: 80–84.

(62). There is a striking similarity between Hegel's formulation of the will's having "universality, or itself as infinite form, as its content" or "object," and Kant's ideas of moral laws as "laws of freedom" and "autonomy," the will's property of being a law to itself simply by virtue of its form.

The deep point is that whereas an agent's deliberative perspective in (α) is focused externally on the objective world and what external action to perform, and not on their own will and practical reasoning, morality as Hegel (and other modern moral philosophers like Kant and the British rationalists) are concerned is focused on the will itself – on how agents freely determine their wills as autonomous moral agents. For what we might call a "naïve practical reasoner," the agent's will and practical reasoning is not in the deliberative foreground; it is focused on a confronting practical situation in the external world (Darwall 1983, 2006: 216–218). The agent's own reasoning and will are, as Pettit and Smith say, in the "background," or, perhaps more accurately, out of the agent's deliberative field entirely (Pettit and Smith 1990).

"With right in the strict sense," Hegel observes, "it made no difference what my principle or intention was" (Hegel 1991: 135). Abstract Right – that is, right, as Kant and Fichte strictly understand it – concerns only persons' external actions. It does not look behind their actions and concern itself with their motives, with their "principles," as Hegel calls them. Only within Morality does the "question of the self-determination and motive [*Triebfeder*] of the will and of its purpose now aris[e]" (135). Within Morality, "the worth [moral goodness] of a human being is measured by his inward actions" (136). Therefore, "the point of view of morality is that of freedom which has being for itself" (136).

Morality, in its modern conception, ushers in various "rights" of subjectivity, as Hegel calls them: the "right of the subjective will" and "right of subjective freedom," as well as the related "right of knowledge" and "right of intention" (136, 144, 148, 151). By determining themselves, and making their wills' own freedom an object of their wills, moral agents seek to actualize or give "existence" to their free, morally good agency. They seek to make it objective in a recognizable way. And they seek to claim that whatever is attributed to them as part of what they *are* be something they can *recognize* as issuing from their own free will:

> The moral point of view therefore takes the shape of the *right of the subjective will*. In accordance with this right, the will can *recognize* something or *be* something only in so far as that thing is *its own*, and in so far as the will is present to itself in it as subjectivity (136).

Hegel will argue that this right cannot, however, be actualized within Morality. As he sees it, Morality remains an abstract conceptual structure, like Abstract Right. Worse, unlike Abstract Right, Morality exclusively values agential "inward[ness]," abstracted from the external sphere in which the morally good will seeks recognizable expression (136–141).

In Abstract Right, all that matters are external "deeds." However, the "*moral* element" is the "*motive* of a deed" (149). In Hegel's view, this is a distinctively modern focus. "In recent times, especially, it has become customary to enquire about the motives of actions" since actions' moral quality is supposed to reside uniquely there. "Now, we seek to look into people's hearts, and thereby presuppose a gulf between the objective realm of actions and the inner, subjective realm of motives" (149). This means that Morality, strictly conceived, is unrealizable in an objective realm of recognizable actions. Morality's right of subjective will cannot be realized in its own terms.

Hegel is clear that a central reason why Morality requires the right of subjective will is its connection to *accountability*. "I can be made *accountable* for a deed," he says, "only if my *will was responsible* for it" (144). This is "*the right of knowledge*" (144). Actions are morally evaluable on the condition that the agent knew what they were doing. When we hold someone accountable for moral wrongs, we necessarily presuppose that they knew they were doing something wrong and that they had the freedom to determine themselves to act otherwise because of it. We assume, that is, not just that their action was intentional in a thin sense, but that they had what Cudworth called "moral free will" and not just "animal free will" (Cudworth ~1670: 4980.171, 4982.20, 4982.89, 1678: I.iv.9). Morality also requires the "*right of intention*," that morally evaluable actions be intentional (Hegel 1991: 148).

Together, these rights of subjectivity comprise the "right of subjective freedom." Moral action necessarily involves an agent's subjective will expressed in a particular objective action. It is an enduring problem for Morality, Hegel thinks, that subjective will and objective action are metaphysically distinct things since Morality must assume they can be identified – that moral agents can recognize and identify themselves as subjective wills in their objective actions. It must assume that the objective action for which someone is recognizably accountable is identical with what the agent subjectively willed.

Hegel stresses that the "right of subjective freedom" is a distinctively modern conception. It is, he says, "the pivotal and focal point in the difference between *antiquity* and the *modern age*" (151). "The legal codes of antiquity attached less importance to the subjective element, to responsibility, than is the case today" (144). By contrast, the right of subjective freedom is woven throughout modern life. Related to its centrality to moral accountability is the distinctive role modern moralists give to "conscience," which, Hegel says, "expresses the absolute entitlement of subjective self-consciousness to know *in itself* and *from itself* what right and duty are, and to recognize only what it thus knows as the good" (164).

Especially interesting is the way Hegel also implicates the right of subjective freedom in modern conceptions of the good or "welfare." Against ancient theories of the good, such as objectivist Aristotelian accounts of *eudaimonia*, modern Morality identifies the good or well-being with satisfaction of the subjective will, with what Hegel calls the agent's "particular and subjective existence" (141). We can trace this thought throughout modern moral philosophy, from hedonist theories, like Locke's, that understand pleasure in terms of the agent's own subjective attitudes, to theories like Butler's and Kant's that take happiness to consist in satisfaction of desires, to ideas of the good as preference satisfaction, as these enter into contemporary welfare economics.

The deep point that Hegel grasps is that these modern conceptions are all ultimately grounded in a view of the normative significance of *freedom*. The "particular and subjective existence" in which Hegel says modern Morality takes welfare to consist is that of subjective will. When moderns reject paternalistic direction for individuals' own good, it is fundamentally because they regard it as inconsistent with individuals' right to subjective freedom. There seems to be a fundamental difference between philosophers, like Hutcheson, who embrace the principle of utility out of benevolence, and those who support it for freedom-based reasons that are closer to "consumer sovereignty."

Morality's central problem, as Hegel sees it, is that it stresses inwardness and the subjective will – the right of subjective freedom – while insisting also on objective recognizability, all the while lacking anything that can link subjective and objective together. Action necessarily occurs within an objective, public realm, but its distinctively moral properties result from its issuing from moral agents' self-determining wills. Moral duties purport to concern actual objective actions, but moral accountability must engage agents' subjective wills. Morality cannot, therefore, be actualized in its own terms. It remains an abstract conceptual structure. Only in Ethical Life, Hegel will argue, with modern practices and institutions in which individuals can share and express publicly recognizable wills, can duties be valid and actually binding.

Kant's moral philosophy provides, for Hegel, the purest expression of Morality and also, therefore, the clearest illustration of Morality's abstract formality and unrealizability. Kant holds that moral worth and morally good will consist in acting "from" or, Hegel puts it, "for the sake of," duty (Hegel 1991: 161; Kant 1996a: 4:398–4:400). It is crucial for Kant (and for Morality, in Hegel's view) that action "from duty" be read *de dicto* rather than *de re*. The right of subjective freedom requires that morally good action be *conscientious* action; it must be what agents *themselves* judge or perceive to be their moral duty and be done under that description. The morally good agent, according to Kant, is moved not by desires to avoid, say, dishonesty and cruelty, the specific things we are required not to do. They rather avoid violating their moral duty, as they conceive it, for that very reason. Recent critics of this Kantian outlook, like Nomy Arpaly and Michael Smith, agree with Hegel in holding that this *de dicto* concern involves a kind of *alienation*, which Hegel holds to be a hallmark of Morality as a distinctively modern conception (Smith 1994; Arpaly 2004; see also Stocker 1976; Williams 1985).[10]

Hegel's most famous critique of Kant is that conceiving of Morality in terms of autonomy or self-legislation, however true it may be to Morality as an abstract concept, lays bare Morality as an "empty formalism" (Hegel 1991: 162). In *Groundwork* I, Kant attempts to ground duty in, and derives its content from, conscientiousness ("respect for law") as the uniquely moral motivation or character (Kant 1996a: 4:400). Having shown that the moral agent's "representation of" a law must determine the will "even without regard for the effect expected from it," "in order for the will to be called good absolutely," Kant asks: "What kind of law" could make the will good absolutely (Kant 1996a: 4:402). Since the good will's motive is entirely *de dicto*, "nothing is left but the conformity of actions as such with universal law" (Kant 1996a: 4:402). Kant answers with the *Groundwork*'s first formulation of the categorical imperative: *I ought never to act except in such a way that I could also will that my maxim should become a universal law* (4:402).

There is an apparent gap in Kant's reasoning between acting only on principles one can *regard* as universal law and acting only on principles that one can *will to be universally regarded* as universal law (Darwall 2023a: 293). There is a gap, even, between acting on principles *because* one sees them to be universal law and acting on principles one can will to be (universally

[10] Cf. Hegel's (1991) remark that the morally "good will consists in" the "willing of *good in the abstract*" as the "sole prerequisite, for the goodness of the action itself" (173).

regarded as) universal law, as the example of a *principled* egoist shows. The most that conscientious subjective will can ground, Hegel says, "is abstract universality," and that may be insufficient to ground even this initial formulation of the categorical imperative in terms of what can be *willed* (be universally regarded) as universal law (Hegel 1991: 162).

Hegel thinks further, however, that even if the categorical imperative in its universal law formulation (FUL) could be grounded in autonomy or subjectively free will, it would still reduce to an "empty formalism" (162). Suppose, for example, that we attempt to derive from the categorical imperative the duty not to steal by reasoning that we cannot consistently will that everyone act on a principle that would license theft because that would lead to the undermining of property itself. To this Hegel replies, "the fact that *no property* is present is in itself [*für sich*] no more contradictory" than the existence or non-existence of anything else (162). So, an agent *can* consistently will that a principle that permits theft be universally followed.

Hegel allows that there are some principles that cannot be universally followed and so willed to be universally followed, but he argues that some of these are principles on which we think it is entirely permissible to act. Kant argues, for example, that we are obligated to help the poor because we cannot rationally will that everyone act on a contrary principle that would permit ignoring indigent need, including when we ourselves are in need. Against this, Hegel claims that the categorical imperative does not even *permit* helping the poor, much less require it. The reason is similar to the one that Kant himself gives concerning the wrongness of insincere promises, namely, that if everyone were to act on a principle that permitted such promises, it would make promising itself impossible (Kant 1996a: 4:422). Because that is so, Kant argues, one cannot even conceive a possible world in which everyone acts on a principle permitting insincere promises. Similarly, Hegel argues, in a world in which everyone helped the poor when they are in need, there would be no poverty. "The maxim, 'Help the poor,' tested by being elevated into a principle of universal legislation, will prove to be false because it annihilates itself . . . either there [will be] no poor left or there [will be] nothing but poor" and "no one . . . left to help them" (Hegel 1975b: 80).

Kant has resources to respond to Hegel's critique since a Kantian maxim includes the agent's end within it. The will of anyone who helps the poor in order to help eliminate poverty will not conflict with their will that everyone act on their maxim. To the contrary, the universalization is something they will welcome. By contrast, Kant can argue, ordinary theft is motivated by the aim to have the other's property and not by the desire to eliminate property itself. Were everyone to act on the agent's theft-permitting maxim, and were that to undermine the practices and institutions in which property consists, that *would* undermine something the agent themselves is attempting to employ. So that shows that it is morally unacceptable to act on that maxim.

There are, however, further replies that are available to Hegel. We can imagine a Proudhonian anarchist thief who steals, not to gain property but to help destroy the practices and institutions of property themselves. There would be no contradiction in the universalizing of the will of such an agent. What this brings out is that the "universal law" formulation of the categorical imperative directly concerns not moral duty or obligation to perform *acts* considered independently of their motivation but rather the moral permissibility of *actions* on certain *reasons* or maxims.

Further replies are, of course, available to Kant. Most obviously, the Formula of Humanity gives Kant a way of arguing for the wrongness of acts independently of motive, specifically, the wrong of treating persons merely as means, for whatever reason. And there are also ways of interpreting Kant's related Kingdom of Ends formulation along the contractualist lines Rawls proposed that might provide promising grounding for a theory of duties. However, Hegel might himself proffer Kant's Formula of Humanity as yet further grist for his mill. The requirement not to treat others as ends may not have significantly more specific content than Abstract Right's requirement to respect persons and therefore be, by Hegel's lights, no more capable of being actualized.

Hegel thus holds that Morality involves free subjectivity, principled conscientious determination of the will or autonomy in Kant's sense. But the morally good will's actions also necessarily occur in the objective external world. Together, these elements set Morality's fundamental dilemma. "This subjectivity, as abstract self-determination and pure certainty of itself alone, *evaporates* into itself all *determinate* aspects of right, duty, and existence" (1991:166). "Modern" deontic notions, like right and duty, are distinctive among ethical notions in calling for actualization in a public order of free, mutually accountable persons, in a way that axiological or aretaic concepts like good or virtue do not. However, Morality also insists on a subjective conscientious certitude that is incompatible with the common, public, objective determinacy that right and duty call for. Morality's "subjectivity" "*evaporates*" its intended "determinacy," so that "the good" can be nothing more than an "obligation" rather than "valid" and "binding" "duties," which are realizable only in Ethical Life (165–166, 191–192).

For modern Morality, "subjectivity, in its universality reflected into itself, is the absolute inward certainty of itself"; "it is ... *conscience*," which "expresses the absolute entitlement of subjective self-consciousness to know *in itself* and *from itself* what right and duty are" (163–164). Only with the "point of view of the modern world," has "this consciousness, this descent into the self" been achieved, in the "moral point of view" (163–164). The problem is that the moral perspective is abstract and formal in a way that defies actualization in an objective public order, even as it calls for it. Hegel notes anticipations of this modern predicament in earlier periods:

> In the shapes which it more commonly assumes in history (as in the case of Socrates, the Stoics, etc.) the tendency to look *inwards* into the self and to know and determine from within the self what is right and good appears in epochs when what is recognized as right and good in actuality and custom is unable to satisfy the better will. When the existing world of freedom has become unfaithful to the better will, this will no longer finds itself in the duties recognized in this world (166).

The predicament of a good will in a world in which it "no longer finds itself in the duties recognized" is that of an alienated critic. The distinctive form the alienated consciousness of a good will takes in the modern world, viewing things from the perspective of Morality, is criticism of current practice expressed with "ought" and "obligation."

Unable to conceive its ethical relations as recognizably valid and binding "duties," as Hegel calls them, the morally good will is reduced to thinking in terms of "obligations" to which it cannot give recognizable determinacy, and of "how the world ought to be" in contrast to how it is (23). The moral perspective thus faces a "perennial *obligation*, with the "moral point of view ... simply drift[ing] to and fro" in the actual objective world "without being able to resolve" itself in ways that can give it actuality and enable it to "be with" and "recognize itself" (163, 17, 42). Only within Ethical Life can the free will "get beyond obligation" (163).

Hegel's distinction between "obligation" and "how the world ought to be," on the one hand, and "valid," actually "binding" "duties," on the other, may sound odd to contemporary ears attuned to the synonymy of "duty" and "obligation." It is grounded, however, in a distinction we saw Hegel making at the outset of *Elements* between proper philosophical science, which pursues "*comprehension of the present and the actual*, not the setting up of a *world beyond*," and any philosophy that attempts to "*issu[e] instructions* on how the world ought to be" (23). It is also implicated, as we saw, in Hegel's distinction between "laws of nature" and "laws of right," which recalls, but importantly differs from, Kant's distinction between "laws of nature" and "laws of freedom" (Hegel 1991: 13; Kant 1996a: 4:387). As Hegel puts his disagreement with Kant in *Phenomenology*, Morality's "laws of freedom" "stop short at Ought, they have no actuality" (Hegel 1991: 13; 1977: 256). They are not, therefore "laws" in the sense that "laws of right" are. They are "merely commandments" (1977: 256). When Hegel draws his distinction between "laws of nature" and "laws of right" in *Elements*, he says, somewhat tendentiously, that any conflict between "what is," in the sense of what is actualized in an actually accepted public order of right, and "what ought to be," amounts to that between the "right which has being in and for itself," and "the arbitrary [subjective] determination of what is supposed to be accepted as right" (1991: 13).

Morality's ambition to be actualized in an objective public order of mutual accountability is unrealizable. The most that can be achieved within Morality is subjective determination of the will, which necessarily lacks the determinacy of publicly recognizable right. Of "conscience," "it is required that its determinations should be universal and objective" (162, 185). But owing to Morality's "empty formalism," the most conscience can achieve is "the indeterminate which *ought* to be determined" (185). In its own terms, Morality can advance no farther than an "abstract good which merely *ought to be*, and an equally abstract subjectivity which merely *ought to be good*" (185). As postulated within Morality, morally good (subjective) will and objective right or good are both "abstract" and "one-sided." Both, Hegel says, are "posited in their negativity," so "cancel themselves out ... and are thereby reduced to moments" (185).

To make both subjective freedom and the will, on the one hand, and the good – according to Hegel, "objective" or "realized freedom" – "concrete" rather than abstract, Morality's formal "one-sided" character must be superseded (157, 185). Hegel holds that this is possible only within what he calls "Ethical Life." "The unity of the subjective with the objective good which has being in and for itself is *ethical life*, and the reconciliation which takes place in it is in accord with the concept" (186). Neither Morality nor Abstract Right are left behind entirely, however. Though neither can "exist independently" (either in themselves, or independently of one another), both are given concreteness and "life" within the practices and institutions of modern Ethical Life. Both "must have the ethical as their support and foundation" (186):

> For right lacks the moment of subjectivity, which in turn belongs solely to morality, so that neither of the two moments has any independent actuality. Only the infinite, the Idea, is actual. Right exists only as a branch of a whole or as a climbing plant attached to a tree which has firm roots in and for itself (186).

Thus, any attempt to theorize either philosophy of right as its own ethical domain, as Kant and Fichte do, or Morality as a distinctive ethical conception, in the manner of modern moral philosophy, is doomed to unrealizable theoretical abstraction. Philosophy's proper task, by contrast, is to comprehend the actual freedom-realizing customs and institutions of modern Ethical Life in which both Abstract Right and Morality can be brought to life.

Ethical Life

Hegel devotes *Elements*' Part III, which takes up over half the book, to "Ethical Life." Along the lines we have just been discussing, Hegel defines "Ethical Life" as "the *Idea of freedom* as the living good which has its knowledge and volition in self-consciousness, and its actuality through self-conscious action" (189). The way self-consciousness enters into Ethical Life is not in the one-sided, abstract ways it does in Morality and Abstract Right. Self-conscious action within shared practices, customs, and institutions of modern life is self-*recognizable* action, conduct that is recognizable as one's own by both oneself and others within a common public space. Through ethical action, persons can "be with" and recognize themselves in the world (42, 286). They can reconcile themselves with modern life and overcome the alienation that is the besetting malady of attempting to live with modern moral theorists' abstractions.

The ethical conception that Ethical Life realizes is deontic; it is a realm of right. Even though Hegel's use of "right" in Ethical Life is more capacious than it is in either Abstract Right or Morality, he is clear that the "substantial determinations" of the "Idea of freedom" that Ethical Life realizes are "*duties* which are binding on the will" (189,191). An actual ethical duty is not, however, "merely an *obligation*" like Morality's requirements (197).

Unlike the obligations of Morality, which emanate from an abstract point of view, the provenance of ethical duties is "immanent" rather than transcendent (192). They are rooted in actual practices of the modern world – in institutions of the modern state and informal practices and customs that become "second nature" to engaged participants (195). It is not sufficient to ground binding duties, however, that practices in which they are rooted simply exist. "In laws of right . . . the thing is not valid because it exists" (13). The practices must also adequately develop the Idea of Freedom, as is required by Hegel's dialectical logic. Though existence is not sufficient, however, it is necessary. "Binding" duties must be at least implicit in current law and custom (191–192). "An immanent and consistent theory of duties can be nothing other than the development of *those relations* which are necessitated by the Idea of freedom, and are therefore *actual* in their entirety, within the state" (192). Determining what our ethical duties are is thus akin to legal interpretation within a body of case and common law.

Although Morality necessarily involves self-consciousness, Hegel argues that it actually prevents self-*recognition*. Morality alienates individuals from a common life in which they can be "at home" and "reconciled" (36, 377). Moreover, despite Kant's view that moral laws are "laws of freedom," moral obligations necessarily present to finite moral agents as "constraints" on their freedom of action. Indeed, that aspect is actually essential to their being *obligations* in Kant's technical sense (see Darwall 2023a: 335). In Hegel's diagnosis, the phenomenologically constraining character of obligation derives from the unlimited, indeterminate subjectivity that Abstract Right and Morality both presuppose. "A binding duty," he says, "can appear as a *limitation* only in relation to indeterminate subjectivity or abstract freedom" (Hegel 1991: 192).

In Ethical Life, by contrast, "the individual . . . finds," not limitation, but "*liberation* in duty" (192). He is "liberated from his dependence on mere natural drives" (like Kantian finite moral agents) and "from the burden he labours under as a particular subject in his moral reflections on obligation and desire . . . In duty, the individual liberates himself so as to attain substantial freedom" (192). As Brandom and Wood emphasize, Hegel plausibly holds that participation in shared practices of modern Ethical Life enables a self-actualizing form of freedom that cannot be realized otherwise (Brandom 1979; Wood 1999: 46–50). Modern customs and practices make possible new forms of norm-defined conduct, thereby creating "expressive freedoms" (in Brandom's phrase) that otherwise would not exist and that, Hegel holds, more completely develop the Idea of Freedom itself.

"Ethical substance" is Hegel's term for what realizes the developed "Idea of freedom" and "Right" in the "realm of spirit" in Ethical Life (Hegel 1991: 35, 189). Hegel says that "the ethical substance, as containing self-consciousness which has being for itself and is united with its concept, is the *actual spirit* of a family and a people" (197). Note Hegel's language: "*a* family" and "*a* people." Ethical substances in Hegel's sense are *collectivities* of persons (and others related to them). And they are *particular* collectivities, existing in specific spatiotemporal and social locations. Unlike Kant, for whom right is grounded in universal laws for any possible rational agent as an end-in-itself who is thereby part of an assumed transcendental moral community or Realm of Ends, Hegel holds that right is ultimately a property of particular collectivities of human beings who are related by familial, social, and national ties in specific times and places with particular shared histories.

Recall Hegel's claim about the third moment of the will, (λ) – which can be realized only in Ethical Life – that in it "'I' is with itself in its limitation" (42). In relations of love and friendship, Hegel says, by way of illustration, "we are not one-sidedly within ourselves, but willingly limit ourselves with reference to an other, even while knowing ourselves in this limitation as ourselves" (42). We see limitations of choice by the duties of Ethical Life not as universal moral obligations but as duties of particular "stations," to use Bradley's term, within our familial, social, and political collectivities.[11] When we are bound by ethical duties, the bonds are those of family, social group, and country. Here there is no clear distinction between love and duty, between bonds of love, friendship, and comradeship and binding duties owed to family, friends, and country. We *identify*, moreover, with family and country; these particular relations penetrate our practical identities, and give us and our lives a sense of significance and meaning they would otherwise lack. Wholeheartedly embraced limitations like these are experienced less as limiting the self than as opportunities for self-actualization and "liberation" (192).

Hegel divides Ethical Life into three parts – the Family, Civil Society, and the State – where these are conceived as distinct, but overlapping collectively constituted spheres. The family is "the *immediate substantiality* of spirit"; so it partly constitutes the "realm of spirit" in which right can be realized (35, 199). Hegel calls the family "*natural* ethical spirit" (198). The family has "as its determination the spirit's *feeling* [*Empfindung*] of its own unity, which is love" (199). The feeling of love is "ethical life in its natural form." "Love means in general," Hegel says, "the consciousness of my unity with another" (199). Its "first moment" is the "wish" not to be "independent," where that possibility feels "deficient and incomplete"

[11] In "My Station and its Duties," in Bradley 1988.

(199). And in its second, loving family members "find" themselves "in" one another and "gain recognition" in the family (199).

It is clear enough how persons can find recognition and be "with themselves" "in an other" in family life and other loving relations. But self-recognition and reconciliation are also realized, according to Hegel, in Civil Society and the State. Since our focus is ethics rather than political philosophy, we will omit Hegel's account of the State, as we did similarly in discussing Fichte's philosophy of right. To set up our consideration of the role of recognition in Hegel and Fichte, with which we shall conclude this chapter, however, we would do well to try to understand something of Hegel's views of recognition and right in Civil Society.

Civil Society, for Hegel, is "an association of members as *self-sufficient individuals* [*Einzelner*] ... occasioned by their *needs* and by the *legal constitution* as a means of security for persons and property" (198). "Person" and "property" clue us to Civil Society's essential connection to Abstract Right, whose fundamental command is to "*respect others as persons*" and in which to be a person is to be an owner of property. As I argued previously, Hegel's concepts of personality, property, and Abstract Right constitute a mutually entailing circle. In Abstract Right, persons "have existence [*Dasein*] for each other" "only as owners of property" (70).

In Hegel's analysis, "civil society ... intervenes between the family and the state, even if its full development [*Ausbildung*] occurs later than that of the state" (220). Civil Society is constituted by the practices and institutions – which come increasingly to depend upon and be subsumed by the state – in which persons interrelate as owners of property. Mostly, these are market relations in which individuals encounter one another for property exchange and the legal infrastructure this requires. Hegel discusses market relations under the heading of "The System of Needs" and much of the legal infrastructure under "The Administration of Justice."

"The creation of civil society," as Hegel understands it, "belongs to the modern world, which for the first time allows determinations of the Idea to attain their rights" (220). Only in the modern period, Hegel believes, has a system of Abstract Right been conceived and the practices and institutions been created in which individuals can reciprocally *recognize* one another as persons thereby having rights to hold and exchange property.

"The System of Needs" sets out the characteristic economic institutions of modern civil society. Reciprocal recognition enters here not just in the Smithian way that exchangers of property implicitly recognize (so respect) one another as equal independent persons but also in Rousseauean fashion, as modern tastes and preferences are formed socially through *amour propre*.[12] "That abstraction which becomes a quality of both needs and means [in modern economies] also becomes a determination of the mutual relations [*Beziehung*] between individuals. This universality, as the *quality of being recognized*, is the moment which makes isolated and abstract needs, means, and modes of satisfaction into *concrete*, i.e., *social* ones" (229). "*Imitation* as the process whereby people make themselves like others," Hegel follows Rousseau in thinking, inevitably brings to the fore issues about equality that Rousseau discusses in his *Discourse of the Origin of Inequality* (Hegel 1991: 230; Rousseau 2011).

"The Administration of Justice" is concerned with the practices and institutions necessary to adjudicate claims of Abstract Right as these arise in market and other property-involving relations. Only here, Hegel says, can right be given "an *existence* [*Dasein*] in which it is *universally recognized*, *known*, and *willed*, and in which, through the mediation of this quality of being known and willed, it has validity and objective actuality ... The objective actuality of right consists partly in its being present to the consciousness and ... *known*"(Hegel 1991: 240). But what Hegel calls "the power of actuality" adds that the right must also have "*validity*." And this requires that it be "*known as universally valid*" and, crucially, that it be *recognized as such* (240). For property rights to be objectively *valid* and, therefore, to entail "binding duties," it is insufficient that everyone has these rights *in mind* ("present to the consciousness"). This is true even in Abstract Right (191–192, 240). It is also necessary that these rights be "*universally recognized*" – mutually acknowledged in a common public space – so that it is public common knowledge that they are valid and binding.

Recall how Hegel handles the "administration of justice" in Abstract Right. Lacking universally recognized practices, individuals are thrown back upon an irresolvable dilemma, one horn provided by Abstract Right and the other by Morality. On the one horn, abstract property rights license coercive attempts to repel or "cancel" any coercive property violations, that is, any "force directed against the existence [*Dasein*] of my freedom in an external thing [*Sache*]," and render their action a "nullity" (120–121, 123). In Abstract Right, however, this always risks appearing to the others as simply substituting my subjective will for theirs. So far conceived, there is no *recognizable* difference between the will of a would-be property taker and that of a would-be property right enforcer. Similarly,

[12] For Smith on the implicit respect in property exchange, see Smith 1976: 25.

there is no recognizable difference between "avenging" and "punitive" justice, that is, between a personal retaliatory response and a valid meting out of justice (131). Abstract Right offers no alternative to this horn of the dilemma in its own terms.

Any alternative would have to involve a change of consciousness beyond the terms that Abstract Right itself makes available. It would have to enable persons to distinguish between unjustified "personal" retaliation or "revenge" (what Hegel calls, somewhat confusingly, "avenging justice"), on the one hand, and "punitive" justice, on the other (129–131). Morality goes some way to providing an alternative, since, Hegel says, it enables those who think in its terms to regard merely "personal" "revenge" as "immoral" (129–130). Moreover, if individuals themselves believe that their action would violate another's person or property, Morality gives them a perspective, "the moral point of view," from which they can will that *they themselves* not pursue it, as a particular instance of willing universally that no person do so (132).

Morality marks a development in the concept of the will in that it can now make a distinction between the "universal will" and the "individual will" (131). Coercive nullification of the nullification that crime itself involves within Abstract Right leads, Hegel says, "through punishment . . . to affirmation, i.e., to *morality*" (132). Morality thus provides a second horn to the dilemma.

But Morality, for Hegel, is no less an abstract conceptual structure than is Abstract Right. Individuals reasoning within either cannot get beyond their own private reasoning to achieve anything public and mutually recognizable. Morality's grasping of the second horn does not resolve the dilemma, therefore. Individuals within Morality are still left without the public *recognition* necessary to judge as objectively valid and binding even the actions they believe to be morally necessary to protect their rights as persons ("punitive" justice).

This is precisely what Hegel believes "The Administration of Justice" provides in Ethical Life. When modern practices and institutions protect property rights of persons through publicly recognized means, they do so in a way that individuals who participate in them can accept and publicly acknowledge as valid and binding. And to the extent that moderns recognize *themselves* within these practices and institutions, their membership penetrates their own identities and so they are able to be reconciled with themselves and be "with themselves" in this modern form of publicly recognized life.

Recognition in Hegel and Fichte

Recognition (*Anerkennung*) is thus at the very foundation of Hegel's philosophy of right, as it was at the foundation of Fichte's. But how does Hegel understand recognition, and what role can it play in grounding his philosophy of right? We saw that the form of recognition in which Fichte grounds the right is the *summons*, which is an essentially second-personal form. A summons is an address to another person that implicitly acknowledges their shared status or authority as mutually presupposed common ground. I argued that the most promising way of interpreting Fichte's philosophy of right is as grounding his "rule of right" in this shared (second-personal) authority, along the lines of Grotius's claim that "sociability" is the "fountain of right" (Grotius 2005: I, 86). But what about Hegel?

Hegel's most extended discussion of recognition occurs in the well-known section of *Phenomenology of Spirit* on "Lordship and Bondage" (Hegel 1977: 111–119). Hegel titles this section, "Independence and Dependence of Self-Consciousness." It is *Phenomenology*'s first under the heading, "Self-Consciousness." Hegel makes the section's main claim in its first sentence: "Self-consciousness exists in and for itself when, and by the fact that, it so exists for another; that is, it exists only in being acknowledged" (111). Self-consciousness, in other words, is dependent on recognition by another self-conscious person for its very existence. Moreover, Hegel says that this recognition must be *mutual*; both "*recognize* themselves as *mutually recognizing* one another" (112). The requisite recognition must be "acknowledge[ment]" (111).

We can hardly do justice here to the complexity and depth of Hegel's discussion in "Lordship and Bondage" nor to its role in his overall phenomenology of consciousness.[13] On a relatively cursory analysis, however, Hegel's claim certainly seems very similar to Fichte's thesis that consciousness of oneself as a free agent requires the kind of acknowledgment by another that Fichte holds a summons to presuppose. But is the recognition that Hegel is talking about anything like a Fichtean summons? Hegel, like Fichte, conceives of self-consciousness as consciousness of our own freedom. But does Hegel hold, like Fichte, that the recognition necessary for this must involve anything second-personal like a summons?

An indication that he does not is his description of the process leading to self-consciousness as a "struggle for recognition," specifically, as

[13] For excellent discussions, see Brandom 2019 and Pinkard 1994.

a "life-and-death struggle" (Hegel 1977: 114, 1991: 87). It is important for Hegel that the kind of self-consciousness in question is awareness of oneself as a subjective "infinite will," having "being in and for itself" (moment [α]) as opposed to [β]): "the determinateness in which it is posited" (1977: 111). To be conscious of oneself as free in this sense, a person must gain recognition of themselves as a being who can self-consciously choose what to do in *abstraction* from any of the things they happen to desire or are inclined to commit their agency toward (β).

This is why Hegel thinks it necessary for any struggle that can achieve recognition of oneself as free be a life-and-death struggle. Only if each "stakes his own life" on mastering the other can mastery show that one valued freedom more than anything, more, indeed, than one's own life (114). In accepting defeat, and so bondage to the victorious master, the bondsman reflects this image of freedom back to the master. The acceptance of defeat recognizes the master's identity as a free agent in the requisite sense. Hegel recognizes that any such putative recognition cannot really be received as genuine recognition, even in its own terms; indeed, that is his point. To accept the defeated bondsman's reflected view as genuine recognition, the lord must see the bondman's view as the result of a freely exercised power or authority rather than as an inauthentic, manipulated view exacted by force. Once the lord accepts his dependence on this assumed authority of the bondsman, any assumption of his own absolute authority is exposed as a self-undermining myth or ideology.

The crucial point for our purposes, however, is that even this authority differs fundamentally from the *right-grounding* practical authority that is implicitly attributed by a Fichtean summons. Any authority to confirm someone's awareness of themselves as free in Hegel's metaphysical sense (as exemplifying [α]), or to confirm their *identity* as free in the sense that their freedom is essential to their practical identity (that they cared about being free above all else), is a fundamentally *epistemic* authority. It is an authority to see others as they really are. A Fichtean summons, by contrast, presupposes a shared basic *practical* authority – that summoner and summoned have in common an authority to make claims and demands of one another. And whereas, I have argued, this latter authority can play a fundamental role in grounding claims of right, it remains totally unclear how either metaphysical freedom, as Hegel conceives of it, or even a recognized practical *identity* as free, bears at all on the practical normative question of what rights we have against each other, or, indeed, how we are morally obligated to act toward one another.

I have been arguing that although Hegel is a critic of morality, as he understands it, he nonetheless makes essential use of the conceptual connection between morality and accountability that is so central to much modern moral philosophy. According to Hegel, indeed, it is this connection that is the source of Morality's disabling challenge. Accountability requires mutual recognition in a common public space, and this can be provided only immanently, within modern institutions and practices in their actuality, and not by any forms of thought that are realizable in individuals' reasoning, even from the "moral point of view." If Fichte is right, however, the form of recognition that is necessary to ground the normative idea of right, so much at the heart of modern liberal practices and institutions, may itself presuppose the equal practical authority of persons as a necessary transcendental assumption. And if that is right, rights and right may be less detachable from morality than Hegel, and, it should be said, Kant and Fichte, suppose. Arguably, both morality and basic human rights may require a common grounding that adequately respects their common conceptual connection to mutual accountability.

Coda: Douglass on Slavery and Accountability

Hegel puts forward his dialectic of lordship and bondage as part of a phenomenology of consciousness and not to theorize any actual modern institution, like chattel slavery. It is worth noting in conclusion, however, that principled resistance to modern chattel slavery – both early opposition to the slave trade leading to its abolition in Britain in 1807 – the very year Hegel's *Phenomenology* was published – and by American Black people, prominently in Frederick Douglass's famous speech, "What to the Slave is the Fourth of July?" delivered in 1852 – issued powerful *moral* arguments for abolition that made effective use of Fichtean accountability-seeking summonses.

Elizabeth Anderson points out the role of accountability in morally based social protest in British abolitionism in the eighteenth and early nineteenth centuries (Anderson 2014). This was arguably one of the first and most successful social protest movements in history (Hochschild 2005). Begun by Quakers in the early 1780s, the movement solidified with the establishment of the Society for Effecting the Abolition of the Slave Trade in 1787. The society achieved remarkable early successes. By the end of its first year, 10,000 (or one-fifth) of the citizens of Manchester had signed a petition to Parliament calling for abolition (121). And by 1791, approximately 300,000 Britons were taking part in a boycott of slave-produced sugar (Crawford 2002: 178).

The movement pioneered a number of techniques that might be called "accountability-seeking" mass protest.[14] In 1787, Josiah Wedgwood's pottery produced a medallion of an enslaved person kneeling in chains with the inscription: "Am I Not a Man and a Brother?" which circulated widely to significant effect. The medallion's inscription is a Fichtean summons addressed to viewers that implicitly holds them accountable for the summoner's continued enslaved position. To whom, after all, would the question be posed except to those who bear some responsibility and have some power to help end the slave trade? Moreover, it does not merely presuppose a shared dignity or authority in the way Fichte holds any summons does. It implicitly asserts it in the summons's content: You and I share a common humanity as part of the human family. We are thus, it implies, accountable to one another as fellows.

This, too, is the theme of Douglass's speech, but in much greater detail, at greater length, and with greater depth. "What to the Slave is the Fourth of July?" is among the best known of Douglass's extensive writings, and arguably the most important speech in American abolitionism. It, too, can be read as an extended Fichtean summons, indeed, one that includes a Fichtean moral philosophical commentary.[15]

There are 69 occurrences of "you" and 116 of "your" in Douglass's speech, along with 13 occurrences of "fellow citizen," 28 occurrences of "we," and 26 of "our" in a speech of approximately 10,000 words. Douglass goes back and forth between exclusivist and inclusivist forms of second-personal address, between accusations, on the one hand, and calls to "Fellow Citizens" to live up to a shared obligation to the nation's founders to complete their vision of equality and equal liberty, and not to free ride on their efforts, on the other (Douglass 2018: 63). Even here, Douglass's call takes the form of an accountability-seeking charge: "You have no right to enjoy a child's share in the labor of your fathers, unless your children are to be blest by your labors. You have not right to wear out and waste the hard-earned fame of your fathers to cover your indolence" (66).

Some of Douglass's most effective rhetoric is an entreaty to "behold the practical operation of [the] internal slave trade." "The crack you heard, was the sound of the slave-whip; the scream you heard, was from the woman

[14] Anderson discusses the role of accountability in this general phenomenon, drawing on Tilly and Tarrow 2006.

[15] I can give only a short treatment of this topic here. For a more extended analysis of Douglass's speech along these lines, see Darwall 2024.

you saw with the babe" (73). Here, Douglass's "you" makes his audience imagined *witnesses* to slavery's crimes, giving them, at least imaginatively, heavy consequential responsibilities.

Perhaps most interesting for our purposes, though, is a point Douglass makes in the course of replying to the complaint that he should "argue more, and denounce less ... persuade more, and rebuke less" (69). Douglass replies: "Must I undertake to argue that the slave is a man? ... The slaveholders themselves acknowledge it in the enactment of laws for their government. They acknowledge it when they punish disobedience on the part of the slave ... What is this but the acknowledgement that the slave is a moral, intellectual and responsible being?" (70). And in this acknowledgment, he concludes, slaveholders are also committed to whatever follows from the *Declaration of Independence*'s assertion of equal inalienable rights to liberty for "all men." When we hold others accountable, and summon them to comply with recognized law, we are also committed to their standing to hold us accountable in return – to our mutual accountability for compliance with the demands that we can make of one another as equal moral persons.

This leaves us with an irony. Immanent reflection on actual practice, including principled resistances, when it is as philosophical and deeply comprehending as Douglass's, can reveal aspects that commit us to the mutual accountability of persons as an inescapable transcendental assumption. Perhaps this is where Hegelian immanent philosophy of right and modern moral philosophy meet.

PART II

Morality Critique

In this section, we turn to three thinkers – Karl Marx (1818–1883), Søren Kierkegaard (1813–1855), and Friedrich Nietzsche (1844–1900) – all of whom have an agonistic relationship to modern moral philosophy. Each offers philosophically acute criticisms of modern moral theorizing and, like Hegel, criticisms of (thus theorized) morality itself, though for very different reasons. Moreover, each advances, explicitly or implicitly, *nonmoral* ethical conceptions that draw on and develop distinctively modern ideas of *freedom*, arguably, of "subjective freedom," in senses related to Hegel's. Although they all write in Hegel's (and Kant and Fichte's) wake, none are followers of German idealism, to put it mildly. Elements of Hegel's thought certainly influenced all three – its dialectical and historical character, for example – but the explicit rejection of German idealist claims is a main feature of the thought of each of Marx, Kierkegaard, and Nietzsche.

This is perhaps most obvious with Marx, whose *Critique of Hegel's Philosophy of Right* sets the stage for his own historical and political-economic theorizing, including its most philosophical aspects. In place of Hegel's dialectical idealism, Marx famously substitutes dialectical materialism. The engine of sociohistorical change is not, as Hegel argued, conceptual developments of dialectical logic, but fundamental political-economic contradictions deriving from conflicting relationships different socioeconomic classes have to the means of production. Kierkegaard and Nietzsche form key aspects of their thought in response to central planks of German idealistic orthodoxy as well. A main inspiration for Kierkegaard's thought, for example, was Schelling's critique of Kant's view of noumenal freedom (Kosch 2006). This ultimately led Kierkegaard to a view of radical freedom and commitment from which the twentieth-century existentialists Sartre and de Beauvoir draw core aspects of their doctrines, including those of authenticity and "bad faith."

It is hard to miss Hegel's three-part dialectical-historical structure – Abstract Right/Morality/ "Ethical Life" – in the thought of all three of

Marx, Kierkegaard, and Nietzsche. In Marx, it is the passage from feudalism to capitalism to communism, explained not by Hegelian conceptual development but by class struggles that are inherent in differing relations to the means of production. Marx holds that this explanation is entirely materialistic. However, there are, as we shall see, Hegelian, and conceptually nonmaterialist, elements in Marx's notion of class, since it turns out that Hegelian recognition relations construct the different socioeconomic identities on which Marx's political-economic explanations depend.

In Kierkegaard, a three-part structure is set, first, by the two elements that comprise Parts I and II of *Either/Or*, the "esthetic" and then the "ethical life" (Kierkegaard 1987a, 1987b). A subsequent, third stage comes with a "teleological suspension of the ethical" (by which Kierkegaard means "suspension of the moral" in the modern sense) and a committing "leap" of faith (Kierkegaard 2006: 46; 2009b: 13). Unlike Marx's version, Kierkegaard's dialectic takes place not at the social level, but within an individual's life in a way that can bring about an essentially *individual* authenticity and what Kierkegaard called "existential inwardness" (Kierkegaard 2009b: 226). But if Kierkegaard's dialectic, unlike Hegel's and Marx's, is decidedly not world historical, differently from Hegel's and Marx's, the notions of individuality and authenticity that Kierkegaard develops are nonetheless *themselves* distinctively modern ethical ideas, more modern, indeed, than any idea of individuality that is in place in early modern moral philosophy (Wahrman 2006). Kierkegaard's concept of the "single individual" is more closely related to Nietzsche's "sovereign individual," to "individuality" in John Stuart Mill, and to the radically free subject of the twentieth-century existentialists, than it is to the "*forensic*" notion of the individual person or moral agent as, for example, in Locke or Kant (Kierkegaard 2009a: e.g., 115).[1]

Nietzsche's three-part dialectical structure can be seen as combining sociohistorical elements, like those in Hegel and Marx, with something like the path to individuality we find in Kierkegaard. His "genealogy of morality" is mainly sociohistorical. The model for Nietzsche's first stage – the "aristocratic" ethos of noble and base – is ancient Greece during a period when it is insulated from the religions of the book: Judaism, Christianity, and Islam. These religious movements then bring a whole new set of ethical – or, better put, moral or proto-moral – ideas onto the scene, at a second stage. "Good" now contrasts with "evil" rather than with

[1] Hannay claims that Kierkegaard held that this was the unifying theme of his work (Hannay 2001).

"bad" in the aristocratic sense of low or base. Indeed, the sense of "good" that is "evil"'s contrary is not the aristocratic sense of high or noble, but that of "*morally* good" (Nietzsche 2007).

Modern moral philosophy, in Nietzsche's view, inherits a conceptual scheme brought on by "the slaves' revolt in morality," led by a "priestly" or "clerical caste" (Nietzsche 2007: 15–18). Through these first two stages, Nietzsche's account is primarily sociohistorical, though accompanied by a rich theory of the unconscious psychic mechanisms in the "man of ressentiment" that give rise to self-deceptive acceptance of moral ideas (22). From here, however, Nietzsche's dialectical account is more individualist in the fashion of Kierkegaard's. His "sovereign individuals" transcend the moral ideas they are bequeathed by their culture and achieve, individually, an ethical conception that is "beyond good and evil" (Nietzsche 2002, 2007: 37). They create themselves as "autonomous, supra-ethical individual[s]" (Nietzsche 2007: 37). And they thereby realize a form of freedom that is like Kierkegaard's, although not, of course, through anything like religious faith.

Finally, we should highlight the theme of freedom in the sense of *emancipation* or *liberation*. This runs through the positive ethical views of all three of Marx, Kierkegaard, and Nietzsche. Marx's (and Engels's) call to "working men of all countries," who "have nothing to lose but their chains," to "unite" aims at their "emancipation" (Marx and Engels 1975b: 503, 519). The proletariat, for Marx, is a "universal" class with "radical chains," whose freedom is the crucial step to achieve the liberation of all humankind (Marx 1975a: 186). "The emancipation of the workers contains universal human emancipation" (Marx 1975b: 280). "*Man*," Marx says, "*is the highest being for man*, hence . . . the *categorical imperative to overthrow all relations* in which man is a debased, enslaved, forsaken, despicable being" (Marx 1975a: 182). This language, like Marx's focus on exploitation as capitalism's besetting flaw, recalls Kant's "humanity" formulation of the categorical imperative: to treat human and rational beings always as ends in themselves and never as means. As we shall see, however, Marx steadfastly avoids the deontic terms of moral obligation and right in which moral imperatives are most naturally cast. In their place, he points to a nonmoral substitute for moral recognition respect that is more like solidarity, as well as a companion conception of equal human relations as a common good.[2]

[2] For a discussion of moral recognition respect, see Darwall 1977.

For his part, Kierkegaard stresses a kind of emancipated authenticity that individuals can realize, not in free moral agency in the modern or Kantian sense, but in authentic religious faith. Kierkegaard does not use language this explicit, but Schelling, whose views are arguably in the background of Kierkegaard's views on freedom, does. The will, Schelling says, "long[s] for its own liberation" (Kosch 2006: 119).[3] Schelling holds that the requisite freedom is from what Kosch calls the "universal . . . rational moral law" that is "the inner law of ethical conduct" (119). Kierkegaard follows Schelling in this and thus holds that authentic freedom as a subjective individual consists not in moral conscientiousness but in a "suspension of the ethical [moral]" through faith.[4]

We find a similar pattern of ideas in Nietzsche, but with a critique of free will as it figured in modern moral philosophy and with a decidedly nonreligious conception of liberation. The (modern) conception of morality that Nietzsche places under genealogical suspicion and argues against presupposes, he claims, a kind of freedom of the will that simply does not exist. But that does not mean, he urges, that human beings cannot achieve a very different species of freedom: autonomy. Nietzsche's "*Übermensch*" is a "sovereign individual" whose "autonom[y]" is "supra-ethical" (Nietzsche 2007: 37). As with Kierkegaard, it is clear that by "supra-ethical," Nietzsche means "supra-moral" (in what Leiter calls the "pejorative sense" of "morality" that Nietzsche criticizes [Leiter 1995]). As we shall see, much of Nietzsche's critique of morality is itself ethical, as when he says that he aims in *Genealogy* to question "the *value* of morality" (Nietzsche 2007: 6). Unlike Schelling and Kierkegaard, however, the liberation Nietzsche proposes is not from the rational in favor of arational faith. It arguably itself involves the cold-eyed view of reason.

[3] Kosch's translation of *Philosophische Einleitung in die Philosophie der Mythologie oder Darstellung der reinrationalen Philosophie* [*Philosophical Introduction to the Philosophy of Mythology or Presentation of Pure Rational Philosophy*] 11:569 (in first [1856–61] edition of Schelling's works).

[4] See also Kierkegaard's discussion of the "moment of liberation" when a "learner" is freed from "untruth" by a "teacher" who is a "savior" (Kierkegaard 1985: 16–17). I am indebted here to Rachel Dettelbach.

CHAPTER 3

Marx

In the process of forming his own ideas in relation to Hegel, the young Karl Marx wrote in 1843, at the age of twenty-five, to the older "Young Hegelian," Arnold Ruge, about the discouraging prospects for liberation in Germany:

> One will have to reawaken in the breast of these people the sense of the self-worth of men – freedom. Only such a sense, which vanished from the world with the Greeks and evaporated into the blue with Christianity, can transform society again into a community of people for their highest ends – a democratic state (Padover 1979: 25).

Already we find a number of philosophical themes that run throughout Marx's corpus. Foremost is his focus on free social and political relations – on emancipated people governing themselves together rather than being mastered by others. Here Marx refers to this ideal as a "democratic state." Later, his collaborator, Friedrich Engels, will say that under the communist vision of social order that he and Marx favor, the state will "die out" (or "wither away") (Engels 1975: 321). But whether that was Marx's view or not, there is no doubt that Marx was a sharp critic of law, justice, and right (*Recht*) – which Kant had argued can only be realized in a state – and that Marx's communist social ideal is nonjuridical.

A second theme is that although Marx will reject the modern deontic conception of morality, he is very much aware that his own ideal of freedom is a modern conception, which is based, like modern morality, in a view of the unique value of human persons – the "self-worth of men" as "free." In Kant's moral philosophy, the dignity of persons is an essentially juridical value that grounds the humanity formulation of the categorical imperative, requiring that persons always be treated as ends in themselves (Kant 1996a: 4:429). A key question will be how to interpret Marx's (partial) embrace of this Kantian idea, as in his theories of exploitation and alienation, without Kant's *rechtlich* implications.

A third is Marx's communitarian emphasis on "a community of people [organized] for their highest ends": a "democratic" society of free people, whether organized as a state or not. Marx plainly conceives of this as a modern idea, one that was not adequately recognized either by "the Greeks" or by "Christianity." However, it is important, again, that Marx does not ground his democratic conception as orthodox liberal moderns do in a deontic conception of fundamental equal human *authority*. Ultimately, Marx's ideas must be understood as a liberal egalitarianism of *the good* rather than of *the right*. He must be read as claiming that a properly communist social order will end "the cleavage ... between the particular and the common interest," and so have no use for a theory of the right (Marx and Engels 1975c: 47).

In arguing that a communist democratic order occludes any distinction between individual and common good, Marx may be thought to be echoing Hegel on love and love's capacity to overcome individuals' alienation and to allow them to be "at home" together in a shared social world (Hegel 1991: 36, 42, 199).[1] There is something to this, but Marx makes clear that what he is proposing is not a "love-imbued opposite of selfishness" (Marx and Engels 1975d: 41). If Marx's favored ethical motivation is a form of love, it is not one that focuses on individuals' goods out of concern for them for *their* sake.

This creates something of a fundamental challenge for Marx's view: how to ground his communist ideal without falling into a juridical doctrine of equal dignity and respect, on the one hand, or into a view of love he seems to want to avoid and that is impotent to ground democracy as a sociopolitical ideal in any case. I suggest that Marx's best candidate is something like *solidarity*: a sense of comradeship of people working together for the common end of their own emancipation. This, after all, would seem to be the sentiment to which Marx and Engels appeal when they call on "working men of all countries" to "unite" (Marx and Engels 1975b: 519).

Although Marx is an unremitting critic of the modern conception of morality, it can be difficult, as Lukes and others have pointed out, to interpret Marx's critique of capitalism in other than moral terms (Lukes 1985). When Marx steadfastly denies that capitalist exploitation is unjust, one can be left with the impression, as Elster remarks, that Marx "did not really understand what he was doing" (Elster 1986: 92). But Marx's position is a principled one, even if it is mistaken. He has good reasons to think that

[1] See the discussion of these passages in the last chapter.

the natural rights views with which he was familiar were insufficient to mount an adequate critique of capitalist exploitation. Partly this was because of their focus on "negative" rights. But mostly it was because they failed to appreciate the essentially *structural* character of political-economic exploitation, especially when it involves "free" market relations. The problem with capitalism is not that individual capitalists treat individual laborers unjustly. We cannot even understand the interactions between capitalists and workers unless we take account of the political-economic structures within which they occur.

Marx's focus on oppressive social *structures* as a fundamental site of moral and ethical critique is arguably his most significant contribution to the history of ethical and political thought. Ancients, like Plato in the *Republic*, made social structure fundamental to their ethical philosophy, but without modern conceptions of equality and freedom. From a modern perspective, Aristotle's doctrine of natural slavery makes his political philosophical views a nonstarter, at least in that respect. There are moderns before Marx who focus on structure also, for example, Hume's discussion of justice as an "artificial virtue" that depends on shared practices and "conventions." Even Kant argues that natural rights grounded in the equal dignity of individual persons are mostly "provisional" and that they can be realized only in a shared political order. However, none of these philosophers places social and, especially, political-economic structure at the center of their ethico-political thought in the way Marx does.

In *A Theory of Justice*, John Rawls argues that what he calls the "basic structure" of society is the "primary subject of justice" (Rawls 1971: 7). Without Marx's substantial influence on the history of moral and political thought, it is hard to believe that Rawls would have found this a natural starting place for theorizing about justice. The very idea of "distributive justice" is itself a structural notion; it concerns distributive "patterns" that result from a political-economic structure, to use Nozick's term (Nozick 1974).[2] Fleischacker argues that the focus on distributive justice, in the contemporary sense, only became a preoccupation of moral and political philosophers after the early modern period (Fleischacker 2004). But though Marx is, as Fleischacker notes, a steadfast critic of justice, he nonetheless looms large in Fleischacker's history of distributive justice. Ultimately, however, Marx's communist idea is less a distributivist ideal than one in which free social *relations* are realized as a quintessential

[2] Nozick argues against Rawls that "liberty upsets patterns" (Nozick 1974: 149–182).

common human good. It is, in Elizabeth Anderson's sense, a "relational egalitarian" view (Anderson 1999, 2012).

Lukes describes what he calls a basic "paradox" in Marx's writings. On the one hand, Marx claims "that morality is a form of ideology, and [is] thus social in origin, illusory in content, and serv[es] class interests" (Lukes 1985: 3). On the other, "no one can fail to notice that Marx's . . . writings abound in moral judgments, implicit and explicit" (3). Lukes attempts to resolve the paradox by distinguishing between "the morality of *Recht* and the morality of *emancipation*" (27). In Lukes's view, Marx rejects the former and accepts the latter. I shall argue that this is (mostly) correct. Marx's critique of modern philosophies of right and morality is a central feature of his view, but so is his propounding of an ethical ideal of "human emancipation." Lukes's description of Marx's positive view as "the morality" of emancipation may not be the most felicitous given the modern conception of morality as fundamentally deontic (and, therefore, *rechtlich*). But this is a terminological quibble. I will be arguing that Marx's ethics amounts to a liberal egalitarian or "human emancipationist" theory of the good rather than of the right.

As I argue in Darwall (2023a), the account of moral motivation that fits most naturally with the modern conception of morality is the kind of shared respect for equal dignity of all persons that we find in Kant (and before him in Pufendorf). This will leave the question of what account of ethical motivation can play an analogous role in relation to Marx's emancipatory ideal. Lukes does not directly address this question. I suggest that the answer is a form of motivation that is, roughly, as close as possible to equal (recognition) respect while lacking its *rechtlich* character: solidarity with others as fellow pursuers and members of a shared emancipated social order. Under capitalism, this will be solidarity and identification with the proletariat: fellows in a class struggle whose object is a classless society that is free of oppressive social relations and structures.

The Critique of Hegel: Philosophy of Right, Alienation, and Recognition

Marx's early philosophical education centered on Hegel and Kant. Marx's father, with whom Marx was close during this period, was an avid follower of Kant and Fichte (Heinrich 2019: 75). What we remember of Marx's early writings begins primarily with his philosophical works on Hegel and

Feuerbach.[3] Those concerning Hegel consist in a lengthy critical commentary on portions of Hegel's *Elements of the Philosophy of Right* that concern the state (roughly from §261 through §309) and in an "Introduction" to this critique (Marx 1975a, 1975c).[4]

In addition, there is a highly revelatory letter to Ruge ("For a Ruthless Criticism of Everything Existing") and Marx's *Theses on Feuerbach* (Marx 1978a, 1978b), which clarify Marx's relationship to Hegel and the fundamental direction of his materialism. The former calls for a "worldly" philosophy that is unafraid to engage in "ruthless criticism of everything existing," including the state, which, of course, Hegel takes to be the self-realization of reason. The state presupposes "private being," which is inconsistent with "the humanistic principle" (Marx 1978a: 13). As Hegel argues, "the state everywhere presupposes that reason has been realized," but, Marx claims, there is an irresoluble "contradiction between [the state's] ideal mission and its real preconditions" (14).

In *Theses on Feuerbach*, Marx contrasts his materialism with Feuerbach's. This concerns the *perspective* from which materialism is incorporated into thought. "All hitherto existing materialism," Marx claims, has treated material reality as an "object . . . *of contemplation*" rather than "as *human sensuous activity, practice*," that is, "not subjectively" (Marx 1978b: 143). Although Feuerbach makes an advance on naïve religion in revealing its origins in human projection, he is unable to "grasp the significance of 'revolutionary,' of practical-critical, activity" (143). The alternative, Marx argues, is to bring our best (materialistic) science into the practical point of view. This actually harks back to Kant and Hegel. It makes Marx a kind of phenomenologist in the spirit of Fichte and Hegel, but one who is steadfastly materialist rather than idealist. "The question whether objective truth can be attributed to human thinking is not a question of theory but is a *practical* question" (144).[5] We might think of Marx as pursuing a materialist "critique of practical reason."

There is much in Marx's *Contribution to the Critique of Hegel's Philosophy of Law* that is not relevant to our purposes. Exceptions are some comments that Marx makes about the relationship between the state and Civil Society in Hegel. Hegel's Civil Society is a realm where economic actors encounter one another as self-interested consumers and

[3] Marx's earliest works were literary, including poetry (Heinrich 2019).

[4] For more details about these works and their relation, see Joseph O'Malley's editor's introduction to Marx 1970.

[5] The resonance with Korsgaard's views about the "sources of normativity" in the practical point of view is unmistakable (Korsgaard 1996a).

producers against a background of private, state-enforced property relations. The interests of citizens and public officials, however, are supposed to be "general" or "universal." Hegel calls civil servants a "*universal estate* [that] has the *universal interests* of society as its business" (Hegel 1991: 237). Marx notes that this establishes civil servants and economic actors as "two hostile armies" (Marx 1975a: 50, 70). Since actual individuals function both as members of Civil Society and as citizens (and even as civil servants), this creates a fundamental opposition in their recognized identities (Irwin 2009: 236). Even more worrying, in the Marxist view, is that the state functions to support Civil Society and that state institutions and actors are corrupted and taken over by private, capitalist class interests.

To this, Marx's "Introduction" adds matters of fundamental significance to his political-economic analysis and relevance for his view of human liberation and his communist social ideal. To the Hegelian claim that civil servants of the state form a "universal estate," Marx opposes his claim that the proletariat are effectively a universal "class," whose liberation, he will say in *The Economic and Philosophic Manuscripts of 1844*, "contains universal human emancipation" (Marx 1975b: 280).[6] The proletariat is a "class with *radical chains*" (Marx 1975a: 186). This gives it the revolutionary potential to bring about a classless society, to end the class struggle that Marx holds to be the driving force of history, and, therefore, to realize human emancipation. The proletariat is, Marx says, with characteristic paradox, "a class of civil society which is not a class of civil society, an estate which is the dissolution of all estates, a sphere which has a universal character by its universal suffering and claims no *particular right* because no *particular wrong* but *wrong generally* is perpetrated against it" (186). This last point resonates with Marx's critique of rights. The exploitation of workers under capitalism is neither an injustice to them nor a violation of their rights, though it is, of course, radically criticizable in other terms.[7]

Just at this point, Marx makes some fascinating comments about the proper role of philosophy. Against Hegel, Marx says that the engine of historical change is not conceptual but material. Thought and philosophy are impotent to achieve human liberation. The impetus must be material, and only the proletariat can provide it. The workers may require philosophical support and perhaps direction, but only the proletariat's victory

[6] On this point, see Kain 1988: 38–41and Daly 2000: 352–353.

[7] It's worth noting that Marx does say here that the causing of needless suffering under capitalism is "wrong generally." This opens up the possibility that his target might only be doctrines of natural rights and justice and not the modern conception of morality itself.

and the end of class struggle can make philosophy, rather than class-biased ideology, possible. "As philosophy finds its *material* weapons in the proletariat, so the proletariat finds its *spiritual* weapons in philosophy" (187). The only genuine liberation is "*the emancipation of the human being*" (187). "The *head* of this emancipation is *philosophy*, its *heart* is the *proletariat*. Philosophy cannot be made a reality without the abolition of the proletariat, the proletariat cannot be abolished without philosophy being made a reality" (187).

The point of departure for Marx's own philosophizing is thus Hegel. In the rest of this section, we shall consider two further aspects of the Hegelian framework that loom large in Marx's thought. The first is Hegel's view of *alienation*, its role both in his theories of property, recognition, and social identity, and in his complaint that modern moral and political theorists before him leave individuals with but an abstract notional existence in Morality (*Moralität*) and Abstract Right that can only be remedied by Ethical Life (*Sittlichkeit*), which provides reconciliation and enables individuals to be "at home" and "with themselves" in the world. The second concerns the notion of *recognition* itself, which plays an implicit role in virtually all of Marx's thought, even if it is rarely explicit.[8]

As we saw in the last chapter, alienation is a core, defining concept of Hegel's theory of property and, therefore, of his account of Abstract Right. In this guise, alienation is a juridical idea. It is the process by which individuals acquire rightful ownership of property through externalizing their wills on unowned things in ways that others can recognize as making them theirs. The fundamental "commandment of right" is to respect persons as individuals who have thus alienated their wills.

At the same time, Hegel also works with a nonjuridical notion of alienation, which is in play in his claims that the world postulated by modern moral and political theories is one in which actual individuals are alienated and cannot be at home and with which they cannot be reconciled. This is the sense of "alienation" that Pippin has in mind when he says that Hegel is the first philosopher for whom modernity is itself a philosophical problem (Pippin 1997: 19, 158, 439). The social world that modern moral and political philosophy has created is an alienated one. We will consider Marx's responses to both of these aspects of Hegel's views when we analyze his critique of "alienated labor" in *The Economic and Philosophic Manuscripts* in the next section.

[8] See Furner 2019 for a study of some ways that recognition is involved in Marx.

A central tenet of Marx's political-economic history is that, as Marx and Engels put it in *The Communist Manifesto*, "the history of all hitherto existing society is the history of class struggles" (Marx and Engels 1975b: 482). But what does Marx mean by "class"? Of course, the notion of class that is most directly of interest to Marx is one of economic class, defined in relation to the means of production. But it is clear that by economic class, Marx cannot simply mean economic strata as these might be defined in terms of the distribution of economic goods like income or wealth. That is why I said earlier that Marx's fundamental dispute with the oppressive social forms from which he believes human beings must be liberated is not with how they distribute goods. It is with oppressive *social* relations that place some people under the power and control of others, most especially, of course, in their political-economic relations.

The sense of class that is involved in any such complaint must be fundamentally *social.* Social classes in the relevant sense are constituted by patterns of *recognition* in which some are seen and *treated* as though they are below and appropriately under the control of others, who are regarded as their (recognized) betters. The only form of class from which *emancipation* is possible are forms of socially *recognized* governance and mastery. Moreover, Marx was no less opposed to noneconomic forms of oppression, like systems of caste he wrote of in India, than he was to economic oppression (Marx 1975c: 217). Marx was fundamentally concerned with oppressive social *relations* (Anderson 1999, 2012).

In the previous chapter, we considered important differences between the idea of recognition as it functions in Fichte and Hegel. It is fair to say that the notion that Marx works with is Hegel's rather than Fichte's. He is concerned with the way patterns of recognition establish oppressive social *identities* that impede genuine human liberation. Perhaps the richest exploration of these is Marx's chapter on "Alienated Labour" in *The Economic and Philosophic Manuscripts*, to which we now turn.

"Alienated Labour"

There are many different but related senses in which Marx claims that labor under capitalism involves what translators term "alienation," "estrangement," or "objectification."[9] I count some twenty distinct but

[9] As translations of "*Entäusserung*," "*Entfremdung*," *and* "*Vergegenständlichung*," respectively. Buchanan 1982 provides a very helpful analysis of these differences and their role in "Alienated Labour."

related claims that Marx makes with this vocabulary in "Estranged [Alienated] Labour":

1. Labor tends to produce steadily increasing "alien," "hostile" power, steadily decreasing workers' own power (Marx 1975b: 272).
2. Both labor and workers themselves become commodities (272).
3. Labor helps to produce a commodified, devalued, less human world (272).
4. Labor's products confront workers themselves as "alien" (272).
5. Labor is "objectif[ied]" (272).
6. Labor activity vitiates the workers (272).
7. Labor activity creates bondage to commodities it creates (Marx calls this the "objectification of labor") (272).
8. Labor activity impedes self-realization (272).
9. Labor activity alters workers' relations to the natural world (273).
10. Labor produces its own replacement through "labour-saving" machinery (242, 273).
11. Labor is self-denying rather than self-fulfilling (274).
12. Labor activity "mortifies [the worker's] body and ruins [their] mind" (274).
13. Workers can feel "at home" – or like themselves – only when they are not working (274).
14. Work has only instrumental and no intrinsic value for workers (274).
15. Work estranges workers from their "species-being" (276).
16. Therefore, work estranges workers from self-conscious ("free" and "universa[l]") species-activity (276).
17. Work estranges workers from products of their labor in a socially recognized public world (277).
18. Work estranges workers from other human beings (277).
19. Labor produces capitalism and capitalists (279).
20. Therefore, labor produces the source of every aspect of workers' alienation, estrangement, and commodified world (279).[10]

Marx himself distinguishes three main species of phenomena that "constitut[e] the alienation of labour" (274). The first concerns the relation workers have to the *products* of their labor "as alien object[s] exercising power over" them (275). The second comprises various alienating aspects of workers' relation to the "*act of production* within the *labour* process"

[10] There is obviously nothing definitive about this list, but it may be useful to give some idea of the complexity of Marx's claims.

(275). And the third, which Marx says follows from the first two, consists in workers' alienation from what Marx calls their "species-being". This third aspect brings Marx closest to the traditional ethical view that Terence Irwin calls Aristotelian naturalism since it suggests the view that human beings can flourish and realize their common good only when they actualize their rational human nature in ways that capitalism makes impossible (Irwin 2007, 2008, 2009). However, Marx's ethical naturalism departs substantially from any premodern view like Aristotle's, owing to Marx's (modern) emphasis on "human emancipation" (Marx 1975b: 280). (Irwin argues that, in effect, Marx attempts to "reconcil[e] Kantian with Aristotelian moral theory" [Irwin 2009: 251].) Marx holds that human beings can realize their "species-being" only by treating themselves as "*universal* and therefore . . . free" beings (Marx 1975b: 275). This they can do under capitalism only through class struggle in solidarity with the proletariat, whose "radical chains" make them a universal class (Marx 1975a: 186). Class struggle is the engine of historical change, culminating with the establishment of a classless communist social order, which necessarily excludes oppressive social structures because it lacks social classes.[11]

Under capitalism, labor activity is deprived of the essentially rational and social character of human species-activity. Work becomes routinized in ways that require no rational thought and that are replaceable (and increasingly replaced) by advancing technology, itself made possible only through profits (exploitatively) generated by labor. Workers work not for any fulfillment or to express and realize intrinsic values but only to enable

[11] See "Comments on James Mill":

> Let us suppose that we had carried out production as human beings. Each of us would have *in two ways affirmed* himself and the other person. 1) In my *production* I would have objectified my *individuality*, its *specific character*, and therefore enjoyed not only an individual *manifestation of my life* during the activity but also when looking at the object I would have the individual pleasure of knowing my personality to be *objective, visible to the senses* and hence a power *beyond all doubt*. 2) In your enjoyment or use of my product I would have the *direct* enjoyment both of being conscious of having satisfied a *human* need by my work, that is, of having objectified *man's* essential nature, and of having thus created an object corresponding to the need of another *man's* essential nature. 3) I would have been for you the *mediator* between you and the species, and therefore would become recognised and felt by you yourself as a completion of your own essential nature and as a necessary part of yourself, and consequently would know myself to be confirmed both in your thought and your love. 4) In the individual expression of my life I would have directly created your expression of your life, and therefore in my individual activity I would have directly *confirmed* and *realised* my true nature, my *human* nature, my *communal nature* (Marx 1975e: 227–228).

I am indebted to Jacob McNulty for directing me to this passage.

themselves to continue a kind of existence they share with other animals. They feel free, not in their labor but in their life off the job and, even there, primarily in nonrational activities that enable them to escape and dull the pain and boredom of their labor.

Returning now to the first form of alienation, Marx summarizes this by saying that "the worker is related to the *product of his labour* as to an *alien* object" (1975b: 272). The point is not that any objects workers create are external to them. After all, this is an essential feature of Hegel's three-moment analysis of the will. (β) is the will's second moment in which it makes itself determinate by willing something external to it (Hegel 1977: 111). This externalization of the will is, moreover, essential to Hegel's theory of property and, therefore, to his account of persons as it figures in Abstract Right and its "commandment of right" – "*be a person and respect others as persons*" (Hegel 1991: 69). Persons, for Hegel, are essentially property holders, which they become through externalizing their will and acting on objects in the external world in a publicly recognizable way. This is the juridical sense of "alienation," in which property can be alienated, but also in which the will can externalize and thus alienate itself by "plac[ing]" itself "in any thing" in a publicly recognizable manner (75, 95–98).

Marx explicitly distinguishes this Hegelian sense from the sense in which he claims labor under capitalism involves the worker being (pejoratively) alienated from the products of their labor:

> The *alienation* [Entäusserung] of the worker in his product means not only that his labor becomes an object, an *external* existence, but that it exists as . . . something alien to him, and that it becomes a power on its own confronting him. It means that the life which he has conferred on the object confronts him as something hostile and alien (Marx 1975b: 272).

Most obviously, the objects workers produce under capitalism do not thereby become theirs. To the contrary, because of capitalists' state-enforced legal property right in the means of production, they belong to the capitalist. And every hour of labor increases capitalists' profits and, thereby, capitalists' power over workers. Far from workers being able to express themselves and their values through the products of their work, their products are thus a publicly visible sign of their disempowered and miserable condition. And not just in welfare terms. Workers' labor and products help constitute capitalists' power and control *over* workers and the workers' subservient social position. Workers' products confront them "as something hostile and alien."

Labor's products are, essentially, commodities, and in producing them, workers add to the "fetishism of commodities" Marx will describe in *Capital* (Marx 1975f: 81–103). But so also is labor itself a commodity that workers produce. The worker-created commodity social world thereby becomes yet a further form of alienation, giving rise to an alienated relation to the natural world.

Concerning what he cites as his second form of alienation, workers' alienated relation to "the *act of production* within the *labour* process," Marx mentions several important aspects (Marx 1975b: 274). Most significant is labor activity's failure to be "species-activity" (302). Marx cites many aspects of capitalist labor – its routine, energy-sucking, and mentally and physically deteriorating character – which both make it impossible for work to express free and universal human values and are, severally and jointly, alienating aspects in themselves. Work wears down workers and makes them disposable.

Perhaps most important for our purposes, however, are Marx's views in the 1848 manuscripts about the ways in which relations in a capitalist economy impede the realization of workers' species nature as "a *universal* and therefore . . . free being" (275). When we combine these with Marx's remarks in his 1843 letter to Arnold Ruge about freedom as "the self-worth of men" and a "democratic" "community" being the "highest end" for which human beings can be organized, we may be better able to see both exactly how capitalism alienates workers from their species-being *and* what the fundamental form of communist social order must be (Padover 1979: 25). What's more, I shall be arguing, we can gain a philosophically interesting and plausible way of understanding Marx's doctrine of capitalist exploitation that is different from orthodox interpretations, as well as independent from Marx's labor theory of value.

Marx's idea that capitalism alienates workers from their species-being or human nature can sound like an Aristotelian naturalist critique. And that is undoubtedly part of Marx's thought. Capitalism deprives workers of the ability to thrive in distinctively human ways, and communism, Marx argues, makes up this lack. Whereas capitalism's division of labor stunts human growth, communism will enable its members to develop and actualize a wide variety of human skills: "to hunt in the morning, fish in the afternoon, rear cattle in the evening, criticise after dinner, just as I have a mind" (Marx and Engels 1975c: 47). But even if he does not put it in so many words – certainly never in deontic or juridical terms – there is also, as Irwin suggests, a Kantian aspect to his thought, namely, that capitalism fails adequately to appreciate or respect human dignity. It is hard to read Marx's theory of exploitation (*Ausbeutung*) of labor under capitalism without hearing resonances of

Kant's idea of treating people as means only and not as ends in themselves. Elster notes, indeed, that although "exploit" can have nonnormative senses, "*ausbeuten*" means "to take unfair advantage of" (Elster 1986: 92). How could Marx avoid the implication that capitalism treats workers as mere means when he explicitly says that capitalism treats workers as replaceable by literal instruments or machines? In a capitalist political economy, workers "decline to a mere machine" (Marx 1975b: 238).

Recall now Marx's language in his 1843 letter to Ruge: "freedom" is the "self-worth of men." And democracy is the "highest end" of a community of free people (in Padover 1979: 25). In Kantian terms, democracy is the form of social order that befits the dignity of each and every human being. Only this form of collectivity enables each person to realize their species nature as "universal" and "free" beings. If we carry these thoughts into the workplace, we get an "economic democracy" of some form. In order to realize workers' species-being, they must themselves be given standing and voice in the laboring process. To deny workers this standing and to dictate their work to them, is, by definition, to place them in a position of social subservience from which proletarian class struggle hopes to emancipate them.

I shall argue that Marx's theory of exploitation can be interpreted similarly so that he can plausibly claim that capitalists exploit their workers, without having to rely on a controversial labor theory of value. A society in which workers have voice and the standing to play a role in determining how work is to be conducted as a collective activity of equal rational human beings is one in which all are treated as having equal dignity. This is the deep significance of Marx's claim that the proletariat has "radical chains" and that their emancipation is "universal human emancipation" (Marx 1975b: 280). A genuine democracy with workplace democracy promises a social order in which, in Kantian terms, all are treated as ends in themselves.

Again, Marx steadfastly rejects the deontic and juridical terms in which Kant puts his claims about human dignity. Most specifically, he rejects Kant's claim that universal human rights can be so grounded. We turn next to Marx's critique of rights and justice.

Marx's Rejection of Rights and Justice

Marx's main critique of justice and rights occurs in *On the Jewish Question*.[12] The central topic of this work is *emancipation*. Marx

[12] But see Buchanan 1982 for discussion of a passage in *Critique of the Gotha Program* in which Marx criticizes the notions of rights and justice (Buchanan 1982: 68–69).

engages with Bruno Bauer, who had argued that Jews can achieve what Marx calls "political emancipation," that is, equal rights as citizens, only if they relinquish their Jewish identity. Marx makes two arguments against Bauer. The first, and less important for our purposes, is Marx's claim that having full rights as an equal citizen *is* consistent with maintaining religious, hence Jewish, identity, at least in nonpolitical contexts (Marx 1975c: 155). This will seem uncontroversial to modern liberals who see the separation of church and state as established common sense. Marx's second, more significant argument is that although political emancipation is consistent with Jewish (or any other religious) identity, "human emancipation" is utterly inconsistent with religious life (159–160). Being emancipated as a human being requires not just that religious identities be excluded from political life and that the state be made fully secular, but that human beings be freed from religious belief altogether. Here Marx follows Feuerbach, who had argued that religious faith inevitably involves alienation, in effect, human beings relating to their own humanity in an alienated form, as though it could be perfectly instantiated in a nonhuman being (God) (Feuerbach 1989). Feuerbach thus makes basically the same point about religious belief that Marx makes about labor under capitalism. Religion, like capitalism, alienates those involved in it from their "species-being."

But this is only one way in which political emancipation falls short of full "human emancipation." Even a fully secular state in its most emancipated form – in which all have equal citizenship – is characterized by the coercive legal forms of right and justice that Marx argues in *On the Jewish Question* are incompatible with a fully emancipated social order. Only a communist society, free of the juridical trappings of the state, is capable of being a "community of people" organized "for their highest ends" of "freedom" and "democra[cy]," as Marx puts it in his earlier letter to Ruge (in Padover 1979: 25).[13]

Democracy is the form of collective decision-making in which members of a community relate to one another in their (rational) "species-being," all treating one another's rational humanity as ends, in the Kantian sense. Not just any equal vote-counting mechanism will count as democratic in this sense. To most fully realize human (rational) "species-being," a democratic

[13] Of course, Marx does not say in the letter to Ruge that the juridical state is incompatible with the highest human end of freedom – indeed, he there characterizes this end as "a democratic state." It is in *On the Jewish Question* that Marx makes this claim.

collective order must be a "deliberative democracy" (Fishkin 1991). Only if democratic processes involve shared *collective reasoning* can those taking part in them achieve human emancipation and mutual relations in which none are alienated from their "species-being."

Again, Marx's view is that this can be actualized only in a classless, communist society. Social class inevitably distorts human relations in an alienating way. People relate to one another not as individuals sharing a common life, but through the hierarchical lens of stereotyping or "characterizing" emotions like contempt (from above) and shame (from below) (Darwall 2018b). The burden of Marx's argument in *On the Jewish Question* is to show that any social order that instantiates legal standards of justice and right – that is, any state in the classical liberal sense – must also alienate its citizens from their common "species-being" and thus be incompatible with human emancipation. Any collective order that permits socioeconomic *classes* will create alienation and unfreedom in the relevant sense. And any collective order that enforces individual rights and justice – even the most liberal political state – will necessarily permit socioeconomic classes.

Within rights and justice, Marx distinguishes "civic" or "*political rights*, rights which can only be exercised in community with others," from other "rights of man," that is, human rights that do not require political community for their exercise and that, Marx will argue, provide the only justification for the liberal state itself (Marx 1975f: 160–161). Marx has already argued that "political emancipation," or "political freedom," as he also calls it, is fully compatible with religious identity. What political emancipation requires are rights of equal citizenship, an equal status in the political order – for example, having the right to run for office, vote, and so on – that one can hold irrespective of religious identity. The problem with equal citizenship, from Marx's perspective, is that it is a membership in a juridical, political order. Equal citizenship is the best form of citizenship; it is *political* emancipation. But it is still only *political*, and not *human*, *emancipation*. It still involves alienation from human species-being and so unfreedom in the sense with which Marx is most fundamentally concerned.

Marx reserves his most focused arguments for the "rights of man" since it is only these nonpolitical rights, in his view, that can provide a juridical, political order with whatever justification it might have. The major problem, as he sees it, is that the conception of the person that is involved in the "rights of man" is as a member of *civil society*.

> The *droits de l'homme*, the rights of man, are as *such* distinct from the *droit du citoyen*, the rights of the citizen. Who is *homme* as distinct from *citoyen*? None other than the *member of civil society*. Why is the member of civil society called "man," simply man; why are his rights called the *rights of man*? How is this fact to be explained? From the relationship between the political state and civil society, from the nature of political emancipation (162).

Marx takes his analysis of civil society and its relation to the state largely from Hegel. Recall that in the "Introduction" to his *Contribution to the Critique of Hegel's Philosophy of Law*, Marx argues that there is an unbridgeable gap between the *private* economic order of civil society, on the one hand, and the civic and political realm, on the other. Hegel's citizens and civil servants (the "universal class") and economic agents stand as "two hostile armies" in opposition to one another, as Marx sees it (Marx 1975a: 50, 70). Marx's critique of Hegel is that member of civil society and civil servant are both roles that actual human individuals must play, and this opposition necessarily alienates individuals from themselves and from each other.

Again, these conceptions of civil society and the state are drawn directly from Hegel's *Elements of the Philosophy of Right*. "Civil society," for Hegel, is "an association of members as *self-sufficient individuals* [*Einzelner*]" (Hegel 1991: 198). It is a private "free market" society, in which property owners relate to one another *as such*, each directly pursuing their own, and only their own, interests, with any common interest or general welfare being realized only through a Smithian "invisible hand." As Hegel puts it, "*subjective selfishness* turns into a *contribution towards the satisfaction of the needs of everyone else*" (Hegel 1991: 233). In relation to civil society, the state's function is to legally enforce the rights constituting Abstract Right, that is, the sanctity of "persons" as owners of private property.

Marx picks up on both of these Hegelian themes but uses them against Hegel. Marx argues that since the life of Abstract Right is one of alienated individuals (a point Hegel himself makes in support of Ethical Life), any state that seeks to enforce the "rights of man" (as Hegel's state does) is incapable of overcoming alienation and achieving "human emancipation." Marx thus uses Hegel against himself. The "so-called rights of man," Marx says, are "the rights of egoistic man" (Marx 1975e: 162). Commenting on the French Constitution of 1793's declaration that the right to "liberty . . . is the right to everything that harms no one else," Marx says that this is "the liberty of man as an isolated monad, withdrawn into himself" (162). This right to liberty "is based not on the association of man with man, but on the separation of man from man" (162). "It is the *right,*" Marx continues, "of this separation, the right of the *restricted* individual, withdrawn into himself" (162–163).

This entails that any state whose function is to legally enforce the rights of man will simultaneously (a) have subjects who are alienated both from their "species-being" and from one another ([14] and [17] in the list of Marx's kinds of alienation under capitalism given earlier) and (b) will be incapable of realizing human emancipation. "It makes every man see in other men not the *realisation* of his own freedom, but the *barrier* to it" (163). The state achieves not human emancipation but the alienation of "man from man" and from human "species-being."

How effective is Marx's critique of individual rights and justice? A reasonable initial response is that since Marx bases his critique of rights and justice entirely on negative rights to liberty and property it can easily be avoided by embracing a more capacious conception of justice as including positive rights, for example, to equality of opportunity, healthcare, education. Indeed, given that Marx is criticizing the very idea of rights and justice, an opponent might even take the position that justice might require not just equality of opportunity but equality of condition or outcome. One might reply on Marx's behalf that any such rights cannot really be considered "rights of man" in Marx's sense since they cannot be established or realized outside of a political order, so perhaps they should count as "political rights." But to this it is entirely reasonable to reply that there would still be a natural, nonpolitical right underlying any such "political right," namely the right of individuals to organize themselves into a juridical, political order to actualize the relevant political rights. This after all is the position that Kant takes with respect to the right to acquire and own property, which Marx counts as a paradigm "right of man." Any right to property holding in a state of nature, Kant holds, is only "provisional," and individuals are obligated to leave the state of nature and become citizens of a legitimate state that can suitably establish and secure property rights (Kant 1996c: 6:256–264). It is very hard to see how this aspect of Marx's critique of justice and rights can satisfactorily reach its target.

On the other hand, Marx's argument that any social order with socioeconomic classes of the kind he is concerned with must be rife with alienation and social oppression, hence incompatible with "human emancipation," is entirely persuasive, for the reasons we have canvassed. If Marx can argue that any juridical state, even the most just polity, will have socioeconomic classes, and so alienation and forms of oppression from which its members should be emancipated, then, arguably, he will have made his case.

Now, the central problem Marx is focusing on is not, again, the way capitalism distributes benefits and burdens. That it is distributively unjust is no doubt a justified criticism of capitalism, but it is not Marx's critique. Indeed, some commentators plausibly argue that Marx himself believed that capitalism was just in its own terms (Tucker 1969; Wood 2004).[14] But whether Marx believed that or not, his critique is, in Anderson's terms, a "relational" rather than a distributivist critique (Anderson 1999, 2012). Marx is arguing that even the most liberal state, realizing whatever standard of distributive justice you like, will admit of social classes, and therefore fall short of the human emancipation that only a classless, communist society can provide.

As we noted earlier, "classes" in Marx's sense are nothing that can be captured in socioeconomic data about wealth, income, or distributive patterns of benefits and burdens more generally. They are realized by essentially social, *recognitional* facts concerning how members of certain groups are treated, related to, and seen by members of others. Emancipation is, by definition, release from a condition of servitude, subservience to or mastery by others, which relations are established by patterns of recognition. Human emancipation for Marx, I am claiming, can only be realized by forms of collective order that involve mutual relations as equals. Marx argues that this is impossible in a juridical state, even one that is distributively just by the most demanding standards.

But would that establish the conclusion that justice is a defective social ideal since it is compatible with alienation and oppression? Not necessarily, since the most promising theory of justice might be, as Anderson argues, a relational egalitarian one rather than any theory of distributive justice (Anderson 1999, 2012). Moreover, it might be, as Anderson clearly thinks, that there are forms of liberal states that could pass relational egalitarian muster. We could even stipulate that such a state would be some form of democratic socialism. Marx would then have to argue that even the best such relational egalitarian state would nonetheless be consistent with alienation and oppression owing to its establishment of relational egalitarian *law*.

Exploitation

Marx's most well-known and widely received critique of capitalism is mounted in terms of *exploitation*. This is advanced most prominently in

[14] For an excellent discussion of the issue and of these commentaries on it, see Buchanan 1982: 50–85.

volume I of *Capital*, which was published in 1867 (Marx 1975f). Because Marx's arguments about alienation, especially those concerning "species-being," are more clearly philosophical, they can seem to violate the more rigorously empiricist standards of Marx's later dialectical materialist writings. For this reason, many who are attracted by this aspect of Marx's later work are skeptical of his earlier, more philosophical critique and so prefer his analysis of capitalist exploitation in *Capital*. The earlier critique certainly involves claims of ethical philosophy. Whether these are consistent with radical empiricism or materialism, however, are substantive questions of metaethics.

In volume I of *Capital*, Marx gives a theoretically precise definition of exploitation in terms of other theoretically defined notions of "constant capital" (the "exchange value" of the means of production), "variable capital" (the "exchange value" of workers and their labor), and "surplus value" (the exchange value created by combining constant capital with variable capital less the exchange value of labor). Marx then defines what he calls "the rate of surplus value" as the ratio of surplus value to variable capital, and he also calls this the "degree of exploitation" (196–251). So with "s" being "surplus value" and "v" being "variable capital," the degree of exploitation involved in a given labor produce is then equal to s/v.

To operationalize these definitions, we need observable measures. How do we calculate the relevant (exchange) values? Marx answers with his labor theory of value, which he largely takes from Smith and Ricardo. Roughly, the value of any commodity is a function of the "socially necessary" labor time required to produce it (220). The basic idea is that the labor required to produce the worker's laboring itself (which determines the exchange value of variable capital) is whatever labor is needed to keep the worker alive and in working order. Only some of the worker's day is required to produce this value (v); during the remaining time, the worker produces surplus value (s). And the degree of exploitation can then be determined as the ratio of these measures: s/v.

Most, though not all, followers of Marx now reject Marx's labor theory of value and therefore any standard of exploitation that is based on it. It would seem, in any case, that nothing with critical bite can follow from such a nonnormative standard without additional normative premises. Some followers of Marx, like Elster, think that the claim that capitalism involves objectionable exploitation can convincingly be made without depending on the labor theory of value in any way (Elster 1986: 60–102).[15]

[15] For an excellent interpretation of Marx's labor theory, see Harvey 2018.

If it is not necessary to analyze exploitation so that it can pass positivist scruples in order to sustain the claim that capitalism is criticizable as endemically exploitative, then perhaps Marx's earlier, more philosophical critique of capitalism as involving alienating oppression from which human beings must be emancipated should not be rejected by Marx's followers. I want to conclude by proposing that one way to understand Marx's exploitation critique is in the very same terms that he makes his alienation critique.

In particular, I want to focus on Marx's claim that a capitalist economy impedes the realization of workers' species nature as "a *universal* and therefore . . . free being" (Marx 1975b: 275). Recall Marx's remarks in his 1843 letter to Arnold Ruge about freedom being "the self-worth of men" and a "democratic" "community" being the "highest end" for which human beings can be organized. When we combine those remarks with the former claim, we can infer that realizing our species nature is something we can do only collectively through joint processes and procedures of deliberation and decision that involve everyone equally as individual human beings. Bearing in mind the Kantian dictate to treat every individual as an end, and that this involves relating to them in ways that include and respect their wills as individual rational human beings, gives us a way of understanding a nonexploitative political economy in similar terms.

A political economy involves exploitation when the roles individuals occupy are inconsistent with mutual relations as "free" and equal human beings. Arguably, these relations require both that the economy be governed by a "democratic" "community" – whether communist, democratic socialist, or social democratic – and that workplaces be organized so that all have voice. It is up for normative debate – whether theoretically or politically and democratically – exactly what form the economy itself should take: what ownership relations concerning the "means of production" and what mix of public and private ownership there should be, and how markets should be utilized and restricted. Approaching Marx's critique of capitalist exploitation from the perspective of his earlier "philosophical" critique gives him a way of theorizing exploitation that is normatively plausible in its own right, that avoids dependence on the labor theory of value, and that seems truest to Marx's central concern with "human emancipation."

We concluded the previous chapter with a discussion of the differences between Fichte and Hegel on recognition and of the different ways in which their conceptions of recognition enter into their ethical and political thought. I have been emphasizing the way recognition is also implicitly involved in Marx's. To this point, the role I have focused on has been Hegelian, namely, recognition's function in establishing social identities and classes. At this juncture, however, we see a role for a form of recognition that is Fichtean. Political economy can involve nonexploitative *relations* as equals only through Fichtean summonses that are implicit in all genuine communication and shared deliberation.

Finally, we should note the connection between these last themes and the solidarity or comradeship that, I have been suggesting, is a natural candidate to play the motivational role that is most consonant with Marx's ethical philosophy, if only implicitly. Marx faces the problem of motivation at two stages. There is, first, the question of what can motivate individual members of the proletariat to develop class consciousness and engage in revolutionary action that may benefit the class at the cost of individual disadvantage. It is central to Marx's analysis of capitalism that workers are alienated from each other and therefore lack any incentive for collective revolutionary action (Buchanan 1979). And then there is the question of what can motivate collectively beneficial action after the revolution. If workers come to identify with the community good, this will tend to diminish conflicts of interest. It is hard to see, however, how it can completely eliminate them or, even more, eliminate the suspicion that interests conflict. To what can members of a communist order appeal when they want to call out those they perceive to be injuring them?

Marx might reply that although he rejects the idea of a Fichtean summons of *right*, that doesn't mean that a summons of some form would not play an essential role. After all, the *Communist Manifesto* is an explicit summons to "working men of all countries" and to their allies (like Marx and Engels themselves) to "unite," which not only *expresses* solidarity with the proletariat but partly *constitutes* it. This suggests that solidarity is like Strawsonian "reactive attitudes" in having not just intentional objects but implicit addressees (Strawson 1968). Solidarity involves an implicit Fichtean summons; it is a form of motivation that presupposes a "participant" (or second-personal) standpoint. If this is right, then although the form of recognition that constitutes social classes is the Hegelian variety that constructs social identities, the form of recognition involved in the solidarity that Marx holds to be necessary for *de-constructing* social classes, and therefore for human emancipation, is ultimately Fichtean. The form of the summons would not be deontic. If someone steps on another person's foot, the second might not respond with "Hey, you can't do that. I'm a person." But perhaps they could respond with something like, "Hey, I'm Nick," calling the first to a recognition of them as the particular individual with whom they are in a relation of reciprocal comradeship.[16]

In this way, we might think of a Marxian community as modeled on a family or other group whose members identify with concern for the family as a whole but also for each individual member. In such groupings there may be no way to specify what members should want and do independently of some process of joint decision. Such an understanding would harken back to Marx's championing of democracy in his 1843 letter to Ruge.[17]

16 I am indebted here to Nick Jacobson, Angel Nwadibia, and other members of my seminar on "The Ethics of Marx, Kierkegaard, and Nietzsche" at Yale University in Spring 2023 and to Will Darwall.

17 See p. 101.

CHAPTER 4

Kierkegaard

Quite unlike Marx, Kierkegaard first came to philosophy through his study of theology. However, like Marx, his early philosophical education was steeped in the idealism of Fichte and Hegel, from which he also radically departed, including with ideas around the realization of human freedom and freedom's relation to reason. Kierkegaard takes his model for the "ethical" outlook of volume II of *Either/Or* from Fichte and Hegel, though he later argues that it is supplanted by the "life-view" of faith (Kosch 2006). Thus, Kierkegaard and Marx both end up holding that what Marx calls "emancipation" can only be achieved *beyond* morality, by realizing non-deontic ethical conceptions. But whereas Marx seeks human liberation in nonjuridical egalitarian *social* relations, Kierkegaard thinks that we can live "in freedom" only internally, through forms of inwardness – faith and love – that realize our "particularity" as "single individual[s]" (Kierkegaard 1987b: 349; 2006: 46, 54). And quite differently from the relentlessly secular Marx, Kierkegaard holds that emancipation comes through loving faith in God.

Faith involves a "teleological suspension of the ethical [moral]" that makes "the particular . . . higher than the universal" (Kierkegaard 2006: 46–58).[1] God, however, is not only the ultimate object of the forms of ethical consciousness that enable individuals to live "in freedom" as "single individual[s]" beyond morality (Kierkegaard 1987b: 349; 2006: 54). God is also, as we shall see, the source, for Kierkegaard, of deontic morality. And that sets for Kierkegaard the basic problematic of free moral agency in a way that is familiar from the modern moral philosophy of Pufendorf, Locke, the British rationalists, and Kant. Consciousness of ourselves as morally obligated necessarily brings with it an awareness of ourselves as free, as capable of doing what we are morally accountable for doing (as in Kant's "fact of reason").

[1] Again, Kierkegaard generally uses "ethical" to mean moral in the modern sense.

It is also a fundamental feature of Kierkegaard's view, however – one he arguably gets from Schelling – that we must also be capable of *not* doing our moral duty, that we are radically free in a way that goes beyond Kant and Hegel's doctrine of freedom as practical reason (Kosch 2006). We often freely choose to do wrong, thereby turning away from God and violating His will. We can only accept God's love and live "in freedom," consequently, if we "choose [ourselves] as guilty" and "repent" (Kierkegaard 1987b: 216–217).

Radical freedom, for Kierkegaard, is the human existential predicament because we are subject to moral duty. Thus far, Kierkegaard is simply drawing out implications that are already central to modern morality. There are not simply good and sufficient reasons for doing what is morally right; we are *obligated* to do our moral duty. This, again, is Suárez's distinction between law and counsel, which runs through so much of modern moral philosophy and which brings agential freedom in its train. We cannot intelligibly be held accountable for doing what we are incapable of doing.

But Schelling and Kierkegaard go farther than Kant and the German idealists, who identify freedom with practical reason. Kierkegaard holds that moral action could not be genuinely free unless *not* doing what is right, wrongdoing, were a genuine agential alternative also. In this, Schelling and Kierkegaard are arguably taking Suárez's distinction and its implications for human freedom more seriously than Kant and the idealists do.

In addition, as Kosch shows, Kierkegaard also follows Schelling in maintaining the theological voluntarist thesis that morality has these features just because it depends on God's will (Kosch 2006: 113–114, 180–182). Schelling writes, "God is outside of and above all law, for he himself is the law . . . The good is only *what* he wills and it is good *because* he wills it (not in itself). If he did not will it, it would not be good."[2] Similarly, Kierkegaard holds that it is awareness of God's loving will that shows us our duty to do His will and love Him in return. Accepting God's love necessarily involves "repentance." The "basis" for our guilt is "that he has loved me first" (Kierkegaard 1987b: 216). We must repent of the "evil[s]" (wrongs) we have done and will do. "Repentance specifically expresses that evil essentially belongs to me and at the same time expresses that it does not essentially belong to me" (224). This is a "paradox of apology": we

[2] This is Kosch's translation of a passage from *Zur Geschichte der neueren Philosophie*, quoted in Kosch 2006: 113.

simultaneously own our wrongdoing and, as Kierkegaard puts it, "choose [ourselves]" as upright selves.[3]

Schelling and Kierkegaard contrast "impersonal" (idealist) ethics of universal practical reason with genuinely deontic standards that presuppose, they hold, like Pufendorf and other voluntarists, a relationship of *personal* accountability to God (see Kosch 2006: esp. 118–120). Without God's personal address to make us morally responsible, "a person could live without coming in touch with the ethical [moral]" (Kierkegaard 1987b: 225). Not every choice has the meaning and significance that puts one's identity on the line – as Kierkegaard phrases it, choice "of oneself" as a "single individual." It is only from the perspective of a seriously committing choice in which one "choose[s] oneself absolutely," that the concepts of "good and evil" come into view (224). Only "someone who views the personality ethically [morally] has at once an absolute difference: namely, the difference between good and evil" (225–226). Individuals like Kierkegaard's A in *Either/Or*, who seek to evade their radical freedom by living an "esthetic" life, "never think in the categories of good and evil" (223). They "continually think relative differences, never the absolute difference" required to choose themselves "absolutely" (1987a: 223). They evade the serious choices we confront when we see ourselves as morally obligated and occupy the (second-personal) perspective of individuals addressed by God's will.

Radical freedom thus structures the human existential predicament or standpoint, what Kierkegaard calls our "life-view."[4] It is worth pausing to note the originality and significance of this focus on the perspective of lived human experience, especially for the continental thinkers who follow. Kierkegaard is interested less in traditional issues of ethical philosophy than in what Husserl and later philosophers will call the "life-world," the phenomenology of human life.

Kierkegaard names three importantly distinct evaluative outlooks – the esthetic, the ethical, and the life-view of faith. As we shall see in the next section, the esthetic "life-view" is marked by the attempt to evade responsibility and "escape from freedom" through esthetic role play, as in Sartre's waiter whose "bad faith" consists in seeking to cancel his freedom by absorbing his identity in the role of a waiter (Fromm 1941; Sartre 2020: 117–118). The ethical life-view, by contrast, takes life choices seriously – as

[3] I am indebted to Francey Russell for this helpful term.

[4] As Alastair Hannay notes, Kierkegaard criticized the Danish novelist Hans Christian Andersen, in Kierkegaard's first publication, for writing novels that "fail to evince" a life-view (Hannay 2001: 107).

"either/or"'s – conscientiously coming to terms with moral duties. But ultimately, Kierkegaard argues that the moral life, conceived by *Either/Or*'s Judge William in terms of universal practical reason, is wholly impersonal and incapable of authentic individuality and particularity. (Judge William is also called B, as I will refer to him henceforth for convenience.) Neither can the ethical outlook dispel the despair that Kierkegaard holds to be also unavoidable from the esthetic perspective and replace it with the joy of loving faithful relationship.

Outside the life-view of faith, the human condition is one of anxiety and despair. "Anxiety," Kierkegaard says, "is the dizziness of freedom" (Kierkegaard 1980: IV.331). Aware of our moral responsibility, we cannot deny that we are free to live up to it, but also that we often do not. And we also cannot deny that when we violate our moral duty, we *choose* to do wrong. This brings us to despair, which, for Kierkegaard, is the fundamental problem of human existence: how to live with the awareness of our inevitable guilt and sin in the knowledge that we (will) have freely chosen it.[5] Here we might note that the subtitle of Kierkegaard's (1980) *The Concept of Anxiety* is *A Simple Psychologically Orienting Deliberation on the Dogmatic Issue of Hereditary Sin*. This, of course, is ironic; nothing in Kierkegaard is simple, and much of it is ironic. Indeed, Kierkegaard's (1989) dissertation and first philosophical publication was *The Concept of Irony*.

Either: The Esthetic Life-View

Kierkegaard's irony and dizzying literary devices are on full display in volume I of *Either/Or*, the first of his pseudonymous works. This does not have a formal author but only an "editor," Victor Eremita (Latin for hermit). Eremita does not write *Either/Or* in the book's fictional world. Rather, in a secret compartment of a writing desk he has purchased secondhand, he discovers two sets of papers that purport to be by two different authors. One is an "esthete," whom Eremita calls "A." A's papers, which include the lengthy "Diary of the Seducer," comprise volume I. The second set, comprising volume II, purport to be by a second author, whom Eremita calls "Judge William" and also "B." Whereas A's essays and diary are addressed to no one in particular, as perhaps befits an esthete

[5] It is not too farfetched to consider in this connection Anne Case and Angus Deaton's *Deaths of Despair and the Future of Capitalism*, which discusses the decline in life expectancy among the white working class in the United States through, among other things, suicide, drug overdose, and alcoholism during the past two decades. They argue that this results from socioeconomic decline for which those afflicted see themselves as responsible (Case and Deaton 2020).

(though the diary includes letters written to his seduction's target), B's compositions are explicitly addressed to A, earnestly entreating A to abandon his esthetic life, accept his moral responsibility, and take his existential choices seriously.

Neither A's nor B's words can be taken as directly expressing anything that Kierkegaard himself would wish to stand behind; but in context, they both provide rich materials from which to infer Kierkegaard's views about the esthetic and ethical life-views. Sometimes a character will say something we can be reasonably confident Kierkegaard himself believes, for example, when B describes A as evading responsibility, denying his freedom, and being unable within the esthetic life-view to do or think anything to dispel or displace an inescapable state of despair and even depression.

At other points, however, A and B will not so much explicitly assert things we can conclude Kierkegaard believes as *show* us truths of which we can infer Kierkegaard is trying to convince us. For example, A describes in "The Diary of the Seducer" how he manipulates the woman he wishes to seduce, Cordelia, by promoting a rumor, which she hears, that he might have another lover, in order to increase her interest in him. A purposely avoids declaring love to Cordelia directly, seeking to create appearances that can successfully effect seduction without direct avowal. Of course, this is impotent to create genuine relationship, substituting esthetic play, and not even mutual play at that, for serious engagement. Kierkegaard's message, that a fulfilling relationship is incompatible with the esthetic outlook, is unmistakable.

Kierkegaard himself engaged in similar play in the actual writing and publication of *Either/Or*. In addition to employing only pseudonyms, Kierkegaard deployed complex subterfuges to maintain the secrecy of his authorship. Kierkegaard wrote in his journals that if he "wanted to tell about it, a whole book could be written on how ingeniously I have fooled people about" his patterns of life during the period he was writing the book (Kierkegaard 1987a: xiv). Known for spending endless hours walking and conversing in the streets of Copenhagen, he was faced with the problem of how to maintain his secret since he had "almost no time" during the time of writing to continue his usual patterns. "Every evening when I left home exhausted and had eaten at Mini's, I stopped at the theater for ten minutes, not one minute more. Familiar as I was, I counted on there being several gossips at the theater who would now say: Every single night, he goes to the theater; he does not do another thing" (Kierkegaard 1987a: xiv). Kierkegaard took a secret esthetic pleasure in being able to show himself "that one can work hard without seeming to, that one can privately concentrate while every bungling student dares look upon one as a loafer" (xix). We can imagine him thinking, "Now, the joke's on them." He concludes this journal entry with an ironic, self-mocking estimation of *Either/Or* and its philosophical milieu: "Even if the book itself were devoid of meaning, the making of it would still be the pithiest epigram I have written over the maundering philosophic age in which I live" (xix).

Clearly, Kierkegaard was not a complete outsider to the esthetic life-view. Hannay describes him as an "esthetically inclined young man" (Hannay 2001: 8). And though Kierkegaard was utterly serious about the one romantic love of his life, Regine Olsen, aspects of their courtship and breakup were eerily similar to those of Cordelia and A's. Both A and Kierkegaard cause their respective breakups and manipulate their lovers' beliefs about their real feelings and intentions (Hannay 2001).

A central theme of *Either/Or*'s volume I is the difference between thinking and "living" in a narrative, perhaps fictional, world, with characters and plots, as exemplified by A's esthetic life-view, on the one hand, and genuine existence and serious engagement, which A decidedly does not exemplify, on the other. A has an active mental life, but nothing is ever at stake; he can never "choose himself," as B will complain in volume II. Sometimes, as in his method of "rotation," A's focus is on keeping himself occupied by contemplating "interesting" objects, *seriatim*, not in order to advance a particular line of thought or to discover something out of curiosity or out of some other passion with which he might identify, but simply to stave off boredom (Kierkegaard 1987a: 281–300). At other points, as in "The Seducer's Diary," A's object is mostly the playful spinning out of interesting seduction scenarios, which may or may not be executed in real life. And even when A's writings purport to describe actual events, these typically consist in his playing a character in relation to a woman, Cordelia, whom he has cast in a role of his own esthetic choice. Whenever his letters address Cordelia, or even when he speaks to her "in real life," A writes and speaks "in character" (Kierkegaard 1987a: 301–445).

The significance of "characterization" and its moral psychological function is suggested already in volume I's "Preface," in which Victor Eremita describes how he came to possess the text of *Either/Or* and presents to us its central characters, A and B. For weeks, Eremita says, he had passed by a writing desk in the window of a secondhand shop (in which, as it transpires, the papers that would comprise *Either/Or* were secretly contained). He admired the desk and came gradually to want so much to view it that on the "rare occasion that it was necessary to make a detour for its sake, [he] did not hesitate" (4). (Note, by the way, the irony of "for its sake," which plays on the difference between Eremita's longing looks and a loving gaze that really would have its object's "sake" in view.) The desk was, Eremita says, a piece for which he "had no use, and it would [have been] a prodigality" for him to have purchased it (4). Eremita continues: "But desire, as is known, is very sophistical. I found a pretext for going into the secondhand shop, inquired about other things, and as I was about to leave I casually made a very low offer for the writing desk" (4). Since Eremita wants to maintain his self-characterization as prudent, not "prodigal," a very low offer is the most he will permit himself. The "casual" character of the offer also suggests that it is nothing anyone need concern themselves with, least of all Eremita himself, and he thereby distracts himself from his prodigality. (Compare here J. L. Austin's description of akratically "succumb[ing] to temptation" in taking an extra portion of ice cream "bombe" at High Table, "with calm and even with finesse" [Austin 1956–1957: 24].) As it happens, the owner will not accept Eremita's offer. Undeterred, he continues to pass the shop daily, "gaz[ing] at the desk with enamored eyes" (Kierkegaard 1987a: 5). It is important that this happens less self-recognizably, in steps. Finally, Eremita rationalizes purchasing the desk at the higher price and does so, encouraging himself with the following thoughts as pretexts: "This is the last time you are going to be so prodigal." His evidence? With "every time you look at [the desk] you will be reminded of how prodigal you were; with this desk commences a new period in your life. Ah, desire is very eloquent," Eremita concludes, "and good intentions are always on hand" (Kierkegaard 1987a: 5). Here Kierkegaard gives voice, through Eremita, to a thought that Eremita himself could not have had at the time and remained "in character."

We learn from Plato's *Republic* that desire focuses only on its object and we require some other perspective in order to make the "all-things-considered" judgments of practical reason (Plato 1997). But – Plato to the contrary notwithstanding – we do not always automatically do what we think we have the most reason to do. As we have noted, Kierkegaard is especially concerned to stress this point in the case of doing what we think we morally should. He insists that we sometimes, perhaps frequently, freely choose to do what is morally wrong. It is evident from Eremita's words that Kierkegaard also thinks we often freely do what we think is imprudent or "prodigal" as well. However, the point involved here is that we normally "permit" ourselves to do so only when we can save face with ourselves through some "pretext" or rationalization. The central point is the contrast between accepting our freedom and acting on what we genuinely think we morally or prudentially should do, plainly and honestly without self-deceiving self-characterizing flourish, on the one hand, and on the other, acting with "pretexts" and rationalizations in ways that save face with ourselves, enabling us to continue to characterize ourselves as we wish and find esthetically pleasing.

Throughout volume I of *Either/Or*, it is A whose own words show him to be interested solely in (interesting) esthetic appearances. In "Diapsalmata," A says in a quite amazing passage:

> If anyone should keep a diary, I am the one, in order to refresh my memory a bit. It frequently happens that with the passage of time I have completely forgotten the reasons that moved me to this or that, with regard not only to trivialities but also to the most crucial steps. If the reason occurs to me, it can sometimes be so strange that I cannot even believe that it was the reason. This doubt would be removed if I had something written to refer to (Kierkegaard 1987a: 32).

The irony, of course, is that it is simply not true that A's doubt would, or at least should, be removed by having a written record since his self-serving rationalizations are often so persuasive to himself (that is their function, after all) that what he will have written down as his reason at the time will not have been the (desire-driven) reason he actually acted on as a matter of psychological fact. His "sophistical" desires will likely have expressed themselves in pretexts or rationalizations that are quite distant from his actual motivating reasons.

"On the whole, a reason is a curious thing," A writes next. "If I regard it with all my passion, it develops into an enormous necessity that can set heaven and earth in motion; if I am devoid of passion, I look down on it derisively" (Kierkegaard 1987a: 32–33). When the weight of normative reasons fortunately coincides with the strength of relevant desires or passions, then it will be to the agent as if they are incapable of freely choosing against their practical reason, as, indeed, Kierkegaard takes Fichte and Hegel to hold. Their normative reasons will then seem to create psychological, and not just normative, "necessit[ies]." But this is only appearance, which, after all, is what the esthete, A, deals in. Frequently, Kierkegaard thinks, we (and esthetes) freely choose what is contrary to what we (and they) know morally or rationally should be done, with our choices being motivated not by our judgments of normative reasons but by contrary passions. When we are "devoid of passion[s]" that fortunately align with our judged normative reasons, "we look down derisively at" the reasons and save face by attending to some rationalization or "pretext" that puts our action in a better light, as seeming to us to be sufficiently justified by less weighty reasons in a way that enables us to remain "in" a character we like to think of ourselves as being.

A's (honest, for the moment) admission that when he is devoid of a cooperating passion he "look[s] down on [normative reasons] derisively" suggests two further important themes of volume I. One is the connection between self-serving characterization and social hierarchy. "Looking down derisively" is something one does as if from a position of superiority. The second theme is the incompatibility between characterization and genuine engagement with others (and ourselves) that seriously attempts to come to terms with the way things actually are.

Consider, then, in the first connection, the relation between characterization and hierarchy. In volume I's "Diapsalmata," A imagines being "transported to the seventh heaven" (42) and being asked to make a wish. "I choose one thing," he responds, "that I may always have the laughter on my side" (43). To have laughter on one's side is precisely to be laughing *at* someone from an implied position of a superior "side." Laughter *at* that takes "sides" is a form of contemptuous ridicule – a "put down," as we say – in an implied social hierarchy. Consider, in this connection, Du Bois's remark in *The Souls of Black Folks* that Black people must carry with them as one part of a "double consciousness" the internalized regard of a socially oppressive superior racial caste, which regards and treats them with "an amused contempt and pity" (Du Bois 1987: 364).

Characterization need not always be contemptuous, as racist characterizations plainly are. But the reverse is true: Contempt invariably involves characterization (Darwall 2018a). And even when characterization does not portray the other as inferior, or as someone essentially in an inferior state – for example, the pitiable poor – it invariably *distances* characterizer from characterized in a way that prevents genuine engagement on equal terms.

This is the second theme. A's characterizations invariably fix their objects in an implied observer's third-personal gaze, substituting an imagined fantasy or appearance for the reality of the particular individual and their subjectivity or inwardness, which can only be revealed through reciprocal (ultimately, for Kierkegaard, loving) engagement. As B emphasizes, "life is a masquerade" for A providing "material for amusement" so that "no one has succeeded in knowing [A]," or, we might add, being known by A (Kierkegaard 1987b: 159).

In the twentieth century, Iris Murdoch will also contrast what she calls "self-consoling [characterizing] fantasy" with "loving" "attention" and argue that only the latter can bring us into rapport with another person as a particular individual in a way that allows us to see them as they really are (Murdoch 2001: 33, 83). Similarly, Kierkegaard's fellow Danish philosopher K. E. Løgstrup, a contemporary of Murdoch's, will argue that "self-enclos[ing]" "picture[s]" are at odds with the default second-personal trust and disposition to loving engagement that Løgstrup calls the "sovereign expressions of life" (Løgstrup 2007: 52; 2020a: 13). An implication is that the esthetic "life-view" is not a genuine form of *life*.[6]

We will pursue presently the incompatibility that Kierkegaard emphasizes between the esthetic life-view, in which characterization is endemic, and the forms of love he holds to be necessary to dispel and displace the esthetic view's necessarily besetting despair. First, however, we should note some extraordinary passages in which Kierkegaard connects a particular form of characterization to what Nietzsche calls the "aristocratic" ethos and anticipates Nietzsche's view of the genesis of "slave morality" (Nietzsche 2007: 12, 20).

"All human beings . . . are boring," says A in a characteristically world-weary way (Kierkegaard 1987a: 288). A then connects this to Nietzschean themes in a remarkable manner:

> The very word ["boring"] indicates the possibility of a classification. The word "boring" can designate just as well a person who bores others as someone who bores himself. Those who bore others are the plebians, the crowd, the endless train of humanity in general; those who bore themselves are the chosen ones, the nobility . . . Generally, those who do not bore themselves are busy in the world in one way or another, but for that very reason they are, of all people, the most boring of all, the most unbearable (Kierkegaard 1987a: 288).

You can see the Nietzschean theme coming. The "aristocratic" evaluative categories of base and noble distinguish two classes of people: one of whom, the "crowd," are worthy of the contempt of those in the other class, Kierkegaard's "nobility" (288). The aristocratic evaluative categories precisely map onto the two hierarchical social classifications. Plebians, who, doing the work of the world, have no time to be bored, bore the higher ups for that very reason (who bore themselves). Boring is a "classification," A says. It defines a lower social class, the members of which are put in their place by the contemptuous regard of their social

[6] I pursue these themes in Darwall in press.

betters. That regard defines them evaluatively: "They are unbearable bores." Of course, A's remark that "all human beings . . . are boring" threatens to empty the upper class. This may suggest something deep about the esthetic perspective, namely, that it aims to occupy a standpoint higher than any available within humanity, decisively rejecting and derisively looking down upon human "species being," in Marx's phrase. "A adds a yet further Nietzschean theme: the genealogy of 'slave morality.' Idleness, we are accustomed to say, is the root of all evil. To prevent this evil, work is recommended. But it is just as easy to see . . . that this whole view is of very plebian extraction" (289). The idea that idleness is the root of evil is, of course, a central plank of the Protestant work ethic, which B would certainly count as a core thesis of the ethical (moral) life-view.[7] Like Nietzsche, A presents this as the ideology of the herd. It follows that it is of the nature of the esthetic life-view to look down on ethical concerns with amused contempt. Morality thereby suffers the worst possible esthetic put down: "Boring!" And morality is a conceptual product of the boring to boot. Ultimately, however, all human beings and their creations become boring to the esthetic outlook, whether they issue from plebians or not. The esthetic life-view thus threatens to cannibalize those who hold it, if they cannot disguise from themselves their own humanity.

To this A adds a significant final remark. Among the boring crowd are "apostle[s] of empty enthusiasm" who "make a profession of being enthusiastic everywhere . . . are present everywhere and, no matter whether what happens is significant or insignificant, shout: Oh! Or Ah!" (290). An especially annoying feature of the boring, from A's point of view, is that they presumptuously enter into your presence and *speak* to you! And since the natural human tendency is to speak back, their boring engagement risks social contagion. This threatens their social betters with becoming boring themselves and not just to themselves in the way that would classify them as superior. To engage boring plebians is to risk catching "their" boredom, that is, to risk becoming someone who is boring to the superior class, whose disdain keeps the boring in their place.

From A's perspective, it is interacting with those who seriously engage with other people (and with the real world more generally) that risks making one déclassé. This takes us to our second theme. Not only does characterization create and sustain social hierarchy, it is also incompatible with genuine human (second-personal) engagement on equal terms. Most

[7] On the history of the Protestant work ethic and its role in both progressive political movements on behalf of workers and in conservative reactions that turn it against them, see Anderson 2023.

importantly for Kierkegaard, it is incompatible with the loving connection he holds to be the only antidote to the despair that is intrinsic to the esthetic outlook. Indeed, Kierkegaard suggests that it is lack of love and faith – ultimately, love of God – that creates the psychic hole in the esthete's soul or spirit, which they seek misguidedly to fill with ever new and interesting entertainments. In volume II, B says to A:

> At this point I shall not add my voice to the frequently heard lament about you that you are insatiable; I shall rather say: In a certain sense you are right, for nothing that is finite, not even the whole world, can satisfy the soul of a person who feels the need of the eternal (203).

Kierkegaard's point is not that A's desires to contemplate this or that shiny object cannot be satisfied individually, nor even is it the Hobbesian point that every desire is always followed by others, *seriatim*, until death. It is rather that A is insatiable *himself*, because he, like any human being, has a need for (eternal) love, which identifies him as a subjective individual. And *that* need cannot possibly be satisfied through any esthetic technique.

Partly this is the point on which Løgstrup will insist. The esthetic perspective is steadfastly an observer's third-person standpoint, whereas the point of view from which we give and receive love, God's or anyone else's, is the second-person standpoint of reciprocal feeling and concern. The fundamental psychic point is that what sets the esthete on the desperate and futile search for satisfying esthetic activity is the misguided thought that they can thereby fill their spiritual hole, which can only be filled by love.[8]

B follows this by saying that "the spirit does not allow itself to be mocked; it avenges itself on you and binds you in the chains of depression" (204). By "spirit," B (and Kierkegaard) mean that aspect of the human psyche through which we are capable of love, faith, and, therefore, love of God. But it is also where Kierkegaard locates the affective state of "depression," or "esthetic" or "reflective sorrow," which he takes to be the affective upshot of the despair that is the inescapable existential framework of esthetic life-view (211). Depression is a sadness or sorrow that is the inevitable consequence of lacking love, which is the only thing that can dispel it and give us joy.[9]

[8] This is also a theme of twentieth-century psychoanalytic "attachment" theorists like John Bowlby and Mary Ainsworth.

[9] Cf. A's remarks on "the relation between sorrow and joy": "Joy is communicative, sociable, open, wishes to express itself. Sorrow is inclosingly reserved, silent, solitary, and seeks to return into itself" (1987a: 169).

But what, again, is despair? And why is the esthetic outlook necessarily subject to it in Kierkegaard's view? Despair is like anxiety in having no specific object; it is a general condition. Indeed, Kierkegaard believes, it is the besetting malady of modern life, though at this point he is focusing only on the esthetic life-view. A speaks of anxiety as having a "self-preoccupation ... with sorrow" (155). But not just any form of sorrow, since that, too, can have a specific object, as fear does in contrast with anxiety.

The form of sorrow that is the affective upshot of despair is a distinctively modern form of sorrow, which Kierkegaard calls "reflective sorrow." Lacking a specific object, "reflective sorrow ... is continually seeking its object; this seeking is the sorrow's restlessness and its life" (178). Anxiety is to fear as despair and its affective upshot of reflective sorrow or depression are to loss of hope and sadness concerning specific things. (B distinguishes between despair over some "particular matter," and A's reflective "thought-despair" [194–195].)

Again, this is a modern phenomenon. "A feature in which our age certainly excels that age in Greece," A remarks, "is that our age is more depressed and therefore deeper in despair" (142). A then adds: "Our age is sufficiently depressed to know that there is something called responsibility" (142). Crucially, "responsibility" here is *moral* responsibility, which is what Anscombe (and many others) identify as the distinctive feature of "modern moral philosophy" (Anscombe 1958).

The modern notion of moral obligation, I argue, is that of what we are morally responsible or accountable for doing, where this is taken essentially to involve the exercise of the *will* (Darwall 2023a). A contrasts guilt as it operated in ancient Greek tragedy with the essentially "subjective" notion of guilt of (modern) morality. "What specifically characterizes ancient tragedy is ... that the action is not subjectively reflected enough" (Kierkegaard 1987a: 143). "In the modern period," by contrast, "situation and character are in fact predominant. The tragic hero is subjectively reflected in himself" (143). "The more the subjectivity is reflective, the more Pelagianly one sees the individual thrown solely upon himself, the more ethical guilt becomes" (144).

This is the situation of modern moral agents, who see themselves as bound by the moral law and as having, as free individuals, the full moral responsibility to comply with it by exercising the capacities of (free) will that make them subject to it. The Pelagian view is that we have all that it takes *in ourselves* to discharge our moral obligations in every instance. To this, Kierkegaard adds the awful, despair-engendering thought that we frequently will not so comply, indeed, that we will freely *choose* not to do so. Realizing this, we despair. Despair is thus the unavoidable condition of the modern moral agent. It is the inevitable consequence, as is the anxiety that is "self-occupied," of recognizing our radical freedom. This recognition brings the "dizziness" of freedom and the depression of despair.

Or: The Ethical Life-View as Dutiful Love and Universality

Volume II of *Either/Or* is an extended letter (running to more than 300 pages!), divided into three sections. Written from B to A, it is presented as an earnest entreaty to A to abandon his esthetic outlook, acknowledge his free choices (his "Either/Or"'s), and take his life seriously, thereby adopting the ethical life-view. Although personally addressed, and replete with second-personal pronouns, it is actually mostly an impersonal treatise on the basic contrasts between the esthetic and ethical life-views. "A" functions less as a name than as a variable that can be instantiated by anyone occupying the esthetic standpoint.

B seeks to show that the esthetic life-view is necessarily beset with pervasive depression and despair and that the ethical life-view's serious commitment to dutiful love for God and for a beloved partner in "marital love" enables one to avoid the esthete's besetting maladies and, indeed, to experience enduring joy (47, 103). A central feature of *committed* love is what Kierkegaard calls *resignation.* Resignation is a fundamental Kierkegaardian concept that will be especially important when we seek to understand later Kierkegaard's "teleological suspension of the ethical," in *Fear and Trembling.* There his point will be that resignation, which the ethical essentially involves, is necessary, but not sufficient, for the faith that "suspends" the ethical. Kierkegaard's point here, however, is that resignation, in his sense, is an essential aspect of committed love, which he understands as "marital love" (e.g., 29): "marriage has an ethical and religious element that erotic love does not have; for this reason, marriage is based on resignation" (36).[10]

For Kierkegaard, the crucial element of resignation is that it involves a committing exercise of the *will.* The signal difference between "erotic" or "romantic love" and "marital love" is that the latter involves committed *intention.* "Intention is," B says, "resignation in its richest form, in which

[10] "Religious" here evidently does not imply faith of the kind that Kierkegaard contrasts with the ethical in *Fear and Trembling.* More on that is given in the next section. It is important that throughout his writings, Kierkegaard takes the fundamental ethical (moral) obligation to be to love God, and our neighbors as ourselves, which he takes to be owed to God.

the concern is not for what is to be lost but for what is to be gained by being held fast" (61). Marital love holds to a commitment to stand by the beloved lovingly, "for better, for worse." A core meaning of "resignation" is "readiness to endure adversity without complaint" (*Oxford English Dictionary* 2024). In Kierkegaard's sense, though, resignation is not so much a "readiness" as the result of a committed willing. And this actually fits better with "resignation"'s original sense, which is the result of an act of resigning, which publicly expresses a committing will, as in resigning an office or surrendering a title to land. If relinquishing title to complain is now "resignation"'s core meaning, Kierkegaard's usage expresses something closer to committing oneself to concern "for what is to be gained" rather than giving up the standing to "concern" oneself with "what is to be lost."

The burden of B's argument to A is to show that the erotic or romantic form of love that A sometimes pursues, although only playfully through an esthetic lens, is not only compatible with marital love but intrinsic to it. B argues to A that he cannot achieve romantic love in its actual form within the esthetic life-view, but that he could in an ethically committed loving marriage.

The most essential thing to which B calls A, however, is ethical choice itself, to confronting Either/Ors, and most fundamentally, what B calls the "absolute Either/Or." "Wherever in the stricter sense there is a question of an Either/Or, one can always be sure that the ethical has something to do with it. The only absolute Either/Or is the choice between good and evil, but this is also absolutely ethical" (Kierkegaard 1987b: 166–167). "What is important in choosing," B says, "is not so much to choose the right thing as the energy, the earnestness, and the pathos with which one chooses" (167). This has a distinctly Kantian flavor. Granted, "energy" and "pathos" are hardly central moral virtues for Kant. But the idea that "earnestness" in trying to determine and discharge moral duties is a basic moral good, indeed, *the* moral good, is akin to Kant's doctrine of the unique goodness "without limitation" of the good will (Kant 1996a: 4:393).

B then enunciates an aspect of the ethical life-view that Kierkegaard takes to be central to Kant's and the Idealists' doctrine of the ethical as practical reason, which Kierkegaard is anxious to reject: that it is impossible to choose freely not to do what is morally right:

> What, then, is it that I separate in my Either/Or? Is it good and evil? No, I only want to bring you to the point where this choice truly has meaning for you. It is on this that everything turns. As soon as a person can be brought to

> stand at the cross-roads in such a way that there is no way out for him except to choose, he will choose the right thing (Kierkegaard 1987b: 168).

This is a remarkable passage. What, one might think, can B possibly mean by saying that *his* Either/Or is not really between good and evil? As we read on, we see that B asserts that when a person is brought to a point where an Either/Or "truly has meaning" for them, they can (freely) choose only the right thing. B's frequent complaint against A is that ethical choices seem insignificant and without meaning to him. A does not feel the weight of the choice between good and evil because he simply does not care about ethical choice. B, however, *does* care.[11]

What B is saying is that for someone who treats ethical choices seriously and clearly sees their moral duty, there really is no practical alternative to doing what is right. B is never really faced with a serious choice about whether to do his duty, an absolute Either/Or. B holds what Kierkegaard regards to be Kant's and the Idealists' doctrine of freedom as practical reason. There is no such thing as a clear-eyed, non-self-deceptive, fully free choice of moral evil. A may choose moral evil frequently enough, but he does not (indeed, cannot) do so after fully exercising his practical reason. To the contrary, he engages in reason-subverting rationalizations and self-deception.

This is a doctrine that Kierkegaard decisively rejects. Following Schelling, Kierkegaard holds that agents can fully exercise their practical reason, determine clearly that they are morally obligated to do something, and nonetheless freely choose not to do it (Kosch 2006). Moreover, there is, for Kierkegaard, as we shall see, a kind of freedom, in the sense of ease and grace, that is possible only beyond the exercise of moral practical reason, through faith and love. As B himself says, "when you are in love you are in freedom" (Kierkegaard 1987b: 349).

Kierkegaard also follows Schelling in connecting a rejection of idealist freedom as practical reason to a parallel rejection of the idealist identification of morality (the ethical) with practical reason. As they see it, this amounts to rejecting a universal, impersonal conception of morality in favor of a particular, personal conception that grounds morality in the relation every individual has with God personally (see Kosch 2006, esp. 118–120). Moral duty involves personal accountability to God.

[11] All of B's "energy" and "pathos" are directed to doing what is right and loving in accordance with his moral duty. Although there are puzzles that we will explore later about how there can be a duty to love, B apparently does not think so. He tells A that "though you regard duty as the enemy of love, I regard it is as its friend" (Kierkegaard 1987a: 146).

B makes this universalist, impersonal, or as he calls it, "abstract" conception of morality an essential feature of the ethical life-view. "The ethical is the universal," he says, "and thus the abstract" (Kierkegaard 1987b: 255). "The person who lives ethically works toward becoming the universal human being," B says, in words that recall Kantian universalization (255). The fundamental moral obligation, for B, is "to love God with all your heart" (255). But this gives rise to a second obligation, namely, to love one's "neighbor as oneself," as is made clearest in Kierkegaard's (1995) *Works of Love* (14, 44). And as befits the universalism of the ethical life-view, by "neighbor," Kierkegaard means every human being. Dutiful love is ultimately universal and grounded in the fundamental duty to love God.[12]

As we shall see in the next section, Kierkegaard's doctrine of the "teleological suspension of the ethical" through faith and love of God places the "particular" individual over the universal and counsels acting "as the single individual" (Kierkegaard 2006: 46, 65). "Faith," Johannes (de silentio), Kierkegaard's pseudonym, says in *Fear and Trembling*, "is precisely this paradox, that the single individual as the particular is higher than the universal" (48). But though a central thesis of this work is that faith enables one genuinely to become a single individual in a way that dispels despair, we shall end this section with a brief consideration of B's claim that in the ethical life-view one also chooses themselves as an individual, but in an importantly different sense.

"The person who chooses himself ethically chooses himself concretely as this specific individual," B says (Kierkegaard 1987b: 250–251). As a moral agent at the point of deliberate choice, "the individual ... becomes conscious as this specific individual with these capacities, these inclinations, these drives, these passions, influenced by this specific social milieu, as this specific product of a specific environment. But as he becomes aware of all this, he takes upon himself responsibility for it all" (251). Of course, it is always particular moral agents who actually face Either/Ors and make choices. But the universality of their ethical choices nonetheless remains. From the agent's point of view in deliberate choice, their particularity completely drops out; they confront a set of practical alternatives in a situation. Their deliberative ethical question is what they should do *morally*. But that is ultimately a universal rather than a particularistic question. It is the question of what someone, anyone, in their situation should do.

[12] It is worth noting a parallel structure in Pufendorf's view: Though all moral duties are owed to God, nonetheless the "fundamental" moral law is to be sociable.

Granted, they "becom[e practically] conscious as this specific individual with these capacities, these inclinations," and so on. But they can deliberate about their practical situation without considering any of these individuating facts. Unless, of course, any such facts are relevant to what they ethically should do. Perhaps the fact that I am inclined to do something is actually relevant to what I ethically should do; maybe it provides a normative reason for acting. But if it does, it is universally relevant; it is relevant to what someone, anyone, with such an inclination in such a situation, should do.

Suppose now that the agent steps back from their deliberative perspective and considers themselves as part of what Kant would call the phenomenal realm, part of the causal network of nature. So viewed he might view his own (particular) action as issuing from these continent causal features, perhaps even with causal necessity. B's claim is that "as [the moral agent] becomes aware of all this, he takes upon himself responsibility for it all" (251). The crucial point is that since the choice is an ethical (moral) one, it is one moral agents are *responsible* for. And since it is, it must be one that they have the capacity to do when they deliberatively determine they morally should do it, abstracting from irrelevant particularistic individuating features. What they should do is whatever anyone should do in the situation, irrespective of (irrelevant) individuating features. B's ethical agent is a product of their social milieu. So be it! They still must, and can, choose to do what is morally right despite being such a product. "He chooses himself as a product. And this choice is freedom's choice in such a way that in choosing himself as a product he can just as well be said to produce himself" (251). Thus it is that although morality is "universal" and "abstract," the ethical individual can still choose themselves as particular, "single," and B also says, "authentic individual[s]" (259).

Faith and the "Teleological Suspension of the Ethical"

When Kierkegaard first published *Fear and Trembling* at the age of thirty, he wrote in his journal that it would "be enough for an imperishable name as an author." "It will [be] read [and] translated into foreign languages as well" (Kierkegaard 2006: vi). The literary ambitions this journal entry evinces could not be farther, however, from the ethos *Fear and Trembling* expresses. The work celebrates a simple religious faith likelier to be found among ordinary people (including "bourgeois philistines") than in sophisticated literary or academic circles. But with characteristic irony, Kierkegaard's style is sophisticated and complex, employing the elaborate literary devices of all his pseudonymous works. Johannes's central theme – and through him, Kierkegaard's – is that the ethical life-view B champions in *Either/Or* cannot defeat the despair that B had argued afflicted A's esthetic life-view. Only an essentially nonphilosophical and unreasoned form of religious faith can do that. Kierkegaard's God is decidedly not the "God of the philosophers."

Johannes's "Preface" begins with a satirical critique of "the momentous march of modern philosophy," which "does not stop at doubting everything but goes further" (3). The reference to doubt evokes Descartes, but Johannes stresses that Descartes himself was a "humble" thinker who "did not doubt with respect to faith" (3–4). Of course, Descartes was a modern philosopher who doubted precisely in order to "go further" in solidly grounding a systematic philosophy. But Johannes notes that in his *Principles*, Descartes emphasizes that the "natural light" of reason "is to be trusted only to the extent that it is compatible with divine revelation" (4). The most important "rule," Descartes says, is "that whatever God has revealed to us must be accepted as more certain than anything else" (4).

Johannes's opponents in *Fear and Trembling* are systematic philosophers who "[do] not stop at faith, but [go] further" and base philosophical systems on reason and experience (4). "The present writer is not a philosopher," Johannes says, "he has not understood the System" (a sardonic reference to Hegel and the Idealists) (5).

The argument of *Fear and Trembling* is carried by a description and analysis of the biblical story of the "binding of Isaac" from Genesis 22, in which God tests Abraham by asking him to sacrifice his son Isaac on Mt. Moriah. There is significantly more complexity and texture than we can go into here. But the central contrast is between how an "ethical" or moral agent concerned to comply with their obligations would act and feel in Abraham's situation, on the one hand, and how Abraham approaches his situation through faith, on the other. Again, Kierkegaard's model for the ethical life-view is the conception of morality as practical reason that he finds in Kant and the German idealists.

Both individuals would take their obligation to God to be supreme but also believe that "to the son the father has the highest and most sacred duty" (23). We need not worry about how B's morally conscientious agent would attempt to adjudicate this conflict within the ethical standpoint. The crucial point is that however they might, they would nonetheless necessarily view things in a way that is profoundly different from Abraham's, from the religious life-view of faith. Whether they were to see their situation as an irresolvable moral conflict, or to assume that God, as a moral exemplar, would not ultimately require them to go through with the awful act, or to reason that, in the circumstances, one choice is morally preferable, they would face an agonizing decision. Even were God to stay their hand, if they had been willing to sacrifice their son, their willingness would unalterably darken their relationship with their son.

Abraham, by contrast, approaches his situation with absolute trust and faith in God. "He believed that God would not demand Isaac of him, while he still was willing to sacrifice him if it was demanded" (29). And when God does stay Abraham's hand, Abraham is able to "receiv[e] Isaac more joyfully" than before, even though he "was willing to sacrifice him if it was demanded" (29).

Abraham is a "hero of faith" who Kierkegaard contrasts with the "tragic hero," exemplified by Agamemnon. Agamemnon faces a superficially similar situation when he sacrifices Iphigenia to enable the Greeks to sail to Troy.[13] Agamemnon makes a tragic moral choice, discharging what he takes to be his weightiest obligation. Johannes says, "I *think* myself way *into*" a tragic hero like Agamemnon (27). We can empathically enter even very difficult moral situations and reason practically from that point of view. After all, the relevant deliberative standpoint is ultimately universal. But, Johannes says, "I cannot think myself into Abraham" (27). And when "I must think about Abraham, I am virtually annihilated" (27).

Unlike the ethical life-view, the religious outlook of faith cannot be reasoned into; neither is it intelligible to an outsider. Faith is simultaneously "absolute devotion" ("for God's sake") and "the expression for the highest egoism" ("doing the frightful deed for one's own sake") (62). Unlike the ethical, which is universal in its nature, faith "cannot be mediated into the universal, for it is thereby annulled. Faith is this paradox, and the single individual is utterly unable to make himself intelligible to anyone" (62). Morality essentially concerns accountability: answerability to others in the medium of justification. Faith, Johannes is saying, is constitutively incapable of giving an account of itself or being accounted for.

The view from faith is also irreducibly *particularistic* in a way that uniquely enables living as a "single individual." Recall B's claim that ethically conscious agents choose themselves "absolutely" as single "authentic individuals" when they choose as representative "universal" agents (Kierkegaard 1987b: 223, 259). A "knight of faith" like Abraham sees themselves, by contrast, as called as the particular individual they are to

[13] As Evans points out in his introduction, Abraham is prominently listed among the "heroes of faith" in Hebrews 11 of the New Testament.

personal relationship with God. In the ethical life-view, the universal always has priority over the needs of any particular individual – most obviously, the moral agent themselves, but also particular beloved others – but faith "teleologically suspends" the ethical. "Faith is precisely this paradox, that the single individual as the particular is higher than the universal and is justified over against the latter not as subordinate but superior to it" (Kierkegaard 2006: 48). The individual is justified, not ethically "by works," but "by faith."

Recall B's point about the role of resignation in committed "marital love." Resignation essentially involves a commitment of will in the same way all committed moral action does. Indeed, for Kierkegaard, resignation is the mark of the ethical (or moral). It is setting yourself to do your duty and to be *satisfied* with the moral life, "resigned" to its personal costs by accepting them fully. Kierkegaard holds that it is resignation that distinguishes the esthetic from the ethical life. Now, although faith goes beyond resignation, Kierkegaard nonetheless holds that resignation is necessary for faith. "Faith . . . is no esthetic emotion . . . precisely because it presupposes resignation" (Kierkegaard 2006: 40). Resignation, though not sufficient, is nevertheless necessary for faith.

Johannes refers to an "infinite resignation" that characterizes a kind of moral ideal like his "tragic hero." Such a "knight of infinite resignation" is committed to doing everything within their power – straining every nerve – to comply with their moral duty as they see it. Such characters are, Johannes says, "easy to recognize," "bold," and of a "noble nature" (Kierkegaard 2006: 31–32). Knights of faith, by contrast, are ordinary folk who "belon[g] entirely to the world" (32). What they have that moral paragons do not is nothing for which they themselves are responsible and of which they might therefore be justly proud. Faith is a gift the faithful receive in loving relation with God (41). Infinite resignation is the "last stage before faith," but is not yet faith (39). Resignation necessarily involves the will, but faith is a form of receptivity rather than agency. Through resignation, we "renounce" what we resign ourselves to not having. "By faith I do not renounce anything; on the contrary, by faith, I receive everything" (41).

Faith is in this way like love. We cannot will ourselves either to love or to receive it. Love involves a receptivity of the spirit or soul, an openness and susceptibility of the "heart" to engaging with the open, loving "heart" of another. Whereas the respect that governs moral agency involves a relation of the will to other wills, love and faith are open-hearted to the hearts of others. They involve a heart-to-heart relation (Darwall 2024). The most important thing we receive through love is love itself, but this also bathes the rest of life in its light.

Finally, the most important aspect of the life-view of faith (and love) is that it is the opposite of and antidote to the despair that Kierkegaard holds to be inescapable for both the esthetic and the ethical life-view. We can see why this is so, according to Kierkegaard, by examining a passage that occurs at the outset of "A Tribute to Abraham," which begins *Fear and Trembling*'s central argument: "If there were no eternal consciousness in a human being, if underlying everything there were only a wild, fermenting force writhing in dark passions that produced everything great and insignificant, if a bottomless, insatiable emptiness lurked beneath everything, what would life be then but despair?" (Kierkegaard 2006: 12). By "eternal consciousness," I take Kierkegaard to mean a consciousness of the eternal, of God, which suitably expands the consciousness of which it is the object. What the right kind of consciousness of the eternal – love, faith, and hope in God – provides is the sense of meaning and purpose without which everything seems "empty" and without real significance. Despair is the sense that nothing really matters; one despairs of being able to do anything or even to *be* in any way that would make any real difference. Loving faith provides compelling answers to "man's search for meaning" (Frankl 1963).

There follows a contrast between those who attempt to use their own powers to make a difference, on the one hand, and Abraham, on the other, who "was greater than everybody," because his "strength is powerlessness" (Kierkegaard 2006: 14). This is the contrast, again, between powers of will and resignation, exemplified by the knight of infinite resignation, on the one hand, and loving faith, on the other, which is not an agential power of will, but a form of receptivity or susceptibility: the ability to respond to love with love. Abraham, "the one who loved God," was "greater than everybody" (13). Only Abraham's love and faith can cure despair.

But why? Isn't the ethical life-view put forward by B as the antidote for thinking nothing matters? Isn't B's whole argument against A that the esthetic outlook treats nothing as mattering and so treats no Either/Or as serious? And isn't B's positive claim that serious deliberation and choice is what defines the ethical outlook?

By the ethical life-view, again, Kierkegaard means (modern) deontic morality. That is what sets up the whole problematic of the moral agent facing the Either/Or between which they must freely choose and for which choices they are personally accountable to God. According to Kierkegaard, the ancients did not face the distinctively modern problems of anxiety (the "dizziness of freedom"), despair, and depression. As A puts it, "our age is sufficiently depressed to know that there is something called responsibility" (Kierkegaard 1987a: 142).

As we shall see, Nietzsche will argue that deontic morality is essentially *negative*; it is life denying rather than life affirming (Nietzsche 2007: 7, 43; Reginster 2009). It may be that we find a version of this thought in Kierkegaard also, albeit in a religious key Nietzsche would abhor. Nietzsche's version holds that while in the aristocratic value scheme of "good" and "bad" (noble versus base), the fundamental notion is the good, and the bad is simply what is not good, this order is reversed in morality. With the moral notions of good and evil (culpable wrongdoing), it is the latter, wrong or culpability, that is the fundamental notion, and moral good is defined in relation to that. Deontic morality's positive notion is no more than the negation of its fundamental (negative) notion.

Moral obligation arguably is defined in terms of the nay-saying attitude of moral blame. It is a conceptual truth that an act is morally obligatory if it is an act of a kind that would be blameworthy to omit without excuse (Darwall 2006: 91–118; 2016). To blame is to express the "negative" thought that the culpable action is something one must *not* do. Often obligations are to perform positive actions, of course. But that does not gainsay the point that conscientiousness is fundamentally about avoiding wrongdoing.

Even the conscientious person, therefore, can be vulnerable to the thought: "Does anything really matter?" I accept that there are things I must *do*, but does anything of what happens in the world independently of my, or anyone's agency, really matter? And if not, what significance does my agency really have, even my dutiful agency?" Something like that thought seems to have been at the bottom of Mill's depression, to which the cure appears to have been values he discovered in the poetry of Wordsworth and Coleridge and his loving relationship with Harriet Taylor. Mill's convictions about his moral duty, which did not waiver, did nothing for his depression (Mill 1981).

Kierkegaard's point would then be that love and faith are correctives to this despairing thought. To love is precisely to care about what happens independently of one's agency and to take guides for action from that. Love of a person focuses on that individual's precious existence; that is what matters and what we should do depends entirely on what would most benefit them.[14]

[14] For an argument along these lines, see Darwall 2002: 69–104.

Works of Love: A Puzzle or Paradox of Love

It is only love of God with its "eternal consciousness" that can securely dispel despair. Love of other persons and ourselves follows in the same train, but it is clearly love of God that is normatively most fundamental for Kierkegaard. Here there are two distinct but related points, which Kierkegaard makes in *Works of Love*. The fundamental moral obligation is to love God and to do His will. Any obligation we have to love others follows from that. And God does, indeed, command us to "love your neighbor as yourself" (Kierkegaard 1995: 17). This is the first point: it is because we are obligated to follow God's commands that it is our moral duty to love others (as ourselves). The second point is that the love that is commanded in each instance is what Kant calls "practical" rather than "pathological" love (Kant 1996b: 5:82–83). It is a condition of the will. After all, something can be commanded only if it is something that one can *do*, indeed, do for the reason that it has been legitimately demanded.

Kierkegaard explicitly contrasts the form of personal loving connection to friends and loved ones with love of "the neighbor." He calls the former "preferential love" and says that it does not accord with God's command to love our neighbors as ourselves since preferential loves "more or less hold together with the self-love in one" (Kierkegaard 1995: 21). The goods of preferentially loved persons are part of our own good. No heartfelt (pathological) feelings of the kind that mediate loving personal relationships are therefore covered by the obligation to love others "as ourselves." Rather, this obligates us to love practically, that is, to take action to promote others' well-being. And Kierkegaard stresses that this includes *all* others. "'The neighbor' means 'all people'" (21). Felt (pathological) love seems never to be morally obligatory, and perhaps, indeed, not to be something that *could* be morally obligatory. For that to be possible, it would have to be possible to love pathologically as a response to a legitimate demand.

But this creates a puzzle, perhaps even a paradox. On the one hand, Kierkegaard seems clearly to hold in *Works of Love* that it is only because there is a *duty* to love that love can dispel despair: "Only when it is a duty to love, only then is love . . . happily secured against despair" (29). On the other hand, this seems to run against the main argument of *Fear and Trembling* that nothing that is conscientious can be proof against despair. This seems to be the point of Johannes's central contrast between the knight of resignation and the knight of faith. Although resignation, as instanced in conscientious action, is necessary for faith, it is not sufficient, and only faith can dispel despair.

This puzzle deepens when Kierkegaard says that "love is a matter of conscience" (137). This partly means, he says, that "the sum of the commandment is love" (137). But if it is, he adds, then love must simultaneously "be out of a pure heart and out of a good conscience and out of a sincere faith" (137). This seems to identify exactly what *Fear and Trembling* is at pains to distinguish.

In the twentieth century, we will see Kierkegaard's fellow Dane K. E. Løgstrup attempt to work out a view of the centrality of love that, while it owes a good deal to Kierkegaard, clearly departs from him in rejecting the identification of the "pure heart[ed]" and the conscientious. This remains a puzzling aspect of Kierkegaard's view. In the end, it gives Kierkegaard a deeply ambiguous relationship to mainstream modern moral philosophy.

CHAPTER 5

Nietzsche

Recall Johannes's statement in *Fear and Trembling* that without "eternal consciousness," a "bottomless, insatiable emptiness [would] lur[k] beneath everything" (Kierkegaard 2006: 12). As we noted, this idea sets the stage for twentieth-century existentialism: Without a divinely provided framework of meaning, human life can seem insignificant and absurd. We find a similar thought in another important figure for the existentialists: Friedrich Nietzsche. If "God is dead," as Nietzsche famously proclaims in *The Gay Science*, "Are we not continually falling? And backwards, sidewards, forwards, in all directions? Is there still an up and a down? Aren't we straying as though through an infinite nothing?" (Nietzsche 2001: 109, 120). In a "disenchanted" world, life can seem directionless and lacking in meaning (Weber 2002). "Man . . . *suffer*[*s*]," as Nietzsche puts it in *On the Genealogy of Morality*, "from the problem of what he mean[s]" (Nietzsche 2007: 120).

Kierkegaard bequeaths to the twentieth-century existentialists the idea that the human condition is one of radical freedom, as well as the "anxiety" of "the dizziness of freedom" (Kierkegaard 1980: IV.331). For Kierkegaard, it is deontic morality that sets this existential condition. Morality poses the fundamental Either/Or, making us aware that we are free to choose between right and wrong. Nietzsche agrees that morality presupposes freedom of the will, but he denies that this metaphysical freedom obtains. His critique of the modern conception of morality on this basis continues to have influence today.

Nietzsche also agrees that the idea of morality is deeply tied to Christian religious belief. Perhaps Nietzsche's most famous critique of morality is that it is a mere ideology that is rooted in unconscious psychological mechanisms of "*ressentiment.*" Those mechanisms lead a "priestly caste" and their "herd" of followers to fashion new ethical concepts – those of deontic morality – that project repressed anger and hatred rather than responding to anything true or really valuable (Nietzsche 2007: 17, 19).

Feeling themselves the object of contempt – like A's contempt of "the boring" – and being impotent to retaliate for such insults personally, the herd repress natural retaliatory impulses, feeling them as *impersonal* indignation or moral blame, thereby conceiving of the insults as affronts to humanity or moral persons in general: as *culpable wrongs*.

In these respects, Nietzsche and Kierkegaard seem light years apart. As we shall see, however, there are also significant affinities between these two otherwise opposed philosophers. One concerns the role of faith. To be sure, Nietzsche is no friend of religious faith. "From the beginning," he says in *Beyond Good and Evil*, "Christian faith has been sacrifice: sacrifice of all freedom, of all pride, of all self-confidence of the spirit; it is simultaneously enslavement and self-derision, self-mutilation" (Nietzsche 2002: 44). On the other hand, Nietzsche emphasizes that the "free spirit" of his favored "overmen" – those who live beyond both "faith in . . . morality" and the religious faith from which that springs – also involves faith, but of a different kind (25, 76). Speaking on behalf of those he calls "*new philosophers*," Nietzsche proclaims: "We . . . have a different faith" (Nietzsche 2002: 91). And this new faith is, indeed, a "self-confidence of spirit" of the kind that Christian faith requires sacrificing, in Nietzsche's view (44).

A second point of agreement between Nietzsche and Kierkegaard concerns the signal importance of the *particular individual* and the claim that authentic individuality can only be achieved outside and *beyond* morality. For Kierkegaard, this is because it is only by receiving God's love that morality's impersonality can be overcome, enabling individuals to realize themselves as "single individual[s]" (Kierkegaard 1987b: 349; 2006: 65). For Nietzsche, the "free spirit" of a "new philosophy" is only possible once the sociocultural consequences of deontic morality have been fully worked through in a way that enables individuals to become their own "sovereigns" and take responsibility for their own lives without the crutch of morality. Only then can there be "autonomous, supra-ethical individual[s]," by which Nietzsche means individuals who have rejected the deontic morality of their own culture (Nietzsche 2007: 36–37). Such "overmen" are hardly supra-ethical in a broader sense; Nietzsche holds that they, of all people, live the most valuable lives. And the same goes for Kierkegaard's view of people of religious faith. They, too, live the best lives by "suspend[ing]" morality (Kierkegaard 2006: 46). Nevertheless, Kierkegaard and Nietzsche remain sharply divided on what it takes to realize authentic individuality.

Given Nietzsche's antipathy to religion, and to Christianity in particular, it may come as a surprise that Nietzsche grew up an enthusiastic Lutheran in his father's congregation, that his first academic study was in theology (at the University of Bonn), and that, according to his biographer Julian Young, "for most of his youth, Nietzsche intended to enter the [Lutheran] priesthood" (Young 2010: 18). This last was no doubt due at least in part to Nietzsche's identification with his beloved father, who died when Nietzsche was very young. Fairly quickly, however, Nietzsche's own religious thinking was influenced strongly during his year in Bonn by the kind of metaphysically deflationary hermeneutics that he encountered in David Strauss's *Life of Jesus*. The metaphysically realist aspects of Christian orthodoxy were the initial casualty. But at first, Nietzsche remained "a Christian, specifically a Lutheran Protestant," at least "emotionally" (Young 2010: 60). And even when he later turned decisively against religion, it was not through emotional reaction against his own religious youth. To the contrary, as we shall see presently, Nietzsche retained the spiritual yearnings that he had once experienced as religious faith.

Early Years

Nietzsche left Bonn in 1865 to continue his studies at the University of Leipzig, but now in philology rather than theology. Philology would provide Nietzsche's only field of academic employment.[1] In 1869, he left Leipzig to take up a chair in classical philology at the University of Basel at the extraordinarily young age of twenty-four. It would be the only academic position Nietzsche ever held.

Apart from his philological studies, which provided important background for Nietzsche's *Genealogy* arguments concerning the nonmoral concepts expressed by "good" and "bad" and the contrasting moral concepts expressed by "(morally) good" and "evil," the most important event in Nietzsche's intellectual life during his time in Leipzig was his exposure to the thought of Arthur Schopenhauer (1788–1860). Nietzsche's relationship to Schopenhauer provided one of the most dramatic reversals of his philosophical life, so we shall want to know more about this philosopher who was so important for German philosophy of Nietzsche's era, but of whom so relatively little is known or appreciated today.

Nietzsche first encountered *The World as Will and Representation* in a second-hand bookshop in Leipzig and "immediately became a Schopenhauerian" (Young 2010: 81). Nietzsche had already heard glowing

[1] We should note that the kind of philology Nietzsche always favored was concerned with "the universal-human ... shaped by the moulding hands of philosophy" (in his words, quoted in Young 2010: 68).

reports about Schopenhauer from his other early idol, also later turned nemesis, Richard Wagner. When he first met him, Wagner told Nietzsche that Schopenhauer was "the only philosopher who understood the nature of music" (quoted in Hollingdale 1999: 40). This was surely part of Nietzsche's attraction to Schopenhauer. First, by association with the great Wagner, but also because of Nietzsche's own keen appreciation of music.[2] Nietzsche had a serious interest in music throughout his life and by this period had already composed music for the piano (as his father had before him) (Young 2010: 27).

More significant, however, were two things that Nietzsche found philosophically compelling in Schopenhauer. One concerned Schopenhauer's whole approach to philosophy. Young plausibly claims that Schopenhauer was the first philosopher to put the fundamental human existential question – in Camus's formulation, "whether life is or is not worth living" – "on the table" (Young 2010: 86). When Nietzsche first read Schopenhauer, he said, "every line cried out renunciation, denial and resignation, I saw a mirror in which I espied the whole world, life, and my own mind depicted in frightful grandeur" (quoted in Young 2010: 81). As he did for the twentieth-century existentialists, Schopenhauer set for Nietzsche the basic philosophical question of human existence.

The second concerned Schopenhauer's own response to this question, which, however satisfying Nietzsche found initially, eventually left him deeply unsatisfied. Ultimately, Nietzsche thought that Schopenhauer's response was about as unsatisfying as any philosophical reply to that question could possibly be. This was because Schopenhauer held that human existence is one of irredeemable suffering and despair and is so, indeed, as a matter of metaphysical necessity. Schopenhauer also thought, however, that there is a perspective available to human beings that transcends the egocentric standpoint from which we normally live our lives. From this perspective, we can achieve something like Hutcheson's "calm extensive benevolence" (see Darwall 2023a: 180) and also appreciate that all temporal suffering is metaphysically illusory. Nietzsche turned out not to be keen on this aspect of Schopenhauer's thought either.

But Nietzsche's first response to Schopenhauer's philosophy was overwhelmingly positive. Young claims that this was at least partly because Schopenhauer recast for Nietzsche "the essence of the Christianity of his childhood in a form fit for adults" (Young 2010: 87). Nietzsche wrote that what he found in Schopenhauer was an account of human "sickness and

[2] Which fit with Nietzsche's enduring Dionysian streak, most evident in *Thus Spake Zarathustra*. On this, see Gooding-Williams 2001.

recovery, banishment and refuge, hell and heaven" (quoted in Young 2010: 87). This admiring response would dramatically change. It was not long before Schopenhauer became for Nietzsche something like the philosophical devil incarnate. Whereas the project of Nietzsche's "new philosophy" would center on what Bernard Reginster calls "the affirmation of life" in response to the problem of nihilism, Nietzsche came to see Schopenhauer's philosophy as cynical, pessimistic, and ultimately nihilistic (Reginster 2009).

Schopenhauer

It is worth pausing to inquire more into Schopenhauer's moral philosophy, both because Schopenhauer was such an influential philosopher at the time – Nietzsche called him "the most read German philosopher" – and because he was such an important figure for Nietzsche (Nietzsche 1982: 101). We can focus on Schopenhauer's relatively short *On the Basis of Morality*, which, though it was not what first attracted Nietzsche, contained much of what ultimately repelled him.

Viewed from the perspective of the history of modern moral philosophy, this is a remarkable work. The question it contends with is nothing less than modern moral philosophy's fundamental problem. *On the Basis of Morality* is Schopenhauer's response to a question that was posed in 1837 by the Royal Society of Denmark: "Is the source and foundation of morality to be looked for in an idea . . . which lies immediately in consciousness (or conscience) . . . or is it to be sought in another ground of knowledge?" (Schopenhauer 1995: 38). The society introduces this question as follows: "The original idea of morality or the principal notion of the moral law appears with a necessity peculiar to it by no means logical," "which shows itself partly in the judgment passed by our conscience on our own actions, partly in our moral censure of the actions of others" (37).

There it is. The issue Schopenhauer is charged with addressing is morality's "basis" in the sense of what can account for or ground the distinctive normativity or "necessity" that deontic morality purports to have. Moral necessity is clearly different from logical necessity, not to mention natural necessity. How, then, are we to account for the "must" with which we express moral duties and obligations *and* that we take to be tied to conscience and censure? This is arguably *the* metaethical question concerning deontic morality. It is, in effect, a formulation of Anscombe's challenge in "Modern Moral Philosophy" (Anscombe 1958; Darwall 2023a: 1–4).

It quickly becomes clear, however, that Schopenhauer steadfastly refuses to answer the question in this form. The reason, as it turns out, is that

Schopenhauer is no less an opponent of *deontic* morality than Nietzsche is! That is not, however, because Schopenhauer shares Nietzsche's love of the ancients or because he distrusts the modern turn. To the contrary, Schopenhauer praises Kant for "having purged ethics of all *eudaimonism*" (Schopenhauer 1995: 49).[3] Although Schopenhauer holds, pessimistically, that almost all human actions are motivated egoistically and so cannot be moral, he nonetheless holds that purely benevolent action is possible *and* that it is uniquely moral (much like Hutcheson and Leibniz).

Where Schopenhauer departs from Kant is in Kant's claim that morality necessarily takes a deontic imperatival form, at least, that it does for human moral agents (see Darwall 2023a: 325–333). "A practical philosophy," Schopenhauer reports Kant as holding, is concerned "with giving laws as regards what *ought to happen*" (Schopenhauer 1995: 52). "What justification" does Kant have, Schopenhauer asks, "for forcing on us, as the only possible one, a system of ethics framed in the legislative imperative form" (52). Schopenhauer goes on then to make the Anscombean claim that the "concept of duty . . . together with its near relatives, such as those of *law*, command, obligation, and so on, taken in [an] unconditional sense, has its origin in theological morals" (54).

Like Anscombe, Schopenhauer holds that deontic morality requires divine command, although unlike her, he denies that God exists. Schopenhauer does not deny, however, that deontic concepts have any meaningful use, for example, in criminal law. But when they do, "they deriv[e] all sense and meaning simply and solely in reference to threatened punishment or promised reward" (55).

It is, indeed, a good thing, Schopenhauer thinks, that societies do have laws threatening sanctions since he holds pessimistically that almost all human action is motivated egoistically and that without the state there would be something like a Hobbesian war of all against all. Schopenhauer denies that moral conscience exists with its own power to motivate. (Putative) conscience's oughts can have no genuine content, and even if they could, conscience would be powerless to motivate.

Schopenhauer does not, however, hold that all human motivation is egoistic. It is *possible* for human beings to be benevolently motivated, and it is here that moral action uniquely resides. In this, Schopenhauer resembles no one so much as Hutcheson, although Schopenhauer's morality of benevolence is

[3] Although Schopenhauer complains that Kant lets eudaimonism in the back door when Kant argues that practical reason requires a "postulate" that connects "virtue and supreme happiness" "in his doctrine of supreme good" (Schopenhauer 1995: 49).

a grim and pessimistic version that is couched in a metaphysical idealism that is far from Hutcheson's empiricist naturalism. (Another, metaphysically more congenial, ally might be Leibniz.) Schopenhauer and Hutcheson both hold that moral goodness consists uniquely in disinterested benevolence. Schopenhauer's preferred terms, however, are 'compassion' and 'pity' (*Mitleid*) (Schopenhauer 1995: 195). Nietzsche is particularly perturbed by the latter, as we shall see.

Schopenhauer and Hutcheson also share their suspicion of deontic language – Hutcheson calls "'ought' an "unlucky Word in Morals" (Hutcheson 2002: 156). Like Shaftesbury and Hume, Hutcheson subversively redefines "obligation" in nondeontic terms. And like Schopenhauer, Hutcheson (2004) recognizes a criticizable sense of 'obligation' connected to "the laws of a superior" (176).

Philosophers, like Hutcheson and Leibniz, who ground morality in morally good *motivation* and hold that moral goodness consists in universal benevolence, nonetheless also often offer principles of moral choice (Hutcheson's "election"). When they do, they are attracted by versions of what becomes known in the nineteenth century as utilitarianism. We owe to Hutcheson and Leibniz some of the first formulations of the "greatest happiness principle" (see Darwall 2023a: 172–182). It is worth noting that there is no such tendency in Schopenhauer's thought and considering why that is so since it reveals what is arguably the most pessimistic aspect of his philosophy. Schopenhauer holds that, however well motivated, action can never successfully relieve suffering since suffering is endemic in human will. So, it is futile even to try. Ultimately, Schopenhauer is led to a "denial of the will" itself and to the idea that transcendental knowledge involves a "transition from virtue to ascetism" (Schopenhauer 1969: I:380).[4]

What Nietzsche ultimately found most disturbing about Schopenhauer was Schopenhauer's pessimism and his championing of an ethical perspective outside of any normally available within life since the latter is frequently self-regarding. Nietzsche ultimately finds what he calls Schopenhauer's "Euro-Buddhism" maddening (Nietzsche 2007: 7). It amounts, Nietzsche claims, to "nihilism" since Schopenhauer's moral perspective cannot affirm life but must rather "withdra[w]" from it (Schopenhauer 1969: I:380).

Schopenhauer's "Buddhism" enters into his *Basis of Morality* in his formulation of the master moral virtue as "boundless" "compassion" or "loving-kindness" "for all beings," and most especially in his "metaphysical

[4] For discussion, see Young 2010: 85.

foundation" of morality in the book's final chapter (Schopenhauer 1995: 172, 199–214). It is here that we find remarks that will remind contemporary readers of Derek Parfit's *Reasons and Persons*, which Parfit also connects to Buddhism (Parfit 1984: 502–503). The key metaphysical point is Schopenhauer's denial of what Rawls calls "the separateness" of individual persons and what Parfit terms any "further fact" of personal identity (Rawls 1971: 259–262; Parfit 1984: 197–348). The classical discussion of personal identity, on which Parfit depends, of course, is Hume's in the *Treatise* (Hume 1978: 259–262).

Like Parfit, Schopenhauer holds that there is no metaphysically real distinction between distinct individuals that makes one the individual they are and another the individual *they* are. The morally good agent who is able to transcend the inevitable self-absorption of living beings, Schopenhauer says, "makes less of a distinction than do the rest between himself and others" (Schopenhauer 1995: 204). Their more enlightened valuing is rooted, moreover, in a metaphysical insight, namely, that the worldly temporal dominion is only a "phenomenal" realm of appearance that has no existence "in itself." Here Schopenhauer simply borrows from Kant the idea that space and time are forms of intuition that have no metaphysical reality. To see things as they really are, we must "withdraw" from any perspective that is available to us within temporal living. And this means, Nietzsche concludes, that it is impossible on Schopenhauer's view to provide a philosophical affirmation of life *from within life*, which is precisely what Nietzsche's "new philosophy" will attempt to do.

Daybreak: Nietzsche's Early Critique of Morality

Ultimately, in the *Genealogy*, Nietzsche presents his "new philosophy" as the third stage in a three-stage sequence. The first stage is an original hierarchical ("aristocratic") ethos – whose contrasting concepts are *good* (noble) and *bad* (base) – and the second stage is a later conception of (deontic) morality – whose contrasting concepts are (moral) good and evil (understood as culpable wrongdoing). Nietzsche's greatest influence in the history of ethics comes from his searching critique of (modern deontic) morality, which he presents in its most mature form in the *Genealogy*, published in 1887. Aspects of *Genealogy*'s critique are anticipated in two earlier works that are worthy of our attention: *Daybreak* (1881) and *Beyond Good and Evil* (1886). *Human, All Too Human*, which was published from 1878 through 1880, has less interest from our perspective. The chapter of greatest interest to us topically, "The History of the Moral Sentiments," is mostly superseded by Nietzsche's discussion of Paul Rée and those Nietzsche calls the "English psychologists" in *Genealogy* (Nietzsche 2007: 10).

Nietzsche's critique of morality will ultimately focus both on morality's *form* and on its *content*. Morality's form consists in its deontic obligating character: its issuing putatively legitimate demands with which moral agents are accountable for complying and with which, consequently, they have to be assumed capable of complying *freely*. With this formal aspect of Nietzsche's critique, Schopenhauer is in complete agreement. There are no moral imperatives, and even if there were, we lack the metaphysical capacity necessary to comply with them freely. This formal critique might go through, however, entirely independently of morality's content.

It is with the second, substantive critique of morality's content – in Schopenhauer's view, benevolence, compassion, or pity (*Mitleid*) – where Nietzsche and Schopenhauer end up at loggerheads. It is not that they disagree about what morality's content is. They agree that moral goodness is other regarding and altruistic. What they disagree about is what Nietzsche will call the "value" of moral goodness so understood (Nietzsche 2007: 6). "Apart from a few philosophers," Nietzsche wrote in *Human, All Too Human*, "men have always placed pity fairly low in the order of rank of the moral sensations, and rightly" (Nietzsche 1996: 56). "Pity," he also says, "is felt as a sign of contempt" (Nietzsche 1996: 322). If, consequently, moral goodness is, as Schopenhauer supposes, *Mitleid* or pity, then moral goodness can hardly be anything valuable. In effect, what Nietzsche and Schopenhauer disagree about is whether moral goodness is really an *ethical*, that is, genuinely normative, form of goodness at all.

Related to this is Nietzsche and Schopenhauer's divergence on the importance of the *individual*. Morality seeks, Nietzsche (1982) says in *Daybreak*, the "abolition of the individual" (83). Behind "the praise of useful impersonal actions" is "fear of everything individual" (105). Schopenhauer sides with morality here, whereas Nietzsche will argue that a more advanced and valuable form of human life is realized by "autonomous supra-ethical individuals" who reject morality.

Moralities and Morality

We should note an important distinction between two different things that "morality" can mean in Nietzsche's critique that it is necessary to keep separate. This is, roughly, the difference between what Hegel called

Sittlichkeit (customs or *mores*) and what he termed *Moralität* (morality, in our modern moral-philosophical sense). This distinction is already in play in *Daybreak*, as Clark and Leiter note in the introduction to their edition (Nietzsche 1997: xxix–xxxi). It is the distinction that English speakers mark between "morality" in a count-noun sense and "morality" in a noncount-noun sense.

In the count-noun sense, moralities are realized in actual customs and mores and in moral codes that individuals or groups subscribe to. "Morality" in this sense refers to something in the actual world that can be studied by the empirical methods of psychology and sociology. Nietzsche does not of course deny that moralities exist in this sense. Part of his argument for why there is no such thing as Kantian *Moralität* runs, indeed, through the character and origins of moralities in this sense, especially those that came about as a result of monotheistic, mandating religions.

What Nietzsche opposes is the idea of morality in the noncount-noun sense. He rejects any notion of a transcendent, universal, nonempirical, essentially *normative* deontic standard: *Moralität*. He argues, beginning in *Daybreak*, that morality in this sense simply does not exist. And he holds that (count-noun) moralities that implicitly claim *Moralität*'s normative support for complying with their customs have no normative force and should be superseded.

This distinction between different senses of "*Moralität*" (or "*die Moral*") is already implicit in *Daybreak*, which Nietzsche subtitles "Thoughts on the Prejudices of Morality" (Nietzsche 1982). Section 9 of book I is titled "*Concept of morality of custom*" (10). This would seem to refer to "morality" in the count-noun sense. The only sense of "morality" that is tied to custom *conceptually* is the sense in which there are as many moralities as there are different systems of custom.

Nietzsche (1982) then says that a "chief proposition" is that "morality is nothing other (therefore *no more*!) than obedience to customs, of whatever kind they may be" (10). Nietzsche does use "*Sittlichkeit*" here, but if he intends it simply to mean the customs themselves, that is, current morality in the count-noun sense, then this can hardly be a "chief proposition"; it is an empty tautology. He must be intending a substantive use that implies moral wrong in the noncount sense, as when we say that someone did not even show common decency. It is hard to see what else he could have in mind other than the *normative* proposition that conduct that has the empirical nonnormative property of according with custom also invariably has the additional normative property of being moral, where this latter use of "moral" is understood in the intrinsically normative noncount-noun sense.

We do best to interpret Nietzsche as making the same claim here about social custom that legal positivists frequently make about law. Although positivists hold that the existence of laws and systems of law consists in positive, empirical facts, they nonetheless also hold that the law necessarily *implicitly claims* to have normative force, to be normatively binding, from what Hart called the "internal point of view" (Hart 1961: 56, 89; Green 2003). Without such a normative claim being sufficiently widely accepted, what we have is not a legal system, but "the gunman situation writ large," that is, social practices that can *compel* obedience, but not *legally obligate* their subjects to it (Hart 1961: 7). Legal systems must have *de facto* authority in order to exist as a matter of positive empirical social fact. But *de facto* authority itself consists in sufficiently wide acceptance of the system's normative *de jure* authority. Similarly, in order for mandatory social customs to exist as a matter of positive empirical fact – in order, that is, for a society to have *a* morality – the customs must themselves purport to have normative moral force in the (intrinsically normative) noncount sense of "moral." Of course, this does not entail that they do.

That this must be how Nietzsche is thinking becomes evident later in the same paragraph:

> If an action is performed not because tradition commands it but for other motives (because of its usefulness to the individual, for example), even indeed for precisely the motives which once founded the tradition, it is called immoral and is felt to be so by him who performed it: for it was not performed in obedience to tradition (Nietzsche 1982: 10–11).

The presence of the feeling of immorality means that one has not simply gone against a current tradition since that can be perfectly appreciated without any feeling at all. One feels as if one has done wrong in a normative sense, as if one has violated morality in the noncount sense.

Nietzsche (1982) continues: "What is tradition? A higher authority which one obeys, not because it commands what is *useful* to us, but because it *commands*" (11). The analogy with a positivist picture of law is clear. Deontic custom has no intrinsic *de jure* normative authority itself, so its existence is a matter of positive social fact. But it nonetheless implicitly claims to have *de jure* authority. It therefore implicitly demands *obedience* and implies that those subject to the custom are obligated by it morally (in the noncount-noun sense). Deontic custom also thus implicitly claims that obligated agents have sufficient normative reason to comply in that fact alone. From the "internal" point of view of mandatory social custom, it simply does not matter whether or not there are prudential reasons of "usefulness" for compliance, even indeed, Nietzsche says, whether there are reasons that might make the obligating custom a useful one for the society to have (Nietzsche 1982: 10–11).

Part of Nietzsche's critique then is, first, that no such essentially normative thing as morality in the noncount-noun sense exists, and second, that customary moralities (in the count-noun sense) must always therefore lack the "higher" authoritative normative backing they invariably implicitly claim. Nietzsche thus contends that a fully adequate causal account of customary moralities will leave them without any transcendent "cause" or ground. And once "one has destroyed a countless number of imaginary causalities hitherto believed in as the foundations of customs," then one will have undermined any basis "of respect for the authority of custom" (Nietzsche 1982: 12).[5]

"There are," Nietzsche (1982) says in *Daybreak*, "two kinds of deniers of morality" (60). One thing it "can mean" "to deny morality" is to deny that "the moral motives which men *claim* have inspired their actions really have done so" (60). For this issue, Nietzsche can allow those who affirm morality to stipulate what the moral motive is. For philosophers like Butler and Kant, it is conscience or free practical reason; for philosophers of (nondeontic) virtue like Hutcheson or Leibniz, it is disinterested benevolence or charity. Nietzsche's first kind of morality denier will then deny that human actions can ever actually be motivated in these ways, that any human action ever is purely conscientious or free willed, or that disinterested benevolence ever exists in a purely psychological sense. Nietzsche cites La Rochefoucauld as the kind of unremitting psychological egoist who denies the existence of moral actions in this first sense. (As Clark and Leiter [1997] point out, in *Human, All Too Human*, Nietzsche might have fit this category too [xx–xxv].) By the time of *Daybreak*, however, Nietzsche (1982) accepts that the motives moralists identify as moral, like compassion, "really are motives of action" as a matter of human psychology (60).

In *Daybreak*, Nietzsche (1982) denies morality in a different, second way. He denies morality, he says, as one might "deny alchemy" (60). He does not deny that alchemists sincerely believe in alchemy; what he denies is that any such belief is true. Similarly, with morality, Nietzsche does not now deny that people are sometimes sincerely morally motivated. He just denies that any moral judgments that might be involved in moral motivation are

[5] Clark and Leiter have a good discussion of this passage in Nietzsche 1997: xxiii.

ever true. Nietzsche holds that "it is *errors* which, as the basis of all moral judgment, impel men to their moral actions" (60). The situation is clearest in the case of conscientious action, when agents are moved by their considered moral judgments. If there is no such thing as morality in the normative, noncount-noun sense, then all moral judgments are false; therefore, such moral motivation is moral *in error*. All (putatively normative) moral judgment is mistaken.

Daybreak's Rejection of Morality, Its "Natural History" of Morality, and Its Moral Psychology of Drives

Of course, Nietzsche's major arguments for this claim are in *Genealogy*, but one that is partly anticipated in *Daybreak* is his assertion that free will, an ineliminable presupposition of morality, simply does not exist. As he puts it in *Daybreak*: "If only those actions are moral which are performed out of freedom of will . . . then there are . . . no moral actions" (93).[6]

Despite this, *Daybreak* contains a remarkable section (112) in which Nietzsche (1982) gives what he calls "the natural history of rights and duties" (66–67). There are three reasons to consider this small section carefully. One is that it actually provides a very different "natural history" of the concepts of right and duty than Nietzsche's *Genealogy*. Second, parts of it can be interpreted as a rational reconstruction of the second-personal aspects of morality like those of Grotius and Pufendorf grounded in sociability or of Adam Smith and Fichte on justice and rights (Darwall 2023a). And third, it departs from these accounts in ways that resonate with Hume's theory of justice.

First, Nietzsche asserts a correlativity of rights and duties. "Our duties," he says, "are the rights of others over us" (Nietzsche 1982: 66). How does the idea of such equivalent duties and rights arise? And how have others acquired these rights and, therefore, how we have acquired duties to them? Nietzsche's answer recalls the "sociability" line in Grotius, Pufendorf, Smith, and Fichte: "By taking us to be capable of contracting and of requiting, by positing us as similar and equal to them, and as a consequence entrusting us with something, educating, reproving, supporting us" (Nietzsche 1982: 66). Voluntary exchange and contract require both parties to take one another as sharing an equal authority or "normative power" to exchange or contract. Nietzsche (1982) notes that this also requires the parties to attribute shared powers to

[6] Technically, this critique might allow that there might be nonhuman agents having free will who are subject to deontic morality.

one another: "The rights of others can relate only to that which lies within our power; it would be unreasonable if they wanted of us something which we did not possess" (66). And Nietzsche sees, and says, that both parties must share this belief. The "feeling of duty," he says, "depends upon our having the same *belief* in regard to the extent of our power as others have" (1982: 66–67). All this must be reciprocal and shared.

Thus far, *Daybreak*'s "natural history" is similar to a line of thought encountered in the philosophers just mentioned, who stress what Grotius and Pufendorf call "sociability" and its connection to reciprocally recognizing respect. For these philosophers, the psychological powers necessary to ground what Nietzsche will call in *Genealogy*'s second essay "the prerogative to promise," are assumed to be basic equipment of fully developed human beings. Nietzsche decisively rejects this picture. In *Genealogy*, he argues that the competence to make binding promises that parties can trust one another to keep has its own genealogy. It requires the centuries-long shaping of individuals' psyches through customary moralities that initially "social[y] straitjacket," but whose overthrow can eventually bear the "fruit" of "autonomous supra-ethical individual[s]" who are able to stand surety for themselves (Nietzsche 2007: 35–37).

At this point in *Daybreak*, however, Nietzsche's natural history shifts decisively toward an account that is more like Hume's theory of the emergence of social "rules of justice" in the *Treatise* (and Fichte's account of rights, on a voluntarist interpretation). The need to join others in contract and Humean conventions of justice depends on continued mutual advantage and that depends on relative power. "If power-relationships undergo any material alteration, rights disappear and new ones are created" (Nietzsche 1982: 67). Everything depends on relative power and consequent mutual interest. "The rights of others constitute a concession on the part of our sense of power to the sense of power of those others" (67).

It is hardly remarkable that Nietzsche tempers his more Smithian passages with this Humean addition. That he goes so far in the Smithian (et al.) direction, however, is remarkable. But what is more remarkable is that even an approach to justice like Hume's would give Nietzsche a much more congenial account of deontic morality than Nietzsche's thoroughly debunking argument in *Genealogy*.[7]

[7] Perhaps Nietzsche realizes that Hume's account fails to give justice the kind of normativity "rules of justice" necessarily aspire to have. Of course, Nietzsche also thinks that any account that meets this aspiration will be no better than alchemy.

A central line of *Genealogy*, hinted at in *Daybreak*, is that the moral concepts of good and evil are the projection of distorted natural instincts or drives to retaliate that are repressed by the impotent herd. Those feelings simmer unconsciously as hatred and *ressentiment* and express themselves consciously as impersonal – better, impartial – feelings of moral praise and blame, with all manifesting the "will to power." In a section of *Daybreak* titled, "*Praise and blame*," Nietzsche discusses how conflict and war inevitably spawn these consciously felt emotions. "Failure brings with it a depression of spirits against which the sole remedy is instinctively applied: a new excitation of the *feeling of power* – and this is to be discovered in the *condemnation* of the 'guilty'" (88). Nietzsche also speaks here of the "drive to praise or blame," though what does the work in his mature *Genealogy* theory are unconscious drives to retaliate.

The idea that much of human motivation is a product of unconscious instincts and drives that can be repressed or sublimated, which plays a starring role in Nietzsche's *Genealogy* argument, has had enormous influence among psychologists and psychoanalytic theorists, most prominently, Freud. Nietzsche says more about drives in *Daybreak* than he does in *Genealogy*, and more yet in *Beyond Good and Evil*, as we shall see in the next section.

Nietzsche proclaims in *Daybreak* that "however far a man may go in self-knowledge, nothing ... can be more incomplete than his image of the totality of *drives* which constitute his being" (119). Human beings, for Nietzsche, are bundles of drives lacking any definite unity. Nietzsche is thus a "bundle theorist," like Hume, but Nietzsche's bundles are not Humean perceptions, but practical dispositions realized in our bodies in the same way they are in any animal. What distinguishes human from other animal drives, for Nietzsche, is that our drives can be unconsciously repressed or sublimated so that we are ignorant of them as they receive quite different conscious expression owing to other psychic forces. Because they operate in the "dark workshop" of the unconscious, as Nietzsche puts it in *Genealogy*, even the most self-knowing person will have an "incomplete" knowledge of them (Nietzsche 1982: 119; 2007: 27).

As Paul Katsafanas has shown, instincts and drives differ, for Nietzsche, from ordinary desires and aversions; they lack definite objects and so are incapable of directly motivating definite action. They are rather primitive dispositions to form more specific desires and aversions (Katsafanas 2016: 77–107). The natural animal instinct to respond to perceived threats with fight, flight, or freeze is a drive-in Nietzsche's sense. It is a disposition that gives rise to more specific desires, for example, to flee from this angry grizzly. The drive that will play the central role in Nietzsche's genealogy of morality is the natural drive to retaliate attacks and avenge insults, which the impotent herd unconsciously shape into moral blame in their "dark workshop." No drive has, Nietzsche says, "any moral character at all" (Nietzsche 1982: 26). It is consciously felt as moral "only when it enters into relations with drives already baptized good or evil" (Nietzsche 1982: 26).

Beyond Good and Evil: Drives, the "Instinct for Rank," and Hierarchical Values

Nietzsche's most extensive discussion of drives and their moral psychological role is in *Beyond Good and Evil*, which appeared in 1886, five years after *Daybreak* and one year before *The Genealogy of Morality*. Subtitled *Prelude to a Philosophy of the Future*, *Beyond Good and Evil* lays out some central aspects of Nietzsche's "new philosoph[y]," both its hierarchical character, rooted in the human "instinct for rank," and its focus on "teach[ing] humanity its future" (Nietzsche 2002: 91, 160). Against Kant's idea that the distinctive value of humanity consists in a dignity that all rational human beings share, Nietzsche argues that the moral notion of equal dignity is "an abased (more specifically a diminished) form of humanity" (91). Morality fosters "a mediocritization and depreciation of humanity in value" (91). (Accordingly, *Beyond Good and Evil* also lays out aspects of Nietzsche's "historical" critique of morality, which are more fully developed in *The Genealogy of Morality*.)

Nietzsche connects his theory of drives to his well-known "will to power." "Physiologists," he says, "should think twice" before saying, with Hobbes, that "self-preservation" is "the cardinal drive" of human and other "organic being[s]" (Nietzsche 2002: 15). What a living being wants "above all" is to "*discharge* its strength – life itself is will to power" (15). All animals, humans included, are bundles of drives; what drives do is simply exert themselves, thereby "discharg[ing] [their] strength." By the "will to power," Nietzsche does not mean that some faculty, the will, exercises and seeks to increase its own power or that we seek to do so through our will. Rather, each and "every drive craves mastery"; it seeks to exert itself and, indeed, to enlist other aspects of the psyche in helping it do so (9). The will to power may be nothing more than the cumulative phenomena of drives manifesting and fostering their own power. Nietzsche is a bundle theorist here as well.

What we might call the "cunning of drives" is their ability both to exercise their power and to coopt other, more rational modules into helping them beneath our notice. Philosophers, for example, may believe that a "'drive for knowledge' is the father of philosophy." What they fail to notice is that they are moved by other, more "basic drives" that seek "knowledge (and mis-knowledge!) merely as a tool" to their own satisfaction (8–9). With individual drives themselves, therefore, "there might really be something like a drive for knowledge" (9). But anything we might ordinarily call philosophers' drive for knowledge is at best an instrumental motivational tendency – actually, usually the *presentation* of such a tendency, at which the philosophers' more basic drives aim.

Nietzsche lampoons the tendency to see the mind as a single conscious (and self-conscious) entity, or as an organized whole of intellectual capacities hermetically separated from a physical body having multiple needs and instincts, as putting a "scientific head on an ape's body" (Nietzsche 2002: 28). On Nietzsche's psychoanalytic picture, conscious thought and activity is as likely to result from subconscious drives and instincts as it is from clear and distinct thought and reasoning carried on by the conscious mind itself. Nietzsche gives an example that anticipates his *Genealogy* account of morality as an unconscious projection of *ressentiment*:

> The angry man, and anyone who is constantly tearing and shredding himself with his own teeth (or, in place of himself, the world, or God, or society), may very well stand higher than the laughing and self-satisfied satyr, considered morally. But considered in any other way, he is the more ordinary, more indifferent [or herd-like] . . .. And nobody *lies* as much as the angry man (Nietzsche 2002: 28).

The angry, embittered person, motivated by their drives to ignore their own weakness, impotence, and relatively miserable condition, lies to themselves and to others about their own bitterness; they consciously feel cool, impersonal moral blame and disapproval – expressed in judgments of deontic morality – thereby masking their unconscious personal *ressentiment* (see Nietzsche 2007: 22). "Thinking," Nietzsche says, "is only a relation between ... drives" (2002: 35). "Drives ... subjugate not only our reason but our conscience as well" (2002: 71).

Now, it is a central plank of Nietzsche's argument against deontic morality that the free will it presupposes simply does not exist. But Nietzsche acknowledges that the *feeling* or "affect" of free will does. What he calls an "act of willing" involves a "plurality of feelings" that uncannily mimic phenomena to which modern moral philosophers have pointed (18). He says that willing involves feelings of Hobbesian desires and aversions, feelings "towards" and "away from" their respective objects (18). Even more remarkably, Nietzsche describes the "affect" of the "act of willing" in terms that resonate with Cudworth and, most especially, Locke (19). Locke describes "volition" as an "Act of the Mind knowingly exerting that Dominion it takes it self to have over any part of the Man" (Locke 1975: 240–241).[8] Here now is Nietzsche: "What is called 'freedom of the will' is essentially the affect of superiority with respect to something that must obey . . . [of] command[ing] something inside himself that obeys, or that he believes to obey" (Nietzsche 2002: 19). Of course, unlike Cudworth and Locke, Nietzsche holds that any such feeling is illusory. It is, at best, in Marxian terms, an epiphenomenal superstructure resulting from a base of actually motivating drives.

Brief Interlude on Nietzsche and Metaethics

Nietzsche says something similar in *Beyond Good and Evil* about the relation between affect and moral judgment. "Morality," he says, "is just a *sign language of the affects*" (Nietzsche 2002: 77). This would seem to have metaethical implications.

It is worth taking a brief interlude at this point to consider what can reasonably be concluded from this and other things Nietzsche says about metaethics. There is no question that much of Nietzsche's ethical writings are metaethically suggestive and that they have been influential in contemporary metaethical debate. Nietzsche is one of a group of modern philosophers, including Hobbes and Hume, who approach their ethical philosophizing in a decidedly naturalistic way and whose ideas have genuine currency among contemporary naturalistically inclined philosophers, especially those whose naturalism gives them doubts about deontic morality. A search of *Philosophers' Index* shows many more articles written on Nietzsche and metaethics than on Hobbes and metaethics (though fewer than Hume and metaethics).[9] A book exists titled *Nietzschean Metaethics*, and Nietzsche has been enlisted on behalf of constitutivism, constructivism, subjectivist naturalism, anti-realism, and fictionalism, and perhaps other metaethical views (Schacht 1983; Katsafanas 2013; Silk 2015; Rowe 2019).

[8] Cudworth says something similar about what he calls the "autexousious power" (Cudworth ~1670: 4982.17). For discussion see Darwall 1995.

[9] On September 7, 2021: Nietzsche forty-nine, Hobbes six, and Hume seventy-three.

Caution, however, is required in attempting to attribute any definite metaethical position to Nietzsche. Before Moore and the development of metaethics as a subfield of ethical philosophy in the twentieth century, philosophers lacked the vocabulary and sharpened concepts necessary to think about metaethical questions as they have come to be defined and, therefore, to develop definite answers to them, as we observed with Hobbes and Hume. Moreover, as Brian Leiter and Nadeem Hussain have observed, Nietzsche's texts radically underdetermine specific answers in any case (Leiter 2000; Hussain 2013). The most sensible approach is simply not to attempt to assign definite metaethical positions to Nietzsche (Hussain 2013).

All that said, it is worth noting the anti-realist thrust of so many of Nietzsche's remarks. Clearly, he is an anti-realist or "error theorist" about *moral* judgments. There are, Nietzsche says, "no moral facts."[10] And though Nietzsche's statement that "morality is just a *sign language of the affects*" is technically restricted to (deontic) morality, it is hard not to hear a more general ethical expressivism there, of the kind encountered in Hobbes's idea that we call "good" what we desire and "bad" that to which we are averse (Hobbes 1994: VI.7; Darwall 2023a: 46–48). This does not mean, however, that Nietzsche is likely to have thought of the value judgments he makes, for example about the "[dis]value of morality," simply as expressions of his desires or tastes, rather than as evaluative convictions to which he was seriously committed and for which he was prepared to offer reasoned support (Nietzsche 2007: 6). Surely a good part of what Nietzsche is doing in his ethical works, most clearly in *Genealogy*, is offering reasons for thinking that living with the priestly caste's conception of morality is genuinely *disvaluable*. Nietzsche (2007) there explicitly calls, after all, for a "*critique*" of "*the value of these* [*moral*] *values*" (7).

Moreover, as we shall see presently, Nietzsche is clearly invested in making *positive* value judgments. He argues in *Beyond Good and Evil* that human beings have an "instinct for rank" that expresses itself in hierarchical value judgments of higher ways of living that merit respect and lower forms of humanity that deserve contempt (Nietzsche 2002: 160, 167). There can be no doubt that Nietzsche shares these hierarchical judgments. They are central to his "new philosoph[y]" – his "philosophy of the future" – which celebrates the reversal of "*the total degeneration of*

[10] This is from Kaufmann's translation of *Twilight of the Idols*, quoted in Hussain 2013.

humanity" that was the necessary consequence of the "democratization" of modern morality (Nietzsche 2002: 91–92, 134).[11]

This celebration of "higher," "exceptional," affirmative types is central also to Nietzsche's whole anti-nihilist project. His "affirmation of life," in Reginster's terms, results from a double negation that is part of *Genealogy*'s three-stage dialectic. "All noble morality grows out of a triumphant saying 'yes' to itself" (Nietzsche 2007: 20; Reginster 2009). This is the first stage, where good contrasts with bad rather than evil. "Slave morality," by contrast, "says 'no' . . . to everything that is 'outside'" itself, especially to the "good" or "noble" types toward whom the herd feel *ressentiment* (Nietzsche 2007: 20). If "sovereign individuals" or "autonomous supra-ethical" types are to emerge, therefore, they must reject morality's "No-saying" (37). In doing so, they make themselves "noble Yes-saying types" and advance a postmodern morality. The most genuine "affirmation of life" can come only dialectically, through this double negation.

This will be clearer presently. My point here is that Nietzsche means these hierarchical, "supra"-moral *ethical* judgments with utmost seriousness. And this must surely cut against any attempt to read him as a straightforward noncognitivist, like Ayer or Stevenson, whose interest is primarily in anti-realist metaethics rather than in normative ethical philosophy. Even if early noncognitivists and other anglophone metaethicists avoided "moralizing" on principle, there is no doubt that Nietzsche does not avoid what we might call "ethicalizing" (Hudson 1970: 13). Even though he was not a normative *moral* philosopher, he certainly was a normative *ethical* philosopher. But while this cuts against Nietzsche's having to hold any simple-minded version of noncognitivism or anti-realism, it certainly does not show that he would not have been attracted by forms of expressivist anti-realisms that were first put forward in the late twentieth century, like Gibbard's "norm expressivism" and Blackburn's "quasi-realism" (Blackburn 1984; Gibbard 1990). Ultimately, however, it is ahistorical and foolhardy to try to pigeonhole Nietzsche metaethically.

"Instinct for Rank," Aristocratic Ethics, and "Higher Men"

That the ethos of the first stage of Nietzsche's three-stage sequence in *Genealogy* is "aristocratic," structured by the nonmoral concepts of the noble and base, is widely recognized. Less well appreciated is the way

[11] See Nietzsche's characterization of *Beyond Good and Evil* as a "Prelude to the Philosophy of the Future" in *Ecce Homo* (Nietzsche 1967: 310).

Nietzsche sets up *Genealogy*'s discussion of this and other stages in *Beyond Good and Evil*. There, Nietzsche advanced an idea that will underlie his entire genealogy of morality: the "instinct for rank" (Nietzsche 2002: 160).[12] As will become clearer when we consider *Genealogy*, the plausibility of Nietzsche's explanation of the origin of moral concepts in *ressentiment* ultimately depends on this instinct.

"Aristocratic value judgments" figure not only in *Genealogy*'s first stage but also in its third, in which the "supra-ethical [moral]" individuals – or "higher men," as they are called in *Beyond Good and Evil* – transcend the second stage's "slave morality" (Nietzsche 2002: 39; 2007: 17, 20, 37). The "instinct for rank" is what puts human beings in touch with essentially hierarchical "rank-ordering and rank-defining" value (Nietzsche 2002: 160; 2007: 11). It is not a desire for status or social power, but a sense of higher and lower *values* and a ranking that these define. "Rank," as Nietzsche defines it, is very different from status or relative power.

"There is," Nietzsche says, "an *instinct for rank* that, more than anything else, is itself the sign of a *high* rank; there is a *pleasure* in nuances of respect that indicates a noble origin and noble habits" (Nietzsche 2002: 160). Nietzsche ties the "instinct for rank" to "the soul's *instinct for respect*," which shows itself in "an involuntary hush" of respect when "the soul *feels* the presence of something deserving the highest honors" (160). Respect of this kind is a form of esteem, the feeling that its object is deserving of esteem and "honors." The instinct for rank and respect is thus a felt sense of higher values – of what is estimable and deserving of honor.

Notice in this connection Nietzsche's remark that a (cultivated) instinct for rank "is itself the sign of *high* rank" (160). This recalls a point that Aristotle makes in the *Nicomachean Ethics* while arguing that virtue rather than honor is the highest good. In book I, section 5, Aristotle notes that unlike those who are "slavish in their tastes," those in "high places" tend to want honor over pleasure (Aristotle 1998: I.5). So far, this concerns status rather than rank in Nietzsche's sense. Status is socially constructed through publicly expressed forms of hierarchical honor respect, so those who want to maintain their status want to be honored in fact (Darwall 2013d). Aristotle points out, however, that we do not want to be honored by just anyone – whether higher ups or not, we want to be honored by those *we* honor (Aristotle 1998: I.5). And the reason we do is that we take them to be more discriminating in *their* honoring so that we take them to be better

[12] For a discussion of the "instinct for rank" and its role in Nietzsche's thought, see Ganesh 2017, from which I here draw.

judges of whether we *deserve* honor or are, in Aristotle's terms, "excellent" or "virtu[ous]" (I.5, 1.12).[13] But this just means, in Nietzsche's terms, that we take them to have a more discriminating "instinct for rank." Their being worthy of our respect goes together with their being better judges of *our* being worthy of respect, as they might show by (sincerely) honoring us. Rank, in this *normative* sense, is the object of our desire or "instinct."

What is important for Nietzsche's *Genealogy* account is the *internal, valuing* aspect of the instinct for rank. "Rank," in Nietzsche's lexicon, refers to a normative and *evaluative* hierarchy rather than a socially constructed one, like social status. The instinct for rank is thus an internal sense, which can be more or less discriminating, of "rank-defining," hierarchical value. The implications for Nietzsche's *Genealogy* account of moral values as the psychological projection of *ressentiment* are significant. Higher social status can be fully acknowledged publicly without inner feeling, or even belief. Without the instinct for rank, contempt from above, however unsettling, need not lower the herd's self-esteem. But if even lower classes have an "instinct for rank," then being the object of contempt from those above will get under the herd's skin. They will be susceptible to internalizing the contempt as shame, to *feeling* contempt for themselves.

And that will set their unconscious – what Nietzsche calls their "dark workshop" – to work (Nietzsche 2007: 27). Unable to bear consciously their subconscious shame and self-hatred, they will feel these as a new kind of conscious "moral" feeling. They will feel *moral blame* for those who have put them in this dark place, not as from the perspective of someone who has been *personally* wounded (that is too painful to acknowledge), but as from the impartial perspective of an imagined moral community. They will feel the injury not as personal insult but as an insult to *a person*.

Finally, we should note how in *Beyond Good and Evil*, Nietzsche makes clear that hierarchical rank-defining values are not simply the core of (what will be) the first stage of *Genealogy*'s three-stage sequence but also of its third stage, in which "higher men," embodying a "philosophy of the future," live their lives "beyond good and evil." Nietzsche bemoans the democratic trends and liberal egalitarian ideals he finds around him in nineteenth-century Europe. When, "at the beginning of the Revolution," the French "aristocracy ... [threw] away its privileges ... and [sacrificed] itself to an excess of its moral feeling ... [i]t was really just the final act of that centuries-long corruption in which the aristocracy gradually

[13] Adam Smith makes a similar point about the human desire for merited or "proper" esteem (Smith 1982: 190).

relinquished its dominant authority" (Nietzsche 2002: 152). Morality's form of reciprocity, "placing your will on a par with [all] other[s]" in the way morality prescribes, Nietzsche will argue, ultimately seeks to "*negate* life" (152–153). To affirm life, it is necessary to negate morality's negation. It is necessary "for raising an exceptional being up to its higher duty and to a higher state of *being*" (152). Morality's rejection of hierarchy must be rejected to give rise to a new, genuinely evaluative hierarchy of rank.

The idea of "a single morality" obligating all equally "is harmful precisely to the higher men" (119). "There is," Nietzsche says, "an *order of rank* between people, and between moralities as well" (119).[14] The "English utilitarians" come in for special opprobrium for two reasons. First, their hedonism and emphasis on avoiding suffering flattens the good life and seeks to remove sources of resistance, the overcoming of which the highest human achievements and flourishing depend upon. And second, their moral goal of the general happiness flattens natural hierarchy and undermines "exceptional . . being[s]" (119, 152). Both subvert evaluative hierarchy. The aristocracy of higher men reverses this. It seeks and (would realize) an order in which all serve, not the general happiness but the instantiation of higher values: "enhancement ... in the type 'man'" (151). For "higher men," this will mean realizing them in their own noble, life-affirming activity. However, the less gifted are cast in, at best, a supporting role, indeed to the point of what Nietzsche calls "slavery" (151) "Aristocracy," he says, "accepts in good conscience the sacrifice of countless people who have to be pushed down and shrunk into incomplete human beings, into slaves, into tools, *all for the sake of the aristocracy*" (Nietzsche 2002: 152). This obviously turns Kant's idea of equal human dignity as ends in themselves on its head.

The Genealogy of Morality

Nietzsche's *Genealogy of Morality* famously begins: "We are unknown to ourselves, we knowers: and with good reason. We have never looked for ourselves – so how are we ever supposed to *find* ourselves?" (Nietzsche 2007: 3). The theme of critical self-scrutiny is almost as old as philosophy itself. Nietzsche's focus is on the examination of our ethical, more specifically, our *moral* beliefs. How can we expect to critically examine these, he

[14] For a discussion of "higher men" and their role in Nietzsche's ethical hierarchy, see Leiter 2015: 91–100.

asks, if we do not inquire into how we came to have them, including how we acquired the very concepts necessary to frame them?

This is *Genealogy*'s eponymous project: a psychosocial account of the origin of our moral convictions and of the very idea of morality. Nietzsche's aims in *Genealogy* are threefold. He seeks, first, to show that morality is a mere ideology, a set of concepts and beliefs whose origins in *ressentiment* have nothing to do with their application or truth. Living with these concepts and convictions provides only misleading evidence of their validity.

Second, noting that "people have taken the *value* of these [moral] 'values' as given," Nietzsche seeks to destabilize this assumption genealogically (8). In addition, he seeks, third, "a *critique* of moral values" themselves (7). Nietzsche's genealogy cannot contribute to that directly, however; it can only undermine commonsense moral beliefs without arguing directly against them.

This third critical aim seeks to criticize the value of morality head on and to show on that basis that morality's pretensions to supreme value are "chimerical," in Kant's term (Kant 1996a: 4:445). Nietzsche argues that morality cannot possibly have the value it purports to have. Partly, this is because necessary presuppositions of morality – such as freedom of the will – are simply false. But Nietzsche also argues that morality must lack value because it is fundamentally *negative* – it "says 'no' on principle to everything that is 'outside' [or] 'other'" (Nietzsche 2007: 20). So, morality must be revealed not just as an ideology but also as a modern *malady*, as both an "illness" and a "symptom" of that illness (7, 56).

Morality is, Nietzsche argues, nihilistic. It says "no" to life, whereas value is positive almost by definition, the affirmation of life and all that makes life good: health, vigor, physical exploits, joy, creativity, human excellences, and cheerful community with others who both exemplify and appreciate higher values, what Nietzsche sometimes calls a "higher community" (Nietzsche 1999: 18; Reginster 2009).[15]

Nietzsche tells us that he "was given the initial stimulation to publish something about [his] hypotheses" on the genealogy of morals by reading Paul Rée's *The Origin of the Moral Sensations*, published a decade before in 1877. Here hangs a fascinating tale about Rée's role in Nietzsche's life.

[15] Young stresses that the desire to live in community with esteemed peers was a recurrent theme in Nietzsche's own life (Young 2010).

Genealogy and Nietzsche (Human, All Too Human)

Perhaps no significant ethical philosopher's views are more intimately connected to the details of their life than Nietzsche's. There is little doubt that Nietzsche was trying to exemplify the "new philosoph[y]" that his writings celebrate in his own life. But influence may have gone in the other direction also: from Nietzsche's life to his philosophy. Given Nietzsche's call to examine the sources of our moral beliefs, perhaps we should hold his *Genealogy* critique to the same standard and inquire into possible connections between Nietzsche's life and the strikingly emotion-laden terms of his *Genealogy* critique. This is where Nietzsche's relation to Rée (and their respective relations to the great unrequited love of Nietzsche's life, Lou Salomé) come in.

Julian Young calls Nietzsche's relation to Rée one of "the two most important philosophically friendships of Nietzsche's life" (Young 2010: 212).[16] You wouldn't know it from reading *On the Genealogy of Morality*, however, as we shall see presently. Rée's and Nietzsche's friendship was confined mostly to the period before Lou Salomé entered their lives. When that occurred, Nietzsche initially prevailed upon Rée to help promote a hoped-for romance with Salomé, but Rée had his own designs. After Nietzsche's plan failed, Nietzsche suggested that the three of them form a "higher community" as second best. However, after a short period, the threesome broke up, and Salomé and Rée subsequently went to live together in Berlin. Ultimately, Salomé decided that she had had enough of both Nietzsche and Rée. The upshot was that Nietzsche never forgave Rée. By 1882, their friendship was effectively over (Young 2010: 339–356).

Nietzsche's own *ressentiment* drips all over the pages of *Genealogy*'s preface, though he makes every effort to hide it. Nietzsche begins by saying that he had been "stimulat[ed] to publish something" of his own genealogical "hypotheses," by reading Rée's *Origins of the Moral Sensations* (Nietzsche 2007: 5). The appearance he presents is that Rée was otherwise unknown to him, even though they were close friends and almost collaborators, pursuing in their different ways what they together called "historical philosophy" (Young 2010: 233). In *Genealogy*, Nietzsche repeatedly belittles *Origins* as a "clever, even too-clever little book" (though he adds that it is "clear" and "honest") (Nietzsche 2007: 7). And Nietzsche repeats: "the little book" (7).[17] The belittlement of Rée is obvious enough, but the

16 Young excludes Nietzsche's relationship with Richard Wagner. The other relationship Young includes was with Heinrich Köselitz (Young 2010: 212).

17 It is worth noting that *Der Ursprung der moralischen Empfindungen* had 142 pages and Nietzsche's *Genealogie*, only 40 more (182).

text attempts to blind us to its source in Nietzsche's own subconscious *ressentiment*. (No doubt this would all have been evident to Salomé (and also to Rée).)[18]

Simply to reject his critique of Rée's *Origins* on these grounds would be a genetic fallacy of the kind morality's supporters point to in justifying a refusal to draw philosophical or normative conclusions from Nietzsche's genealogical critique. We should therefore ask, what it is that Nietzsche objects to *substantively* in the "origin" accounts of Rée and other "English psychologists," as Nietzsche calls them in another subtle put down (5, 10). The "English kind" "of genealogical hypotheses" is, Nietzsche says, "back-to-front and perverse" (5). In Nietzsche's view, "English" genealogical psychology is like what is sometimes called "whiggish history"; it sees current moral conceptions as the natural and inevitable result of the past. It complacently supports the normative and conceptual status quo and sets out its (illegitimately derived) genealogy to help it do so.

In Rée's case, this was because he sought to show the evolutionary origins of both altruistic conduct and moral conscience. *Origins* closely follows Darwin's account in *Expressions of Emotion in Man and Animals*, as Nietzsche himself notes (Darwin 1872; Nietzsche 2007: 7). Against these, Nietzsche will point to plausible psychoanalytic sources of moral motivation and belief that such "English" accounts ignore. But this raises a further puzzle. Since Darwin actually was an (especially prominent) English psychologist, at least, of an evolutionary kind, why does Nietzsche not take *him* on? Why Rée? Part of the answer is that Nietzsche was himself an acknowledged Darwinian (Young 2010: 198). But surely, we can appreciate another important reason why Nietzsche substitutes Rée for Darwin when, like Nietzsche, we attend to the subconscious backstory. Here Nietzsche shows himself to be human, all too human (or, one is tempted to say, male, all too male).

This suggests that, at least while he was writing *Genealogy*, Nietzsche was himself a "man of *ressentiment*" (Nietzsche 2007: 21). It is notable that all three of Nietzsche's most virulent critiques of morality date from the period after his disaffection from Rée in 1882. Although it is almost impossible to believe that it really could be, the question naturally arises whether not only Nietzsche's rhetoric in *Genealogy* but also his critical attack on morality itself in all three of *Daybreak*, *Beyond Good and Evil*, and

[18] Salomé went on to a notable career as a psychoanalyst during which she was known as Lou Andreas Salomé, her middle name coming from the linguist Friedrich Carl Andreas, with whom she had a celibate marriage.

Genealogy might be at least partly a product of his own "dark workshop" (27), After all, what better way to get back at the "English psychologist" whose *Origins of the Moral Sensations* had anchored moral ideas not in *ressentiment*, but in naturally selected psychic sources (Rée 2003).

From Good and Bad to Good and Evil

Nietzsche lays out his psychosocial account of the genesis of morality in *Genealogy*'s first essay. Its basic structure is simple. In an initial "aristocratic" stage, the "rank-ordering, rank-defining" concepts of good and bad (noble and base) are established in hierarchical valuing attitudes. In a second stage, the contempt of those above for those below provokes resistance by the contemned "herd" and their "priestly" leaders.

It is the form that the resistance takes in the second stage, unconscious *ressentiment*, that is Nietzsche's distinctive contribution. As Scheler put it, "Nietzsche's discovery that *ressentiment* can be the source of" moral judgments and attitudes was "most profound" (Scheler 1994: 27). The herd's repressed *personal ressentiment* is projected impersonally and consciously through genuinely new evaluative concepts: moral good and evil. This gives rise to another reaction in turn and creates the possibility of a post-moral hierarchical ethics embodied in the lives of "autonomous, supra-ethical individual[s]" who, for the first time, can genuinely take responsibility for themselves (Nietzsche 2007: 35–37).

To see how Nietzsche thinks *ressentiment* can give rise to new evaluative concepts, we will need to keep in mind that "*ressentiment*," for Nietzsche, cannot mean what "resentment" means for Smith and other modern moral philosophers. These philosophers take resentment already to be a moralized attitude that is conceptually tied to the deontic idea of injustice. Since Nietzsche is trying to account for the origin of this idea as an unconscious projection from a pre-moral stage, he can hardly hold that *ressentiment* is already a consciously moralized attitude.

A key to Nietzsche's meaning is given by Scheler, who characterizes *ressentiment* as "a self-poisoning of the mind . . . caused by the systematic repression of certain emotions and affects," including "revenge, hatred, malice, envy, the impulse to detract, and spite" (Scheler 1994: 29). Unable to bear the conscious pain of wounding insult from above or to retaliate openly, the herd repress their *ressentiment* and feel it consciously as impersonal moral blame.

But first things first. Differently from the "English psychologists," Nietzsche argues that an earlier notion of good that is not morally inflected originated "aristocratic[ally]," from "'the good' themselves, meaning the noble, the mighty, the high-placed and the high-minded" (Nietzsche 2007: 11). A noble class "judged themselves and their actions as good," and judged those below as bad, not as morally bad, but as contemptible or base, as deserving their lower social status (11).

Because Nietzsche talks in terms of nobles "creat[ing]" the reigning value hierarchy, it can seem that his story is one of power all the way down (11, 14). Those with greater power force their evaluations on those with less. As we saw, however, this fits poorly with what Nietzsche says earlier about the "instinct for rank" and its capacity to generate *feelings* of inferiority (Nietzsche 2002: 160). *Genealogy*'s story is much more plausible psychologically, not to mention more philosophically interesting, if we recall that rank for Nietzsche is ultimately a status in a(n) (imagined and felt) normative or evaluative order rather than a position of relative power or social status. It is more like the normative status of deserving an honored social status.

The evaluative concepts in play in the aristocratic ethos are "rank-defining" (Nietzsche 2007: 11). They involve a kind of value that admits not just of more and less (like more and less benefit) but also of *higher* and *lower*. It is important that for Nietzsche, "good" in the first stage is not *das Wohl* (well-being or a person's good) but *das Gute*. It signifies a kind of value that is conceptually tied to "looking up to" and "looking down upon" attitudes – the attitudes of esteem, emulation, and admiration, on the one hand, and disesteem, contempt, and disdain, on the other. "Good" and "bad" in the aristocratic ethos refer to the *noble* and the *base*, respectively, to forms of merit and demerit that are justifiably regarded with esteem, admiration, emulation, and pride (the estimable), on the one hand, and with contempt, disdain, and shame (the contemptible), on the other. These valuing attitudes, moreover, are not restricted to the nobles; they are also shared, if unconsciously, by the herd. As the Scheler scholar Lewis Coser puts it, "*ressentiment*-imbued persons secretly crave the values they publicly denounce" (Scheler 1961: Introduction, 24).

It is also important that Nietzsche does not restrict "*ressentiment*" to the repressed form it takes in the weak.[19] Indeed, he explicitly contrasts *ressentiment* as it appears in the strong with the poisoning form it takes in the weak. "When *ressentiment* does occur in the noble man himself, it is consumed and exhausted in an immediate reaction, and therefore it does not *poison*, on the other hand, it does not occur at all in countless cases

[19] My account here closely follows that in Darwall 2013i.

where it is unavoidable for all who are weak and powerless" (Nietzsche 2007: 22). What is common to both strong and weak is the occasion and impulse to retaliate against attack or insult. In the strong, retaliatory impulses and feelings are "exhausted in an immediate reaction," whereas in the weak, who are powerless to retaliate, simmering feelings of *ressentiment* are "unavoidable" and must be shamefully suffered or repressed. The noble man "shakes from him, with one shrug, many worms which … burro[w] into" the weak (22). *Ressentiment* is the repressed shame and self-hatred that those below feel when they are empathically infected by the contempt of those above.

Nietzsche says,

> The beginning of the slaves' revolt in morality occurs when *ressentiment* itself turns creative and gives birth to values: the *ressentiment* of those beings who, being denied the proper response of action, compensate for it with only imaginary revenge. Whereas all noble morality grows out of a triumphant saying "yes" to itself, slave morality says "no" on principle to everything that is "outside", "other", "non-self": and *this* "no" is its creative deed (20).

Ressentiment responds, by its very nature, to *personal* attacks or insults. To take something *personally* just is to see oneself as that thing's target and to see it as intended to hurt, injure, or devalue *one* in some way. It is, therefore, to see it as calling for some defensive, retaliatory response, a counterattack that turns tables and defends oneself. Vengeance is personal in its nature; it avenges a personal injury.

When nobles are attacked or insulted, any *ressentiment* they feel is above board and immediately "exhausted" in retaliatory action (22). But the weak's impotence drives *ressentiment* below; *ressentiment* "burrow[s] into" the weak, into their "dark workshop," where its creative work can be done subconsciously (22, 27). Though "the noble man is confident and frank with himself," "the man of *ressentiment* is neither upright nor naïve, nor honest and straight with himself. His soul *squints*; his mind loves dark corners, secret paths and back-doors" (21).

Impotent to prompt personal vengeance, *ressentiment* becomes "creative" through a putatively impersonal response to an imagined impersonal attack (20). "Priestly vengefulness" and impotent "hatred" prompt a "reversal" of the "aristocratic value equation (good = noble = powerful = beautiful = happy = blessed) … 'Only those who suffer are good, only the poor, the powerless, the lowly are good'" (17). The revenge of the weak and their priests comes from turning the aristocratic ethos upside down. By reversing the value hierarchy, they can view the strong with contempt.

Notice, however, that so far as the processes described to this point are concerned, we do not yet really have a new evaluative *concept*, moral evil, that requires a different conceptual framework in place of the aristocratic one. All we have thus far is a reversal *within* the earlier framework – that what was deemed noble and worthy of esteem and pride is actually worthy of contempt and shame. We get closer to Nietzsche's idea if we notice a further element that plays a central role in his well-known parable of the lambs and the "birds of prey," namely, that the lambs do not simply look down on the birds for their preying character, but "blame" the birds of prey and claim a "right to make [them] *responsible* for being birds of prey" (25–27). They imaginatively resist the preying attacks of the birds through *blaming* the birds and conceiving of their predation as *culpable* wrongdoing.

This brings in an element of the concept of moral evil – that perpetrators are morally responsible or accountable for intentional wrongdoing – that is essential to morality, and that is centrally implicated in moral resentment, as we have seen with Smith and other modern moral philosophers. And it brings with it the presuppositions necessary to hold someone accountable, namely, that they had a kind of freedom of the will necessary to hold themselves accountable and freely comply with moral demands.

Crucial background for Nietzsche's analysis of the parable is his view that just as different species have different natures, so also do different kinds of human beings. The good, noble qualities of the strong are natural to them, as are the weak's unimpressive features to them. When the birds of prey manifest their greater strength to the detriment of the lambs, the lambs absurdly question this. Nietzsche replies on the birds' behalf: "it is just as absurd to ask strength *not* to express itself as strength . . . as it is to ask weakness to express itself as strength" (28). *Ressentiment* leads the lambs to see both the birds' and their own actions not as unavoidable expressions of their different natures but as *freely chosen*. This enables them to see their own submission and deference not as natural expressions of an inescapable nature but as "a voluntary achievement, something wanted, chosen, a *deed*, an *accomplishment*" (27).

The greatest injury the strong inflict on the weak is less any physical damage or disadvantage the weak suffer at their hands than the insult of their contempt, which the weak cannot avoid feeling empathically as shame, however repressed their shame may be. The weak cannot stand to see themselves as the strong see them to feel the shame of their base condition. So they invent the fantasy that they have chosen to be the way they are and to act as they do because this is actually better. "This type of man *needs* to believe in an unbiased 'subject' with freedom of choice, because he has an instinct of ... self-affirmation in which every lie is sanctified" (27). It is the need for self-*esteem*, to see one's life as valuable, to be proud rather than ashamed of oneself, that fuels their mendacious inversion of the noble/base hierarchy.

At the end of the day, however, it remains unclear how the psychological mechanisms Nietzsche's account employs can explain genuinely new, distinctively deontic moral concepts rather than simply a reversal in the aristocratic valuations. So far as *ressentiment* is concerned, why would it not be a sufficiently satisfying victory over the nobles to infect them with the weak's contempt for the strong, *viewed as from an objective impersonal perspective*? "We *are* a sorry lot," they might be brought to think and feel, when, empathically, they view themselves as the weak see them, thereby ceding an authority to the weak to see and evaluate them (the strong) as they really are.

But what can get the weak from contempt for the strong to the attitude of moral *blame*? And what would get the strong from empathically felt self-contempt, or shame, to self-blame or guilt? This remains a lacuna in Nietzsche's account, one, indeed, that might plausibly be filled by twenty-first-century evolutionary accounts that descend from "English psychologists" like Darwin, which hold that the psychological capacities for mutual accountability were the result of human natural selection (see esp. Tomasello 2016; Buchanan and Powell 2018).[20]

Taking Responsibility: The Supra-Moral Autonomous Individual

Genealogy's second essay presents another Nietzschean route to the development of a distinctively moral conscience ("bad conscience," as Nietzsche calls it), which, although it involves *ressentiment*, also makes use of other elements. Perhaps it can close the gap we have noted in the first essay's account.

The essay begins with a sentence that announces its theme: "To breed an animal with the prerogative to *promise* – is that not precisely the paradoxical task which nature has set herself with regard to humankind? Is it not

[20] Tomasello, especially, argues that psychological mechanisms of perspective taking necessary for mutual accountability are both selected for by biological evolution and evident in young human children, though they are lacking in other animal species (Engelmann and Tomasello 2019).

the real problem *of* humankind?" (Nietzsche 2007: 35). Since the second essay concerns the development of moral conscience, we might initially assume that by "the prerogative to promise," Nietzsche means the default standing that we normally think persons have *within* morality to give and receive promises and, more broadly, to exercise normative moral powers of the kind Pufendorf explicated in his moral theory (Darwall 2023a: 65–86). And, indeed, much of the essay is concerned with the social cultivation of habits of mind – specifically, of memory and the "forgetfulness" necessary to defer gratification ("the active ability to suppress") – required for ordinary moral agency. The standing to make ordinary promises depends on presupposed psychological capacities to hold promises in mind and to distract oneself from attractive opportunities for breaking them. Only societies with established "moralit[ies] of custom" can socially straitjacket members to make them sufficiently "predictable" that others will want to have a promissory relation to them (Nietzsche 2007: 36).

It later becomes clear, however, that although Nietzsche is partly focused on the development of moral conscience, the feeling of guilt, and the capacity to enter into *moral* promissory relations, his ultimate goal is to explain the acquisition of a *higher* "prerogative to promise" that can occur only "at the end of this immense process" of social and moral disciplining (36). Only then does the process bear its "ripest fruit": the "*sovereign individual*," who, "freed . . . from the morality of custom" and, indeed, from morality itself, genuinely has a "privilege of *responsibility*" *for themselves* (37). Only such freed individuals, unconstrained by moralities and morality, can genuinely take responsibility for themselves both for their own life and when they give their word to other higher individuals in a Nietzschean "higher community" (Nietzsche 1999: 18; Young 2010: 373).

We shall return to Nietzsche's vision of a post-moral individuality that can uniquely affirm life in our final section. First, however, we should consider whether Nietzsche's account of the development of moral conscience in the second essay can fill the gap we noted in his first essay account. Does Nietzsche have materials there that can explain the emergence of the conscientious feeling of *guilt* along with the deontic moral concepts – accountability, moral obligation, culpability, and so on – that are necessary to make sense of that feeling?

Nietzsche tauntingly asks of other "genealogists of morality" – his "English psychologists" – whether they have "up to now ever remotely dreamt that, for example, the main moral concept '*Schuld*' ('guilt') descends from the very material concept of '*Schulden*' ('debts')? Or that punishment, as *retribution*, evolved quite independently of any assumption about freedom or lack of freedom of the will?" (Nietzsche 2007: 39). The idea of debt is arguably as old as social humanity itself (Graeber 2011). People have been incurring debts and settling accounts as long as they have been able to borrow, whether objects or fungible currency, or to set a price on dishonoring insults and injuries in honor cultures. Systems of credit and debt of all kinds depend on mutually agreed and acknowledged methods of repayment. And this can be done entirely through socially established conventions that are not actually normative in the philosopher's sense. Most importantly, no assumption of free will is required, and it does not matter what goes on in creditors and debtors' minds. No feeling of obligation that presupposes freedom, as in Kant's "fact of reason," is required (Kant 1996b: 5:30–31). Indeed, for any "ordinary" debt, we can sensibly ask whether we are morally obligated to pay it in a way that guarantees normative reason for us to do so.[21]

Primitive systems of punishment, Nietzsche argues, were, similarly, systems of strict liability. There was no assumption that law breakers were justifiably sanctioned because they had freely chosen to act as they did in full knowledge that they should not have so acted and with the capacity to choose not to do so out of that very knowledge. The capacities that modern moral philosophers like Pufendorf and Kant treat as necessary for the very possibility of moral obligation and accountability were not assumed. "Throughout most of human history, punishment has *not* been meted out *because* the miscreant was held responsible for his act," Nietzsche writes. "Rather, as parents still punish their children, it was out of anger over some wrong that had been suffered" (Nietzsche 2007: 40).

So far, this makes punishment the same as angry retaliation not only without assumptions of moral agency but also without any notion or measure of what the violator (or scofflaw, in the case of ordinary debts) owes as a consequence. This element came along with sociocultural development. "No form of civilization has been discovered which is so low that it did not display something of this relationship. Fixing prices, setting values, working out equivalents, exchanging – this preoccupied man's first thoughts to such a degree that in a certain sense it *constitutes* thought" (45). Ultimately, Nietzsche argues, "the feeling of guilt, of personal obligation" resulted (45). For it to do so, however, the payment of debt had to include an *internal* price. It was not enough for violators and scofflaws to give up

[21] For an argument that moral obligation or debt can be understood as a kind of ordinary debt, see Hockett and James 2020. For a criticism, see Darwall 2023b.

some external good ("money, land or possessions of any kind") (41). Otherwise, wrongdoers would view their punishment as we often view the payment of a parking fine. In addition, those to whom the debt was owed were given an additional benefit, a "*pleasure*" consisting in "the right to exercise power over the powerless" debtor and thereby cause them *pain* (41).

This gets us closer to a feeling of guilt and what Nietzsche calls "bad conscience," but we are still not there. Guilt is no doubt a painful feeling, but it is one that is experienced as *deserved* and through which one appreciates the culpable wrong one has freely chosen to do. It involves the sense, as Pufendorf put it, that any evil the violator suffers "falls upon him justly" (Pufendorf 1934: 91). Nietzsche is clear, however, that even with all the materials he has assembled thus far, "punishment [only] makes men harder and colder, it concentrates, it sharpens the feeling of alienation; it strengthens the power to resist," as anyone who knows much about contemporary carceral states can readily attest (Foucault 1995; Nietzsche 2007: 54). It is worth noting, by the way, that with this very observation, Nietzsche himself implicitly attributes a sense of justice and deontic morality to illegitimately punished prisoners. Usually what hardens and alienates the imprisoned is the vivid sense that they are being unjustly treated, as they themselves feel in their consciences.

For Nietzsche, however, conscience in this "bad" form is a creation of *ressentiment*, which, when "not discharged outwardly *turns inwards*" (Nietzsche 2007: 57). Not able to retaliate against those who have them in their power, the person "of ressentiment" turns against and "persecute[s]" themselves (21, 57). Their pain is not simply caused by an alien force but by them themselves. This is aided and abetted, Nietzsche argues, by the religious ideology of the West, most obviously by Christianity. Once we have the idea that "moral" debts are all owed to God, who has given his only son to redeem our debts, we are saddled with two infinite debts (61–63). We owe God for any and every moral violation, and on top of that, we owe God an infinite debt of gratitude. This is, Nietzsche says, "*Christianity*'s stroke of genius": "None other than God sacrificing himself for man's debt, none other than God paying himself back, God as the only one able to redeem man from what, to man himself, has become irredeemable – the creditor sacrificing himself for his debtor, out of love (would you credit it? –), out of *love* for his debtor!" (63). Brilliant as this is, however, it gets us no closer to moral conscience conceived in terms of moral accountability. Even if a debt is infinite, unless it is already framed as a normative *moral* debt, one to which the fitting response is moral guilt, we simply have an infinite "ordinary" debt with respect to which the normative question of whether to pay it remains conceptually open. And *ressentiment* can add nothing that really helps close the gap here anymore than it could in the first essay. Even if it gives both ordinary folk and higher types a vivid sense of how shameful we all are for our transgressions of God's will and for putting ourselves in infinite arrears, that cannot give us a feeling of guilt of having acted culpably, unless we already have what it takes to conceive of ourselves as morally responsible, in this case, to God.

Nietzsche's Positive Ethical View: Affirmation of (Higher) Life

As we noted, Nietzsche reserves "the prerogative to promise" and "the privilege of responsibility" for "higher men" who live beyond morality. Clearly part of what Nietzsche means is that the "sovereign individual" can take a kind of responsibility for their own lives, in relation to their "own *standard of value*," which is quite different from that of ordinary moral agents (37). But given the centrality of "higher communities" to Nietzsche's vision of the life of "higher men," it seems likely that he also has in mind a kind of "prerogative to promise" that involves the standing to be trusted within such a higher community. Dannenberg plausibly interprets Nietzsche in this way and gives the vivid illustration of twentieth-century Idaho cattlemen who reserved for honored peers the prerogative to promise and be taken at one's word (Dannenberg 2017).[22] For these ranchers, as for Nietzsche's "higher men," who would not lower themselves to break their word, it was sign of respect; it thereby included them in a "higher community."

This kind of higher integrity within a community that sees themselves as realizing and mutually appreciating higher values and also their "sovereign individuality" (the men in Dannenberg's example are, quite literally, "cowboys") is essential to Nietzsche's positive post-moral ethos. In this final section, we shall fill in some (but only some) of the other elements that Nietzsche holds to be central to the higher post-moral life. For various reasons, we can be relatively brief here.

First, Nietzsche is significantly less detailed and systematic in laying out his positive vision than he is in his critique of morality. Much of his positive view is expressed in *Thus Spake Zarathustra*, which is significantly more literary than the more philosophical works we have considered. Second, those modern ethical philosophers who have been influenced by Nietzsche's

[22] Including Dannenberg's grandfather. Steven Pinker argues that, unlike farmers, cattlemen, and herders more generally, are likely to form honor cultures (Pinker 2011).

critique, like Bernard Williams, Philippa Foot, and Annette Baier, though they heartily endorse certain broad elements of Nietzsche's view – for example, its emphasis on physical and emotional health, esthetic experience, and affirmation of life. But many, if not almost all, also reject central aspects of his positive view: for example, its sexism, racism, and other forms of contemning exclusion (Williams 1985; Foot 1991; Baier 1993: 448). Probably no current philosopher moved by Nietzsche's morality critique, or even by other aspects of his positive view, would endorse the celebration of exploitative hierarchy expressed in the following passage from *Beyond Good and Evil*: Aristocracy "accepts in good conscience the sacrifice of countless people who have to be pushed down and shrunk into incomplete human beings, into slaves, into tools, all *for the sake of the aristocracy*" (Nietzsche 2002: 152).[23] We can therefore be relatively brief when it comes to Nietzsche's own positive view (especially since his vision of a society that says yes to life is one that says no to so many people). It is his critique of morality that has had a greater footprint in modern ethical philosophy.

Still, there is much in Nietzsche's positive view and even, indeed, in his devaluing of (distorted conceptions of) morality, that is appealing. As we can see in more orthodox critics of deontic morality like Shaftesbury, Leibniz, Hutcheson, and Hume, there is a strain of religiously based moralism, some of it springing from what Hume calls "superstition," that can give rise to what he calls the "monkish virtues," the deprecating names he gives them (see esp. Hume 1985b: 270). Especially against this dismal background, Nietzschean virtues of creativity, health, vigor, cheerful community, and joyful affirmation seem refreshing and attractive.

Here as elsewhere, we learn much about Nietzsche's positive values by looking to his life. Afflicted with severe health problems, Nietzsche devoted great attention to his health, specifically, walking and hiking countless hours, especially in his beloved Swiss alps near Sils Maria. He was also someone who was remarkably cheerful in his interactions with others (see, e.g., Young 2010: 182). Although he was a sharp and steady critic of the altruism championed by Schopenhauer (and, indeed, Rée), he nonetheless championed a kind of giving to others rooted in the power and vigor of the giver (like God's overflowing goodness) (see Young 2010: 348).[24] Nietzsche's "heroic" egoist's giving to others is an expression of their will to power.

[23] In *Twilight of the Idols*, Nietzsche remarks that the modern "doctrine of equality," which he associates there with Rousseau, should be regarded "with *disgust*" (Nietzsche 2005: 221).

[24] Young there quotes a fascinating letter from Salomé to Nietzsche in which she says that she prefers the Nietzschean form of giving to the vision she finds in Rée's thought.

Finally, it is difficult to imagine a more emphatic expression of affirmation for life than Nietzsche's doctrine of "eternal recurrence" or *amor fati*. Expressed in *Beyond Good and Evil* and other works, this is Nietzsche's idea that the test of affirmation for one's life is whether one would want to live it all over again, eternally (Nehamas 1985).[25] "The ideal of the most high-spirited, vital, world-affirming individual, who has learned not just to accept and go along with what was and what is, but who wants it against *just as it was and is* through all eternity, insatiably shouting *da capo* not just to himself but to the whole play and performance" (Nietzsche 2002: 50–51). This is a vision that has inspired even many who deplore several other aspects of Nietzsche's ethical views.[26]

[25] Young provides plausible evidence that Nietzsche first formulated this doctrine in connection with his discovery of Spinoza in 1881 (Young 2010: 319–320).

[26] A striking example is Anne Boyer, a committed communist, who wrote an unflinching memoir of her experience with breast cancer as a single parent at the age of forty, which included radical mastectomy and extensive chemotherapy: "Nietzsche has this thing, *amor fati*, in which his hope is to so embrace fate . . . the suffering and the ugliness as well as the goodness – that eventually he is a complete 'yes,' an embodied . . . 'yes.' Inside of my essay [*The Undying*], the 'no' serves as this invisible armor around a deeper mystery, which is what we can truly love, what we truly want to say yes to" (Boyer 2019).

PART III

Sources of Naturalistic Utilitarianism

When Nietzsche disparaged the "English utilitarians" in *Beyond Good and Evil* in 1886, he was referring to followers of Jeremy Bentham (1748–1832), most prominently to John Stuart Mill (1806–1873), whose *Utilitarianism* was published as a series of articles in 1861 and then as a book in 1863. Mill took the term "utilitarianism" from Bentham, who coined it in his "Article on Utilitarianism" in 1829, though he had provided a canonical version of the theory in his landmark *Introduction to the Principles of Morals and Legislation*, published f in 1780, but more authoritatively in 1789 (Bentham 1983, 1996). There was, however, a lot of utilitarian theorizing before Bentham, much of it quite sophisticated.[1]

Although Bentham was influenced as much by Helvétius's *De l'esprit* (1758) and Beccaria's *On Crimes and Punishments* (1764) as by Hume's *Treatise* (1740), Nietzsche was certainly right in characterizing utilitarianism as a distinctively "English" (more accurately, British) doctrine (Helvétius 1759; Beccaria 1986; Hume 1978). Albee calls Richard Cumberland, whose *Treatise of the Laws of Nature* was published in 1672, "the true founder of English Utilitarianism" (Albee 1957: 1; Cumberland 2005). Two better-known British writers, Hutcheson (1694–1746) and George Berkeley (1685–1753), also developed utilitarian theories. Berkeley formulated what is arguably the first version of rule utilitarianism and Hutcheson advanced a utilitarian theory of rights that anticipated by over a century Mill's more famous version. In addition, there was a long British tradition of *theological utilitarianism*, beginning with John Gay (1685–1732), and running through Berkeley, Abraham Tucker (1705–1774), and others, culminating in William Paley (1743–1805), whose *Principles of Moral and Political Philosophy* (1785) became a frequently assigned text in Cambridge and helped shape the British intellectual elite of the late

[1] For extensive discussions of Cumberland, Hutcheson, and Hume, see Darwall 2023a.

eighteenth and nineteenth centuries (Albee 1957: 98).[2] It was the appearance of this work that prompted Bentham to publish the fuller version of his *Introduction to the Principles* in 1789 (Bentham 1996: li).[3]

Utilitarianism was also the ideology of capitalist development in England during this same period. A particularly dramatic illustration is Dickens's *Hard Times* (1854) and its character Mr. Gradgrind. Dickens depicts Gradgrind as a strict utilitarian who is concerned only with profit and quantitative economic analysis. At the same time, utilitarianism provided the theoretical underpinnings of English social and political reform. Legal reform, especially of common law, was the primary impetus for almost all of Bentham's works, and Bentham was surrounded by a circle of "Philosophical Radicals" – including James Mill (1772–1836, John Stuart's father) – who were bent on extending the suffrage and undermining traditional British legal and customary hierarchy (Seth Pringle-Patterson 1907; Postema 1986). This group gave Mill his early education, and he carried forward its reformist spirit, both in early essays on legislation benefitting vested interests, like the Corn Laws, and, most prominently, in his later feminist collaboration with Harriet Taylor (1807–1858), *The Subjection of Women*, published in 1869 (1984). Bentham was a supporter of women's legal rights as well (Williford 1975).

The "English Utilitarians" were also prominent critics of the Atlantic slave trade. Hutcheson argued strongly against chattel slavery in his *System of Moral Philosophy* (Hutcheson 1755: v. ii. 301) (Barry 2014). And Mill provided a devastating reply to Thomas Carlyle's racist tract, which Mill titled, civilizing Carlyle's, "On the Negro Question."[4] Slavery, Mill said, "can have no place in any society even pretending to be founded on justice" (Mill 2004: 112).

[2] See Mahieu's foreword (Paley 2002: xi).

[3] If Bentham hoped his secular version of utilitarianism would supplant Paley, his success would not come for quite a while. Schneewind points out that "it was not until the middle of the 1830s that [Bentham] began to be taken seriously as a philosopher by philosophers" (Schneewind 1977: 130). According to Schneewind, it took Whewell's criticism and Mill's defense to bring Bentham's writings into philosophical prominence.

[4] Carlyle's piece was republished as "On the N*gg*r Question" (Carlyle 1853). In it he holds Christian sentimentalists and utilitarian political economists responsible for reluctant free Black labor on sugar plantations in the British colonies in the West Indies, which tended, he argues, to increase poverty in England. This essay is the origin of the characterization of economics as the "dismal science." Although it is often believed that the term derives from Malthus, it seems much likelier that it comes from Carlyle's contention that utilitarian political economy had led to English penury, hence to the "negrifying" of British subjects (Levy 2002). In other words, the condition of the British working classes, Carlyle thought, would become as "dismal" as that of enslaved peoples in the Caribbean.

In this section, we shall consider the development of this remarkable line of British utilitarians. We will mostly concentrate on Bentham and Mill but we will begin with the sources of utilitarian ideas in earlier British writers. Anglophone utilitarianism hardly ends with Mill; its most systematic expositor was Henry Sidgwick, whom we will discuss after Mill. And it runs throughout the twentieth century also, in ideal versions, such as in Moore's *Principia Ethica* (1903) and later similar consequentialisms like Parfit's formulations in *Reasons and Persons* (1984) – and in hedonistic or preference-satisfaction versions that are reminiscent of Bentham's and Mill's, as in R. M. Hare's *Moral Thinking* (1980) and Richard Brandt's "Toward a Credible Form of Utilitarianism" (1963) (Brandt 1963; Hare 1980; Parfit 1984; Moore 1993a).

It is noteworthy that the forms that utilitarianism took before Sidgwick were almost invariably empiricist and naturalist. To such positions, Sidgwick will pose a challenge similar to, but ultimately deeper than, Moore's more famous charge that such positions inevitably commit a "naturalistic fallacy" (Moore 1993a). In Sidgwick's version, empiricist-naturalist theories that attempt to understand ethical concepts and properties in empirical-natural terms all fail to account for their normativity. That accounting can be done, Sidgwick argues, only by recognizing that all ethical judgments contain "the fundamental notion represented by the word 'ought'" (Sidgwick 1962: 25). This is a challenge that confronts all versions of British utilitarianism before Sidgwick, as we shall see.

Also on display in this section will be the remarkable variety of utilitarian positions. Most prominent is the division between theological and secular versions, but even among theological versions, there is an important divide between voluntarist varieties, like those of Berkeley, Gay, Tucker, and Paley, and nonvoluntarist theories, like those of Hutcheson and, on one interpretation, Butler. It may seem odd to classify Butler as a utilitarian, but since he holds that God's benevolent will is the source of conscience, which determines rules of right, he might be thought of as a kind of rule (or perhaps, conscience) utilitarian. In effect, for Butler, it is God who should follow utilitarian principles. Also, although Cumberland presents his view in theological voluntarist terms, these are merely window dressing, since only natural sanctions figure in his theory and the theological and the voluntarist aspects are ultimately reduced away. Not only is Cumberland the first "English utilitarian," he is arguably also the first philosopher to put forward the kind of empiricist-naturalist reductionism that has been such an important strand of empiricist utilitarianism, indeed of empiricist metaethics, ever since.

Another major divide within utilitarianism is that between "direct" or "act utilitarianism," on the one hand, and such "indirect" forms as "rule utilitarianism" (or "conscience utilitarianism"), on the other. Hutcheson and Bentham both seem clearly to hold that a person morally ought always to do whatever would maximize utility. And rule utilitarianism finds adherents in Berkeley and, arguably, Mill.

In Mill's case, this is related to his response to the challenge that issues of rights and justice pose to utilitarianism. Although Hutcheson proposed the first utilitarian theory of rights, he failed to appreciate its conflict with his act-utilitarian theory of morally choiceworthiness.[5] Like Spinoza and Shaftesbury, Hutcheson tended to downplay the concepts and terms of deontic morality, and, against the modern mainstream, he ignored the conceptual correlativity of rights and duties. It is a conceptual truth that a person can have a right to someone else's doing something only if the latter is obligated to the former to do it. For Hutcheson, what a person morally should do is entirely independent of what justice requires of them. Moral choice is dictated for Hutcheson, as we shall see, only by benevolence.

Mill sees the conceptual connection between deontic morality and accountability, and this ends up affecting his view of moral obligation also, so that his normative position turns in the direction of rule utilitarianism. This guarantees that rights and obligations track together. Utility-maximizing practices in which people are held accountable for complying with the rules that structure the practices simultaneously create correlative rights and duties. Mill is quite explicit about the conceptual entailments of deontic morality. "We do not call anything wrong," he says, "unless we mean to imply that a person ought to be punished . . . for doing it . . . [for example], by the reproaches of his own conscience" (Mill 2002: 5.14).

Rights and justice have had at best a tenuous relationship to utilitarianism. Some utilitarians, like Bentham, deny anything like natural rights, although they of course support utility-producing social and legal institutions and practices that encode social and legal rights. As Bentham famously put it, the idea of natural rights is "nonsense upon stilts" (Bentham 2002: 330). Another approach, followed by William Godwin (1756–1836), is to argue that justice is already incorporated into the principle of utility: "it is just that I should do all the good that is in my power" (Godwin 2013: 56).[6] Justice for Godwin is a matter of equality and impartiality, which is

[5] For a more extended discussion of Hutcheson's theory of rights see Darwall 2022b.

[6] Whether Godwin is aptly understood as a utilitarian is discussed in Lamb 2014.

already entailed by what Mill called "Bentham's dictum, 'everybody to count for one, nobody for more than one'" (Mill 2002: V.36). Mill also mentions this as a conception of justice, although it is ultimately not his own (Mill 2002: V.9–10). Mill's considered view is that doing all the good one can be unjust, as in Hume's case of helping those in need rather than repaying a loan to a "seditious bigot" (Hume 1978: 497).

Utilitarians have historically been in the forefront of movements of social and legal reform, as we noted earlier. This was certainly true of Bentham and Godwin, and it was even more obviously of Mill.[7] But again, their support for legal, political, and social rights does not mean that utilitarians uniformly accept *natural* rights. Yet another combination involves supporting natural rights without rejecting an act-utilitarian account of moral choice, as seems required by the correlativity of rights and duties. Hutcheson is a prominent instance of this.

Finally, Hutcheson also provides an example of a kind of utilitarianism that rejects the very categories of deontic morality. Mill's conceptual claim that "we do not call anything wrong" unless it is something we would aptly blame someone for if they had no excuse creates a dilemma for utilitarians. Either they must, like Mill in *Utilitarianism*'s chapter V, opt for some form of indirect utilitarianism or, on the other hand, reject deontic moral concepts and formulate their utilitarian view in terms of moral *choice-worthiness*, as Hutcheson does. In this respect, Hutcheson may be the first example of what today is called "scalar utilitarianism" (Norcross 2020).

[7] Godwin was a strong supporter of women's rights, as was, even more prominently, his spouse, Mary Wollstonecraft (1759–1797). Although Godwin's thought is certainly utilitarian in its most important respects, there seems little reason to think that Wollstonecraft's famous *Vindication of the Rights of Woman* (1792) was utilitarian in any significant respect (Wollstonecraft 1995).

CHAPTER 6

Early Modern Prologue

We turn now to canvassing the rich utilitarian or proto-utilitarian tradition before Bentham, beginning with Cumberland.

Cumberland

Since Cumberland's moral philosophy is discussed at length in Darwall (2023a), we need only rehearse those aspects that are particularly significant for the history of utilitarianism.[1] We have already noted Albee's remark that Cumberland is the "true founder of English Utilitarianism" (Albee 1957: 1). In the same vein, Sidgwick calls Cumberland "the precursor of the later utilitarianism" (Sidgwick 1964: 174). Clearly, what Sidgwick and Albee have in mind when they so characterize Cumberland's thought are such claims as that following the "Laws of Nature" leads to the "greatest Happiness of *all* rational Agents" (Cumberland 2005: 487). Even in this passage, however, there are two elements of Cumberland's thought that are unusual among canonical utilitarians. One is that Cumberland quickly adds that following moral laws leads to "to *our own* [happiness] in particular" (487). What Cumberland calls the "best Effect" is thus the greatest *common* good, that is, the greatest good of all and, simultaneously, the agent's greatest good (258). The second is that Cumberland thinks of himself as, and was understood by his contemporaries and historians to be, a kind of theological voluntarist. It is essential for Cumberland that he present the proto-utilitarian moral law as *"promulg'd by competent Authority* [God] *with Rewards and Punishments annex'd*" (253). As it turns out, however, both the idea of God's competent authority and that of divine punishment or reward are reduced away, so that they can be fully understood in secular, empiricist-naturalist terms.

[1] What follows draws on Darwall 2023a: 100–110.

Since it played such a little role for later utilitarians, we can ignore Cumberland's claim that the best outcome is not just the greatest aggregate happiness but also the greatest happiness of the agent as well. Many later utilitarians – Bentham, for example – hold that the best *rational* outcome of action is always the agent's own greatest happiness, but they tend to deny that this in any way conditions the morally best "effect." Many were (and still are) very much influenced by Cumberland's empiricist-naturalist program, however, so it is worth saying something more detailed about that.

Cumberland is a reductionist both in normative ethics and in metaethics. At the normative level, he argues that "all the Laws of Nature" or "true Rules of Morality" can be "reduc'd to that one, of Benevolence towards all Rationals," where benevolence is understood to aim at the "common Happiness of all rational Beings" (237, 413).[2] And in metaethics, Cumberland's project is to show that "the Whole of *moral Philosophy*, and of the Laws of Nature, is ultimately resolv'd into *natural Observations* known by the Experience of all Men, or into Conclusions of true *Natural Philosophy*" (291). Unlike contemporary naturalists, however, Cumberland hastens to add that he intends "*Natural Philosophy*" to be understood in a "large Sense" that includes empirical inquiry into "the Nature of our *Souls*" no less than "*natural Bodies*" (291).

We will see other forms of theological voluntarist utilitarianism in Berkeley and Paley, but it is important to Cumberland to reduce the theological voluntarist frame of his view to empiricist-naturalist terms also. Partly this was a matter of insisting that the sanctions that enforce God's law are entirely natural and independent of anything involving eternal rewards and torments. The supernatural sanctions that are so important for Locke's account of morality play no role in establishing the law of nature as Cumberland understands it.

Formally, again, Cumberland holds that law must be "*promulg'd by competent Authority*" (253). But God's authority is ultimately not independent of a proper understanding of natural law itself. As Cumberland puts it,

> It amounts to the same thing, when we *say*, "That the Obligation is an Act of the Legislator," or of the First Cause; as if in this place we had *call'd* it, "An Act of the Law of Nature." For the Legislator obliges by the Law sufficiently promulg'd, and he sufficiently promulges it, when he *discovers* to our Minds, "That the prosecution of the Common Good is the Cause necessarily requisite to that Happiness, which every one necessarily desires" (555).

[2] "True Rules of Morality" is Maxwell's translation of "veris Morum regulis" (Cumberland 1683: 118–119).

It turns out, therefore, that both the existence of normative reason for following natural law's "Direction" and the obligatory normative force that is distinctive of moral law are both reduced to the empiricist-naturalistic generalization that is the natural law's content (145). Thus are "*moral Philosophy*" and "the Laws of Nature ... ultimately resolv'd into *natural Observations* known by the Experience of all Men, or into Conclusions of true *Natural Philosophy*" (291).

There are yet other aspects of Cumberland's view that are important for subsequent utilitarianism. When it comes to agency and the will, for example, Cumberland holds the traditional view that all action aims at some good, but he modifies it in two important ways. First, he takes action to be fundamentally *instrumental* and, therefore, to be capable of being justified only by the goodness of natural *effects* it realizes. And second, he takes these justifying effects to include others' goods no less than the agent's, since they are no less good. In the latter modification, he anticipates Sidgwick's well-known claim that "the good of any one individual" is no more important than that of any other from "the point of view ... of the Universe" (Sidgwick 1962: 382).

Cumberland writes: "'The Understanding, is capable of judging, what promotes the Good of others, as well as what promotes our own'; nor is there any *Reason*, 'Why we cannot will those same things, which we have judg'd to be good'" (Cumberland 2005: 473). Thus we can will others' good no less than our own. But whose good is it morally right to realize? "When we are enquiring into the *Right* of Acting, the *Question* is, 'Which among those Actions which are in our *power*, are *lawful?*' ... Any one *can* either hang, or throw down a Precipice, either himself, or any other innocent Person" (359–360).

Having raised the question, Cumberland answers that the good of others is no less good, and so no less choice worthy, than the agent's own good. It follows, Cumberland argues, that "*Reason* will not suffer, that the greatest *Private* Good should be propos'd as the *ultimate End*" (529). Were that so, "*Actions* truly *Good* will be in *mutual opposition* to one another, which is impossible" (529). When people's goods conflict, moreover, "there is no Cause, why the Happiness of one of these should be his ultimate End, rather than the Happiness of another should likewise be his ultimate End" (529). Cumberland therefore concludes that "Reason dictates" to no one that they "should propose to" themselves their "own Happiness only" as their "greatest End" (529). That, rather, is "that *Common Good*, which we contend is to be sought after" (529).

For Cumberland, then, there is one fundamental ethical standard, the good, more precisely, the goodness of "effects." Whether conduct is justified or dictated by practical reason depends only on the goodness of its effects, and others' goods are no less good than the agent's own. It follows that reason must dictate to every agent that they pursue their own good "in conjunction with the Happiness of others" (529). "Let *Hobbes* tell me," Cumberland writes, "what the addition of a *proper name* does, toward making the former Proposition [that each act only for their own self-preservation] a *more evident* Dictate of Reason," than that each should promote the happiness of all (532). What Cumberland is really objecting to is Hobbes's use of the reflexive, first-person pronoun. Ruling out agent-relativity is a deep feature of a view of practical reason that takes the goodness (*simpliciter*) of an effect as what most fundamentally underlies there being reason to aim at it. This will show itself also in Moore's well-known "refutation" of egoism in *Principia Ethica* (Moore 1993a: 99–102).

Cumberland concludes that the "common Good is the best and greatest End, which [rational beings] can propose to themselves" (Cumberland 2005: 269).

> "The Happiness of All is greater than the like Happiness of any smaller Number." But "that Happiness is the greatest, which is greater than any other assignable." Nor is it a different Judgment, that by which we *affirm*, "The greatest Happiness of all Rational Beings is the greatest or chief End, which any Rational Agent can pursue" (537).

Effectively, "The greatest overall happiness" is the naturalistic content of the "best end." Cumberland says that his "*Method*" is to show "how to reduce whatsoever the Moralists have said concerning the Means of obtaining the best End, into *Theorems* concerning the *Power* of human Actions in producing the Effects propos'd" (259). Once "best end" is interpreted naturalistically as "greatest overall happiness," natural philosophy suffices to establish truths concerning what will best promote it. Thus does empirical naturalism ground utilitarianism as a normative ethical theory.

Hutcheson

As with Cumberland, we can dispense with an extended discussion of Hutcheson (see, e.g., Darwall 2023a: 172–182). There are, however, elements of Hutcheson's thought that are particularly important for understanding the history of utilitarianism. Hutcheson provides the first formulation of the greatest happiness principle in English; he anticipates Sidgwick's "dualism of practical reason" in its distinctive hedonistic form, with utilitarianism being one of practical reason's two options (the other being egoistic hedonism); he formulates the first utilitarian theory of rights; and his making overall utility a standard of moral choiceworthiness rather than right anticipates scalar utilitarianisms of our own time.

What is perhaps most remarkable about Hutcheson's utilitarianism, however, is that it is ultimately grounded in an ethics of moral virtue. Unlike what Scanlon calls "philosophical utilitarianism," according to which "the only fundamental moral facts are facts about individual well-being," Hutcheson begins with axioms about morally good motivation and derives his version of utilitarianism from that (Scanlon 1982: 108). Metaethically, Hutcheson is a sentimentalist, or, as he puts it, a "moral sense" theorist. According to Hutcheson, who follows Locke in thinking that every simple idea must have a dedicated sense, the existence of a moral sense is entailed by our having the "simple," irreducibly moral idea of approbation (and its contrary condemnation). Approbation and condemnation are distinctive feelings we have when we contemplate certain motives. A motive's being morally good, then, consists in its being one that "procures" approbation when contemplated disinterestedly in a way that enables us to see the motive as it really is (Hutcheson 2004: 85, 217).

Hutcheson believes that all motives that can be shown in this way to be morally good are instances of benevolence and that the most "extensive" forms of benevolence are morally best (123). The morally best motive, then, is an impartial desire for the happiness of each and every creature (or human being, if we so restrict our attention).[3] It follows, Hutcheson thinks, that the morally best motive is a desire for the greatest happiness of the greatest number. And from that, he concludes that the morally best and most morally choice worthy act is whatever produces the greatest overall happiness: "that Action is best, which procures the greatest Happiness for the greatest Numbers; and that, worst, which, in like manner, occasions Misery" (2004: 125).

This is the reverse of what will come to be the orthodox utilitarian reasoning. A "philosophical utilitarian" begins with claims about human well-being and the goodness of its being realized and derives claims both about the choiceworthiness of acts and the moral goodness of motives from that. Hutcheson turns this on its head. And here lies an interesting story about the passage of utilitarian ideas from Hutcheson to Hume to Bentham. I discuss the details of this story in Darwall (1994) but will sketch the outlines here. Its basic irony is that although Bentham's act

[3] Hutcheson was also a great supporter of the rightness of promoting animal well-being (Garrett 2007).

utilitarianism is much closer to Hutcheson's view than to anything in Hume, and although Hume takes his basic metaethics from Hutcheson, it was Hume rather than Hutcheson that influenced Bentham's moral theory. Bentham wrote that when he read the *Treatise*, he "felt as if the scales had fallen from [his] eyes"; he "learnt to see that *utility* was the test and measure of all virtue" (Bentham 1977: 440–441). This was close to the reverse of Hutcheson's thought.

Hutcheson and Hume agree in being sentimentalists and that a sentimentalist metaethics grounds an ethics of virtue. As Hume puts it, "the external performance has no merit" (Hume 1978: 477). It is the motive that is worthy of esteem, not conduct considered independently of its motive. But whereas Hutcheson thinks that all motives worthy of approbation are instances of benevolence, Hume denies this. He agrees with Butler that virtuous motives include those of honesty and justice, among others, even though, he says, justice is an "artificial" rather than a "natural" virtue. It is, however, what grounds this difference between Hutcheson and Hume that explains Hume's influence on Bentham; so far as we know, Hutcheson had none.

For Hutcheson, approbation is a simple moral idea. Though Hume sometimes uses the language of moral sense to refer to "approbation," it quickly becomes clear that he has in mind a response that is neither simple nor distinctively moral. As a Newtonian, Hume was always trying to explain phenomena with the simplest posits, and he thought he had an explanation for the sentiment of approbation that did not rely on a dedicated "moral sense." Although Hume's explanation was not itself simple, it relied on general human psychological capacities of "sympathy" – in Hume's distinctive meaning, which is closer to emotional contagion – and the association of ideas. Roughly, his idea was that when we contemplate a motive disinterestedly, our attention naturally passes to the usual consequences of the motive; if these include pleasure from people who benefit from the motive, our sympathy then turns the idea of this pleasure into a pleasurable feeling in us. This pleasurable feeling, felt on contemplating some motive, is what Hume takes the moral sentiment to be.

But this means that utility turns out to be the "test and measure of all virtue," just as Bentham said. Moreover, it means that there need be no sharp line between moral virtues and "natural" estimable features that are not moral. A favorite example of Hume's is wit. Wit has value in the same way benevolence does for Hume; it is something that it is beneficial, both to its possessor and to others who enjoy it, and therefore has "merit." Any difference between moral and nonmoral meritorious features is, Hume says, purely "verbal" (Hume 1978: 606). And it also means that the virtues we will want to call "moral" will include many more than benevolence. They will include roughly the virtues Butler insisted on against Hutcheson. They will include all motives and character traits the having of which tends to produce utility.

But there is another respect in which Hutcheson was closer to Bentham than Hume was. And that was that, quite unlike Hume, Hutcheson recognized the moral choiceworthiness of *acts*, and not just the good of motivated actions, *and* that he advanced a version of the greatest happiness principle as the morally preferred standard of choice. This was albeit derivative from his ethics of virtue, but the point is that he made this utilitarian claim about the choiceworthiness of acts in a way that Hume never did.

Another striking utilitarian aspect of Hutcheson's thought was his theory of rights, which is at least as sophisticated as Mill's. "Whenever it appears to us," Hutcheson writes, "that a Faculty of doing, demanding, or possessing any thing, universally allow'd in certain Circumstances, would in the whole tend to the general Good, we say that any person in such Circumstances, has a Right to do, possess, or demand that Thing" (Hutcheson 2004: 182). Moreover, Hutcheson uses this theory to distinguish "perfect," or claim "rights," from "imperfect rights" (2004: 183; see Darwall 2023b).

Mill, however, does significantly better than Hutcheson at accounting for the distinctively deontic character of moral rights. And he does better at relating them to a utilitarian theory of right and wrong that does justice to the right's conceptual connection to accountability, as we shall see.

Hutcheson and Mill broadly agree with Cumberland in grounding their utilitarianism in an empirical approach that Mill calls "inductive" (Mill 2002: I.3), even if they are not as reductivist as Cumberland is. Sidgwick will argue against all such naturalistic attempts, as will Moore, that they necessarily fail to capture the distinctive character of ethical claims, which is irreducibly normative. All "ethical judgments," Sidgwick holds, contain "the fundamental notion represented by the word 'ought'" and so "cannot legitimately be interpreted as judgments respecting the present or future existence of human feelings or any facts of the sensible world" (Sidgwick 1962: 25). Sidgwick holds, against Mill and his empiricist predecessors like Hutcheson, that the method of ethics must be "intuitive" rather than "inductive," in Mill's terms.

Sidgwick's intuitionism is not, however, the sort that Mill most ardently opposes; it is a "philosophical intuitionism," by contrast with the complacent commonsense intuitions that Mill seeks to reform with his inductive utilitarianism. Sidgwick holds that philosophical intuitionism underwrites utilitarianism in the only way an ethical doctrine can be grounded. This is where his dualism of practical reason comes in, which leads us back to Hutcheson. Sidgwick holds that there are two potentially conflicting ultimate rational intuitions: (a) the "axiom of Prudence," which counsels agents to pursue their own greatest good and (b) the "axiom of Rational Benevolence" (Sidgwick 1962: 386–387). And both of these are hedonistic, yielding rational egoistic hedonism and hedonistic utilitarianism, respectively.

Remarkably, Hutcheson agrees with this dualism. Although he denies, like Hume, that there is any such thing as a genuinely practical reason, he nonetheless distinguishes between rationally informed "calm" desires, on the one hand, and violent passions, on the other. And he holds that reason can inform desires from two irresolvable points of view: the agent's own perspective over time and the impartial perspective of moral judgment. When maximally rationally informed, these two perspectives yield two "grand determinations, one toward our own greatest happiness, the other toward the greatest general good, each independent on the other, each capable of such strength as to strain all the particular affections of its kind, and keep them subordinate to itself" (Hutcheson 1755: I.50). Although Sidgwick credits Butler as the source of his dualism, it is really Hutcheson who stands behind it (Sidgwick 1962: xviii).

Again, Hutcheson was no friend of deontic moral categories. He called "ought" an "unlucky Word in Morals," and gave subversive redefinitions of obligation in prudential and moral sentimentalist terms (Hutcheson 2002: 146, 156). This led him to formulate his act utilitarianism not in terms of deontic morality but of moral choiceworthiness. This is a view that finds some favor among utilitarians today who want to avoid the canonical formulation of utilitarianism as a claim about morally right conduct and substitute a "scalar utilitarianism" formulated in terms of moral choiceworthiness (Norcross 2020). As we shall see, defending utilitarianism as a theory of deontic moral right is given particular stress by Mill.

Hutcheson bequeathed to scalar utilitarians even more than the fundamental shape their view should take. He also showed how quantitative techniques can be used to calculate the scalar values of effects that make the acts producing them morally choice worthy to different degrees. Since Hutcheson was steadfastly a virtue ethicist, these must be derived from the scalar values of morally good motives. But Hutcheson showed the way. In early editions of the *Inquiry*, he writes, "$M = B \times A$," where M is the "Moment of publick Good," B is a measure of the agent's benevolence, and A a measure of their ability (Hutcheson 2004: 128).

Berkeley

Berkeley is an interesting foil to Hutcheson in several respects that illustrate some of the diversity of utilitarian approaches. To begin with, Berkeley is a decidedly deontic moralist. Partly this is grounded in his theological voluntarism; but Berkeley has an entirely independent critique of nondeontic ethics that springs from an egalitarian universalist concern and, more specifically, a principled aversion to social class. The second difference is Berkeley's voluntarism. Although Hutcheson and Berkeley are both theological philosophers – it is God, for Hutcheson, who solves the dualism of practical reason by assuring that self-love and calm extensive benevolence ultimately coincide – Hutcheson in no respect shares Berkeley's voluntarism. Finally, Berkeley and Hutcheson differ in their normative views. Whereas Hutcheson gives one of the first expressions of (a scalar form of) act utilitarianism, Berkeley provides perhaps the first formulation of rule utilitarianism.[4]

Berkeley's critique of nondeontic virtue ethics is advanced as a criticism of Shaftesbury (from whom Hutcheson gets the idea of moral sense). Berkeley criticizes both Mandeville and Shaftesbury in *Alciphron* for focusing on virtue rather than moral right and wrong. Shaftesbury, in particular, ties virtue to *virtuosi*, those whose excellence is worthy of esteem, which excellence he believes only *cognoscenti* can appreciate through a cultivated moral taste or "sense." In Berkeley's view, this smacks of class snobbishness, since he doubts that there is any such thing as moral sense as Shaftesbury (and Hutcheson) conceive it. Shaftesbury trivializes morality by placing it "on the same foot with manners" (Berkeley 1964a: 3.1.13).[5]

Berkeley's objections to Shaftesbury include several strands that are worth distinguishing. First, Berkeley thought that the reflective responses that Shaftesbury attributed to a "natural moral sense" could be explained better on other grounds. To the suggestion that we detest villainy spontaneously when we contemplate it, Berkeley has Euphranor reply: "may not this be sufficiently accounted for by conscience, affection, passion,

[4] What follows draws from Darwall 2005.

[5] For some reason, Berkeley does not mention Hutcheson in his critique. Perhaps it was obvious to him that Hutcheson's moral virtue was proto-utilitarian, and hence for "the people," in a way that Shaftesbury's ethics was not.

education, reason, custom, religion; which principles and habits, for aught I know, may be what you metaphorically call a moral sense?" (3.3.6). By "conscience," Berkeley means an awareness that an act is contrary to God's will, together with a knowledge of the sanctions God will apply. What worries Berkeley most is that "moral sense" may be simply a cover for fashion: an arbitrary distinction of manners employed by "people of fashion" who wish to separate themselves from "the middle sort" and the poor (3.3.12, 3.2.3). Not only would this make morality depend on an arbitrary basis; worse, it would rest it on something that can be used to take advantage of the innocent, the vulnerable, and the poor.[6, 7]

Second, even if moral sense faithfully tracks morality as Berkeley identifies it, without divine sanctions there is no adequate motive to be moral. Shaftesbury's proposal, Berkeley writes, "seems just as wise as if a monarch should give out that there was neither jail nor executioner in his kingdom to enforce the laws, but that it would be beautiful to observe them, and that in so doing men would taste the pure delight which results from order and decorum" (3.13). By pretending to make men "heroically virtuous," Shaftesbury has "destroy[ed] the means of making them reasonably and humanly so" (3.3.13). Shaftesbury does not see this, Berkeley suggests, because of his own distance from ordinary folk. He is from "a rank above most men's ambition" and has "a conceited mind, which will ever be its own object, and contemplate mankind in its own mirror!" (3.3.13).[8]

To get to Berkeley's rule utilitarianism, we must go via his general idealist metaphysics together with his theological voluntarist metaethics. Berkeley's voluntarism is quite different from Pufendorf's or even Locke's; it depends in no way on the idea of obligations deriving from God's authority or normative power over us, not even a naturalized version of that, as in Cumberland. Pufendorf holds that God obligates us by

[6] I argue in Darwall 2005 that Berkeley's idealism also has a similar motivation, since it enables him to "speak with the vulgar" (Berkeley 1964d: 51). Those who believe in material bodies are ultimately beset with atheism and skepticism, in Berkeley's view. These are beliefs and attitudes that only those of high status can afford, since only they can order or pay those below to do the kind of labor that cannot brook skepticism.

[7] Berkeley was decidedly not, however, a reformist or "philosophical radical" in the manner of Bentham and Mill. Nor was he, like Hutcheson, a critic of slavery. To the contrary, he owned enslaved persons and justified slavery as a path to Christian conversion. Yale University, whose library began with a gift from Berkeley, also benefitted from Berkeley's slaving. Early scholarships for Yale students – "Berkeley premiums," as they were called – were funded by profits from Berkeley's farm in Rhode Island, which was worked by enslaved people (Blight 2024).

[8] See Darwall 2023a for a discussion of Hutcheson's similar criticism of Shaftesbury. It is important for Hutcheson that what motivates moral action is not moral sense but benevolence, the motive of which moral sense approves.

exercising his authority over us through second-personal address and that that presupposes that we moral agents have the powers of will necessary to hold ourselves accountable for recognizing his authoritative will and complying with it *because* he has so ordered. Locke agrees with Pufendorf on authority and juridical obligation but denies that this can motivate us; Locke claims that we can comply with God's laws only because God attaches eternal sanctions to them.[9]

Berkeley is closer to Locke than to Pufendorf. But the concept of obligating law he accepts is nothing that requires authority or normative power; it needs only the motive force of threatened sanctions. In this way, Berkeley's voluntarism is like that of his contemporaries John Clarke (1682–1757) and John Gay (1699–1745) and the later William Paley (1743–1805), whom we shall consider in the next section.

It is evident, Berkeley says, "by the light of nature," "that a God exists, who alone can make us for ever happy, or for ever miserable; it plainly follows that a conformity to His will, and not any prospect of temporal advantage, is the sole rule whereby every man who acts up to the principles of reason must govern and square his actions" (Berkeley 1964b: 6). All oughts for Berkeley are ultimately prudential. Self-love (that "principle of all others the most universal, and the most deeply engraven in our hearts") leads us to "regard things as they are fitted to augment or impair our own happiness; and accordingly [to] denominate them good or evil" (5). It is, Berkeley says, "the whole business of our lives to endeavour, by a proper application of our faculties, to procure the one and avoid the other" (5).

We ought, therefore, to do whatever God wills, since we are guaranteed to be better off in the longest run if we do. But what does God will? Here Berkeley agrees with Hutcheson. God, as omniscient and omnibenevolent, wills the greatest happiness of all. But why, then, is Berkeley not led to act utilitarianism, as Hutcheson is, albeit in a deontic key? Part of the answer must be the same one we will find in Mill: once a utilitarian goes fully deontic, and sees the conceptual connection between obligation and accountability, it is hard to remain an act, rather than a rule, utilitarian.[10]

But there is a second reason that is more prominent in Berkeley's writings, namely that God's will necessarily takes the form of rules. This becomes evident, first, in the role that God plays in Berkeley's metaphysical idealism. If the only thing that exists are sensible ideas and not material substances, and if these ideas have no way of establishing natural

9 For more detailed discussion of Pufendorf, Cumberland, and Locke, see Darwall 2023a.

10 I argue that the same is true of Parfit (Darwall 2021).

regularities of cause and effect in themselves, then the only endurance of what we take to be material objects must be their continued existence in God's mind. What we take to be causal regularities are nothing but what Hume called "constantly conjoined" ideas whose regular enduring character is that they have an ordered, rule-governed existence in God's mind, even when they are not present in ours.

Of course, any idea that God has depends upon his will, as our having the sensible ideas we have depend on God's will also. So it is simply entailed by Berkeley's theology and his metaphysical idealism that the ideas we experience must take a rule-governed form if we are to experience what seems to be a world with causal regularities. This already brings in God's benevolence. God benevolently wills that we have ideas in a regular fashion so that we can predict what will happen, including what will happen if we take or do not take specific actions (or their idealist equivalents).

Berkeley discusses the function of "laws of nature" and the "language of nature" in regulating human action in several passages. For example,

> The proper objects of vision constitute an universal language of the Author of nature, whereby we are instructed how to regulate our actions, in order to attain those things, that are necessary to the preservation and well-being of our bodies. (1964c: 147)

> Now the set rules, or established methods, wherein the Mind we depend on excites in us the ideas of sense, are called the *laws of nature*: and these we learn by experience, which teaches us that such and such ideas are attended with such and such other ideas, in the ordinary course of things. (1964d: 30)

In these and other passages, Berkeley develops the idea that God causes ideas in us by general rules we learn by experience. These ideas amount to a language, because what we call "cause" and "effect" are really related as sign to thing signified. I come to learn, for example, that the ideas that together make up a falling rock headed for my toe are usually followed, "in the ordinary course," by a painful idea as if in my toe. I take the former as a sign of the latter, or rather, as a sign that the latter will occur unless I do something to alter the normal course of events. This enables me to take evasive action. It is, Berkeley thinks, some of the most impressive evidence we have of God's wisdom and benevolence that he causes our ideas by "the never enough admired laws of pain and pleasure" (1964d: 146).

But how does God will that we act? Since he is omnibenevolent, his will must have some relation to overall happiness. There are, Berkeley thinks, two possibilities. Either God wills that we do what (we ourselves think) will promote the greatest overall happiness; or God wills that we follow "some determinate, established laws, which, if universally practised," will best promote the happiness of all (1964c: 8). Berkeley embraces the latter alternative. God wills that we follow "certain universal rules of morality" rather than that we try, each of us individually, to promote the greatest good overall. These "certain universal rules" are the "laws of nature" to which Berkeley refers as objects of consensus (Berkeley 1964b: 4).

Berkeley thinks, again, that there are only two possibilities:

> ***W1*** God wills that each person aim to do all they can, in each instance, to promote the good directly. Each is obliged "upon each particular occasion to consult the public good, and always . . . do that which to him shall seem, in the present time and circumstances, most to conduce to it." (Berkeley 1964b: 8)

> ***W2*** God wills that each observe "some determinate, established laws, which, if universally practised, have from the nature of things, an essential fitness to procure the well-being of mankind." (Berkeley 1964b: 8)

Corresponding to these two propositions about God's will are the following deontic moral claims about right and wrong.

> ***R1*** On each occasion, what it is right for a person to do is what that person believes (or, perhaps, would believe on available evidence) would best promote overall happiness.

> ***R2*** On each occasion, what it is right for a person to do is what would be permitted by those rules which, if universally accepted and followed, would best promote the overall happiness.

It is a mark of Berkeley's philosophical subtlety that he can see the difference between these alternatives. So far as I know, he is the first philosopher to do so and, consequently, the first to distinguish, much less defend, a rule-utilitarian theory of right.

The key to seeing what Berkeley was up to is to appreciate that in order for his whole system to work, human agents have to be able to give sense to the idea that God holds them *accountable* for acting in certain ways. Berkeley thinks we can believe our eternal interests to be staked on our conformance to God's will only if we can regard God as reasonably holding us responsible for conformance. Or, to put the point another way, whatever it is that God wills us to do must be something we can regard him as reasonably holding us responsible for doing, such that whether we do it or not affects our eternal interests. This rules out *W1* and *R1*. We cannot reasonably be held responsible for consequences of our actions we could not have known about, so God cannot make our eternal benefit depend upon whether our actions *actually* promote the good. Berkeley writes in his notebooks, "Actions leading to heaven are in my power if I will will them: therefore I will them," and further, "Men impute their actions to themselves because they will'd them & that not out of ignorance but whereas they knew the consequences of them, whether good or bad" (Berkeley 1964e: 156).

However we know which rules God wills us to follow, Berkeley is clear that they have the property of being rules it would maximize happiness for all to accept and follow, and that they must be followed even in situations where doing so will occasion "great sufferings and misfortunes ... to very many good men" (Berkeley 1964b: 8). This raises a question familiar from recent discussions of rule utilitarianism. If what justifies establishing general rules is simply the instrumental benefits of doing so, then how can obeying the rules be justified when doing so would be harmful? When the question facing an agent is what to do, the objection goes, the relevant issue concerns the instrumental benefits and costs of the *act*, including, of course, those mediated by instrumentally beneficial, rule-structured practices the act may affect.

Whether contemporary forms of rule utilitarianism can deal adequately with this "rule worship" objection or not, Berkeley's metaethics gives him a way of avoiding it.[11] For Berkeley, a rule has normative force not "merely because it conduceth to the public good, but because it is decreed by the will of God" (Berkeley 1964b: 31). The public good is God's end in decreeing the moral law, but that does not make the public good deontically normative for us. It would be only if God willed that we make it our end and conditioned our eternal interest on our doing so. God would do that, however, only if it would be best for us all to aim directly at this end. Because it would not be, he does not will it. He wills that we accept and follow generally useful rules even on those occasions when the consequences of following them would be worse. Precisely because those rules are what God wills and conditions our eternal happiness on our conformance to, we must conform to them. This is not "rule worship" (Smart and Williams 1973: 6). It is God worship.

Paley

Paley was, like Berkeley, a utilitarian who rooted his normative view in metaethical theological voluntarism. Also like Berkeley, Paley's psychology and his connecting of moral obligation to divine eternal sanctions is

[11] The classic form of the objection is by J. J. C. Smart in Smart and Williams 1973: 16.

grounded in a psychological egoistic hedonism and identification of obligation with necessity for the agent's happiness. Both Berkeley and Paley found these points in John Gay.[12] "Obligation," Gay held, "is the necessity of doing or omitting any action in order to be happy" (Gay 1731: xviii). Differently from theological voluntarists like Pufendorf and Locke, who tie morality to irreducibly juridical law, Paley, Berkeley, and Gay all take it to be grounded in psychological and rational egoism.

Bentham will follow the theological utilitarians in this respect, though he will deny that God is necessary for the requisite motivation. He will agree with Paley, Berkeley, and Gay that the motivation to be moral does not arise naturally, but he will hold that the artifice it requires can be supplied by appropriately sanctioned human convention and law. Showing exactly how the law can most effectively connect the greatest overall happiness to the agent's expectable happiness at the point of action was the great task of Bentham's life.

As we have noted, Paley had an outsize influence on the reception of utilitarian ideas in the nineteenth century, owing to his *Principles of Moral and Political Philosophy*'s having been included in the curriculum in Cambridge. Its appearance in 1785 also contributed to Bentham's decision to republish his *Introduction to the Principles of Morals and Legislation*, which had existed in print since 1780, in 1789 (Bentham 1996: li). As we have seen, Bentham was the first to call his view "utilitarianism," and he doubtless thought it was important to have a clearer formulation of his act-utilitarian version of the view than anything that can be found in Paley. What's more, Paley's view was irredeemably theological.[13]

Although there is a lot of unsystematic unclarity in Paley's *Principles*, there are also interesting aspects that will be important for later utilitarians, most especially Mill. Paley fudges the difference between act and rule utilitarianism in a creative way, making use of the idea of the "tendency" of actions in ways that Mill will pick up in *Utilitarianism* over a half century later.

As previously noted, Bentham said that it was from Hume's *Treatise* that he "learnt to see that *utility* was the test and measure of all virtue" (Bentham 1977: 441). And we also there noted a crucial difference between Hutcheson's and Hume's versions of moral sentimentalism that helped explain why Bentham would have learned his utilitarianism from Hume

[12] On this, see Sidgwick 1964: 237.

[13] Though Berkeley's views were much more clearly formulated than Paley's, they were also grounded in theological voluntarism and were rule utilitarian, rather than act utilitarian like Bentham's.

rather than Hutcheson. Whereas Hutcheson held moral sense to be a separate, distinctively moral module of human psychology, Hume held that our moral sentiments can be explained by more general psychological mechanisms of sympathy and the association of ideas that respond to considerations of utility.

In this respect, Paley's *Principles* also prepared the way for Bentham. Paley criticizes Hutcheson along similar lines. Following upon Hume and David Hartley (1705–1757), whose *Observations on Man*, published in 1749, provided, in Sidgwick's words, an "original and comprehensive application of the laws of association of ideas to the explanation of all our more complex and refined emotions," Paley argued that these associations could explain the phenomena that Hutcheson wished to explain by moral sense (Sidgwick 1964: 218; Paley 2002: 9–10).

Paley also makes Berkeley's point against Hutcheson and Hume that whatever moral sentiments we have are impotent to make human beings avoid moral wrong. For that purpose, nothing short of divine eternal sanctions can suffice. Moral sentimentalists lack, Paley says, any account of "these instincts['] . . . authority" (Paley 2002: 12). The "secret remorse of conscience . . . may be borne with." If "the sinner . . . finds the pleasure of the sin to exceed the remorse of conscience . . . the moral-instinct man . . . has nothing more to offer" (12).

This suggests that the authority of obligation is, as Gay said, "the necessity of doing or omitting any action in order to be happy" (Gay 1731: xviii). But that is not quite Paley's view. "A man is said to be *obliged*," Paley says, "*when he is urged by a violent motive resulting from the command of another*" (Paley 2002: 34). In order to constitute an obligation, the necessity for happiness must be created by God's commands and his promise of eternal sanctions for violation. Nothing irreducibly deontic is required, as with Pufendorf, but motivating eternal sanctions are.

This brings us to Paley's normative view and his formulation of utilitarianism, which is not nearly so careful as Hutcheson's form of act utilitarianism or Berkeley's rule utilitarianism. "Virtue," Paley says, "is *the doing good to mankind, in obedience to the will of God, and for the sake of everlasting happiness*" (25). This provides the content of moral rightness: "doing good to mankind"; its form: obeying God's command; and its motive: that so acting is necessary to our "everlasting happiness." Paley gives another formulation, however, that brings out some other elements of his view. "So then actions are to be estimated by their tendency. Whatever is expedient, is right. It is the utility of any moral rule alone, which constitutes the obligation of it" (42). Here we have three different elements that more analytically minded philosophers, like Hutcheson and Berkeley, are anxious to separate: (a) an act's expediency, in the sense of its actual good consequences; (b) an act's tendency, in the sense of what consequences acts of that kind tend to have; and (c) "the utility of any moral rule" that might require or permit the rule: as in Berkeley's form of rule utilitarianism. And this last element might concern the utility of people *accepting* the rule or the utility of their actually conforming to it, and even here, either "as a rule" or without exception.

We will have occasion to delve more deeply into the differences between these when we get to Mill. "The 'greatest happiness principle,'" Mill says, "holds that actions are right in proportion as they tend to promote happiness; wrong as they tend to produce the reverse of happiness" (Mill 2002: II.2). Although it is not often noticed, this is formulated in terms of tendencies rather than actual consequences.[14] Mill also discusses general rules of thumb, what he calls "secondary principles," in a way that recalls Paley's talk of "moral rules." And, as I have emphasized (and will again), in chapter V of *Utilitarianism* Mill stresses the conceptual connection between moral right and accountability in a way that leads him to a form of (acceptance) rule utilitarianism. For Mill, in that chapter, at least, the relevant utility calculations concern not accepting a rule as a normative guide, but accepting it as a binding rule, violations of which are blameworthy absent excuse.

Paley does not clearly see the distinctions between these different formulations, but the main tendency of his thought is in the direction of evaluating actions by the utility of performing them as a "general rule." "Moral Philosophy," he says, "cannot pronounce that any rule of morality is so rigid as to bend to no exceptions (Paley 2002: 458). And where other philosophers see distinctions, Paley sees nothing to get bothered about. "Why am I obliged to keep my word?" he asks (33). He considers philosophical responses of different kinds, from "because it is agreeable to the fitness of things" (Clarke) to "because it is conformable to truth" (Wollaston), to "because it promotes the public good," to "because it is required by the will of God" (Pufendorf, et al.). Paley thinks any apparent differences between these answers do not matter, since they "ultimately coincide" (33).

When it comes to what "public good" consists in, Paley is a quantitative hedonist in the manner of Bentham. "Any condition may be denominated happy, in which the amount or aggregate of pleasure exceeds that of pain;

[14] Mill continues this "tendency" formulation in his essay on Whewell (Mill and Bentham 1987).

and the degree of happiness depends upon the quantity of this excess" (13). On the matter of whether there are "higher" pleasures that are intrinsically better than "lower" ones – say, the intellectual over the sensual – Paley sides with Bentham against Mill. But this difference may wash out for him quantitatively, since he holds that intellectual pleasures are almost always better extrinsically; they are more reliable, easier to acquire, less likely to be followed by pain. These are all features that Bentham will cite also to calculate pleasure and pain's *extrinsic* value. For Paley as for Bentham, quantity of happiness is a net aggregate of the value of the pleasurable and painful experiences that comprise it.

CHAPTER 7

Bentham

Although there were certainly earlier versions of utilitarianism before Jeremy Bentham, as we have seen, and although Bentham's formulations also draw from earlier writers, it is Bentham who gave the doctrine its name and put it on the map, both as a philosophical theory and as a reforming social and political doctrine. Bentham's primary interests were social, legal, and political. He was less a philosopher – or, at any rate, a philosopher's philosopher – than a philosophical lawyer and social reformer. Sidgwick characterized him as having an "all-comprehensive desire for the amelioration of human life" (Sidgwick 2000: 204).[1]

He was certainly skilled at distinctions, and some of his insights in the philosophy of language were truly revolutionary. Quine said that Bentham took "a crucial step forward" in developing an understanding of the nature of scientific terms and concepts that ultimately led to Russell and Carnap (Quine 1969: 72).[2] But in all of his philosophizing, Bentham was most fundamentally concerned with its relevance for law and, ultimately, for a distinctive kind of legal, social, and political reform.

As Gerald Postema has shown, much of Bentham's concern with law was in opposition to the British common law tradition (Postema 1986). Mill called Bentham "the great questioner of things established" (Mill and Bentham 1987: 177). Bentham was unalterably opposed to legal and political doctrines whose only grounding was in tradition and any commonsense tradition informs. This extended also to his views about morality. His

[1] He is never too busy to help in experiments which may enrich mankind with a new grass or a new fruit. At one time he is anxious to learn all about laughing gas; at another he corresponds at length about a Frigidarium, in which fermentable substances may be preserved from pernicious fermentation while remaining unfrozen. Nothing seems to him too trivial an object for his restless impulse of amelioration. (Sidgwick 2000: 203)

Sidgwick provides a detailed and insightful treatment of Bentham's reforming efforts in "Bentham and Benthamism" (203).

[2] Quoted in Harrison 1983: 64.

defense of the principle of utility or "greatest happiness" is not grounded, as Sidgwick will argue any moral principle must be, in intuition, either an intuition of common sense or a matter of philosophical intuition. But neither does Bentham ground his utilitarianism in an empiricist-naturalist metaethics, as do Cumberland and Mill, though his metaphysics certainly has that character. As we shall see, Bentham holds that the ultimate grounding of utilitarianism must be *political*. The utility principle is the only one that can play the role that a moral principle must be able to play in informed noncoercive public debate. It is the only principle that provides what Bentham calls an "extrinsic ground," that is, one whose satisfaction anyone can, in principle, confirm without having to hold moral or political opinions that may be in dispute (Bentham 1996: 25). Rawls famously says that his theory of "justice as fairness: [is] political, not metaphysical" (Rawls 1985). I shall argue that we might aptly characterize Bentham's theory similarly – utilitarianism: political, not metaphysical.

We will see the same concern to oppose traditional, intuition-based moral theory and moralizing in Mill. Mill begins *Utilitarianism* with a contrast between "intuitive" and "inductive" moralists and places himself very much on the inductive side. This is like Bentham, but also importantly different (Mill 2002: I.3). Mill's defense of utilitarianism ends up being on straightforward empiricist-naturalist grounds, whereas Bentham's is more along the lines of Rawls's political liberalism (Rawls 1993). An unappreciated feature of Bentham's view is that he appears ultimately to ground utilitarianism in an independent value of liberty, whereas Mill's view is the reverse. Mill argues for political liberty on utilitarian grounds.

The Principle of Utility I

Introduction to the Principles begins with the following iconic passage:

> Nature has placed mankind under the governance of two sovereign masters, *pain* and *pleasure*. It is for them alone to point out what we ought to do, as well as to determine what we shall do. On the one hand the standard of right and wrong, on the other the chain of causes and effects, are fastened to their throne. They govern us in all we do, in all we say, in all we think: every effort we can make to throw off our subjection, will serve but to demonstrate and confirm it (Bentham 1996: 11).

Here we see two of the many different roles that hedonism plays in Bentham's thought. The "two sovereign masters, *pain* and *pleasure*," figure both in Bentham's account of how we *should* act as well as that of how we *do* act. Concerning the former, Bentham says that "the *principle of utility* recognises this subjection, and assumes it for the foundation of that system, the object of which is to rear the fabric of felicity by the hands of reason and of law" (11). This is Bentham's primary concern: to state a principle that can function as a fundamental justification – an "extrinsic ground," as he calls it – for the normative criticism of law and social custom (25). But Bentham is also concerned with the explanation of human behavior, not least because he believes that any normative standard must be responsive to actual human nature. So Bentham's normative hedonisms – his quantitative hedonistic theory of the good, his utilitarian theory of the right, *and* his hedonistic egoist theory of *rational* action – are all cast in light of his psychological egoistic hedonism: all human behavior is motivated by a desire for pleasure and an aversion to pain, which he calls "the sole standard,"

> in conformity to which each individual ought, as far as depends upon the legislator, to be *made* to fashion his behaviour. But whether it be this or any thing else that is to be *done*, there is nothing by which a man can ultimately be *made* to do it, but either pain or pleasure (34).[3]

This creates the same problem for Bentham that it did for Locke and theological utilitarians like Paley. Law and morality tell us to do one thing – for Bentham, to act or comply with laws for "the greatest happiness of the greatest number" (14). But the only thing we can ever actually do is something else, *de dicto*, at least: whatever will most advance our own happiness or pleasure. And these may, or may not, coincide *de re*.

Locke and the theological utilitarians solve this problem with God's eternal sanctions. Since Bentham is a resolutely secular thinker, he can solve it only through social and legal sanctions. And this sets the basic character of Bentham's project: to create laws and customs that maximize overall happiness and give individuals incentives to comply with them. Any law or custom that does not maximize universal happiness will not serve "the sovereign masters" of pleasure and pain and is to be avoided on that account. And this requires that laws and customs establish sufficient incentives for compliance in terms of agents' own pleasure and happiness. Only thus can law and custom adequately recognize the sovereignty of the agent's own pleasure and pain in their own practical reasoning.

At the conclusion of the passage, Bentham sounds a major theme of his defense of the principle of utility, one that we will see in a somewhat

[3] As Sidgwick points out, Bentham's psychological egoism has its roots as much in Helvétius as it does in earlier English writers like Paley and Gay (Sidgwick 2000: 205–206).

different form in the thought of Mill as well. "Systems which attempt to question [the principle of utility], deal in sounds instead of sense, in caprice instead of reason" (11). As we shall see, Bentham takes all such critical systems to be based on groundless intuition, to be instances of what Mill will call "intuitive" rather than "inductive" moral philosophy. In another sense, which we will need to analyze, Bentham thinks, like Mill, that no further proof of the principle of utility is really possible.

> Has the rectitude of this principle been ever formally contested? It should seem that it had, by those who have not known what they have been meaning. Is it susceptible of any direct proof? it should seem not: for that which is used to prove every thing else, cannot itself be proved: a chain of proofs must have their commencement somewhere. To give such proof is as impossible as it is needless (13).

But whereas Mill's indirect proof of the greatest happiness principle is grounded in his empiricist-naturalist metaethics, Bentham's, as we shall see, is rooted in his political liberalism.

The principle of utility's content dictates "approv[al] or disapprov[al] of every action whatsoever according to the tendency which it appears to have to augment or diminish the happiness of the party whose interest is in question" (11–12). At this level of generality, the principle includes both a principle of morally right conduct and a principle of rational action. It dictates the "greatest happiness of the greatest number" as a moral principle and egoistic hedonism as a prudential rational principle.[4] An action's "utility," therefore, is its "tend[ency] to produce ... happiness" (12). Here we have a particularly clear statement of act utilitarianism, though one that is formulated, as it is in the beginning of Mill's *Utilitarianism*, in terms of acts' *tendency* to produce happiness. As Mill there initially formulates the "greatest happiness principle": "actions are right in proportion as they tend to promote happiness; wrong as they tend to produce the reverse of happiness" (Mill 2002: II.2).

We can abstract from Bentham and Mill's "tendency" talk at this point. It will become especially important when we get to Mill. For now, we can assume the orthodox reading of Bentham as an act utilitarian, as holding that an act is morally right (and not wrong) if, and only if, it is among those acts whose performance would bring about the greatest total net happiness.

[4] We need not concern ourselves with precisely how to understand "greatest happiness of the greatest number." Given Bentham's clear remarks about aggregating the general happiness from the happiness of each individual, it has become standard to understand it as dictating the maximizing the total net happiness, counting "each ... for one and nobody more than one" (Mill 2002: V.36). For discussion, see Rosen's introduction to *Introduction to the Principles* (Bentham 1996: xxxvii).

For any agent and any circumstances, we look at the set of acts available to the agent and consider the total net happiness that act would bring about, counting in the happiness of each affected person from the point of action through the end of time.

Quantitative Hedonism

Utilitarianism combines two distinct normative ideas. It is itself a theory of the right, and its distinctive character as a theory of the right is that it is based on a distinctive theory of the good. All utilitarians are consequentialists, holding that the rightness of acts must be based somehow on the goodness of consequences. But there are many choice points here. Some concern whether the consequentialism takes the direct form of act consequentialism or an indirect form, like rule consequentialism. But others concern the kind of good involved. Some follow G. E. Moore in basing their theory of right on the intrinsic value of states of affairs (Moore 1993a). Although Moore called his idea "ideal utilitarianism," utilitarians generally follow the line of thought represented in this chapter, which Scanlon calls "philosophical utilitarianism," according to which "the only fundamental moral facts are facts about individual well-being" (Scanlon 1982: 108). This is also the idea that Sen calls "welfarism" (Sen 1979).

Philosophical utilitarians agree that the good that is to be maximized is the good *of* human (and, perhaps, other sentient) beings. And they agree that this good is *aggregative*, that the good of all is simply the sum of the goods of each. They can, however, divide on their theories of good or welfare. Bentham is an uncompromising hedonist. He holds that the personal good is identical with happiness and that that is constituted by pleasure and the absence of pain. Mill represents himself as a hedonist also. The "greatest happiness principle," as he interprets it, dictates that "pleasure and freedom from pain are the only things desirable as ends" (Mill 2002: II.2). But whether Mill is a hedonist in fact is less clear, as we shall see. He departs from Bentham's quantitative hedonism, holding that the "quality" of pleasures makes an independent contribution to well-being (Mill 2002: II.4).

Mill's theory of happiness ends up being more like Aristotle's, as Mill holds that human good consists in the realization of natural capacities.[5] Utilitarians can, then, hold an Aristotelian theory of welfare, although they will ultimately require, as Mill does, quantitative measures of welfare so that individual goods can be aggregated to derive measures of overall good. Yet another possibility

[5] Something like this seems to be Cumberland's view also.

for utilitarians that we can find some seeds of in Mill, but that became increasingly popular in the "marginal revolution" of Jevons and other economists and rational and social choice theorists, is to understand welfare in terms of preference satisfaction (Harsanyi 1977). Although economists often put this idea in welfarist or utilitarian terms, it can ultimately seem to be based on more fundamental notions of autonomy or liberty. The idea of consumer sovereignty seems more naturally understood not as the idea that individuals are the best judges of their own well-being, but as the proposition that they have a liberty right to lead their own lives as they see fit. We will see this idea in Bentham's justification of the principle of utility as well.

Bentham's hedonism, however, is clear and unambiguous. Chapter IV of *Introduction to the Principles* makes its resolutely quantitative character evident. When it comes to measuring the value of pains and pleasures, Bentham cites six factors. Four are clearly extrinsic. *Certainty* concerns epistemic matters of how likely it is that a given pleasure or pain would occur as the result of a given action. *Propinquity* and *remoteness* concern the ease or difficulty of bringing a given pleasure or pain about. The other two extrinsic factors concern a pleasure or pain's connection to other pleasures or pains. *Fecundity* is a matter of how likely a given pleasure is to be followed by further pleasures, and a pleasure's *purity* concerns any admixture with, or possibility of its causing, pain.

None of these features concern a pleasure or pain itself. They are therefore irrelevant to a pleasure's intrinsic value or to a pain's intrinsic disvalue. That leaves *intensity* and *duration* as the only features of pleasures and pains that are relevant to their intrinsic value or disvalue. But how long a pleasure lasts is not really a feature of the experience itself. That leaves *intensity* as the only intrinsic value-making hedonic feature. But intensity of what? Experiences can be intense along various dimensions. The taste of the chilis in a dish can be very intense, but whether that gives rise to pleasure or pain, and the intensity of that pleasure or pain, depends on the taste of the person eating the dish. One person may find it intensely pleasurable and another intensely painful.

Bentham follows a long line of British moralists in thinking that what is essential to pleasure is its involving a positive attitude and that what is essential to pain and other negative hedonic experiences (like a foul odor) is its involving a negative attitude. In this way, pleasure and pain are analogues of desire and aversion. Indeed, Mill will say that they are "two different modes of naming the same psychological fact" (Mill 2002: IV.10).[6] We will consider this point in Chapter 8, since it plays a central role in Mill's

[6] Similar thoughts can be found in Hobbes and Butler.

empiricist-naturalist case for hedonism as part of the principle of utility. Its relevance here is that it shows us how to interpret Bentham's language of intensity. The relevant experiential intensity for assessing a pleasure or pain's intrinsic value or disvalue is intensity of the experiencer's positive or negative valuing – how much they like or dislike the experience as they are having it.[7]

Once we have this idea, Bentham's quantitative hedonism is easy to formulate. The value of a pleasure, considered in itself, is a function of two different factors: how much the experiencer likes the experience as they are having it and how long the experience lasts. And contrariwise for the disvalue of a pain. There is no room in Bentham's theory for any features of the *object* of the experiencer's liking or of the kind of pleasure being experienced. "Prejudice apart," Bentham famously writes, "the game of push-pin is of equal value with the arts and sciences of music and poetry" (Mill and Bentham 1987: 173–174). Trying to live this doctrine was part of what sent John Stuart Mill into a deep depression at the age of twenty (Mill 1981). What led him out was the discovery of Romantic poetry and through that the pleasures of poetry, nature, and love. Mill incorporates these into a profoundly different form of hedonism, if it is a kind of hedonism at all, which we can call *qualitative hedonism*, since it holds that the "quality" of pleasures is an independent value-making feature (Mill 2002: II.4).

Recall Bentham's original formulation of the principle of utility as maximizing the happiness or pleasure of "the party whose interest in question" (Bentham 1996: 12). As we noted, this yields both his moral theory – act utilitarianism – and his theory of rational prudence. Both require aggregation. For his act egoistic hedonism of rational conduct, it is necessary to consider all acts available to the agent in a given circumstance by comparing their overall effects on the agent (reckoned by quantitative hedonism) from the point of action throughout the indefinite future. Similarly, Bentham's act utilitarianism reckons moral rightness by the effects of every act available to the agent on all affected individuals from the point of action throughout the indefinite future.

Principle of Utility II

We turn now to the question of how Bentham justifies the principle of utility. Carefully considering what Bentham says yields a position that is very different from what one might have expected. Begin with Bentham's

[7] This idea also is an important aspect of Sidgwick's view of pleasure as "desirable consciousness" (Sidgwick 1962: 131, 397; Darwall 1974a).

relation to his predecessors, Hume and Hutcheson.[8] Hutcheson derives the greatest happiness principle from a more fundamental claim about universal benevolence being the morally best motive together with the fact that a universally benevolent person desires to produce the greatest overall happiness. For his part, Hume "de-moralizes" approbation, arguing that any difference between moral virtues and "natural abilities" is merely verbal and that approbation is responsive to motives and traits that tend to the public good. It was from reading Hume's account in the *Treatise*, recall, that Bentham "learnt to see that *utility* was the test and measure of all virtue" (Bentham 1977: 441).

This brings us to Bentham's defense of the principle of utility. Although Bentham was also committed to act utilitarianism as a principle of morally right individual conduct, he was throughout his life much more concerned with the structure of social and legal institutions and with the conduct of legal actors. His *Introduction* is to the principles of morals and *legislation*, and more than half of the book is concerned with the latter. The topics of the first half, moreover, are dictated by their relevance to questions of legal and political philosophy.

It is not surprising, therefore, that when Bentham discusses the justification for the principle of utility, it is very much within the context of his legal and political philosophical concerns. As he saw it, it is a besetting problem of public moral, political, and legal discourse that participants frequently put forward views in public debate which they base on no more secure foundation than their own intuitive moral convictions or feelings. Bentham's argument in *Introduction to the Principles* is that utility is the only principle that can provide an "extrinsic ground" for normative moral and political claims and is, consequently, the sole principle that can ground noncoercive moral and political debate.

Notice, first, how Bentham describes the principle of utility. "The principle here in question," he remarks, may be taken for an act of the mind; a sentiment; a sentiment of approbation; a sentiment which, when applied to an action, approves of its utility, as that quality of it by which the measure of approbation or disapprobation bestowed upon it ought to be governed (Bentham 1996: 12 nb).

As Bentham is thinking of it here, the principle of utility is less a "first-order" moral principle than a thesis about the form that moral thought and discourse should itself take. It puts forward what he calls an "extrinsic

[8] In what comes, I closely follow Darwall 1994, especially pp. 73–75, "Slouching Towards Bentham."

ground" or "external standard," not for conduct directly, but for approving conduct (25). Again, the standard counsels approving of an action's utility, as "that quality by which the measure of approbation or disapprobation bestowed upon it ought to be governed." To be sure, however, Bentham evidently does hold that this second-order idea entails act utilitarianism as a first-order proposition of moral right.

By calling the standard that the principle of utility imposes on moral thought and discourse "extrinsic" or "external," Bentham means to convey that it is fully independent of any approbation of conduct that it is taken to recommend and that it can, therefore, be uncontroversially applied even by people with sharply conflicting moral views (Bentham 1996: 25). "The various systems that have been formed concerning the standard of right and wrong," Bentham writes, "consist all of them in so many contrivances for avoiding the obligation of appealing to any external standard" (25). The "obligation" here might be conceived either as intellectual or philosophical or as a moral or political debt owed as a necessary complement to the right to participate in political discussion and debate. All previous systems of ethics that lack external standards, Bentham says, are guilty of simply "prevailing upon the reader to accept of the author's sentiment or opinion as a reason for itself" (25–26).

In a remarkable footnote, Bentham attempts to illustrate how pretty much all the major modern British ethical theories – Hutcheson's "moral sense," Reid's "common sense," Price's "rule of right," Clarke's "fitness of things," among several others (notably, Hume's moral sentiment is absent, since Bentham correctly takes it, unlike Hutchesonian moral sense, to be ultimately guided by utility) – merely amount to devices designed to give the appearance of claims entitled to respect, but that actually lack any justification that could command rational assent. Rather, the reader is induced or "prevail[ed] upon . . . to accept the author's sentiment or opinion as a reason for itself" (25–26).

Bentham is of course a positivist and empiricist who is a sharp critic of legal and moral fictions and who thinks, for example, that the idea of natural rights is "nonsense upon stilts" (2002). But he also has a very different argument for the "obligation" to appeal to "external standard[s]" when urging approbation or disapprobation in public moral, political, and legal discourse. This is an idea akin to the thesis of Rawls's "political liberalism" that normative political claims that cannot be justified while bracketing "comprehensive" moral and political doctrines are antithetical to a liberal society (Rawls 1993). It is implicitly coercive, Bentham is suggesting, for people to make a moral claim on others when they are unwilling to offer a reason for doing so that others could be expected to accept without already sharing the same moral views.

Thus Bentham writes of earlier theories:

> The mischief common to all these ways of thinking and arguing (which, in truth, as we have seen, are but one and the same method, couched in different forms of words) is their serving as a cloak, and pretence, and aliment, to despotism; if not a despotism in practice, a despotism however in disposition: which is but too apt, when pretence and power offer, to show itself in practice (Bentham 1996: 28 n).

Of someone who is prepared to put forward their own normative moral and political opinion as self-justifying, he asks, "let him examine and satisfy himself whether the principle he thinks he has found is really . . . not . . . what in another person he might be apt to call *caprice*" (15).

> If he is inclined to think that his own approbation or disapprobation, annexed to the idea of an act, without any regard to its consequences, is a sufficient foundation for him to judge and act upon, let him ask himself whether his sentiment is to be a standard of right and wrong, with respect to every other man, or whether every man sentiment's has the same privilege of being a standard to itself (15–16).

If the person grasps the first horn, then their principle will be "despotical"; they will be forcing their principle on others. If they grasp the second, however, their principle will be "anarchical," and they will be committed to "as many different standards of right and wrong as there are men" (16).

Bentham considers an objector asking, "But is it never, then, from any other considerations than those of utility, that we derive our notions of right and wrong?" He responds:

> I do not know: I do not care. Whether a moral sentiment can be originally conceived from any other source than a view of utility, is one question: whether upon examination and reflection it can, in point of fact, be actually persisted in and justified on any other ground, by a person reflecting within himself, is another; whether *in point of right* it can properly be justified on any other ground, by a person addressing himself to the community, is a third. The two first are questions of speculation: it matters not, comparatively speaking, how they are decided. The last is a question of practice: the decision of it is of as much importance as that of any can be (28, emphasis added).

This suggests that we do best to read Bentham as arguing that the principle of utility is uniquely suited to play an essential role in public normative moral, political, and legal discourse that is: (a) clear and intelligible; (b) noncoercive; (c) about a common issue; and (d) useful in directing action. Bentham's position is that these criteria will be realized only if acts are approved on the basis of their utility. For these reasons,

Bentham approves of approving them on this basis – he asserts the principle of utility, interpreted as a second-order principle.

Let us take these criteria *seriatim.*

(a) *clear and intelligible speech and thought.* Bentham says of the principle of utility: "When thus interpreted, the words *ought*, and *right* and *wrong*, and others of that stamp, have a meaning: when otherwise, they have none" (13). And: "Systems which attempt to question it, deal in sounds instead of sense, in caprice instead of reason, in darkness instead of light" (11).

(b) *noncoercive.* Putting forward normative moral, political, and legal claims without an external standard (like the principle of utility) is "despotical" (16).

(c) *about a common issue.* Permitting everyone to accept their own principles is "anarchical" (16).

(d) *useful in directing action.* Other principles might provide external standards that are not coercive and that are about common issues. To proponents of alternatives to the principle of utility, Bentham says, "let him say whether there is any such thing as a *motive* that a man can have to pursue the dictates of it: if there is, let him say what that motive is, and how it is to be distinguished from those which enforce the dictates of utility: if not, then lastly let him say what it is this other principle can be good for" (16).

Putting these criteria together, we get the conclusion that the principle of utility is the only principle that can structure public normative moral, political, and legal discourse that is clear and intelligible, noncoercive, about a common issue, and useful in directing action.

Bentham has another more direct line of thought leading to utilitarianism, but, as Sidgwick pointed out, it cannot succeed. The argument is simply that "right" and "ought" can only mean action that produces the greatest happiness.

> Of an action that is conformable to the principle of utility, one may always say either that it is one that ought to be done . . . [or] that it is right it should be done . . . When thus interpreted, the words *ought*, and *right* and *wrong*, and others of that stamp, have a meaning: when otherwise, they have none (Bentham 1996: 13).

The problem with defining "right" in terms of maximizing utility is that it makes the principle of utility a tautology that lacks any normative force (Sidgwick 2000: 41). This leaves the argument I have been sketching the only promising line of support that Bentham offers for the principle of utility.

There is an irony here. Mill is much better known as a defender of liberty than is Bentham. Mill's *On Liberty* is one of the canonical documents of traditional liberalism. But Mill's strong defense of individual liberty is grounded in his utilitarianism, as we shall see. The argument of Bentham's that we have just analyzed reverses this. It grounds the principle of utility in liberty. As I mentioned earlier, its motto might be: "the principle of utility: political, not metaphysical."[9]

Act and Motive

To conclude our study of Bentham, we can come full circle back to Hutcheson and Hume – whose ethics of virtue focus on the goodness of *motives* – to see how Bentham turns their doctrine on its head. Bentham holds that ethics is fundamentally concerned with the evaluation of *acts* – what Hume called "external performance[s]" (Hume 1978: 477). For Bentham, the principle of utility is applied in the first instance to acts and only derivatively to motives (reversing Hutcheson's method). "Consideration of utility" is the only "right principle of action" (Bentham 1996: 32).

Though Bentham is clear that motive is irrelevant to the rightness of acts, he thinks it understandable that someone might think otherwise.

> When the act happens, in the particular instance in question, to be productive of effects which we approve of, much more if we happen to observe that the same motive may frequently be productive, in other instances, of the like effects, we are apt to transfer our approbation to the motive itself, and to assume, as the just ground for the approbation we bestow on the act, the circumstance of its originating from that motive (32).

However understandable, this is an error. The only ground for approving of an act is not its motive, or the motive from which it would best eventuate, Bentham holds, but only its consequences.

Finally, Bentham argues directly that no motive can be bad in itself but only instrumentally through its consequences. He has two different arguments for this. The first is that the very same motives can lead to good or bad consequences depending on circumstances.

> 1. A boy, in order to divert himself, reads an improving book: the motive is accounted, perhaps, a good one: at any rate not a bad one. 2. He sets his top

9 On the model of Rawls's "Justice as Fairness: Political, Not Metaphysical" (Rawls 1985).

> a spinning: the motive is deemed, at any rate, not a bad one. 3. He sets loose a mad ox among a crowd; his motive is now, perhaps, termed an abominable one. Yet in all three cases the motive may be the very same: it may be neither more nor less than curiosity (104).

Second, Bentham argues that all motives are instances of a desire for some pleasure or an aversion to some pain. But, to this extent, every motive is intrinsically good.

A motive is substantially nothing more than pleasure or pain, operating in a certain manner.

> Now, pleasure is in *itself* a good: nay, even setting aside immunity from pain, the only good: pain is in itself an evil; and indeed, without exception, the only evil; or else the words good and evil have no meaning. And this is alike true of every sort of pain, and of every sort of pleasure. It follows, therefore, immediately and incontestibly, that there is no such thing as any sort of motive that is in itself a bad one (100).

Thus Bentham's line of thought is the reverse of Hutcheson's and Hume's. Acts are what is morally evaluable in the first instance, and motives can be morally evaluated only based on their instrumental effects.

CHAPTER 8

Mill

Son of James Mill, a member of Bentham's circle of "Philosophical Radicals," John Stuart Mill was raised as a Benthamite utilitarian (Seth Pringle-Pattison 1907; Mill 1981). Mill first read Bentham at the age of fifteen (in 1821), and it gave him what Mill described as "an object in life; to be a reformer of the world" (Mill 1981: 137). From that point, Mill says, he "entirely identified" his own happiness with the greatest happiness of all, understood in Bentham's quantitative hedonist terms (137). In his early twenties, he anonymously edited Bentham's *Rationale of Judicial Evidence* (119).

Like the Philosophical Radicals, Mill dedicated himself to the Benthamite program of social reform. His article on the mercantilist Corn Laws, which kept the price of staples like corn artificially high to the detriment of the working classes, dated from this period (Mill 1967).

Attempting to maximize the greatest overall happiness, understood in Bentham's quantitative hedonist terms, proved increasingly difficult and distressing to Mill, precipitating, at the age of twenty, a depression:

> It occurred to me to put the question directly to myself: "Suppose that all your objects in life were realized; that all the changes in institutions and opinions which you are looking forward to, could be completely effected at this very instant: would this be a great joy and happiness to you?" And an irrepressible self-consciousness distinctly answered, "No!" . . . I seemed to have nothing left to live for (Mill 1981: 139).

What ultimately dispelled Mill's depression was Romantic poetry. Mill writes, "[the] state of my thoughts and feelings made the fact of my first reading Wordsworth (in the autumn of 1828) an important event of my life" (148). "What made Wordsworth's poems a medicine for my state of mind," Mill goes on, "was that they expressed, not outward beauty but states of feeling, and of thought coloured by feeling, under the excitement of beauty" (150). The "love of rural objects and scenery" that Mill found in

Wordsworth would later transfer to Mill's own loving relations, most significantly, with Harriet Taylor, the love of his life (150).

These experiences bore theoretical fruit as well. The most obvious is the substantial departure Mill makes from Bentham's quantitative hedonism. In *Utilitarianism* (1863), Mill argues that pleasures can differ not just quantitively in how intensely the experiencer likes them, but also qualitatively. Pleasures and pains are of fundamentally different kinds, and the most significant pleasures for overall happiness are those that involve engagement with "higher" faculties, such as those necessary to appreciate literature and natural beauty and to have loving relations with others. Another example is Mill's solution to the problem of how to be motivated to work for the greatest happiness of all without the alienating depression that he knew firsthand could accompany Bentham's egoistic motivation. The human motive underlying utilitarianism, Mill says, is "the desire to be in unity with our fellow creatures" (Mill 2002: III.10).

The Project of *Utilitarianism*

Mill puts forward his chief aim in *Utilitarianism* at the very outset of the book. "There are few circumstances among those which make up the present condition of human knowledge more unlike what might have been expected," Mill writes, "than the little progress which has been made ... respecting the criterion of right and wrong" (I.1). This makes clear that Mill's goal is to defend the principle of utility as a deontic "criterion of right and wrong." And it reflects Bentham's agenda-setting influence, since by the mid nineteenth century, utilitarianism's focus has decisively shifted from the moral assessment of virtuous motive and character to a concern with the rightness and wrongness of acts.

Mill quickly sets up a fundamental contrast he will be concerned with between "intuitive moralists" who defend the status quo and "inductiv[ists]" who look to an empirical "criterion" – the principle of utility – to critically evaluate and reform law and custom (I.1, I.3, III.7). And he does this with the most remarkable conceit. "From the dawn of philosophy," Mill says, thinkers have debated this issue. "And after more than two thousand years the same discussions continue, philosophers are still ranged under the same contending banners ... [as] when the youth Socrates listened to the old Protagoras and asserted (if Plato's dialogue be grounded on a real conversation) the theory of utilitarianism against the popular morality of the so-called sophist" (I.1). Mill thus transposes a distinctively modern concern with deontic morality back into ancient Greek philosophy, running right over any differences between the ancients and the moderns, and Anscombe's challenge to "modern moral philosophy" (Anscombe 1958).

Mill also declares that, just as in Victorian Britain, ancient Greek philosophers argued under "the same contending banners" of intuitive and inductive moral philosophy *and* that two of the most prominent spokespersons for these two sides were, respectively, Protagoras and Socrates. In Plato's *Protagoras*, Mill is saying, Protagoras defends "popular morality," that is, customary morality and tradition, against Socrates's assertion of "the theory of utilitarianism" (Mill 2002: I.1). And Protagoras is "old," and Socrates is a "youth." The implication is clear: "intuitive" defenders of the status quo are attempting to prop up a dying order, whereas utilitarian progressives are on the right side of history (I.3).

Mill argues that both inductivist utilitarians and intuitive moralists are committed to seeking the fundamental principles of right and wrong. Both agree that morality is not a matter of "perception . . . in the concrete" (I.3). So both must "insis[t] on the necessity of general laws" (I.3). This is clear with utilitarianism, since everything flows from the principle of utility. But even when intuitive moralists "assume the ordinary precepts of morals [to be] as of *a priori* authority," they must nonetheless grant that "there ought either to be some one fundamental principle or law at the root of all morality, or, if there be several, there should be . . . one . . . rule for deciding between the various principles when they conflict" (I.3).

Utilitarianism's Fundamental Principle: A First Pass

In chapter II, Mill turns to the exposition and defense of the "greatest happiness principle," which, he says, "holds that actions are right in proportion as they tend to promote happiness; wrong as they tend to produce the reverse of happiness" (II.2). Mill then adds his theory of happiness stated in terms that any Benthamite can accept: "By happiness is intended pleasure and the absence of pain; by unhappiness, pain and the privation of pleasure" (II.2). Mill will turn presently to laying out the first of his two major departures from Bentham: an Aristotelian or "qualitative" form of hedonism that holds that higher forms of pleasure are intrinsically better than lower ones.

We will want to analyze this in some detail. But note first Mill's saying that it is the *tendency* to produce happiness and unhappiness that determines right and wrong. We saw this same language in Bentham, who says that the principle of utility "approves or disapproves of every action whatsoever, according to the *tendency* which it appears to have to augment or diminish [overall] happiness" (Bentham 1996: 12, emphasis added). How should we interpret this talk of acts' tendencies? We might pass it off as an expendable homage to Bentham except for the fact that, among other things, Mill defends it some length in his essay on Whewell (Mill 1985: 165–202).[1] Mill argues against Whewell's critique of Bentham's utilitarianism that "the tendency of actions to promote happiness affords a test to which the feelings of morality should conform" (Mill 1985:172).

It is worth noticing this at the outset, since it destabilizes the standard reading of Mill's version of the "greatest happiness principle," as a fairly straightforward statement of act utilitarianism. Of course, the tendency language shows up already in Bentham; that's why it appears in Whewell's critique that "we do not rest our rules of action upon the tendency of actions to produce . . . happiness" (quoted in Mill 1985: 190). Schneewind points out that John Austin in *The Province of Jurisprudence Determined* (1832) was particularly clear about the contrast between utilities of individual acts and those that a "class" of acts is likely to have in formulating the principle of utility in terms of tendencies of "class[es]" (Schneewind 1977: 154).[2] As Mill will, Austin ties his tendency talk to *rules* (Austin 1832: 39).[3]

Whewell objects that these tendencies are empirically impossible to determine. Later in chapter II of *Utilitarianism*, Mill argues against this objection that "secondary principles" are enshrined in the accumulated wisdom of acts' tendencies (Mill 2002: II.24). Of course, these could still just be rules of thumb or "summary rules" in Rawls's sense (Rawls 1955). That would give acts' tendencies no independent relevance; the rules would function only as guides to what consequences an act would actually have if it were taken. Only when we get to chapter V will we see that Mill is driven in the direction of rule utilitarianism by the pressure that justice and rights and, even more, moral right's conceptual involvement with

[1] Whewell is William Whewell (1794–1866), whose *Lectures on the History of Moral Philosophy in England* include an extensive discussion of Bentham (Whewell 1852).

[2] Now the *tendency* of a human action (as its tendency is thus understood) is the whole of its tendency: the sum of its probable consequences, in so far as they are important or material: the sum of its remote and collateral, as well as of its direct consequences, in so far as any of its consequences may influence the general happiness. Trying to collect its tendency (as its tendency is thus understood) we must not consider the action as if it were *single* and *insulated*, but must look at the *class* of actions to which it belongs. The probable *specific* consequences of doing that single act, of forbearing from that single act, or of omitting that single act, are not the objects of the inquiry. The question to be solved is this: if acts of the *class* were *generally* done, or *generally* forborne or omitted, what would be the probable effect on the general happiness or good? (Austin 1832: 30)

[3] Schneewind notes that James Mill's *Fragment on Mackintosh* (1835) makes a similar link between classes of acts and rules (Schneewind 1977: 158).

accountability, put on act utilitarianism. From there we can appreciate that giving the tendency language some independent interpretative weight in chapter II helps to give *Utilitarianism* a coherent overall view.[4]

Qualitative Hedonism

We turn now to Mill's first major departure from Bentham: his rejection of Bentham's quantitative hedonist view of the good. Mill lays out his specific criticisms of Bentham's "theory of human life" in his essay titled "Bentham" (Mill 1985: 94). Bentham's psychology effectively treats every human desire as being for the experiencer's own pleasant feeling. Mill specifically points out Bentham's blindness to moral and aesthetic feelings, to "conscience" and the "love of beauty" (96). Projecting from the perspective of his younger self, Mill diagnoses Bentham's inability to countenance such disinterested feelings as stemming from his having "been early accustomed to keep[ing] before his mind's eye the happiness of mankind (or rather of the whole sentient world)" (96). Of course, Mill is here describing the view of his earlier self rather than of Bentham; Bentham thought that the only possible object of human desire is the desirer's own pleasant feelings.

In *Utilitarianism*, Mill argues that pleasures can differ not just quantitatively, but also qualitatively, in ways that are intrinsically relevant to their contribution to a person's good. Pleasures vary, not just in how much the experiencer likes them but in their *objects* (the kinds of thing in which pleasure is taken) and, therefore, by virtue of that, the human faculties that are required to take pleasure in objects of different kinds.

He notes, first, that even quantitative hedonists agree that "higher" quality pleasures have greater value. "No known Epicurean theory of life," he says, "does not assign to the pleasures of the intellect, of the feelings and imagination, and of the moral sentiments a much higher value as pleasures than to those of mere sensation" (Mill 2002: II.4). However, Bentham holds that this is owing to extrinsic features to the pleasurable experience, for example, that pleasures involving the intellect, sentiment, and the imagination have greater "purity," "propinquity," "fecundity," and so on.[5] Like all quantitative hedonists, he steadfastly maintains that the only thing that affects the intrinsic value of a pleasurable experience is intensity, how much the experiencer likes the experience as they are undergoing it.

[4] See, however, Jacobson (2003) for an argument that Mill is not attempting to argue for a specific form of utilitarianism in *Utilitarianism*.

[5] For more detail, see the previous chapter.

Having personally experienced the disastrous consequences of attempting to live according to this view, Mill rejected it in favor of the position to which his discovery of poetry and love led him. Pleasures of the intellect, imagination, and sentiment are better not just extrinsically but also intrinsically. "Higher" pleasures are so called because they require development of the higher faculties. Obviously, Mill cannot count faculties as higher because they enable appreciation of higher (more valuable and significant) pleasures without circularity. As Mill understands them, the higher faculties can be determined naturalistically, in developmental-psychological and evolutionary terms. Mill's normative ethical claim is that pleasures that engage these faculties are intrinsically better, other things equal. (Of course, Mill need not deny that quantity in Bentham's sense matters also.)

Students of ethics who first encounter Mill's theory of higher pleasures are often suspicious, thinking that it smacks of an objectionable form of elitism. To be sure, Mill's view is definitionally hierarchical in some sense. And the fact that his hierarchical view of the good then grounds his utilitarian view of the right can create the worrisome impression that it privileges higher classes who are either thought to have more refined tastes as a result of some natural process of social sorting or, if there are no such natural processes, nonetheless have significantly greater opportunities to develop their capacities because of their socioeconomic position.

Mill is eager to assuage such concerns. First, notice that activities as diverse as traditional farming and labor union organizing are as likely to call on higher capacities of cognition, sentiment, and imagination, as is reading pastoral poetry or historical scholarship. Mill does not have in mind abilities that are realized in theoretical as opposed to practical activity. And he also thinks that the capacities that higher quality pleasures call upon are within reach of ordinary human beings. When they fail to be realized, the cause is far likelier to be socioeconomic structures than natural endowments.

> Capacity for . . . nobl[e] feelings is in most natures a very tender plant, easily killed, not only by hostile influences, but by mere want of sustenance; and in the majority of young persons it speedily dies away if the occupations to which their position in life has devoted them, and the society into which it has thrown them, are not favorable to keeping that higher capacity in exercise (Mill 2002: II.7).

Now Mill, like Bentham, is an empirical naturalist or "inductive" moralist, so he can hardly simply assert qualitative hedonism without falling into the intuitionism he is so concerned to refute (III.7). So any defense of qualitative hedonism must be on empiricist-naturalist grounds. This Mill does with his "decided preference" test. "Of two pleasures," he says, "if there be one to which all or almost all who have experience of both give a decided preference . . . that is the more desirable pleasure" (II.5). Mill recognizes that it is possible for a person to have the relevant experience of higher and lower pleasures and to prefer the latter, nonetheless. This may be because they are not open to the higher pleasures, or are distracted, or, more usually, because their powers of appreciation are insufficiently developed. So he adds that the test is provided by those who are "competently acquainted with" or "capable of appreciating and enjoying both" (II.5, 6).

Does not, however, adding these conditions raise the specter of intuitionism? The challenge is to formulate a criterion of competent acquaintance and capacity of appreciation without presupposing that there are independent facts about the desirable that such competences and capacities can register.[6]

Mill's "Proof" of the Principle of Utility

The other thought lying behind Mill's defense of qualitative hedonism is the idea that pleasures differ in kind by virtue of their *objects*. As Bentham sees it, a pleasure's object is irrelevant to its nature and value; that is given entirely by how intensely the experiencer likes it. Imagine that I receive the news that a close friend's cancer has gone into remission. By Bentham's lights, all that matters is how much I like the experience of hearing this wonderful and relieving news. What I like hearing *about* is irrelevant. Of course, this can hardly be irrelevant to me as I am having the experience; indeed, it is impossible to explain how much I am pleased by hearing this news without referring to how pleased I am about the fact of which I am hearing.

Mill's arguments along these lines are given in chapter IV, "Of What Sort of Proof the Principle of Utility is Susceptible." Like Bentham, Mill thinks that there cannot be anything like a direct proof of the greatest happiness principle. All that can be done is to provide considerations "capable of determining the intellect" (I.5).

[6] Cf. Sidgwick's remark against "Mill's 'qualitative preferableness of pleasures'": "If the pleasures are not compared in respect of mere pleasantness, we have intuitivism in the garb of hedonism" (Sidgwick 2000: 177).

Chapter IV begins with Mill's well-known argument that just as "the only proof . . . that an object is visible is that people actually see it," so also is the "sole evidence it is possible to produce that something is desirable . . . that people actually do desire it" (IV.3). So stated, this has seemed to many philosophers – most famously, G. E. Moore – to involve a particularly obvious instance of the "naturalistic fallacy," or to run right over the conceptual distinction between the nonnormative and the normative (Moore 1993a: 118–119).

Ultimately, Mill argues that the only things that human beings can desire are pleasure and the absence of pain. So he might improve his proof by claiming that something is desirable only if it is *possible to* desire it. If Mill can plausibly claim that pleasure is the only possible object of human desire, then this will give him a better argument for his hedonist claims that pleasure and absence from pain are "the only things desirable as ends" (Mill 2002: II.10).

Now consider Mill's claims about the relation of pleasure to desire. Although these claims will buttress Mill's thesis that pleasures differ in kind and not just in degree, it will also put pressure on Mill's presentation of his theory of the good as hedonistic.

The context for these claims in chapter IV is Mill's response to the objection that "the utilitarian doctrine . . . maintains that virtue is not a thing to be desired" (IV.5). Mill's response is that "the very reverse" is true. Utilitarianism "maintains not only that virtue is to be desired, but that it is to be desired . . . for itself" (IV.5). Here Mill asserts his famous doctrine that virtue is not simply a means to happiness but an "ingredient" in or "part of" it. "In being desired for its own sake it is . . . desired as *part* of happiness" (IV.6).

So much, Mill argues, follows from the very natures of pleasure and desire. "I believe that . . . desiring a thing and finding it pleasant," Mill says, "aversion to it and thinking of it as painful, are phenomena entirely inseparable or, rather . . . in strictness of language, two different modes of naming the same psychological fact" (IV.10). "To desire anything," he concludes, "except in proportion as the idea of it is pleasant is a physical and metaphysical impossibility" (IV.10).

The basic point is that pleasures, like desires, have intentional objects. Whenever we experience pleasure – just as whenever we desire – there must be an object of our pleasure or desire. Before I hear the news about my friend with cancer, I desire that the cancer will go into remission. When I hear that it has, my prior desire turns into a pleasure having the very same object. Even Bentham must agree with Mill's conceptual claim, since he understands intensity in terms of how much one likes the experience one is having. So Benthamite pleasures have objects also. The issue between Bentham and Mill then becomes an empirical one concerning what the objects of human pleasure and desire actually are. If Bentham is right, all we ever care about are felt qualities of our experience, whereas if Mill is right, we also often care about the objective features of what our experiences seem to be about.[7] On this empirical issue, Mill seems far likelier to be correct.

Even if this gives Mill a strong argument against quantitative hedonism, however, it then raises the question of whether Mill's considered view is actually a form of hedonism at all rather than a more Aristotelian theory that privileges the exercise of developed human capacities.

Once we distinguish between desire and the pro-attitude of liking that is conceptually implicated in pleasure, we can distinguish three different things to which "pleasure" can refer.[8] It can refer, first, to the object of the liking (what pleasure is taken *in*, like the fact of my friend's cancer remission). It can refer, second, to the attitude of liking that is had toward the object. Or third, it can refer to the complex of the liking attitude being caused by the object "in the right way."[9] Only the first of these would seem to be an instance of hedonism, properly so called. Mill's arguments, however, seem to push him more in the direction of the second and third.

Responding to Objections to Utilitarianism: First Pass

So much for Mill's theory of the good. In order to incorporate it into a utilitarian theory of right, Mill will need for a quantitative measure of happiness that takes into account both quality, in Mill's sense, and quantity, in Bentham's. To proceed to consider the distinctive contours of Mill's utilitarian "criterion of right and wrong," let us assume that such a quantitative measure, adequate to the complexities of Mill's theory of the good, is available.

Having laid out his qualitative hedonism, Mill turns in chapter II to considering a variety of objections that have been, and still are, made against the "greatest happiness principle," interpreted in the broadly act-utilitarian way that Mill seems first to formulate it: "actions are right in

[7] This is, of course, what is at issue in Nozick's well-known "experience machine" (Nozick 1974: 42).
[8] On Mill's ambiguous use of "pleasure," see Sidgwick (2000: 82).
[9] For a view of this kind, see Darwall (2002) and Kagan (2009).

proportion as they tend to promote happiness; wrong as they tend to produce the reverse of happiness" (II.2).

One objection is that utilitarianism, in an overly demanding way, requires agents "to be . . . strictly impartial" "between [their] own happiness and that of others" (II.18). Partly, Mill's response is that "laws and social arrangements" should make individual and general happiness coincide, and not just because of Benthamite external sanctions, but by leveraging the human "desire to be in unity with our fellow creatures" (II.18, III.10). But Mill also points out a distinction of fundamental importance to utilitarianism following Bentham between a standard of motives and a criterion of right and wrong. To suppose that utilitarianism requires that agents "always act from the inducement of promoting the general interests of society . . . is to . . . confound the rule of action with the motive of it" (II.19).

What's more, Mill adds, perhaps incredibly, that utilitarianism rarely asks agents to sacrifice their interests for the sake of others or even to act with the intention (never mind the motive) of promoting the general welfare. "The occasions on which any person (except one in a thousand) has it in his power . . . to be a public benefactor . . . are but exceptional" (II.19). In most cases, the "happiness of some few persons [including himself], is all he has to attend to" (II.19). We will want to keep this remark in mind when we consider in the next section reasons for doubting that Mill is a straightforward act utilitarian.

Yet another objection is that it is impossible to know future consequences and "that there is not time, previous to action, for calculating and weighing the effects of any line of conduct on the general happiness" (II.24). Mill's answer brings in yet again his talk of "tendencies." During "the whole past duration of the human species . . . mankind have been learning by experience the tendencies of actions" (II.24). This is as true with "prudence" as it is with "morality" (II.24). Just as no one doubts that the most prudent actions tend to maximize the agent's happiness, so also should no one doubt that normal consequences for the greatest happiness overall are the test of moral action.

At this point, Mill discusses the role of "secondary principles" in codifying the received wisdom of the ages. Whatever "fundamental principle of morality" we employ, Mill says, "we require subordinate principles to apply it by" (II. 24). All moral theories require "subordinate principles." The objection to utilitarianism just mentioned proceeds "as if no such secondary principles could be had, and as if mankind had remained till now, and always must remain, without drawing any general conclusions from the experience of human life." This, Mill says, is "as high a pitch, I think, as absurdity has ever reached in philosophical controversy" (II. 24).

Mill is happy to concede that utilitarianism, owing to its focus on consequences, will have to make use of secondary principles, but he insists that no moral theory can completely avoid them. But how does Mill intend their use in utilitarianism, more specifically? There are numerous possibilities. One is as rules of thumb or what Rawls calls "summary" rules, that is, as heuristics that summarize past experience (Rawls 1955). So understood, secondary principles have no independent normative force; their role is entirely epistemic. On this interpretation, if we know for sure that going against the received wisdom codified in a secondary principle will have the best consequences in a particular case, then the greatest happiness principle will require us to go against the secondary principle and do what we think will be best.

A second possibility that is slightly different is indicated by Mill's saying that "only in ... cases of conflict between secondary principles is it requisite that first principles should be appealed to" (Mill 2002: II.25). This suggests that if one secondary principle is unopposed by another in a particular case, then it should be followed even if following it would be suboptimal, perhaps even disastrous. On this interpretation, the only role for the principle of utility itself is to settle conflicts between secondary principles; otherwise, it is normatively impotent.

It is hard to believe that this was Mill's considered view. A third possibility is to interpret the greatest happiness principle's talk of tendencies in light of what Mill says about secondary principles and vice versa. On this interpretation, the two forms of expression come to the same thing. Secondary principles codify social knowledge about act tendencies.

Yet a fourth possibility, and perhaps the most promising in light of what Mill goes on to say about utilitarianism and justice in chapter V, is to interpret secondary principles as "practice" rather than "summary" rules (Rawls 1955). Practice rules are not guides or rules of thumb. Rather, they structure practices and are taken to have mandatory force within them. Rawls's thought was that although act utilitarians can happily make use of summary rules, practice rules are essential to a very different kind of utilitarian position: rule utilitarianism.

Act utilitarians of course agree with rule utilitarians in favoring the establishing and furthering of publicly useful social and legal practices. Where they part company with rule utilitarians is in holding that agents have no moral reason to comply with useful practice-structuring rules when doing so will not maximize utility in a given case. To think otherwise, act utilitarians like J. J. C. Smart say, is "rule worship" (Smart and Williams 1973: 6). Rule utilitarians, by contrast, hold that agents are morally required to comply with maximally useful practice rules even when doing so will not maximize overall net happiness in the case at hand (e.g., Brandt 1963).

Even before we get to chapter V of *Utilitarianism*, where a rule-utilitarian interpretation seems to fit best with what Mill says there about the conceptual requirements of justice and deontic morality, Mill ends his invocation of secondary principles in chapter II with a remark that suggests a rule-utilitarian interpretation. "There is no case of moral obligation in which some secondary principle is not involved; and if only one, there can seldom be any real doubt which one it is, in the mind of any person by whom the principle itself is recognized" (Mill 2002: II.25). This suggests that moral obligations require secondary principles that can be recognized and applied by those to whom they apply. In chapter V, Mill makes conceptual claims about justice and wrongness that support this claim. We turn to them now.

Justice, Rights, Morality, and Accountability

"In all ages of speculation," Mill writes, "one of the strongest obstacles to the reception of the doctrine that utility or happiness is the criterion of right and wrong has been drawn from the idea of justice" (V.1).[10] Mill devotes chapter V to meeting this challenge and to arguing for a "connection between justice and utility," as he puts it in the chapter's title.

Unlike Bentham, who thinks that the idea of moral or natural rights is "nonsense upon stilts," or Godwin, who thinks that justice is simply the same thing as universal benevolence, Mill takes the ideas of justice and rights, and the challenge they pose to utilitarianism, seriously as independent moral ideas (Bentham 2002; Godwin 2013: 56). The concept of justice, he writes, is connected to a "powerful sentiment" and "apparently clear perception" in our moral experience (Mill 2002: V.1). But that we have this feeling, Mill argues, "does not necessarily legitimate all its promptings. The feeling of justice might be a peculiar instinct, and might yet require, like our other instincts, to be controlled and enlightened by a higher reason" (V.2). And although "mankind are always predisposed to believe that any subjective feeling, not otherwise accounted for, is a revelation of some

[10] The discussion in this section closely follows Darwall (1998a: 132–138).

objective reality," it does not follow that the "feeling of justice" reveals objective ethical facts that are irreducible to considerations of utility.

Still, there is no doubt that Mill thinks justice and rights are absolutely central to morality. Their function is to protect what is most important to people's happiness. And it is worth noting that Mill thinks that equal rights and justice are not only useful instruments in promoting human goods but also essential constituents of some of the most important human goods. Thus, Mill lists a "sense of dignity" as "so essential a part of the happiness of those in whom it is strong that nothing which conflicts with it could be otherwise than momentarily an object of desire to them" (II.6). And the importance of reciprocal relationships of equal respect is an important theme of *The Subjection of Women* and other works (Mill 1984).[11]

Mill begins by canvassing various things justice has been taken to mean over the centuries. He finds much inconsistency but also notes a common element: Judgments of justice are invariably related to the ideas of *law* and *sanctions*. Initially, justice simply meant "conformity to law," and rights referred only to legal rights. This is justice's "*idée mère*" (2002: V.12). Once societies were able to step back from their laws and consider them critically, however, they were able to conceive of justice as including the critical standpoint of the moral point of view. "The sentiment of injustice came to be attached, not to all violations of law, but only to violations of such laws as *ought* to exist, including such as ought to exist but do not, and to laws themselves if supposed to be contrary to what ought to be law" (V.12).

The difference, then, between what was thought morally better for a person to do and what was thought unjust for them not to do was that the latter was held to involve appropriate sanctions. In many cases, these are formally codified in law, as in laws that create penalties for various forms of violence and harm, fraud, breaking of contract, and so on. But notions of justice and rights may be thought to apply in other cases that "neither are, nor is it desired that they should be, regulated by law" also (V.13). Someone may resent an unjust betrayal and feel that their rights as a friend have been violated. But that doesn't mean that we should have a "friends' court" where such cases might be tried. "Nobody desires that laws should interfere with the whole detail of private life" (V.13). Nonetheless, Mill writes, "even here the idea of the breach of what ought to be law still lingers in a modified shape" (V.13). We may think, for

11 Although the ideas in *Subjection* resulted from a collaboration with Harriet Taylor, since Taylor died in 1858 and *Subjection* was published over a decade later (1869), authorship is usually attributed to Mill alone.

example, that the former friend who acted unjustly should at least feel guilty for what they have done.

Justice and rights, Mill thinks, are things it makes moral sense to *protect* with some rule-governed social practice, either with laws or with less formal devices like expressions of reproach or guilt feelings or even gossip. "A right," he says, is "something which society ought to defend me in the possession of" by such formal and informal social mechanisms (V.25). But this, Mill argues, is as far as the idea of rights and justice can take us. What we cannot get from these ideas themselves is answer to the question of which rights we should protect, hence, what moral rights we actually have – what really is just or unjust. To determine that, we need some basis for choosing between alternative laws or choosing between informal social mechanisms. And this, Mill thinks, is precisely what utilitarianism gives us. If he is asked why a given right should be defended, Mill says, "I can give . . . no other reason than general utility" (V.25).

Not only, then, does justice not conflict with utilitarianism when both are rightly understood. To the contrary, utilitarianism provides a moral criterion of laws without which the idea of justice would be incomplete. For something to be unjust, Mill argues, is for it to be contrary to a rule-governed, social practice (laws or less formal rules) that it would promote the general happiness for society to have.

"The idea of justice supposes two things," Mill says: "a rule of conduct and a sentiment which sanctions the rule" (V.23). The sentiment of justice, he says, involves a distinctively human form of the "animal desire to repel or retaliate a hurt or damage to oneself or to those with whom one sympathizes" (V.23). In human beings, "animal" resentment can be regulated by an "enlarged sympathy" and concern for the welfare of all (V.23). Only from this, Mill writes, does "the feeling deriv[e] its morality," making it a sentiment of *justice* rather than mere revenge. Only then is "the natural feeling of resentment . . . moralized" (V.23, 38). And, for moral purposes, such a rule exists if, and only if, it would promote the general happiness for society to have it.

What is perhaps most important for our purposes is that Mill relates these ideas to the more general deontic idea of moral wrongness. When someone's right is violated, they are wronged, which entails that the violator has violated their moral duty and done something that is morally wrong period (Darwall 2013a). We never "call anything wrong," Mill says, "unless we mean to imply that a person ought to be punished in some way or other for doing it – if not by law, by the opinion of his fellow creatures; if not by opinion, by the reproaches of his own conscience"

(Mill 2002: V.14). This means that the very idea of moral wrong is that of conduct that is punishable or *blameworthy* lacking adequate excuse. As Mill thinks of it, therefore, morality is a system of *accountability* in which individuals are held responsible for their conduct. Whether conduct is wrong, consequently, cannot be determined simply by looking at *its* consequences. Rather, conduct is wrong if, and only if, it is the sort of thing for which people can be appropriately blamed in formal and informal social practices of accountability.

Mill thus holds that there is a conceptual connection between moral right and wrong and accountability that is similar to that between justice and resentment. When an agent does something wrong, they are fittingly objects of "reproaches of [their] own conscience," just as injustice is the fitting object of resentment (V.14). Though conceptually connected, the ideas of injustice and moral wrong are nonetheless distinct. Unlike moral wrongs period, injustice and violations of rights require "some assignable person who is wronged" (V.15). But though these are different ideas, the latter entails the former. In addition to requiring a specific victim whose right has been violated, injustice also entails a "wrong done" (V.15).

If, consequently, Mill is to advance a rule-utilitarian theory of rights and justice, he must also hold a rule-utilitarian "criterion of right and wrong" on pain of inconsistency (I.1). When we put this together with the last interpretation of "secondary principles" we surveyed in the last section, this suggests that the most plausible interpretation of Mill's theory of right overall is a rule-utilitarian one.

This fits also with the tendency language of the "greatest happiness principle," and, as well, with what Mill says about conscience being the major "internal sanction" to comply with morality (II.2, III.6–7). This is true, he thinks regardless of morality's content. What makes conscience focus on utilitarian morality is the natural human "desire to be in unity with our fellow creatures" (III.10).

On Liberty and Progressive Politics

Mill's *On Liberty* is one of the great works of classical liberal political philosophy. Because our focus is Mill's moral philosophy, we can be relatively brief. *On Liberty*'s central political philosophical claim is encapsulated in Mill's famous "harm principle": "the only purpose for which power can be rightfully exercised over any member of a civilized community, against his will, is to prevent harm to others. His own good, either physical or moral, is not a sufficient warrant" (Mill 1977: 223). How exactly to interpret the harm principle is controversial, but Mill clearly intends it to support a robust sphere of individual liberty.

What is noteworthy about *On Liberty* from our perspective is that its defense of liberty proceeds along utilitarian lines.[12] And, perhaps most interestingly, in chapter III, "Of Individuality, as One of the Elements of Well-Being," Mill introduces an idea that both has the first importance in itself and is central to a successful utilitarian defense of liberty. The notion that individuals have an autonomy right to lead their own lives was a familiar claim of early modern moral and political philosophy. As a utilitarian, Mill holds that any such right must be grounded in well-being. What is new in *On Liberty* is the idea that at the core of human welfare is self-development as an *individual*.

This thought is a staple of contemporary culture and ethical philosophy. One finds it, for example, in what Bernard Williams calls "integrity" and in Christine Korsgaard's concept of practical identity. Mill may not have been the first to give it philosophical expression – Kierkegaard and Nietzsche come to mind – but his was certainly one of the most influential for anglophone moral and political theory (Smart and Williams 1973; Korsgaard 1996a). Thus Mill's utilitarianism of rights is based on "the permanent interests of man as a progressive being" (Mill 1977: 224). The relevant "progress" moreover is *self*-progress: "the free development of individuality is one of the leading essentials of well-being" (261).

Like Bentham and the Philosophical Radicals, Mill was a social and political progressive. We have already noted his strong opposition to slavery and racism. Surely his most progressive political philosophical work was his collaborative book with Harriett Taylor, *The Subjection of Women* (Mill 1984). *Subjection*'s very title is radical, centering its discussion not on discrimination or inequality in general but on structural patriarchal subjugation. Individuality is central to the argument here as well. Speaking, for example, about the plight of women writers, Mill writes that "it will require generations more, before their individuality is sufficiently developed to make head against that [patriarchal] influence" (Mill 1984: 317).

Finally, Mill was a strong proponent of the moral status of other animals. In his essay on Whewell, Mill defends Bentham's famous claim in *Introduction to the Principles* that the only qualification for moral consideration is the capacity to suffer (Mill 1985). Mill notes its social influence "seen in the laws enacted nearly fifty years afterwards against

[12] Whereas, as we noted, Bentham's defense of the principle of utility in *Introduction to the Principles* seems to proceed in the opposite direction.

cruelty to animals" (186). An "intuitive moralist" (Mill 2002: III.7), Whewell defends the status quo view as follows: "We are bound to endeavour to augment the pleasures of men, not only because they are pleasures, but because they are human pleasures. We are bound to men by the universal tie of humanity, of human brotherhood. We have no such tie to animals" (Mill 1984: 186). Mill argues against this that Whewell's intuitionist defense of "popular morality" (Mill 2002: I.1) commits him to a host of retrograde views that puts him on the wrong side of history. It is worth quoting Mill's critique at length since it can serve as an example of the "inductiv[ist]" (I.3) utilitarian program at its best:

> It is "to most persons" in the Slave States of America not a tolerable doctrine that we may sacrifice any portion of the happiness of white men for the sake of a greater amount of happiness to black men. It would have been intolerable five centuries ago "to most persons" among the feudal nobility, to hear it asserted that the greatest pleasure or pain of a hundred serfs ought not to give way to the smallest of a nobleman. According to the standard of Dr. Whewell, the slavemasters and the nobles were right. They too felt themselves "bound" by a "tie of brotherhood" to the white men and to the nobility, and felt no such tie to the negroes and serfs. And if a feeling on moral subjects is right because it is natural, their feeling was justifiable. Nothing is more natural to human beings, nor, up to a certain point in cultivation, more universal, than to estimate the pleasures and pains of others as deserving of regard exactly in proportion to their likeness to ourselves. These superstitions of selfishness had the characteristics by which Dr. Whewell recognises his moral rules; and his opinion on the rights of animals shows that in this case at least he is consistent. We are perfectly willing to stake the whole question on this one issue. Granted that any practice causes more pain to animals than it gives pleasure to man; is that practice moral or immoral? And if, exactly in proportion as human beings raise their heads out of the slough of selfishness, they do not with one voice answer "immoral," let the morality of the principle of utility be for ever condemned (1984: 186–187).

PART IV

Victorian Anti-naturalism

Schneewind remarks that British moral philosophy from the French Revolution to the twentieth century can be divided into three periods. The first begins in the mid-1780s with Paley, Reid, and Bentham. The second starts in the mid-1830s, "when both John Stuart Mill and his strongest opponent, William Whewell, began publishing their ethical views. And the third begins some forty years later when, just after the death of Mill in 1873, major ethical works by Sidgwick, Bradley, and Spencer appeared" (Schneewind 1977: 3). Henry Sidgwick (1838–1900) published the first of these, *The Methods of Ethics*, in 1874, which has had, and continues to have, a massive influence on subsequent moral philosophy. (Broad and Parfit are only two of the philosophers who have called it the best book on ethics ever written [Broad 1962: 143; Parfit 2011, v. i: xxxiii].)[1] F. H. Bradley (1846–1924) published the second, *Ethical Studies*, in 1876. And Herbert Spencer (1820–1903) wrote the third, *The Data of Ethics*, in 1879.

Although the social Darwinism articulated in Spencer's *Social Statics* (1851) clearly extends beyond the scope of the debates between Whewell and Mill, Spencer's ethical philosophy fits squarely within Mill's inductivist tradition. From the standpoint of ethical philosophy, *The Data of Ethics* failed to make an enduring mark, and Spencer's social analysis and philosophy were happily ultimately rejected, and their racism denounced. So although our focus in this chapter will be on Schneewind's third period, we will not be discussing Spencer. In his place, we will study T. H. Green (1836–1882), whose *Prolegomena to Ethics* appeared posthumously in 1883.

Green and Bradley are both representatives of what came to be known as British Idealism. Green is by far the more philosophically interesting and acute, as we shall see. Both are influenced by Hegel, but Green attempts to

[1] Already in 1885, Rashdall wrote, "*The Methods of Ethics* has long been recognized as a philosophical classic" (quoted in Marcus Singer's introduction to Sidgwick 2000: xxvi).

work out a version of Kant's doctrine of universal equal dignity that finds no place in Bradley. Indeed, he does so in a way that anticipates Rawls's idea that each person is a "self-originating sourc[e] of valid claims" (Rawls 1980: 546). Green's version of the moral community as a Kantian realm of ends is "a community of all men of whom one can communicate with the other as 'I' with 'Thou,'" that is, a society of mutually accountable equals (Green 2003: §216).

Although Sidgwick and the British idealists are starkly opposed – Bradley and Green argue strenuously against both utilitarianism and hedonism – all three nonetheless agree in departing from the philosophical traditions represented by Mill's inductivism and by his intuitivist opponents. The contrast between Mill and Sidgwick is especially significant since both characterize themselves as hedonistic utilitarians. Against Mill, Sidgwick argues that no ethical doctrine can be grounded in empirical psychology in the way that Bentham, Mill, and earlier utilitarians from Cumberland on had attempted to do. All ethical propositions, Sidgwick says, contain a common "fundamental ethical notion represented by the word 'ought' or 'right,'" which is "essentially different from all notions representing facts of physical or psychical experience" that are open to empirical investigation (Sidgwick 1962: 25). This is an idea that will prove especially important in twentieth-century metaethics, beginning with Moore.

Sidgwick argues that inductivism is thus impotent to ground ethical claims; it cannot account for their irreducibly normative element. For that, he holds, nonempirical intuitions are indispensable. But that does not make Sidgwick an "intuitiv[ist]" in Mill's terms (Mill 2002: I.3). Like Mill, Sidgwick is suspicious of what he calls "Common Sense Morality," which the intuitivists claim to be grounded in commonsense moral intuitions (Sidgwick 1962: 373). Their position amounts to what Sidgwick terms "Dogmatic Intuitionism," which he carefully considers but rejects, along with the morality of common sense that intuitive moralists claim it grounds (xxv, 100–103). For the "intuitivist," dogmatic version, Sidgwick substitutes a more abstract form of intuitionism that he calls "Philosophical Intuitionism." And for commonsense morality, he substitutes utilitarianism, arguing that it can be grounded in self-evident philosophical intuition in a way that commonsense morality cannot be. The putative intuitions of dogmatic intuitionism can never achieve genuine self-evidence.

For their part, Green and Bradley reject both empiricist inductivist ethical philosophy and all forms of intuitionism, whether the dogmatic version of Mill's intuitive moralists or Sidgwick's philosophical intuitionism. In contrast, they defend forms of idealism that derive from Hegel and, in Green's case, from Kant. As David Brink and Terence Irwin emphasize, however, Green and Bradley are both eudaimonists in ways that both Hegel and Kant reject (Green 2003: xlix; Irwin 2009: 602–615). Irwin argues, indeed, that Green develops a version of "Aristotelian Naturalism" (Irwin 2009: 602–615). Our greatest good, Green and Bradley both think, consists in a common good that we realize through a life of virtue.

However, Bradley and Green are both decidedly moderns. Both hold that the human good consists in self-realization and, following Hegel, in the instantiation of "infinite Spirit" or of an "infinite whole" (Bradley 1988: 68; Green 2003: §319). Moreover, both identify this with the actualization of a distinctively positive form of freedom in the manner of Hegel (Green 1885–1888: 3:324–330; Bradley 1988: 169).

All three of Sidgwick, Bradley, and Green, indeed, identify themselves as modern philosophers in contrast with the ancient Greeks. The earlier companion to the current volume begins with Sidgwick's contrast between ancient ethics' focus on the good in its various forms and the modern period's emphasis on deontic or, as he puts it, "quasi-jural" questions of moral obligation and duty (Sidgwick 1962: 106; Darwall 2023a: 4–6). The idealists' focus on freedom also carries forward a theme that Hegel cites as distinctively modern. "The right of *subjective freedom*," Hegel writes, "is the pivotal and focal point in the difference between *antiquity* and the *modern* age" (Hegel 1991: 151).

Ultimately, though, it is unclear how any of Sidgwick, Bradley, or Green can sustain the claim to be modern moral philosophers in Anscombe's and Sidgwick's "jural" sense. Sidgwick does motivate a conception of impersonal goodness from "the point of view . . . of the Universe" that is unlike anything to be found in Aristotle. (This forms one of the two poles of Sidgwick's "Dualism of the Practical Reason," and it plays a central role in all forms of consequentialism from Moore on [Sidgwick 1962: x, 382].) But there ends up being nothing in Sidgwick's ethics having the quasi-jural conceptual contours of deontic normativity that Sidgwick identifies. Sidgwick has nothing in his moral philosophy or psychology that can play the role that he says "Conscience" does "in the modern ethical view, when it has worked itself clear" (1964: 198).[2]

It is truer to Sidgwick's conception, as we shall see, to formulate utilitarianism in the terms that Hutcheson suggests, as a standard of

[2] In the preface to the second edition of *The Methods*, Sidgwick says that he "hold[s] with Butler" that "Conscience" along with "Reasonable Self-love are the two chief or superior principles in the nature of man" (Sidgwick 1962: xiii).

what is most morally choice worthy. For Sidgwick, however, the moral point of view is less one of impartial concern or benevolence, as it is for Hutcheson, and more an impersonal perspective – "the point of view of the Universe" – from which one can see no justifiable difference between one person's good and another's. In this way, Sidgwick's justification for utilitarianism is more like Cumberland's (see Darwall 2023a: 107–108). In any case, Sidgwick provides no reason whatsoever that can support utilitarianism as a deontic doctrine, as providing a "criterion of right and wrong" in Mill's terms (Mill 2002: I.1).

This has profound implications for Sidgwick's "Dualism of the Practical Reason" and for his claim that utilitarianism, as he understands it, provides the best explanation of whatever validity commonsense moral intuitions have. It means that Sidgwick's dualism is ultimately not, as he portrays it, between ancient egoism or eudaimonism, on the one hand, and morality conceived in the "quasi-jural" sense characteristic of modern moral philosophy, on the other. It is rather between prudence, conceived as promoting what is best from the agent's own point of view, on the one hand, and promoting what is best from the point of view of the universe, on the other. Second, Sidgwick's argument that moral common sense is "unconsciously utilitarian" because utilitarianism provides the best explanation of moral common sense is undermined by the fact that common sense is unremittingly "jural" or deontic, as Sidgwick himself regularly points out (see, e.g., Sidgwick 1962: 228). However, utilitarianism, as Sidgwick is bound to understand it, is not. It is simply a claim about what would be most choice worthy from a fully impersonal point of view.

A remarkable manifestation of this is that Derek Parfit, one of Sidgwick's greatest admirers and a defender in *Reasons and Persons* of act consequentialism along Sidgwickean (albeit non-hedonistic) lines, later argues in *On What Matters* that Sidgwick's act consequentialism is "better regarded, not as a moral view, but as being like Rational Egoism, an external rival to morality" (Parfit 2011: I. 168). What explains Parfit's change in view is that, much like Mill in chapter V of *Utilitarianism*, Parfit came to appreciate the conceptual connections between the concept of moral wrong and accountability (Darwall 2021).

But so also are Green and Bradley challenged to provide genuinely deontic moral theories. Bradley's famous "My Station and Its Duties" might seem to prove the contrary, since duty is obviously a deontic concept. However, when this essay is fully grasped in its context in *Ethical Studies*, it becomes clear that duties as Bradley understands them have no intrinsic deontic normativity. And when we take account of

Bradley's "Duty for Duty's Sake," it becomes obvious also that Bradley works with a fundamental contrast between "duties" in a count-noun sense that refers to actual social *mores*, and "duty" in a noncount-noun sense that refers to an intrinsically normative standard obligating those who are subject to it (Bradley 1988: 142–213). Duties have the recognized *actuality* that Hegel contrasts with the mere abstractions of *Moralität.* And "duty" Bradley subversively redefines in eudaimonist terms.

Bradley agrees with Hegel's diagnosis of morality as it is standardly theorized in modern moral philosophy. Every person's final end, he thinks, is their own self-realization, which they can achieve only within their social station by complying with its distinctive duties in the count-noun sense. Crucially, this end concerns agents' *good.* This is what rational persons should aim at, not at complying with "duty for duty's sake" (142–159). To put his claim in other words, Bradley fundamentally rejects Prichard's claim that moral philosophy "rests on a mistake" when the right is grounded in the agent's good (Prichard 1912: 21). To the contrary, Bradley, following Hegel, claims that any morality that is not grounded in the agent's self-realization through compliance with their social duties is a mere abstraction.

Green might be thought to fare better than Bradley, since he argues that self-realization – which, he agrees with Bradley, is the final rational end – is achieved not through complying with actual social duties, but through an ideal "universal human fellowship," that is, in an ideal moral community, a Kingdom of Ends, with everyone who is capable of reciprocal recognition (Green 2003: §216). But Green's ethics are no less teleological and eudaimonist than Bradley's. Green would agree with Bradley as against Prichard that to rest moral philosophy on the good cannot be a mistake; it is the only rational possibility.

Recall that in Bentham and Mill's hands utilitarianism was a doctrine of reform, both in conception and in effect. Victorian moral philosophy was, by comparison, more staid and conservative, even in the utilitarian form that Sidgwick gave it. Bradley's views were avowedly conservative, tying self-realization to the status quo. And though Green was more progressive, he was hardly a "philosophical radical" in the manner of Bentham and Mill. Sidgwick's hedonistic utilitarianism certainly provided ammunition for radical reform, arguably even more than Mill's version, since Sidgwick rejected Mill's qualitative hedonism in favor of Bentham's quantitative version and was clearly, like Bentham, an act rather than a rule utilitarian. Despite this, Sidgwick maintains that the public morality that utilitarianism recommends is likely to be close to moral common sense. Utilitarianism, he argues, should be maintained as an "esoteric morality," a doctrine that theorists believe but do not publicly proclaim. Indeed, Sidgwick argues, "it seems expedient that the doctrine that esoteric morality is expedient should itself be kept esoteric" (Sidgwick 1962: 490). It was this aspect of Sidgwick's defense of act utilitarianism – its sharp separation between a standard of moral right and a *publicly* recommended principle – that influenced later defenses of the view – for example, by Parfit in *Reasons and Persons* – but also led critics like Bernard Williams to characterize it as "Government House utilitarianism" (Parfit 1984; Williams 1985: 120).

Although Sidgwick was hardly a philosophical radical, he definitely was an at least cautious reformer. Most notable was his role, along with that of his wife Eleanor, in the founding of Newnham College (for women) at Cambridge and in supporting women at Cambridge more generally (Schultz 2004: 296–297).[3] (Eleanor became the second principal of the college.) Henry was a broadly liberal political thinker and actor, although one who, like Burke, was concerned about the social costs of reform.[4] His estimate of those costs, moreover, frequently bore the imprint of his gender, race, and class, as well as that of a Victorian colonial British perspective. Not always, however. Bart Schultz notes that Sidgwick's *Principles of Political Economy* contains sections on "International Law and Morality" and "The Regulation of War" that advance a "utilitarian impartialism in international affairs" that "continues to attract defenders" (Schultz 2004: 624). But Sidgwick's *Principles* is also riddled by complacency about colonialism and forms of racism that today seem frankly appalling (Schultz 2004: 630–641).

The Methods of Ethics also features shocking examples. While analyzing commonsense morality's treatment of special relations, Sidgwick writes that we would "all agree" about obligations to close family, "kinsmen," "friends," "neighbors," and "countrymen" (Sidgwick 1962: 246). But to this he adds, "perhaps we may [pay more attention to] those of our own race more than to black or yellow men, and generally to human beings in proportion to their affinity to ourselves" (246). And later he refers to the "legal and customary" polygyny "among the lower races of man" (358). As Schultz remarks, Sidgwick "was not immune to the pervasive and offensive – often offensively casual – racism of his environment" (Schultz 2004: 317). "One cannot confront this side of Sidgwick," Schultz continues, "without worrying deeply about just how limited his notions of

[3] Schultz (2004) is an excellent biography of Sidgwick to which I am much indebted.

[4] Schultz (2004) has an extensive and insightful treatment of Sidgwick's political views (as advanced, for example, in his *Principles of Political Economy*, and his political activity in the Liberal Party [Sidgwick 1887]).

'educated common sense' . . . might have been" (317). This side of Sidgwick does not, however, seem to affect the aspects of his thought that have been most influential – his analysis of ethical (indeed, normative) concepts, his defense of philosophical intuitionism and of the role of intuitions in moral philosophy more generally, his dualism of practical reason, and his defense of act utilitarianism. To that, we now turn.

CHAPTER 9

Sidgwick

Henry Sidgwick, like both Bradley and Green, was the son of a clergyman. His Anglican father was also the headmaster of a local grammar school, and Henry's education was well provided for. He went to the Rugby School, where he first met T. H. Green, and then to Trinity College, Cambridge, where he remained for the rest of his life. Although Sidgwick abandoned Anglicanism early on at Trinity, he retained a strong religious or spiritual outlook for the rest of his life. He had a philosophical incentive to do so. In the preface to the second edition of *The Methods*, Sidgwick announced his famous "Dualism of the Practical Reason," his doctrine that rational prudence and rational benevolence are independent final rational principles and, consequently, that practical reason can give unified guidance only if they do not conflict (Sidgwick 1962: x). "Theology apart," however, he could not be confident that this is so (xi). This was not a problem for Bishop Butler, from whom Sidgwick thought he got his dualism, since Butler believed that God in the long run guarantees the ultimate agreement of conscience and self-love.[1] But Sidgwick could not accept such a divine assurance. Arguably, Sidgwick (and Eleanor)'s long interest in psychical research had something to do with the anxieties his dualism created for someone who was perennially concerned with working out what he had most reason, or ought, to do, but who was disinclined to accept Butler's or Hutcheson's theology.

While an undergraduate at Trinity, Sidgwick joined an exclusive "discussion society," the Apostles, which proved especially important to him and a fertile philosophical ground more generally: Moore and Russell would later join (Sidgwick and Sidgwick 1906: 34). Friendships he formed

[1] I argue in Darwall 2023a that Hutcheson rather than Butler is the true model for Sidgwick's dualism, and that Butler holds that ultimately conscience has supreme authority (Darwall 2023a: 168). Hutcheson also held that God guarantees the ultimate harmony of morality and self-interest, in his case, of benevolence and self-love.

in the Apostles remained active throughout his life. Sidgwick wrote in his memoir that "the tie of attachment to the society is much the strongest corporate bond which I have known in life" (35).

When he completed his undergraduate studies, Sidgwick took up a fellowship, also at Trinity. He held the post for ten years, but became increasingly uncomfortable doing so, since it required allegiance to the Thirty-Nine Articles of the Anglican Church. Finally, Sidgwick could no longer justify what he considered to be hypocrisy given his religious unbelief, and he renounced the fellowship, retaining his lectureship. This, again, gave him a reason, beyond his legendary philosophical curiosity, to investigate ethics, conceiving it as the "study of what ought to be, so far as this depends upon the voluntary actions of individuals" (Sidgwick 1962: xxiii). Most importantly, he wondered, does reason give clear practical guidance? This is the subject of *The Methods of Ethics*.

The Methods: An Overview

A "Method of Ethics," Sidgwick tells us at the outset of *The Methods*, is "any rational procedure by which we determine what individual human beings 'ought' – or what it is 'right' for them – to do, or to seek to realise by voluntary action" (1).[2] Already we can glimpse an issue that will occupy us throughout our study of *The Methods*. The practical "ought" or "right" can have a broad, what Gibbard calls a "flavorless," sense – as the most general term of ethics or normative theory – or it can be read in the "quasi-jural" way that Sidgwick holds to be a distinct contribution of modern moral philosophy (Gibbard 1990: 7; Sidgwick 1962: 106). Ancient philosophers like Aristotle, Sidgwick must have thought, implicitly employed the broader sense of "ought" or "right"; even if they were not doing moral philosophy in the modern style, they were certainly doing ethics! In talking about agents' good (*eudaimonia*) or the noble or fine (*kalon*), they must have been referring to what agents have reason or ought to want (perhaps for their own sake) or what anyone has reason to esteem. But Sidgwick also frequently employs "ought" and "right" in their deontic or, as he usually puts it, "quasi-jural" or "jural" senses, especially when discussing commonsense morality. So we shall need to clarify what these terms are intended to mean in the various contexts in which Sidgwick employs them.

[2] In what follows, I am indebted to many Sidgwick scholars, most especially, to Schneewind 1977, which remains a magisterial work. Other important works are M. Singer's introduction to Sidgwick 2000, Phillips 2011, Crisp 2013, and Shaver 2000, 2006, 2014.

A "Method of Ethics," again, is a "rational procedure . . . by which we determine what individual human beings 'ought' . . . to do." The natural way to read "determine" is epistemologically. Sidgwick tends not to concern himself with metaphysical issues about the nature of ethical properties and facts, although he makes conceptual claims, for example, about the irreducibility of the concept of "ought" and the judgment internalist claim that (ethical) judgments that employ this concept standardly (but necessarily) "have some . . . influence on volition" (Sidgwick 1962: 25; Shaver 2000). Moore will argue from Sidgwick's observations about conceptual irreducibility that the fundamental ethical concept – intrinsic goodness, as Moore interprets it – denotes properties that are unanalyzable *metaphysically*. But Sidgwick never makes any such claim. We should therefore read "determine" epistemologically and not metaphysically.

But things are more complicated still. Sidgwick identifies three main ethical methods, to each of which he devotes a "book": "Egoism" is discussed in book II; "Intuitionism," in book III; and "Utilitarianism," in book IV. None of these, however, are epistemological "processes" or "methods." They are all, primarily, at least, normative ethical theories or "principles."[3] Egoism is the normative principle that dictates doing what will advance one's own greatest good. Intuitionism is the set of principles that Sidgwick dubs "Common Sense Morality." And utilitarianism is the principle that dictates doing whatever will bring about the greatest good overall.

Different normative principles can come with different epistemologies (and, indeed, with different metaphysical foundations). Thus, Sidgwick notes that different philosophers, like Bentham, have attempted to argue for ethical egoism from the empirical theory of psychological egoism. Sidgwick famously claims, however, that no (normative) ethical proposition can be justified empirically, as we shall see in the next section. Similarly, Mill argues for utilitarianism on "inductiv[ist]" grounds (Mill 2002: I.3). But here again, Sidgwick argues that no such grounding can work. In both cases, he argues that the theories can be justified through self-evident (philosophical) intuition. (That is what creates the dualism of practical reason.)

Or take intuitionism. We might think the principles of commonsense morality can be "determined" in the way "dogmatic intuitionis[t]s" like Whewell think, by apparently self-evident reflection (Sidgwick 1962: xxv). Or we might attempt to derive these principles in some more fundamental way, as contractualists and rule utilitarians do.

[3] On the relation between methods and principles, see Schneewind (1977: 195).

Where might perfectionism or self-realization fit in Sidgwick's scheme of methods? If the agent's perfection is held to be rationally choice worthy because it is an important (or perhaps the only important) element of the agent's good or happiness, then it is a version of the method of egoism. If, on the other hand, moral excellence or perfection, say, is thought to be choice worthy in itself, and not just because it benefits the agent, then, Sidgwick thinks, it will ultimately have to consist in dispositions to perform right actions. So it cannot really be an independent method, and Sidgwick tends to treat it under intuitionism.

What, then, is Sidgwick's epistemology? There is disagreement between scholars about whether Sidgwick is a foundationalist – resting everything on self-evident intuitions that support egoism and utilitarianism – or whether his method is some version of what Rawls calls "reflective equilibrium" (Rawls 1971: 48–51; Singer 1974; Schneewind 1977: 260–275; Skelton 2010). It seems clear, however, that whatever epistemology Sidgwick himself accepts, whether at the end of the day he is a foundationalist or a coherentist, the moral epistemology that *The Methods* itself employs is some form of reflective equilibrium, albeit a "wide reflective equilibrium" that privileges philosophical intuitions (Daniels 1979).

Sidgwick tells us that the book's "object ... is to expound ... the different methods of Ethics that [he] find[s] implicit in our common moral reasoning" (Sidgwick 1962: 14). In much of *The Methods*, Sidgwick is writing not in his own voice, but in those he finds in the common moral culture, attempting to see how these might be best systematized and justified. In his preface to the Hackett edition, Rawls calls *The Methods* "the first truly academic work in moral philosophy" (Sidgwick 1981: 2).

Schneewind emphasizes for this reason that it is a mistake to view it as primarily a defense of utilitarianism (Schneewind 1977: 192). Even when Sidgwick is presenting arguments for utilitarianism he seems to agree with, he gives some weight to ordinary moral opinion. Thus his argument that commonsense morality is unconsciously utilitarian implicitly gives moral common opinion at least *prima facie* evidentiary weight. And if it be thought that this argument is purely dialectical, when we read *The Methods* in the light of what we know about Sidgwick's own life – for example, his conscientiousness in resigning his fellowship at Trinity – it is very difficult to conclude that Sidgwick did not take commonsense views seriously.

As noted earlier, books II, III, and IV of *The Methods* are detailed investigations of egoism, intuitionism, and utilitarianism, respectively. Book I contains several analytical preliminaries: setting out definitions of key terms, discussing the relations between pleasure and desire, putting aside metaphysical issues of freedom of the will as "practically [un]important[t]," and, most importantly, giving a metaethical analysis of "ethical judgments," which has a significance that still reverberates in moral philosophy today (Sidgwick 1962: 23, 70).[4]

Toward the end of book I, Sidgwick distinguishes three different views that can be called intuitionist: "Perceptional, Dogmatic, and Philosophical" Intuitionism (102). Perceptional or "ultra-" intuitionism is the view that the ethical qualities of specific kinds of actions can be self-evident. Sidgwick holds that perceptional intuitionism cannot be taken seriously. On reflection, no one can think that ethical qualities attach to particulars *barely*, that is without being grounded in other, ethical-making qualities. If a particular action is right or wrong, it must be in virtue of the kind of act it is, or the kind of thing it causes. Dogmatic intuitionism is the variety held by Mill's intuitive moralists who claim self-evident perception of the rightness or wrongness of act types. This is the kind of intuitionist who supports what Sidgwick calls "Common Sense Morality" and whose position he considers in book III. Philosophical intuitionism is the view that Sidgwick himself accepts. It provides the basis for his Axioms of Rational Prudence and Benevolence and, therefore, forms a powerful plank of his argument for utilitarianism.

Ethical Judgments

Far and away the most significant part of book I is chapter III, on "Ethical Judgments." Moore is often credited with beginning contemporary metaethics when, in *Principia Ethica*, he argues that ethical judgments cannot be analyzed in natural (or supernatural) terms without committing the "naturalistic fallacy" (Moore 1993a). As Thomas Hurka points out, however, Moore's claim was perfectly familiar when he advanced it in 1903, since Sidgwick had argued as much in *The Methods* in 1874 (Hurka 2003, 2014). Indeed, as William Frankena pointed out, Sidgwick had a much better version of Moore's thesis than Moore did himself (Frankena 1942). Moore claimed that the fundamental ethical concept was intrinsic goodness (expressed by "good" when used in an ethical sense) and that this concept was simple and unanalyzable. Sidgwick had claimed, however, that "ought" is the fundamental moral concept and that all other ethical

[4] We should note in passing that Sidgwick explicitly connects his discussion of free will to "judgments of right and wrong" and the "morally culpable" and "blameworthy" (Sidgwick 1962: 60–61). A person can only be "morally bound to do," he says, "what is 'in [their] power'" (67).

concepts, including those of the good, must be analyzed in its terms. We shall see presently why Sidgwick's claim is likelier to be correct than Moore's is.

No ethical judgments, Sidgwick claims, can "legitimately be interpreted as judgments respecting the present or future existence of human feelings or any facts of the sensible world" (Sidgwick 1962: 25). Ethical judgments do not concern "actual or possible facts" (25).[5] The fundamental ones employing "ought" – what Scanlon calls "pure normative claims" – do not concern *actuality* at all (Scanlon 2014: 36–37).

We have already noted that "ought" and "right" are crucially ambiguous, having broader "flavorless" and narrower deontic or "jural" uses. Obviously, the sense of "ought" involved in "pure" ethical judgments must be the broader one. If there are two distinct senses, and both are ethical or normative, then one must be the fundamental sense (clearly, the broader "flavorless" sense), and the narrower "jural" sense will ultimately have to be analyzed in terms of that.[6]

Sidgwick, however, also distinguishes between what he calls a "narrower ethical sense" and a broader "ideal" sense in a different way that reveals a consequentialist theory of action underpinning his thought.[7] This is the distinction between what one ought to *do* (what can be "brought about by . . . volition") and what one ought to desire or hope for (Sidgwick 1962: 33). The latter is a broader notion on the (consequentialist) assumption that the only reason for doing something is that it will bring about some desirable state of affairs. Since Sidgwick is mainly concerned with different methods for determining what we ought to do, we can ignore this distinction.[8]

Moore, again, will claim that intrinsic goodness is the fundamental ethical notion. But if, however, any notion of good must, as Sidgwick claims, be analyzed in terms of "ought" (in its broad sense), as Sidgwick claims, then Moore's claim cannot possibly be true. But why think, as Sidgwick does, that "ought" is the more fundamental notion? As Frankena points out, what lies behind Moore's claim about good being irreducible is his "open-question argument" (Frankena 1942: 102). For any proposed

[5] This follows from Sidgwick's rejection of Hume's account of reason on p. 25 together with his view that ethical judgments are "dictate[s] of reason" (36).

[6] See Darwall 2021 for an account that relates these two senses in this way.

[7] This is what Schapiro calls "action as production" in Schapiro 2001.

[8] Sidgwick also later makes a distinction between subjective and objective rightness that we can similarly ignore. Subjective rightness concerns what an agent should do given their beliefs, and objective rightness concerns what they should do given actual circumstances. We need only focus on the latter (Sidgwick 1962: 207).

analysis of good, we can always accept that something has the relevant property but sensibly ask whether it is good. Frankena argued convincingly that this is so because of what we call the *normativity* of any ethical term or property, which consists in entailing that we ought, or have normative reason, to have some attitude or other toward that thing (Moore 1993a: 95; Darwall, Gibbard, and Railton 1997: 4). (Frankena himself talked of "normative character," using "normative" in its current sense for the first time of which I am aware [Frankena 1942: 102].)

This is precisely what Sidgwick says: the fundamental ethical concept is "ought"; its instantiation entails that anyone to whom it applies ought or has normative reason to take some attitude toward what instantiates it. But this means, Frankena concluded, that the fundamental ethical notion of normativity cannot be a simple property as Moore claimed was true of good; the fundamental ethical notion must concern a *relation* between an agent, an act or an attitude, a deliberative context, and specific facts in that context (Frankena 1942; see also Scanlon 2014: 31).

Sidgwick makes a further observation that does a significantly better job than anything in Moore of explaining why the reaction to Moore's open-question argument gave rise to different anti-realist metaethical views, including the emotivism of Ayer and Stevenson, Hare's prescriptivism, the error-theoretic projectivism of Mackie, and Blackburn's and Gibbard's expressivism (Ayer 1952; Hare 1952; Mackie 1977; Blackburn 1984; Gibbard 1990). Sidgwick claims that "in the case of all or most minds," ethical judgments "have some – though often an inadequate – influence on volition" (Sidgwick 1962: 25). He explicitly contrasts his position with Hume's. Like Sidgwick, Hume famously holds that ethical judgments "go beyond the calm and indolent judgments of the understanding" and are intrinsically motivating, but Hume denies on these grounds that ethical judgments could be judgments of reason (Hume 1978: 457). Sidgwick agrees with Hume about what is sometimes called "judgment internalism" – that motivation is internal to ethical judgments – but he affirms, against Hume, that ethical judgments are judgments of reason (Darwall 1983: 54; Deigh 1992).

It was judgment internalism that led so many twentieth-century metaethicists toward forms of anti-realism. But although the proximate cause was Moore's *Principia*, what these philosophers were responding to was something that is actually absent from Moore – who was himself an externalist – but clearly present in Sidgwick's *Methods of Ethics*.

A second notable element of *Methods*' book I are several claims that Sidgwick makes about pleasure, desire, and the good. These claims will have great importance in assessing his hedonistic theory of the good and his assertions about prudence and benevolence. Some can be considered as stipulative. Sidgwick defines pleasure, for instance, as "agreeable feeling" (Sidgwick 1962: xxiv). His more careful definition, which is later put to use in his argument for a hedonistic theory of the good, is "feeling which the sentient individual at the time of feeling it implicitly or explicitly apprehends to be desirable; – desirable, that is, when considered merely as a feeling" (131). Sidgwick concedes that philosophers can define "pleasure" differently and that many, including Mill, do. Sidgwick considers that Mill does so at his peril, since, Sidgwick notes, Mill defines it in contradictory ways (44). What will matter is whether Sidgwick is right that pleasure *so defined* exhausts the intrinsically good. I shall suggest that not only is it not, but that Sidgwickian pleasures are often not intrinsically good at all.

Less controversial is Sidgwick's claim against empirical egoistic hedonists that not all human desires are for the agent's own pleasure so defined (Sidgwick 1962: 42–51). Here Sidgwick is on firm ground that is shared with Butler, Hutcheson, Mill, and many others. We often desire things other than our own pleasure.

Most important is Sidgwick's drawing out of the implications of his view of ethical judgment for the case of judgments about the good. The crucial point is the one that critics push against Mill, namely, that the fact that someone actually desires something cannot show that that thing is good or desirable in the ethical sense of being something we ought to desire. But things are significantly more complicated for Sidgwick.

In book II, Sidgwick is concerned with egoism, the view that agents should promote their own good. This already requires two different notions of good: the idea, first, of what it is good to do in the sense of what one ought or there is most reason to do, and second, the idea of *a person's* good. These are distinct notions, both of which are needed to state egoism as the view that it is good (best) to do whatever will most promote the agent's good. In addition, however, Sidgwick will also need a third notion of good, when he argues that any one person's good is no less good "from the point of view . . . of the Universe" than that of any other (382). In this impersonal sense of "good," it is a good thing that a person's good is realized. This is the sense of "good" – what is a good thing to occur or take place – that plays the starring role in the consequentialisms that derive from Sidgwick and Moore. Finally, Sidgwick also requires the idea of *aggregate* good to formulate utilitarianism as the doctrine that the (impersonally) best thing that can happen is the outcome in which there is the greatest net aggregate good, as he will argue, the greatest net aggregate pleasure. This is not a fundamental notion of good but a derivate one that is constructed out of individuals' goods. At this point in book I, Sidgwick is concerned with sharpening our grasp of a *person's good* so he can critically assess egoism in book II.

And here Sidgwick faces a complication: There is a crucial ambiguity in the idea of something's being good "for someone."[9] Sometimes what we mean by this expression is that the person prefers or desires, or would rationally prefer or desire, that thing. Something is good for someone in this sense if it is desirable from that person's point of view. At other times, however, we use this phrase to mean that something benefits someone or contributes to their well-being. Here the idea is not so much that it is good from the person's own perspective as that it is good, as it were, with a view toward that person. It is important to keep this distinction clear, since, if we don't, it will end up being a tautology that an agent should seek their own good, as Sidgwick himself recognizes (381). That will just mean that a person has reason to desire what they have reason to desire.

Still, for the concept of someone's good to be an ethical concept, Sidgwick recognizes, it must contain the concept of "ought" or a "dictate of reason" (36). Rawls makes use of a passage of Sidgwick's to define a person's good for purposes of his theory of justice as fairness in *A Theory of Justice.* Here is Sidgwick: "My Good on the whole is what I should actually desire and seek if all the consequences of seeking it could be foreknown and adequately realised by me in imagination at the time of making my choice" (Sidgwick 1962: 111; Rawls 1971: 421; see also Brandt 1979: 11). Although this is fine as a first approximation, Sidgwick thinks, it cannot be adequate since it lacks the essential ethical element of "ought" or of a "dictate of reason" (Sidgwick 1962: 112). So far defined, a person's good is not an ethical concept.

A critical aspect of Sidgwick's Axiom of Prudence is that it is irrational to have greater "regard" for one moment of a person's life over any other (381). This is what Rawls calls the irrationality of "pure time preference" (Rawls 1971: 293–298). However, there is nothing that guarantees that if a given agent were perfectly knowledgeable and attentive to each moment of their life they would necessarily care about each, or themselves at each, equally. Realizing this, Sidgwick adds that a person's good is what "I should [i.e., would] practically desire if my desires were in harmony with reason" (Sidgwick 1962: 112).

But that leaves us with the problem we earlier noticed, namely, that although this might work as a (tautologous) account of what a person ought to desire, it seems obviously inadequate as an account of what is good for that person in the sense of what would benefit *them.* Derek Parfit

[9] In what follows, I draw on Darwall 2000b.

offers a well-known counterexample. You might fall into a deep and moving conversation with a stranger on a train who is on their way to receive treatment for an illness, and you might come to have a rational desire that the treatment be successful and that they live a long and happy life. But the satisfaction of that desire would not benefit you, especially if you did not even know about the treatment's success or were dead by the time it worked (Parfit 1984: 151, 468).

This is sometimes called the "scope problem" (Darwall 2002: 27). If a person's good is to concern their rational desires, and not all do, the issue then is how to specify the scope of desires the satisfaction of which would benefit the desirer and contribute to *their* good. One suggestion has been that the desirer must themselves be within the scope of the rational desire (Overvold 1980). However, this cannot work. Consider an intrinsic desire for self-destruction (say, out of self-hatred) (Darwall 2002: 28). However central the desirer is to the object of their desire, satisfying this desire clearly would not benefit them.

What does work, I think, is specifying that the justified desire of the agent be *for the agent for their sake*, that is, out of care or concern for them (Darwall 2002: 1–49). Sidgwick says things that suggest this solution: that he means to restrict his formula to what people desire intrinsically *for themselves*, "not benevolently for others" (Sidgwick 1962: 109). Also, Sidgwick contrasts prudence, the desire for one's own good, with benevolence, which generally is understood in terms of care or concern. That all said, there is reason, as we shall see, to doubt whether Sidgwick ultimately understands either prudence or benevolence as involving forms of care or concern. Having now analyzed Sidgwick's views on the concept of a person's good, we can now turn to his consideration in book II of the view that agents ought to do and desire all and only what promotes their own good. This is the method he calls "Egoism" or "Egoistic Hedonism."

Egoistic Hedonism

Earlier utilitarians, such as Bentham, argued for rational egoism on the basis of the empirical theory of psychological egoism. Just as Sidgwick argues that it is impossible to base utilitarianism on inductivist grounds, however, so also does he maintain that there can be no successful argument from psychological to ethical egoistic hedonism. But neither can egoism, not even what we might call "*pro tanto* egoism" – the view that we ought *pro tanto* to promote our own interest – be assumed as a default view.[10] Sidgwick holds that both require grounding in philosophical intuition (the history of eudaimonism to the contrary notwithstanding).

Sidgwick's full-dress case for egoistic hedonism awaits later parts of *The Methods*, but some important moves are made in book II and just before (and in a separate essay: "Hedonism and Ultimate Good" [Sidgwick 2000: 95]). Recall, again, that in addition to rejecting any argument for hedonism as an ethical doctrine from psychological hedonism, Sidgwick denies the latter empirical theory as well. Sidgwick follows Mill in holding that we desire many different things intrinsically, and not just as a means to pleasure.

Egoistic hedonists, as Sidgwick interprets them, and, indeed, Sidgwick himself, are committed to denying this Millian view. They hold, following Bentham, that nothing other than pleasure, quantitatively considered, can be intrinsically good (Sidgwick 1962: 94). But what arguments can they give against Mill and others who think that things other than pleasurable feeling are intrinsically good and beneficial for those who engage with them? Sidgwick's only possible reply is that while things like knowledge and beauty may be desired, even for their own sake, that is because they are psychologically *associated* with intrinsically valuable (quantitative) pleasures in the way that Mill says money is with intrinsically valuable quantitative pleasures (Mill 2002: IV.6–7). Though we begin desiring money only for the sake of pleasurable experiences we can acquire with it, we can come to want money for its own sake. For his part, Sidgwick says that "as soon as the alternatives are clearly apprehended, it will . . . be generally held that beauty, knowledge, and other ideal goods . . . are only reasonably to be sought . . . in so far as they conduce either (1) to Happiness [i.e., pleasure] or (2) to the Perfection or Excellence of human existence" (Sidgwick 1962: 114).

Sidgwick considers the values of perfection and excellence, at least of the moral varieties, under (dogmatic) intuitionism. So that leaves pleasure, and here we can interpret Sidgwick as offering an error theory for the intrinsic valuation of things other than pleasure, namely, that they are initially valued instrumentally and only come to be valued intrinsically by association.[11] Just as he argues that commonsense morality is "unconsciously Utilitarian," Sidgwick might be seen as arguing here that commonsense pluralist theories of the good are "unconsciously hedonistic" (424).

Earlier we briefly noted Sidgwick's account of pleasure as "agreeable feeling" (Sidgwick 1962: xxiv). We should now examine Sidgwick's

10 "I do not see why the Egoistic principle should pass unchallenged any more than the Universalistic" (Sidgwick 1962: 418). I am indebted here to Colin Marshall.

11 He makes the same argument at Sidgwick 2000: 95.

account in more detail, since his case for hedonism, whether egoistic or universalistic, crucially depends on it. Recall Sidgwick's definition: "feeling which the sentient individual at the time of feeling it implicitly or explicitly apprehends to be desirable; – desirable, that is, when considered merely as feeling, and not in respect of its objective conditions or consequences" (131).

In effect, Sidgwick combines elements of Bentham's and Mill's theories. Bentham takes pleasure to be a sensation of its own; although it can be caused by a variety of things, it is a sensation of its own distinctive kind. Mill, on the other hand, emphasizes that pleasure, like desire, has an intentional object, and that pleasures are differentiated intrinsically by their objects. Desire and pleasure involve, moreover, the same underlying attitude: what we might call liking. It is a conceptual or a metaphysical truth that if I desire something and it occurs, then, unless I have changed my mind, or it is not as I imagined it would be, I will take pleasure in it.

Sidgwick follows Mill in assuming pleasures to have objects; they involve a desire-like attitude toward something in which one takes pleasure. More, they involve something like an ethical intuition, since they include the apprehension that the object of one's pleasure is desirable (in the ethical sense). Of course, the relevant intuition cannot be a philosophical one, at least not if being a priori is a mark of philosophical intuitions, which seems to be Sidgwick's view of the intuitions involved in the Axioms of Prudence and Benevolence.[12]

On the other hand, Sidgwick follows Bentham and departs from Mill in holding that the only objects of the "liking" or "seeming desirable" attitude are our own sensations or feelings. Differently from Bentham, Sidgwick does hold that there are different aspects of different pleasurable feelings in which one can take pleasure. They are not all the same kind of feeling (except in terms of their valence or direction of intuited evaluative apprehension). But what one apprehends as desirable in pleasure is a "feeling . . . considered merely as a feeling" (131).

This account may work well enough for pleasant sensations: the feeling of a hot shower on a cold day. But it just seems hopeless with many other pleasures. Consider, again, the stranger on Parfit's train. Suppose that later you do hear of their fate: Happily, the treatment succeeded; their life was extended; and they passed the rest of their years flourishing. You are thrilled to hear the news, but is the object of your pleasure the feeling you get when you hear the news? It seems undeniable that your pleasure is

[12] Would Sidgwick count these as "perceptional intuitions"?

itself a feeling state of yourself, but obviously the intentional object of that feeling – what you take pleasure in – is not, at least not primarily. What you are pleased by is that of which you have gotten news: the stranger's survival and flourishing.

Sidgwick might accept that, since he does not say that a feeling is the *only* thing one apprehends to be desirable. Parfit's case will not be a counterexample to Sidgwick's account of pleasure if you *also* apprehend your feeling on hearing the news to be desirable considered merely as a feeling. But would you have? Imagine being told the same propositions about the stranger while they are actually false, perhaps as a cruel joke. Upon learning the truth, would you think, "Well, at least I had the pleasant feeling of thinking it was true?" I assume you would not.

Sidgwick can of course reply that such experiences turn out not to be pleasures on his view. When you heard (falsely) that the stranger had the future for which you had wished, that was not actually a pleasure, because you wanted your experience of hearing not to be "fool's gold," as it were. But even if we grant Sidgwick's definition of pleasure as stipulative, that surely will not help his case for ethical hedonism so defined. You might even regard the experience of truly hearing about his wonderful fate, were you to have it, as one of the most significant and happy making of your life.

Even the desirability of pleasant sensations frequently depends on external matters that go beyond feelings as feelings. Pleasant feelings may be caught up in a whole nexus of factors that crucially involve aspects outside the feeling itself. I once heard a painter describing the pleasures of painting as involving the physical engagement with the pigment, feeling its resistance to the brush as she moved it over the canvas to create paintings with color and shape. She loved the feel of painting because of its *physicality*.

Chapter II considers egoistic hedonism as an ethical method. Mostly, Sidgwick is concerned to criticize empiricist attempts to ground ethical egoism, in the way that Bentham and Mill do. The only possible grounding for ethical principles, Sidgwick holds, is intuition. We have just seen, however, that by Sidgwick's lights, the experience of pleasure seems to involve something like ethical intuitions themselves. Might Bentham and Mill then evade Sidgwick's criticisms, so long as they renounce any attempt to reduce ethical concepts and properties to naturalistic ones like pleasure and desire? They might then hold that pleasure and desires involve feelings that are not just *as of* the good but can actually provide empirical evidence of the fact of something's goodness.

In any case, Sidgwick's account of pleasure as involving intuition-like apprehensions of goodness seems to straddle the line between a priori intuition and empirical sense data. Of course, we can still distinguish the a priori intuition that pleasure defined in Sidgwick's way is intrinsically good from the plainly empirical intuition-like feelings that are involved in pleasure itself. Still, to hold that pleasures so defined are intrinsically good and that they are intrinsically good, indeed the only intrinsic goods, does seem to involve something like what Sellars called the "Myth of the Given" (Sellars 1963: 140).

Finally, we should note another aspect of Sidgwick's analysis of the method of egoistic hedonism that mirrors an aspect of his defense of universalistic hedonism or utilitarianism we have already noticed. Just as the public and/or direct pursuit of the greatest happiness may itself be dictated against by utilitarianism, giving rise to what Williams calls "Government House utilitarianism," something structurally identical is true in the egocentric case (Williams 1985: 120). This is what Sidgwick calls "the Fundamental Paradox of Egoistic Hedonism," which he notes that Butler emphasized (Sidgwick 1962: 136). As Butler put the point, "*Disengagement* is absolutely necessary to enjoyment; and a person may have so steady and fixed an eye upon his own interest, whatever he places it in, as may hinder him from *attending* to many gratifications within his reach, which others have their minds *free* and *open* to" (Butler 2017: XI.9). The person who anxiously asks, "Are we having fun yet?" is less likely to have fun than they would if they could forget about their own pleasure per se and dive into pleasurable activities. This means that egoistic hedonism might even recommend that we pay it no mind.

Intuitionism

We move now to book III's treatment of the ethical method Sidgwick calls "Intuitionism," beginning with the "dogmatic" form that he associated with Mill's intuitive moralists who defend the conventions of moral common sense (Sidgwick 1962: xxv, 102). A major focus will be dogmatic intuitionism's, and therefore, moral common sense's, use of the deontic or "jural" sense of "ought," as opposed to the flavorless sense that Sidgwick says is the fundamental ethical notion (106). Toward the end of book I, Sidgwick notes that the difference between these two senses of "ought" is central to a distinction he makes, in my view correctly, between ancient and modern ethics. "The chief characteristics of ancient ethical controversy as distinguished from modern may be traced to the employment of a generic notion instead of a specific one in expressing the common moral judgments on actions" (Sidgwick 1962: 105). For the ancients, Sidgwick says, "Virtue or

Right action is commonly regarded as only a species of the Good" (105–106). When modern moral philosophers ask, however, "What is Duty and what is its ground," they are not seeking to reduce the right to the good (106). This is the question that dogmatic intuitionists address and with which modern moral philosophy is distinctively concerned. Indeed, Sidgwick says, we moderns "can scarcely underst[and]" the ancients' "speculations . . . unless with a certain effort we throw the quasi-jural notions of modern ethics aside" (106). This means that if we are going to understand Sidgwick's own "speculations" about modern moral philosophy, we have to keep "quasi-jural notions" firmly in view and then ask how both relate to the "generic" notion of "ought" with which Sidgwick says self-evident axioms are themselves framed.

Sidgwick's contrast as between the ancients' use of the "generic" ethical notion and the moderns use of a more specific one is misleading. No ethical philosopher can avoid the generic notion of "ought" on pain of not making ethical claims. What characterizes ancient ethical thought is its use of notions of the good – both the agent's good or *eudaimonia* and the noble or fine (*kalon*). To be ethical notions, both must utilize the generic notion of "ought." Arguably, a person's good is what they (or we) have reason to want for them(selves) for their sake, and the noble or fine is what there is reason for anyone to esteem. Similarly, deontic or jural notions of right and "ought" must also be understood in terms of the generic notion of "ought." Arguably, what is morally required or obligatory is an act of a kind that ought to be blamed (i.e., would be blameworthy) if the act were performed without excuse (Darwall 2006, 2013a, 2013b).

It is clear that the deontic or "jural" concept is the more specific ethical notion that Sidgwick is concentrating on in book III. Commonsense morality, as Sidgwick conceives it, is a conception that competes with rival moral theories, like utilitarianism. As I noted before and shall be emphasizing from here on, the narrower concepts of right, wrong, and "ought" have a different conceptual profile than the generic, "flavorless" concept that Sidgwick claims is the conceptual core of all ethical concepts and judgments. Commonsense morality, therefore, is not simply a view about how people should behave in the generic flavorless sense – how, we might say, they have most reason to behave. It provides deontic/jural standards of right and wrong with which those subject to them are accountable for complying.

This is why, Sidgwick implies (anticipating Strawson), that commonsense morality must be formulable in universal "rules of duty" that those subject to them can be assumed capable of knowing. "Rules of duty ought to admit of precise definition in a universal form: and this assumption naturally belongs to the ordinary or jural view of Ethics as concerned with a moral code: since we should agree that if obligations are imposed on any one he ought at least to know what they are" (Sidgwick 1962: 228). The conceptual connections could not be clearer. "Obligations" that are "imposed" are necessarily such that those on whom they are imposed are accountable for complying with them. Commonsense morality thus differs fundamentally from any view about what rational agents have reason to do; the latter lacks the conceptual consequences of deontic morality.

There are numerous passages throughout *The Methods* that implicitly recognize the conceptual connection between the deontic/jural sense of "ought" and accountability and that this is the "ought" of commonsense morality. A particularly notable one comes in Sidgwick's discussion of utilitarianism. "It may conduce most to the general happiness," he there says, "that A should do a certain act, and at the same time that B, C, D should blame it" (491). This comes just after his discussion of esoteric morality as something that utilitarianism may most highly recommend. Sidgwick agrees with Mill in thinking that utilitarianism should favor a public moral code much like commonsense morality. If anything, indeed, Sidgwick's instincts are more conservative than Mill's, who carries forward Bentham's philosophical radical opposition to the status quo. In this passage, Sidgwick is saying that utilitarianism will recommend people blaming an agent for conduct that utilitarianism will simultaneously encourage (although, of course, not publicly!). Part of what it is for a public moral code to proscribe conduct is for it to hold that it is *blameworthy* if done without excuse.

In the end, I shall be arguing, the form of utilitarianism that Sidgwick himself holds and that is supported by his "axiom of Rational Benevolence" is not a deontic moral proposition but a claim about what there is most reason for an agent to do (from "the point of view . . . of the Universe") (387). This would suggest that he restricts his use of deontic/jural vocabulary to describing moral common sense or the public code that would "conduce most to the general happiness." But there are many places where Sidgwick slips into deontic language in his own voice. In chapter V of book I, "Free Will," for example, he discusses the central issue against the background of assumptions of "judgments of right and wrong" and the "morally culpable" or "blameworthy" (60–61). What gives freedom of the will, and not just of action, its force as a philosophical problem is its connection to deontic morality. "In the case . . . of such volitions as are pre-eminently the objects of moral condemnation and approbation, the psychical fact 'volition' seems to include – besides intention, or representation of the results of action – also the consciousness of self as choosing, resolving, determining these results" (61). As Strawson points out in "Freedom and Resentment," our judgments of deontic accountability, and the reactive attitudes connected to them, betray a particular interest not just in what people do but in how they determine their wills (Strawson 1968). We therefore presuppose freedom of the will in the sense that moral agents have the power to determine their own wills.

Sidgwick notes that "'conscience' is the accepted popular term for the faculty of moral judgment, as applied to the acts and motives of the person judging" (99). In his *Outlines of the History of Ethics*, Sidgwick draws his contrast between ancient and modern ethics in the following terms. "In Greek moral philosophy generally, but one regulative and governing faculty is recognised under the name of Reason . . . ; in the modern ethical view, when it has worked itself clear, there are found to be two, – Universal Reason and Egoistic Reason, or Conscience and Self-love" (1964: 198). This presents Sidgwick with a dilemma. Either "conscience" is a descriptive term that refers to the psychology of those who have accepted commonsense morality as a public moral code, in which case, it cannot be regarded as a "regulative and governing faculty" of reason. Or it is an aspect of practical reason that puts us in touch with genuinely normative claims (and perhaps truths), which can be formulated in essentially normative terms (that include the fundamental "generic" "ought").

As we shall see, Sidgwick's considered view is that the "axiom of Rational Benevolence" can be underwritten by a philosophical intuition of "Universal Reason," and that no proposition of deontic morality can be (Sidgwick 1962: 387). Only dogmatic intuitions can be formulated in deontic/jural terms, and these are only *prima facie*. The upshot will be that although the previous passage suggests that "Universal Reason" is identical with "Conscience," that cannot be Sidgwick's own view when, as it were, "it has worked itself clear." This both creates problems with his argument that commonsense morality is unconsciously utilitarian, and it saddles him with the duality of practical reason that, I shall be suggesting, the deontic/jural character of conscience and morality might have helped him solve. In the end, Sidgwick is not as clear as he might be about the relations between the "ought" of commonsense morality and generic "ought" of practical reason, and this creates problems for him.

We should continue with our analysis of Sidgwick's views of commonsense morality in book III, bearing in mind that there will continue to be some ambiguity and ambivalence in Sidgwick's attitudes toward its fundamental terms. Much of book III is concerned with the relation between the duty of "Benevolence," which is most closely akin to utilitarianism, and the other two main areas of moral common sense – "Justice, and the observance of Law and Contract" – which are not (312). It is in the context of discussing common sense's recognition of special permissions and special obligations to those to whom we have special relations that Sidgwick makes the outrageously racist remark I mentioned earlier. Just as we are morally permitted to favor our near and dear, so, Sidgwick says, are we permitted morally to give preference to members of our own race. In the end, however, a nonracist and historically better-informed Sidgwick might respond, as would Mill, that over commonsense morality utilitarianism enjoys the distinct advantage of being significantly less vulnerable to such retrograde views. Although dogmatic intuition may give comfort to racist complacency, utilitarianism will seek to unmask it for the greatest happiness of all. Moreover, utilitarianism can be grounded in philosophical intuitions that have the self-evidence to which dogmatic intuitions can only aspire but never attain.

Sidgwick points out that commonsense morality faces a dilemma of its own. On the one hand, as we noted before, to function as standards of accountability commonsense deontic requirements must aim for universal principles or rules that can be clearly stated and accepted. However, on the other, "as soon as we attempt to give them the definiteness which [they] require[e], we find that we cannot do this without abandoning the universality of acceptance" (342).[13]

Sidgwick holds that commonsense moral standards inevitably conflict and that therefore they can only purport to have a "*prima facie* claim to furnish independent and self-evident rules of morality," anticipating W. D. Ross's notion of "*prima facie* duties" (Sidgwick 1962: 360; Ross 2002). Dogmatic intuition seems impotent to ground any principled way for settling such *prima facie* duties, moreover. (Ross will hold that this is to be settled without further principles by dogmatic intuition on a [kind of] case-by-case basis.) As we shall see in our discussion of book IV on "Utilitarianism" in the next section, Sidgwick holds that the only method of ethics able to settle these conflicts in a disciplined way is utilitarianism, arguing that commonsense morality is unconsciously utilitarian.

Sidgwick lays out "four conditions" that must be satisfied to "establish a significant proposition [that is] apparently self-evident, in the highest

[13] The passage actually says, "which science requires," that is, which a "method of ethics" requires, but other passages we've already noted show that Sidgwick thinks that clarity is also a requirement of commonsense morality itself.

degree of certainty attainable" (Sidgwick 1962: 338). These are, respectively: 1. "the terms of the proposition must be clear and precise"; 2. "the self-evidence of the proposition must be ascertained by careful reflection"; 3. "the propositions accepted as self-evident must be mutually consistent"; and 4. they must agree with what is found self-evident by others' careful reflection. Sidgwick argues that no dogmatic intuition can meet these four conditions. The only intuitionist position that can is "Philosophical Intuitionism," which, Sidgwick argues, grounds the axioms of rational prudence, benevolence, and justice, where "Justice" is a purely formal requirement that like cases must be treated as like (338–342).

Philosophical intuitionism's two substantive propositions are the "axiom of Prudence," which counsels promoting the agent's greatest overall good (pleasure) over time, and the "axiom of Rational Benevolence," which dictates promoting the greatest overall good (pleasure) of all sentient beings (387). Sidgwick argues that these constitute a "Dualism of the Practical Reason," namely, that agents both should promote their own greatest good and that they should promote the greatest good of all (x). It was a problem that Sidgwick wrestled with throughout his life that "theology apart," we have no reason to believe that these two dictates will not conflict (xi). As Andrew Seth noticed, however, this creates a problem for Sidgwick's claim that both are self-evident axioms, since genuinely self-evident propositions must be, as Sidgwick says, "mutually consistent" (Seth 1901; Sidgwick 1962: 341).[14] Either the dictates of the two axioms do not really conflict, or one is not really a self-evident axiom.

Sidgwick notes that both axioms relate parts and wholes. The Axiom of Prudence counsels doing what will be best for oneself "on the whole," treating all the parts of one's life equally (Sidgwick 1962: 381). The agent's good "is conceived as a mathematical whole, of which the integrant parts are realised in different parts or moments of a lifetime" (381). But similarly, the agent's good can also be conceived as a larger whole, namely, the whole of which the goods of all sentient beings are only parts. Though from the agent's point of view, their good takes up the whole of what they have in view, from the point of view of the universe, their good is but a part of this larger whole and no more and no less more significant than any other (382). The axioms of both prudence and rational benevolence concern "the relation which individuals and their particular ends bear as parts to their wholes, and to other parts of these wholes" (382–383).

[14] I am indebted to Marcus Singer's introduction to Sidgwick (2000) for the reference to Seth (Sidgwick 2000: xxxiii).

This makes philosophical intuitions, as Sidgwick is thinking of them, seem more like mathematical intuitions concerning parts and wholes than anything that might seem self-evident from the perspective of universal benevolence or impartial justice. Clearly, Sidgwick is in very different territory here than Hutcheson, and calling the universal axiom one of "Rational Benevolence" seems entirely misleading. An intuition about parts and wholes conceived abstractly from the point of the universe has nothing to do with universal concern for all sentient beings for their own sake.

Sidgwick concludes that philosophical intuition can give utilitarianism a foundation that inductive moralists like Bentham and Mill could never provide: "Utilitarianism is thus presented as the final form into which Intuitionism tends to pass, when the demand for really self-evident first principles is rigorously pressed" (388). It should be clear, however, that the form of utilitarianism that is grounded in philosophical intuition is not, like Bentham's and Mill's versions, a deontic/jural "criterion of right and wrong" (Mill 2002: I.1). To the contrary, taken to its logical conclusion, philosophical intuition yields a form of utilitarianism that is, as Parfit says, "like Rational Egoism, an external rival to morality," rather than a rival moral principle in the deontic/jural sense. Philosophical intuitionism seems to lead away from deontic morality completely (Parfit 2011: I.168).

Utilitarianism

Book IV is devoted to utilitarianism. Because Sidgwick has had so much to say about utilitarianism earlier in *The Methods*, we can be relatively brief. Sidgwick begins with a definition. "By Utilitarianism is here meant the ethical theory, that the conduct, which, under any given circumstances, is objectively right, is that which will produce the greatest amount of happiness on the whole" (Sidgwick 1962: 411). Given utilitarianism's history as a theory of right and wrong in the deontic sense in which Bentham and Mill advance it, readers might be forgiven if they understand Sidgwick along the same lines. We should be careful, however. As we have just seen, what philosophical intuition supports is no such theory, but a claim formulated in Sidgwick's "generic" sense of "ought" and "right."

Sidgwick begins with some clarifying remarks. First, he distinguishes between a standard of right and wrong *acts* and good and bad motives. Utilitarianism, as he understands it, puts forward a theory of right *acts*; it does not hold that "Universal Benevolence is the only right or always best *motive*" (413). Second, utilitarianism considers the pleasures and pains "of any sentient being" (414). Third, Sidgwick calls attention to important cases where average and aggregate utility diverge owing to the fact that current acts affect future sentient beings.

Here Sidgwick uncovers a set of issues that had largely escaped the utilitarian tradition and that became especially salient to his followers in the late twentieth century, like Parfit (Parfit 1984): "If we foresee as possible that an increase in numbers will be accompanied by a decrease in average happiness or *vice versa*, a point arises which has not only never been formally noticed, but which seems to have been substantially overlooked by many Utilitarians" (Sidgwick 1962: 415). Having raised the issue, Sidgwick replies that "if the additional population enjoy on the whole positive happiness, we ought to weigh the amount of happiness gained by the extra number against the amount lost by the remainder" (415). He concludes that the point to which "population ought to be encouraged to increase, is not that at which average happiness is the greatest possible ... but that at which the product formed by multiplying the number of persons living into the amount of average happiness reaches its maximum" (415–416). This would seem to saddle Sidgwick with what Parfit would call the "Repugnant Conclusion," that population should be increased so long as the aggregate happiness is increased, even if the average is lowered or is very low (Parfit 1984: 387).

Chapter II, "The Proof of Utilitarianism," begins with the extremely important point that no substantive ethical principle, neither utilitarianism *nor* egoism, can be assumed by default. "I do not see why the Egoistic principle should pass unchallenged any more than the Universalistic" (Sidgwick 1962: 418). Egoism, in the form of eudaimonism, was certainly the default view before the modern period. But even many modern moral philosophers, including many writing today, simply assume that agents have reason to pursue their own good and that it has to be shown, though not perhaps on that basis, that we have reason to do what we morally ought, or to help others, or to do anything independently of our own benefit. Sidgwick sees that this is mistaken; no ethical view gets a free pass.

Sidgwick then turns to whether utilitarianism can be proved to someone who already holds egoism (or commonsense morality). He concludes that it cannot be. If we start with egoistic hedonism, nothing can get us to the universalistic view (420). But the same thing is true in reverse. If we start with utilitarianism, nothing gives egoistic considerations even *pro tanto* force. Of course, considerations of the agent's good will have force, considered impersonally rather than egocentrically, but that is just because the agent is one sentient being among others. And Sidgwick has just told us that egoism has no default advantage over utilitarianism (or commonsense morality, for that matter). Moreover, the egoist has but to accept that his good matters from the point of view of the universe, and they will be forced to admit that others' goods matter just as much from that point of view. Once egoists credit that perspective, they cannot avoid utilitarianism. We will return to these matters after we consider Sidgwick's final verdict on the relation between utilitarianism and the morality of common sense in the next section.

Utilitarianism's Relation to the Morality of Common Sense

Sidgwick's aim is to conclude that commonsense morality is "unconsciously Utilitarian" (424). He notes, first, that commonsense moral rules, or at least the ones of which we have the *prima facie* intuitions Sidgwick calls "dogmatic," have "in each case some manifest felicific tendency" (425). This recalls Mill's similar claims about "secondary principles" (Mill 2002: II.24). Sidgwick adds, next, that utilitarianism is "naturally called in as arbiter" when commonsense moral rules come into conflict (Sidgwick 1962: 426). Third, there are various "perplexit[ies]" in moral common sense, for example, concerning "the relation of moral excellence to moral effort," that can be explained by utilitarianism (429). One common moral view is that moral excellence shows itself in the overcoming of temptations, while another holds that being temptable is itself a moral imperfection. Both traits, however, have "felicific" tendencies. "Kind services" are likelier to cause pleasure and grateful appreciation when they do not involve willpower but come spontaneously from the kindness of someone's heart (429). Utilitarianism can also explain, finally, why it is felt that we have weightier obligations to those who are near and dear. Even though utilitarianism holds that "every body counts for one, nobody for more than one," it supports moral codes that permit people to do more for those to whom we are specially related (Mill 2002: V.36).

Sidgwick is clear, however, that the utilitarian theory he embraces is act rather than rule utilitarian. And again, he holds that utilitarianism may well support an "esoteric morality"; indeed it might, as Williams put it, "usher itself from the scene" (Sidgwick 1962: 490; Smart and Williams 1973: 134). "A Utilitarian," Sidgwick writes, "may reasonably desire, on Utilitarian principles, that some of his conclusions should be rejected by mankind generally; or even that the vulgar should keep aloof from his system . . . as the inevitable indefiniteness and complexity of its calculations render it likely to lead to bad results in their hands" (Sidgwick 1962: 490).

The Dualism of Practical Reason

The Methods' concluding chapter concerns "The Relations of the Methods" and returns to Sidgwick's "Dualism of the Practical Reason." Since Sidgwick believes he has shown that moral common sense is "unconsciously Utilitarian," he concludes that whatever *prima facie* validity dogmatic intuitions have in their own right, they actually end up providing better evidence of utilitarianism. As we have noted, however, utilitarianism as Sidgwick defines and aims to support it with philosophical intuition concerns an entirely different ethical subject. It does not concern what it is morally right or wrong to do in the deontic/jural sense, but which acts one ought to perform in the "generic" sense. It follows that the facts Sidgwick marshals neither support utilitarianism as Sidgwick defines it nor exclude commonsense morality. Moreover, there are plainly other ways of attempting to ground something in the direction of the morality of common sense than intuitionism, for example, contractualism and metaethical approaches that are congenial to it.

But put that aside. How should we respond to Sidgwick's claim that philosophical intuition only leaves egoism and utilitarianism standing and, therefore, that a dualism of practical reason is inevitable, that there is a "fundamental contradiction in one chief department of our thought" (508)?

Sidgwick credits Butler as the source of his dualism (Sidgwick 1962: xviii). But this is misleading. First, Butler is best interpreted as holding that conscience trumps self-love, since he holds that conscience uniquely has "authority" over all other principles and that self-love only has "superiority" over inferior principles, which latter never include conscience (Butler 2017: II; Darwall 2023a: 168–172). Thus, Butler actually rejects any dualism of practical reason. Only conscience has supreme authority.[15]

The philosopher who really anticipated Sidgwick's dualism was Hutcheson (Hutcheson 2002, 2004; Darwall 2023a: 168). For Hutcheson, the "two grand determinations" are calm self-love and universal ("extensive") benevolence (Hutcheson 1755: 50). Each trumps everything within its respective sphere – egocentric and impartial, respectively – and Hutcheson recognizes no way of deciding between them.

Exactly how to interpret Sidgwick's dualism is a matter of scholarly controversy. Some scholars seek to defang the conflict. Thus, David

[15] Like Sidgwick, Butler distinguishes between the "principle of reflection," which makes generic ethical judgments, and "conscience," which makes deontic moral judgments. He thus holds two distinct authority claims: first, that the principle of reflection has generic authority and second, that conscience has deontic authority *and* that its generic authority is validated by the principle of reflection.

Phillips argues that we might understand Sidgwick as saying that practical reason's dictates are indeterminate when prudence and benevolence conflict (Phillips 1998). Similarly, David Brink argues that there is no ultimate conflict between self-love and benevolence since their judgments are made from different points of view (Brink 1988). It is difficult to see, however, how these interpretations can fit with Sidgwick's claim that practical reason is beset by a "fundamental contradiction" (Sidgwick 1962: 508). It seems likely that Sidgwick really did think that practical reason would be at war with itself unless, somehow, self-love and benevolence always aligned in the long run.[16]

Finally, it is worth noticing how Sidgwick could have avoided his dualism if he had framed utilitarianism in the deontic/jural language of right and wrong as Mill did. If Mill is right that deontic right and wrong are connected to accountability and blameworthiness conceptually, then there is a way of arguing, on conceptual grounds alone, that conscience, in the deontic/jural sense, must always override egoistic considerations. The crucial point has to do with conceptual presuppositions of blame. It is incoherent to blame someone and simultaneously accept that they had sufficient reason to do what one is blaming them for doing (Darwall 2006, 2016). It is conceptually guaranteed, therefore, that there can never be sufficient reason to do what is wrong in the deontic/jural sense. Ironically, then, if Sidgwick had been able to ground utilitarianism as a deontic/jural principle, he would have been able to argue that practical reason dictates that utilitarianism trumps prudence and, thus, to avoid a dualism of practical reason, without denying that prudential and moral judgments are genuinely ethical judgments.

[16] Another reason for not accepting Brink's solution is that, in effect, it denies that prudential and benevolent judgments are ethical judgments with genuine normative force.

CHAPTER 10

British Idealism

Green

Like Sidgwick, T. H. (Thomas Hill) Green was born into a clergyman's family and was educated at Rugby School. Unlike Sidgwick, however, Green maintained a strong Christian faith throughout his life, and, moreover, his religious outlook played a significant role in his moral philosophy. Sidgwick never lost interest in the spiritual life – he helped found the Society for Psychical Research – but his philosophy was relentlessly secular. Rather than subscribe to the Anglican Church's thirty-nine articles, Sidgwick resigned from his Cambridge fellowship (Harrison 1996: 429).

After Rugby, Green went to Oxford, where he received a quite different philosophical education than Sidgwick had at Cambridge. Benjamin Jowett, a well-known classical scholar, was mainly responsible for Green's Oxford studies, and Jowett promoted both the philosophy of the ancient Greeks and post-Kantian German idealism. Jowett fostered in Green, and later in F. H. Bradley, a eudaimonist outlook along with a profound interest in Hegel and Fichte, which was missing from anglophone philosophy until Green and Bradley's British form of idealism. Both were utterly foreign to Sidgwick's philosophical milieu and philosophy.

Green and Sidgwick were alike, though, in spending their adult lives at their undergraduate institutions. Green was Whyte's Professor of Moral Philosophy at Oxford until his untimely death at the age of forty-five in 1882. And Sidgwick remained at Cambridge almost until his death in 1900.

Green was also like Sidgwick in taking a strong interest in British liberalism and in the Liberal Party. And both played an important role, along with their spouses, in advancing the position of women at Oxford and Cambridge, respectively.[1] Together with Charlotte Byron Green, T. H. Green was involved in the founding of Somerville Hall, which would later become Somerville College, site of a remarkable emergence of British women philosophers when Elizabeth Anscombe, Philippa Foot, Mary Midgley, and Iris Murdoch were all there during World War II (Lipscomb 2021; Mac Cumhaill and Wiseman 2022).

Green was active, as well, in advancing working-class interests. As we shall see when we consider his *Lectures on the Principles of Political Obligation* (Green 1885) and *Liberal Legislation and the Freedom of Contract* (Green 1881), Green pursued a "third way" between "Manchester individualism," on the one hand, and Marxist socialism, on the other. Green's approach was an "ethical" or "Christian" form of socialism (Carter 2003). During his lifetime, Green was known more for his political ideas and activity than he was for his moral philosophy, which was published only posthumously (Green 2003: xiii).

Green's moral and political philosophy hang together, however. The justification for political order, and indeed, for any claim of right, Green thinks, is its role in enabling citizens to realize themselves in ethical action through active membership in a community with a common good. Green was a perfectionist eudaimonist, like Aristotle, but he was also a modern who, like Kant and Hegel, advanced an ethics of freedom. For Green, the self-realization that is our final end actualizes a positive form of freedom (cf. Irwin 2009: 581–624). Green's student D. G. Ritchie once remarked that Green "corrected Kant by Aristotle and corrected Aristotle by Kant" (Ritchie 1891: 139–140).

Hegel is another obvious source of Green's ideas. But Green emphasizes Kant's doctrine of fundamental equality more than Hegel does. Still, Green presents himself as an absolute idealist like Hegel rather than a transcendental idealist like Kant.

The fundamental differences between Sidgwick and Green are illustrated by Sidgwick's comment on Green and Bradley's thesis that the good consists in self-realization: "The notion of Self-realisation is to be avoided in a treatise on ethical method, on account of its indefiniteness" (Sidgwick 1962: 91). As Sidgwick sees it, Green's (and Bradley's) claim is sufficiently general to "cover all possible views of the ultimate end of rational conduct" (91). It verges on being an empty tautology.

[1] David Brink's introduction to Green 2003 has details of Green's life as well as an introduction to his philosophical ideas. Bart Schultz's biography of Sidgwick is also helpful (Green 2003; Schultz 2004).

A similar objection might be raised to Aristotle's identifying the chief good with *eudaimonia* or living well. But just as Aristotle avoids truism by fleshing out his account, so also does Green. First, as I mentioned, Green's final end is self-conscious realization of freedom and the instantiation of "eternal mind" or Hegelian absolute spirit (obviously not Aristotle's view) (Green 2003). Second, as will become clear, Green holds that self-realization can only be actualized in community with all beings who are capable of "intercourse" or saying "thou" to one another (Green 2003: §183, 190). This is clearly a characteristically modern way of specifying the more generic notion of choiceworthiness that departs significantly from Aristotle.

The self and the distinctively self-conscious choice that Green identifies with self-realization play no role in Sidgwick's ethical philosophy. There is one place, however, where Sidgwick shows an uncharacteristic sensitivity to the agent's deliberative point of view and its differences from the theoretical perspective. In "Some Fundamental Ethical Controversies," Sidgwick analyzes the problem of freedom of the will and determinism, and he concludes that even if we cannot avoid determinism from the theoretical standpoint when we attempt "to forecast *future* conduct," it is irrelevant from the practical point of view "when we are ascertaining – according to any ethical principles and method – what choice it is reasonable to make between two alternatives of *present* conduct" (Sidgwick 2000: 36–37).

Otherwise, the choosing self drops out of sight in Sidgwick's ethics completely in a way that is diametrically opposed to Green and Bradley. It is true that Sidgwick believes that to make sense of their greatest good on the whole, an agent must view themselves as existing over time. But Sidgwick holds that an agent's good consists simply in a collection of instances of pleasure at a given time. His hedonism is, like Bentham's, entirely quantitative and "pointillist." Moreover, as we saw, neither Sidgwick's conception of personal good nor that of universal good implicates care or concern, at least not explicitly, whether that be an agent's concern for themselves and their good on the whole or benevolent concern for others for their sake and for the good of all as a consequence of that benevolent concern. The parts of which both wholes are made up are instances of pleasure at points in time.[2]

Although Sidgwick does hold that freedom of the will (one of the kinds of freedom that Green recognizes) must be assumed from the practical

[2] In *Reasons and Persons*, Parfit argues on these grounds against egoism and in favor of what he calls the "Present Aim Theory" (Parfit 1984: 117–132).

point of view, he does not think that freedom appears in the foreground of the agent's view. Nothing could be more starkly opposed to Green's outlook, since, as we shall see, a consciousness of oneself as free is central to his theory of voluntary action. Moreover, Green holds that we actualize positive freedom only when we collaborate with others for the common good in a mutually accountable way that recognizes one another's free agency.

We shall examine Green's view of self-conscious agency presently, but first we should note some other, related ways in which Green's ethics diverge fundamentally from Sidgwick's. Whereas Sidgwick's ethics are, as we saw, dualistic – bottoming out in a dualism of practical reason – Green's ethical philosophy is monistic through and through. To begin with, it is eudaimonist, which is directly opposed to Sidgwick's approach. Sidgwick cites eudaimonism as a mark of ancient ethical views that modern views abandon when they have been worked "clear" (Sidgwick 1964: 198). (As I've mentioned, however, Green and Bradley count as moderns despite their eudaimonism, since they follow Kant and Hegel in centering their views on freedom [another important difference with Sidgwick].)

A further substantial difference from Sidgwick is Green's doctrine that there can be no fundamental conflicts of interest. Sidgwick struggled with the practical dualism of egoism and utilitarianism throughout his life and held that, "theology apart," we have no reason to believe that these two dictates will not conflict (Sidgwick 1962: xi). Green, however, is in this respect what Irwin calls an Aristotelian naturalist in holding that rational human persons realize their natural good through the excellent exercise of their rational natural capacities and that this exercise necessarily involves collective action for the common good (Irwin 2009: 607–610). If Green is an Aristotelian naturalist, however, he is, again, nonetheless a modern, holding that the common good consists in realizing a form of freedom that can only be actualized in a community or "fellowship" of all beings who are capable of interpersonal interaction. Differently from Aristotle, Green holds that our capacity for mutually accountable agency makes us natural equals rather than ordering us in a natural hierarchy.

Finally, although Sidgwick is a rational or "philosophical" intuitionist – holding a view with an obvious affinity for a moral realist metaphysics – Green is an idealist, holding that moral truths emerge through the exercise of practical reason and, moreover, not once and for all, as is arguably true on Kant's view, but through a historical process that is akin to the dialectics of Hegel. In this way, Green is clearly a nineteenth-century rather than an eighteenth-century thinker.

Self, Will, and Desire

We turn now to Green's philosophical works. We should bear in mind throughout that although Green and Bradley were, like Sidgwick, academic moral philosophers in the sense that they did philosophy from positions within academic institutions, they were not academic philosophers in the sense Rawls has in mind when he calls Sidgwick's *Methods* "the first truly academic work in moral philosophy" (Sidgwick 1981: 2). Neither Bradley nor Green seek the careful and balanced consideration of different "methods of ethics" that Sidgwick does. Green is, however, considerably less polemical than Bradley. Though, like Bradley, he is influenced by Hegel, much of his work aims at the same analytical precision as that of analytical philosophers.

The fundamental differences between Green and Sidgwick start to show themselves in book II of Green's *Prolegomena to Ethics* on "The Will" (Green 2003: §85–§153). Here we find Green's theory of agency and action. Some of the main points are already made *arguendo* in chapter I on "The Freedom of the Will." Green's picture of voluntary action is roughly Kantian. Agency begins with "impulses which have been previously soliciting the will" (§105). These do not determine action directly nor yet give the agent any specific "motive," without which action is impossible (§103). "Unless there is an object which a man seeks or avoids in doing an act, there is no act of will" (§103).

The key is that it is the *person* themselves that acts and that the action stems from some motive. Motives, "though . . . in [their] own way definitely determined," are not "naturally determined" in the way that impulses are (§95). Rather motives are "constituted by an act of self-consciousness which is not itself a natural event." The motive-constituting act is one "in which the agent presents to himself a certain idea of himself . . . enjoying" something that "forms for the time his good" (§95).

Unpacking these claims reveals a theory of action that is very much like Kant's, but one that is framed, unlike Kant's, in eudaimonist terms. Green's "impulses" are what Kant calls "inclinations." Kant and Green agree that impulses and inclinations cannot determine voluntary action, as Green puts it, "naturally," that is, as a matter of natural necessity. It is only when, as Kant puts it, inclinations are "incorporated" into an agent's "maxim" of action that, using now Green's terms rather than Kant's, we have a "motive" that can determine action not "naturally," but in a *self*-determining way (Green 2003: §95; Kant 2018: 6:24). The key contrast is between some natural phenomenon, like a Greenian impulse, determining behavior "naturally," on the one hand, and a rational agent determining their conduct themselves through their own reasons or motives. The former does not require self-consciousness, though the latter decidedly does.

An important difference between Green and Kant emerges in these passages from chapter I. When a Kantian agent acts, they necessarily do so on maxims that commit them to accepting norms of action ("practical laws"), hence normative reasons. Here is a famous passage: "Everything in nature works in accordance with laws. Only a rational being has the capacity to act *in accordance with the representation* of laws, that is, in accordance with principles, or has a *will.* Since *reason* is required for the derivation of actions from laws, the will is nothing other than practical reason" (Kant 1996a: 4:412). In other words, when a rational being acts, they do so "in accordance with [their] representation of [practical] laws," that is, norms of action or normative reasons for acting on which they thereby act.

Green holds, by contrast, that whenever agents act, they thereby commit themselves to a *eudaimonist* norm of action. The motive-constituting act is one "in which the agent presents to himself a certain idea of himself ... enjoying." And this idea is one "of which the realisation forms for the time his good" (Green 2003; §95). To put it in the language of reasons, they commit themselves to a conception of their good as giving them conclusive reasons for action.

Here Green attempts to "correct" Kant by Aristotle (Ritchie 1891: 139). Green gives no argument for this ancient eudaimonist framework as against Kant's "modern" one. Green's object is rather to lay out a coherent systematic view that can be convincing as a whole.

Green's points are made in a more detailed and systematic way in chapter II of book II: "Desire, Intellect, and Will" (Green 2003: §115–§153). He begins by returning to his distinction between "instinctive impulse, on the one hand, and desire of that kind which is a factor in our [distinctively] human experience," and that functions as "motive," on the other (§118). "The latter," he continues, "involves a consciousness of its object, which in turn implies a consciousness of self" (§118). "It is only in virtue of his self-consciousness ... that he is aware of facts as facts, or that his experience reveals to him a world of related objects" (§129).

This is a very important claim and, I believe, point. As Tamar Schapiro argues, inclinations of the kind we share with other animals can neither aspire to nor have the kind of objective purport had by desires, as Green puts it, "of the kind which ... factor in our [distinctively] human experience"

(Green 2003: §118; Schapiro 2021).[3] The "objects" of natural impulses or inclinations are always seen as cathected from the inclinations' perspective. Consider the fight, flight, or freeze response. From the perspective of a defensive inclination to fight that we share with other animals, there is no distinction between the way the object seems (e.g., as instantiating to-be-foughtness) and the way it really is that might enable us to gain a critical perspective on it in order to decide whether fighting is really worth it (Schapiro 2021: 119). There is, to be sure, a kind of practical reasoning that other animals, and we under the influence of our inclinations, are capable of, but it is entirely instrumental and unself-conscious.

Self-conscious deliberation, by contrast, is putatively *objective*. It attempts a view of its object that is unbiased by inclinations, in which the directive thoughts inclinations provide us are discounted as such, so that we can take account of them *as inclinations*. This is a point about the very nature of self-conscious deliberation, whether it is theoretical reasoning about what to believe or practical reasoning about what to do.[4]

Building on this point, Green argues that when we draw the distinction between self and world in deliberating from the practical perspective, our relation to the world must enter into the potential objects of our choice. If, for example, I decide on reflection to resist an impulse to fight, I will present the peaceful alternative to myself as something that I identify with and that constitutes, even if only momentarily, part of my personal good.

We see the desires with which we identify not as mere impulses by which we are moved – as desires we simply have or that are caused in us – but as *our* desires. When someone chooses, "he desires [a]n object in a quite different sense from that in which he can be supposed to desire that which has come out second best in his choice" (Green 2003: §138). What the agent finally chooses is something "he desires in the sense that for the time he identifies with it" (§138). It is what *the agent* intends and want as a self-reflecting self.

Impulses – desires in the other sense – "tend to move" the agent, but the agent "does not move in them"; agents are not thereby given a motive on which they can act (§144). To do that, the agent must "take it into himself and identify himself with it in a way which wholly alters it from what it was

[3] Schapiro 2021 brilliantly lays a Kantian theory of action and inclination that is very helpful in understanding Green's contrast between "impulse" and "motive."

[4] As Schapiro puts it, "the line we draw between ourselves and the world we confront . . . is one we draw from the participant standpoint," by which she means the perspective of noninstrumental theoretical or practical reasoning (Schapiro 2021: 43).

as a mere influence affecting" him (§144). Desires that assail us are not part of our will and, therefore, nothing we ourselves are (§153).

Earlier we saw that when an agent concludes deliberation by identifying with a desire and its object, they must thereby see the object as "form[ing] for the time [part of] his good" (§95). This may seem strange, but it is simply the consequence of Green's Kantian theory of will and agency, placed in Green's eudaimonist framework. We can put the point in the language of reasons in the following way. Whenever a rational agent decides to do something, there must be some reason for acting that they thereby take as *their reason* for acting and see as sufficient (normative) reason *for* them so to act (see, e.g., Darwall 1983: 28–32). This, in effect, is what Kant is saying when he says that the actions of rational agents involve their acting on a "representation" of practical "laws" (Kant 1996a: 4:412).

As a eudaimonist, Green holds that all reasons for acting must come from the agent's own good. If action requires acting on a representation of norms of action and therefore normative reasons, it follows that action requires acting on a representation of what the agent takes, "for the time," anyway, as their own good.[5]

Good and Moral Good

Book III of *Prolegomena* is devoted to "The Moral Ideal and Moral Progress." Green first consolidates points he made in book II. A key point is that just as there is a distinction between impulses we *have* and what *we desire* on the whole, so there is a distinction between pointillist pleasures that are part of our experience at a given time, and what *we ourselves* take pleasure in and find satisfying.

Green begins with the "*formal* account of willing" he has already laid out (Green 2003: §154). He aims now to give this account some substance so that it can distinguish between "the good and the bad will" (§154). Wills that have moral content and those that do not share the same "form." In all conduct "to which moral predicates are applicable," an agent is an "object to himself" and "express a motive consisting in an idea of personal good," which the agent "seeks to realise by action" (§154). In all action, an agent seeks to "direct himself to the realisation of some idea, as to an object in which for the time he seeks self-satisfaction . . . Self-satisfaction is the form of every action willed" (§154). The quality of the will, its being good or bad,

[5] On this point, see Skorupski (2006: 52).

"depend[s]" upon the "specific difference of the objects willed under the general form" (§154).

Mill and Sidgwick both argue that the only content of a good or rational will is pleasure. So Green turns to arguments that refute hedonism in all its forms: psychological and ethical, egoistic and universalistic. He begins with psychological egoistic hedonism against which he gives a version of Butler's argument. Action necessarily seeks self-satisfaction, but though self-satisfaction is necessarily pleasant, that does not mean that what the agent seeks is simply their own pleasure. "The pleasure of self-satisfaction can never be that with which he seeks to satisfy himself" (§160).

The point, as in Butler and Mill, is that pleasures and desires both have objects. When something satisfies us by giving *us* pleasure, that must be because we take pleasure in it. If you are on Parfit's train and desire the welfare of a stranger who tells you of an impending medical procedure, and you take some steps to try to bring about the success of their procedure, then the "form" of your action is to will your own self-satisfaction (see Parfit 1984: 151, 468). For that to be actually realized, however, the stranger's welfare must be furthered in fact, and you must want their welfare to be furthered for its own sake. Although the stranger's flourishing satisfies your desire and gives you pleasure, should you be fortunate to hear of it, it does so by being the object of your desire and pleasure. What satisfies you is not itself pleasure. One and the same pleasure cannot be its own object; that is logically impossible.

So psychological hedonism is a nonstarter. Nor is ethical hedonism in significantly better shape. It is a coherent doctrine, but one that is manifestly implausible given what we care about. Green uses Mill here against himself. He agrees with Mill that we desire (and take pleasure in) many things other than our own pleasure. To Mill's claim that we can desire intrinsically many things other than our own pleasure, including being virtuous, but that these thereby become "parts" of our own happiness, Green makes the following reply:

> But this . . . is no more than saying that they are desired by a self-conscious subject, who in all desire, or at any rate in all that amounts to will, is seeking self-satisfaction . . . . It leaves the question open what the ideal object is, in the realisation of which self-satisfaction is sought. It does not exclude the possibility of its being even the endurance of pain (Green 2003: §170).

By and large, Green agrees with Mill about what objects we do find self-satisfying: virtue and the excellent exercise of our "higher" rational faculties (Mill 2002 II.6; Green 2003: §164–166). But like Sidgwick, Green thinks that Mill's qualitative hedonism amounts to a "virtual surrender of the doctrine that all desire is for pleasure" as does ethical hedonism, whether egoistic or universalistic (Green 2003: §167).

Ethical hedonism is thus to be rejected also. Now it follows from Green's "formal" theory of willing that all desires of the kind that are identical with motives are for the agent's own self-realization, where that involves the exercise of their agential capacities. So much is guaranteed formally. But what should be the object or matter of the agent's will? What is the "moral good"? The "moral good," Green answers, "is the realisation of the moral capability," adding that "we cannot fully know what any capability is till we know its ultimate realisation" (§172).

This is the point in *Prolegomena* where Green starts out talking like Aristotle and ends up sounding like Fichte and Hegel. Green's Aristotelian naturalism shows itself in his perfectionist eudaimonism; he holds, like Aristotle, that the final good consists in virtuous activity, that is, excellent activity involving distinctively human capacities. And following the Aristotelian tradition, Green takes this to involve activities that advance a common good. Where he departs from Aristotle is in tying this activity, like Fichte and Hegel, to the reciprocal recognition of free agents on terms of mutual accountability, and through the historical progress of recognition, the realization of "eternal consciousness" or "mind" (§67, §187). As becomes clearest in *Principles of Political Obligation*, however, Green's view remains fundamentally eudaimonist. The justification for human rights is not, as with Fichte, that they are presupposed by a "summons" to mutual accountability, but that socially recognized human rights are an essential feature of the common good, and hence of self-realization.

The idea of the "further realisation of . . . capacities" and a "better state" of the agent is certainly Aristotelian, as is the idea of this including a "common good" (§181, 183). But that this requires a community of mutually accountable equals, potentially involving all others capable of human intercourse, is surely not. Unlike Aristotle, Green embraces a version of Kant's realm of ends. "Each," Green says, is "recognised by each as an end, not merely as a means, and thus as having reciprocal claims, that the capacity is actualised and that we really live as persons" (§183). "Our ultimate standard of worth," Green continues, "is an idea of *personal* worth. All other values are relative to value for, of, or in a person" (§184). To this broadly Kantian doctrine, Green adds the Hegelian thought that the worth of persons "is only actualised through the habits, institutions, and laws, in virtue of which the individuals form a nation"

(§184).[6] This involves nothing less than the "spiritual progress of mankind" (§185). Thus is "eternal mind" "gradually realised" (§187).

It follows, Green argues, that the ideal object of the morally good will, the "absolutely desirable," can never be finally defined (§193). "Of this object it can never be possible . . . to give a sufficient account, because it consists in the realisation of capabilities which can only be fully known in their ultimate realisation" (§193). Only though as the circle of moral concern expands from family to tribe, to nation, and beyond throughout the course of history can human beings realize their ideal object: self-actualizing community with everyone.

Brink emphasizes the way in which Green extends Aristotle's idea of a common good to a community including everyone, using a vision of other selves arising out of the common exercise of our rational human capacities in friendship (Green 2003: xlii–liii). It is important to realize, however, that, unlike even a universally extended Aristotle, Green emphasizes that the community of all is a community of mutual accountability, mediated by a "common language of right" (§216). This is no part of an Aristotelian account of friendship, even one of friendship between all.

"Some practical recognition of personality by another, of an 'I' by a 'Thou' and a 'Thou' by an 'I,' is necessary to any practical consciousness of it" (§190). And this requires recognition of "reciprocal rights and obligations" (§190). Human beings do this initially in families, tribes, and nations. Human progress, however, ultimately extends recognition to everyone.

> Given the idea of a common good and of self-determined participators in it – the idea implied, as we have seen, in the most primitive human society – the tendency of the idea in the minds of all capable of it must be to include, as participators of the good, all who have dealings with each other and who can communicate as "I" and "Thou" (§209).

This entails the idea that "there is something due from every man to every man, simply as men" (§211).

What seems to lie behind Green's view is not some notion of Aristotelian species good but rather something like Fichte's notion of the presuppositions of a second-personal "summons" or Hegel's ideas about the full logical development and actualization of concepts. "The Greek philosophers," Green says, lacked an "adequate notion of the claims in response to which the good will should be exercised." "'Human brotherhood' had no meaning

[6] Green develops this thought further in his *Principles of Political Obligation*.

for them" (§279). Moderns, on the other hand, have "formed" "the idea . . . of the possible inclusion of all men in one society of equals . . . And the idea of this social unity has been so far realised that the modern state, unlike the ancient, secures equality before the law to all persons living within the territory over which its jurisdiction it extends" (§280). The common good, Green emphasizes, includes "consciousness of the claims upon us on the part of other[s]" (§280).

The State, Rights, and the Good

This brings us to Green's account of the state and rights, and their relation to the final good of self-actualization, as he lays it out in *Principles of Political Obligation* and other essays. *Principles* begins by distinguishing senses of "'freedom' as applied to the will and to the moral progress of man" (Green 1921: I.§1–§25). Following Brink, we can identify three different senses: (a) a political sense in which someone is free when they are unconstrained by others or subordinated to them, (b) a "moral" sense that is presupposed by accountability, and (c) what Green calls "real freedom," which is the positive sense we have been discussing that is actualized when we realize ourselves (including in mutually accountable relations with others) (I.§1).[7] *Principles* is, of course, primarily concerned with social and political freedom; however, it is central to Green's view that relations of social and political freedom are ultimately to be justified not by anything like natural rights but by their relation to advancing self-realization and, therefore, "real freedom" (I.§1).

"'Natural rights,' so far as there are such things," Green says, "are themselves relative to the moral end to which perfect law is relative": the common self-realization of all in mutually accountable community (II.§20). He remarks that utilitarianism takes a similar view; as Mill puts it, a right is something that it promotes utility "to defend me in the possession of" (Mill 2002: V.25). Green disagrees with utilitarianism's hedonism, of course, since it recognizes "no vocation of man but the attainment of pleasure and avoidance of pain" (Green 1921: II.§23). For Green, ethics gives everyone the "vocation" of self-realization, and everyone's helping to further self-realization, he holds, is a necessary condition for the existence of rights (II.§25).

Thus Green actually agrees with Bentham's dictum that rights are "nonsense upon stilts." Bentham was, after all, a proponent of utility-

7 See Brink's "Introduction" to *Prolegomena* (Green 2003: lxx).

maximizing *legal* rights (Bentham 2002). But he was opposed to the idea of *natural* rights. Green agrees; there are no natural rights, only morally justified legal rights. Where Green and Bentham (as well as Mill) disagree is on the nature of the ends that rights must serve. According to Bentham, reciprocal recognition of rights and equal dignity is no part of the end, whereas for Green, joint self-realization itself consists, at least partly, in reciprocal recognition of equal rights. Still, Green agrees with the utilitarians that any reason to comply with rights must come from the good; the right has no independent normative status.

It is the necessity of legal structures of right to the final ethical end, the "vocation of man," that provides the justification for the state in general. The "true idea of the state," Green says, consists in the reciprocal recognition of "individual right, founded on the capacity of every man for free contribution to social good" (Green 1921: II.§174). "Social right," he says, is a "right belonging to a society of persons recognising a common good, and belonging through membership of the society" (II.§181 n). An ethically justified state, he continues, "is in principle or possibility a society of all men as rendered capable of free intercourse with each other by the organisation of the state" (II.§180 n).

Similarly, the state's right to punish depends on punishment's role in furthering this ethical end. Green steers a middle path between retributive and consequentialist justifications in their pure form. For punishment to be justified, he argues, "the criminal, being susceptible to the idea of public good, and through it to the idea of rights," must "se[e] in the punishment its natural expression" (II.§186). Punishment must encourage them to see their own act "returning on" themselves (II.§186).

In addition to thinking that familiar "negative" rights, for example, against force and fraud, can be justified by their role in furthering each person's ethical ends, Green holds that individuals have justified "claim[s] to be enabled positively to realise that capacity for freely contributing to social good" that identifies them as persons (II.§207). This is what marks Green's "third way" between Manchester individualism, on the one hand, and Marxist socialism, on the other – what Matt Carter calls his "ethical socialism" (Carter 2003: 144).

Particularly notable are Green's views about the sanctity of contract and property. Since rights of property and contract are justifiable only through their relation to furthering the self-realization of all, both can be restricted by the state when that is justified by the same ethical end. In *Liberal Legislation and the Freedom of Contract*, Green writes that property is "justifiable as a means to the free exercise of the social capabilities of all"

(Green 1881: 11). Tellingly, he says that "there can be no true right to property of a kind which debars one class of men from such free exercise altogether" (11). There can be a negative right to property, in other words, only to the extent that it is consistent with the positive right of all to the "free exercise of the social capabilities" in mutually accountable cooperation. This also entails restrictions on contract, including on the "sale of labour" if the sale makes "it impossible for the person selling it ever to become a free contributor to social good in any form" (11).

Property cannot, therefore, be entirely private. And any capitalist right to property in the means of production must be socially restricted in the requisite way. Green's mention of class here is an obvious reference to Marx, and his remarks about debarring the working class from exercising their social capabilities has clear resonances with Marx's claims about alienation in *Economic and Philosophic Manuscripts* (Marx 1975b).

Despite these similarities between Green and Marx, the two disagree about the role of individual rights in the ideal society. Marx famously criticizes all juridical notions as capitalist ideology, while Green holds them to be central to the ethical ideal. Still, Green and Marx are agreed that juridical or deontic notions have no independent normative force. Though Marx is not a eudaimonist like Green, he does hold, as Green does, that only the good can provide normative reasons for action.

Bradley

Francis Herbert Bradley was born in 1846 into a talented and well-connected family that included his father, Charles, a prominent evangelical clergyman, and his younger brother, A. C., who became a distinguished Shakespearean scholar (Brasile and Candlish 2021). Like Green, Bradley spent his academic career from his undergraduate years on at Oxford. He attended University College, and from 1870 until his death in 1924, Bradley was a fellow at Merton College.

Green had a more visible public face than Bradley, owing to his political writings and activities. Bradley was more reclusive as well. R. G. Collingwood remarked that although he had "lived within a few hundred yards of [Bradley] for sixteen years, [he had] never to [his] knowledge set eyes on him" (Brasile and Candlish 2021). During their lifetimes, however, Bradley was by far better known as a philosopher than Green was. Stewart Candlish calls Bradley "the most famous, original and philosophically influential of the British Idealists" (Brasile and Candlish 2021).

For the most part, Bradley's philosophical fame was due to his metaphysical and logical works, most especially, his *Principles of Logic* (Bradley 1883) and *Appearance and Reality* (Bradley 1893). On their basis, Bradley was "widely held to be," Brasile and Candlish say, "the greatest English philosopher of his generation" (Brasile and Candlish 2021). A polemical and passionate writer, Bradley argued for controversial metaphysical positions in ways that were broadly influential both within philosophy and within the wider reading public. His philosophical monism and famous argument against relations ("Bradley's Regress") have been thought to be philosophically powerful, and they retain influence today (Perovic 2017; Della Rocca 2020).

Bradley's moral philosophy is advanced in *Ethical Studies*, published in 1876. Although argued with similar passion and polemics, it has not had, it is fair to say, the same influence as Bradley's metaphysics. It did have an emotional effect, though, at least, on Sidgwick. Sidgwick reviewed the work in *Mind*, and it is hard to miss his annoyance and antipathy.

> I should have thought, on the contrary, that [Bradley's] chief aim was not merely directly dogmatic, but even vehemently propagandist; and that he had used all the rhetorical resources at his command – more perhaps, than the canons of good taste would permit – to bring his reader to the acceptance of a set of doctrines, chiefly derived from Hegel, which if they are not really coherent were at least believed by himself to be so (Sidgwick 1876: 545).

Sidgwick's own vehemence "perhaps" transgresses "the canons of good taste" also. And his characterization of Bradley's Hegelian views as incoherent is not only unfair but inaccurate. Sidgwick had a real blind spot for idealist approaches to ethics, as Moore would also, and Bradley proved remarkably astute, as we shall see, at pointing that out in a clear and convincing way. Still, Green's development of the idealist position is both significantly clearer and philosophically deeper than Bradley's. What is more, Bradley's ethical position is ultimately more conservative and complacent than Green's, as I have already suggested, even disturbingly so. Thus although Bradley's ethical writings are definitely worthy of study, I shall devote less attention to them than I did to Green's.

Before turning to *Ethical Studies*, we would do well to note criticisms that Bradley makes of Sidgwick in his own book-length review of *The Methods*: *Mr. Sidgwick's Hedonism: An Examination of the Main Arguments of The Methods of Ethics*, published in 1877, one year after Sidgwick's *Mind* review of *Ethical Studies*. A particularly trenchant point is an objection that

Bradley makes to Sidgwick's argument for hedonism that nonhedonistic theories of the good – which hold, for example, that virtue and excellent functioning are intrinsically beneficial for the agent – are unconsciously hedonistic, since we do not value these goods except when they also give rise to pleasure. Sidgwick concludes from this empirical fact that such goods are only instrumentally beneficial and that the only intrinsic good is pleasure.

Against this, Bradley makes the convincing objection that the facts Sidgwick cites are consistent with pleasures themselves being explained by excellent functioning, rather than *vice versa*. Indeed, as we shall see, Bradley defines pleasure as "felt self-realizedness" (Bradley 1988: 131). Excellent activity is the object of the pleasure, rather than merely the pleasure's extrinsic cause (like a CBD gummy). When we are "in the flow," excellently exercising our faculties, we certainly feel pleasure, but the relation between the pleasure and the activity is not simply causal; the excellent functioning is what our pleasure consists in (Csikszentmihalyi 1997).[8]

Bradley is happy to concede that virtuous self-realizing activity is better (and actually more virtuously self-realizing) when it is enjoyed than when it is not. But that does not detract one iota from the British idealist thesis that the good consists in self-realization. To say that self-realizing functioning is good is not, he says, "to say, Pleasure is not good." Rather, "it is to say, Pleasure is an inseparable element in the human end," and "is necessarily included in the end" (Bradley 1877: 31).

Ethical Studies Chapters I and II:

Moral Accountability and "Why Should I Be Moral?"

Composed of seven essays, *Ethical Studies* begins with two that help set up the next three, with the latter forming the dialectical heart of the book. Essay I concerns the "vulgar notion of responsibility" and its relation to "theories of free-will and necessity" (Bradley 1988: 1–57). Essay II, "Why Should I Be Moral?," discusses that perennial question in connection with Bradley's Hegelian account of the will and the central Aristotelian eudaimonist-naturalist, and also British idealist, claim that human good consists in excellent functioning or self-realization (Bradley 1988: 58–84).

[8] These points are, of course, familiar from Aristotle and Butler.

The commonsense idea of responsibility that is essay I's topic is the familiar modern moral philosophical notion of moral accountability and its relation to deontic morality. This, again, is what Sidgwick calls the morality of common sense and also what Hegel means by *Moralität*. Here Bradley covers familiar ground. Moral responsibility is *answerability*, rather than what Gary Watson calls "attributability" (Bradley 1988: 3; Watson 1996). The moral agent must "answe[r]," Bradley says, for what they "have done" (Bradley 1988: 3). They are "accountable" and "must . . . give an account" for all their actions (4, 7). The idea of moral accountability requires companion deontic moral concepts. And the latter essentially include the idea of a natural or moral *law*, the violation of which makes the emotion of guilt fitting.

This is the point Mill makes when he says that "we do not call anything wrong, unless we mean to imply that a person ought to be punished . . . for doing it . . . [for example], by the reproaches of his own conscience" (Mill 2002: V.14). Bradley echoes Mill; there is, he says, a "necessary connexion between" moral "responsibility and liability to punishment," including, he continues, "the finding of guiltiness before the law of the moral tribunal" (Bradley 1988: 4). "Wrong," Bradley says, is necessarily something that "can be imputed to me" (27).

For action to be imputed to an agent and for guilt to be a fitting response, certain conditions of action must be satisfied. Most obviously, Bradley claims, some kind of freedom, not just of action, but also, of *choice* is required, what he calls "self-determination" (10). Bradley agrees with Green in distinguishing between the agent's self-determined "will," on the one hand, and "desires" that they simply have, on the other. "My will is myself, and myself is superior to my desires" (10). Moral agency necessarily involves the will.

By the same token, however, Bradley rejects any identification of the free will and "chance" or the liberty of indifference (11–12). The doctrine of "Necessity" is not to be rejected wholesale, since it includes what Bradley regards as the true claim that moral actions are made necessary by a person's "character." Although we are rightly disturbed by the idea that our actions might be predicted by factors that are extrinsic to the moral self, "the prediction which is not objected to" is one "founded on knowledge of character" (16–17). We are, Bradley thinks, identical with our character, which necessarily expresses itself in our will. We are, however, "horrified" by any putative "deduc[tion]" of our will "from that which is not [ourselves]" (18).

Concerning the second stage-setting essay, "Why Should I Be Moral?," Bradley's view is that this question is ultimately meaningless (58–84). "It is simply unmeaning," he says, "unless it is equivalent to, *Is* morality an end in itself; and if so, how and in what way is it an end?" (64). This gives Bradley an opportunity to say what he thinks a positive answer is. "The most general expression for the end in itself" can be found, he says, "in the word *self-realization*" (64). This of course is the same answer we found in Green, and it raises the same questions around the reduction of the moral right to the good, perhaps even more vividly with Bradley than with Green.[9]

Bradley surely knows that what gives "Why be moral?" at least apparent force is that those who raise it do so using two different normative notions: the deontic "ought" that defines what Sidgwick calls "commonsense morality" and what Bradley calls "vulgar" moral notions, on the one hand, and a more fundamental practical normative notion – the "generic" ought, as Sidgwick calls it, or the notion of what there is most normative reason to do – on the other (Sidgwick 1962: 87, 105; Bradley 1988: 1). So framed, the question is, "Why do I have conclusive normative reason to do what I am morally obligated to do?"

In taking the question to be meaningless, Bradley reinterprets it as, "Why should I do what I should do?" with both "should"s being understood in the "generic" sense. This is especially puzzling, since he has just spent essay I laying out with great analytical insight the conceptual contours of the deontic, rather than the generic "ought." Moreover, by interpreting the question as he does, as what makes "morality an end in itself," so that he can give his and Green's answer of self-realization, Bradley forces the question into a eudaimonist framework. Self-realization, Green and Bradley hold, is what any person's welfare or good consists in and is, therefore, what their conduct should ultimately aim at (when "should" is interpreted generically).

To interpret "Why should I be moral?" as meaningless, we must interpret "moral" not as referring to deontic morality but as the generic normative term, which seems to change the subject. This is also signaled by Bradley's use of "end in itself," which is entirely different from Kant and Green's idea that *persons* are ends in themselves and, therefore, Green concludes, beings who are always already in the relation of mutual accountability within an assumed ideal moral community. We saw above how

[9] Who got what idea from whom is difficult with Bradley and Green. Bradley's book was certainly published earlier, but Bradley also attended some of Green's lectures.

Green seeks to locate this Kantian idea within a eudaimonist framework that holds self-realization to be the chief good. We shall consider in the next section but one, in connection with Bradley's essays IV and V, how Bradley handles these issues.

To conclude our study of essay II, we should note two further things. One is Bradley's holistic interpretation of self-realization. It is important to Bradley's ethics – and it follows, moreover, from his metaphysical monism – that the self one is to realize is not a free-standing entity but an aspect of larger wholes, including most prominently the social whole within which one occupies various stations with their respective duties, to anticipate essay V, "My Station and Its Duties" (Bradley 1988: 160–213). "To realize self," Bradley says, "is always to realize a whole" (69). We will return to this crucial aspect of his thought later. "Each member," Bradley will argue, "can not find the function, which makes him himself, apart from the whole to which he belongs" (163).

A last point we should note in essay II is Bradley's laying out of his version of Hegel's "three-moment" analysis of the will from *Philosophy of Right* (Hegel 1991: 35–37).[10] If an agent has desires for two conflicting alternatives, A and B, the agent must choose between them. To do so, they must step back from the perspective that is offered them by their respective desires for A and B and take up a new perspective from which they can consider both alternatives. This is the first, "universal factor" or moment. The agent identifies themselves with neither desire but just as *a* rational agent considering both (Bradley 1988: 72). So far, however, the agent is reflecting "universal[ly]" on what *someone* should do in the presenting situation, and that is insufficient to actually decide between the alternatives. To act, the agent "must will something" in particular. This is the second moment or "particular side" (72).

However, simply plumping for A or B in particular is not really choosing between them or forming a will. A randomizing device might do the former without being capable of volition and choice. It is only when the agent synthesizes the universal and particular moments in a third moment that we get a genuine "volition": "the volition as a whole" in which universal and particular are made into a unity. This we may call, Bradley says, "the individual whole, or again the concrete universal" (72). If we are looking for a way of interpreting these remarks, we might say that the agent chooses to do something for reasons that thereby become *theirs*. Or in

[10] For discussion see Chapter 1.

Green's terminology, the agent thereby identifies themselves with a conception of their good.

In his introduction to the 1988 edition of *Ethical Studies*, Richard Wollheim remarks that the book is not only "Hegelian in many of its ideas," but "to an even greater extent Hegelian its method" and "*dialectical* in its structure" (Bradley 1988: xv). This is borne out by essays III, IV, and V. These replicate the three-moment dialectical structure of Hegel's account of the will, although in a different order. Essay III, "Pleasure for Pleasure's Sake," is particularistic in that it describes the self as wholly absorbed in some particular in which it takes pleasure. Essay IV, "Duty For Duty's Sake," involves the "universal factor," by contrast, since it concerns not particular actual *duties*, but the abstract notion of duty. Only in essay V, "My Station and Its Duties," do we get a Hegelian resolution of the abstract moments to yield a "concrete universal" or "individual whole." Here the abstract notion of "duty" is given concrete reality in actual social duties. We shall proceed by taking each of these essays in turn.

Pleasure for Pleasure's Sake

Essay III is concerned with hedonism. Many of Bradley's arguments are familiar from Green.[11] Like Green, Bradley criticizes Sidgwick's "pointillist" conception of pleasure and its value. Pleasures so conceived, Bradley says, are "a perishing series." "This one comes, and the intense self-feeling proclaims satisfaction. It is gone, and *we* are not satisfied" (96). Just as there is a difference between desires that we *have* – Green's "impulses" and Kant's "inclinations" – and what *we ourselves desire*, so also is there a difference between pleasant sensations that we feel at a time, and what pleases *us* and gives us satisfaction over time.

This contrast between quantitative hedonisms like Sidgwick's, on the one hand, and idealisms, like Bradley's and Green's, on the other, is related to the roles of the self in these different views. It is crucial to the idealists that the self is an organizing whole that seeks, in turn, membership in larger wholes. This connects selves together in the idealist view in contrast to the way they are separated in Sidgwick. Sidgwick's dualism of practical reason – between what is best for the agent and what is best for all – cannot arise for Bradley and Green, "if my self which I aim at is the realization in me of a moral world which is a system of selves, an organism in which I am a member, and in whose life I live – then I cannot aim at my well-being

[11] Again, I am not saying he got them from Green.

without aiming at that of others" (116). Recall, in this connection, that the language of parts and wholes also plays an important role in Sidgwick. Taking the perspective of wholes is what gets Sidgwick's agent from the benefits of particular pleasures to the agent's greatest good on the whole (Prudence), *and* from the idea that their good is but a part of the good of all to the rationality of promoting the greatest good of all on the whole (Benevolence). But Sidgwick's vision of the whole differs radically from the idealists' vision. The wholes that Bradley and Green are concerned with, both that of the self and larger wholes of which the self is a part, are organic, having "members" with distinct, but interrelated, functions. They are "organisms," whereas Sidgwick's wholes are simply aggregates of parts; the latter's value, consequently, can be nothing other than the sum of the value of the parts (Bradley 1988: 72–73, 79). For Bradley and Green, however, individual members are defined by their functions within the whole. Sidgwick "tacitly assume[s]," Bradley says, "that the individual and the universal are two independent things" (126).

Bradley counters Sidgwick's definition of pleasure as feelings apprehended as desirable independently of their objects. He claims that pleasure "is the felt assertion of the will or self. It is felt self-realizedness" (Sidgwick 1962: 131; Bradley 1988: 131). This is in the tradition of Aristotle's view that "pleasure completes the activity . . . as a sort of supervenient end, like the bloom on the faces of [the] young" (Aristotle 2000: 1174b 32–34). For Bradley, as for Aristotle, what is desirable is not a feeling considered in abstraction from its objective correlates, but self-realizing activity itself.

To complete our discussion of essay III, we should note Bradley's trenchant analysis of a blind spot in Mill and Sidgwick's division of moral philosophers into "inductive" utilitarians and "intuitive moralists," whether they are "dogmatic" or "philosophical intuitionis[ts]" (Sidgwick 1962: xxv, 101–103; Mill 2002: I.3, III.7). Bradley notes that idealism does not fit comfortably into this framework. It is, he says, a "false assumption," "that the 'either-or' of 'intuitive' and 'utilitarian' is complete and exhaustive" (Bradley 1988: 90). This also is a blind spot in Moore's *Principia Ethica*, as I shall argue in the first chapter of *Modern Moral Philosophy in the Twentieth Century* (Darwall in press).

Duty for Duty's Sake

If the problem with hedonism is that it is excessively particular, the problem with Kant's "duty for duty's sake," is that it is excessively abstract and universal. In essay IV, Bradley pursues a critique of Kantian ethics along the same lines as Hegel's. "Its fault," Bradley says, "is the opposite, since for mere particular it substitutes mere universal" (Bradley 1988: 142).

The fundamental problem with Kant's analysis of *Moralität* and the idea of doing one's duty because it is one's duty, from Hegel and Bradley's perspective, is that it provides form without content. And because it lacks content, Bradley says, it can give no specific guidance: "that which has no content can not be willed" (150).

Bradley's view is that the idea of moral "duty" is an abstraction that cannot be realized. He recognizes *duties*, of course. But *duties* are to *duty* as what we called *morality* in the count-noun sense is to *morality* in the noncount-noun sense.[12] Moralities we can count are actualized in social *mores*; they are deontic norms some society or group actually accepts and to which it holds its members. Morality in the noncount-noun sense, by contrast, is no part of actuality; it is a set of essentially normative deontic standards, "ought"s rather than "is"'s.

Following Hegel, Bradley holds that duty cannot be actualized; only duties can be. Now there is a sense, of course, in which duties can be counted without being actualized. "Dogmatic intuitionists" like W. D. Ross or Richard Price hold that there is an irreducible plurality of deontic normative standards. But these are not duties in the sense that Bradley has in mind, since he holds these to be defined by stations in an actual society.[13]

My Station and Its Duties

Essay V ends with a dialectical recap of essays III and IV. In essay III, we learned "that the self to be realized is not the self as this or that feeling" (160). In essay IV, we passed "to the opposite pole, to the universal as the negative of the particulars, to the supposed pure will or duty for duty's sake," and "found that too was an unreal conception" (160). Just as Bradley's Hegelian theory of the will brings the particular and universal together in the "concrete universal" of a "volition as a whole," so his account of the duties as an essential aspect of a living, organic social whole, synthesizes the abstract moments of particularity and universality represented by hedonism and Kantian ethics (72). "The good will (for morality) is meaningless," Bradley says, "if . . . it be not the will of living

[12] In our discussion of Nietzsche's *Daybreak* in Chapter 2.

[13] And even then there is a distinction between the actualized, socially recognized, *more* that gives the agent one of their *duties*, and the *duty* (in the essentially normative, nonactualized, sense) to comply with their *duties* in Bradley's former, actualized sense.

finite beings" (162). Its being realized in an actual social whole, however, makes it a "concrete universal." "It is an organism and a moral organism" (162). It organizes each "member" and thereby every other and the social whole they together constitute: "It is the self-realization of each member, because each member can not find the function, which makes him himself, apart from the whole to which he belongs" (163). This "solve[s]" the "contradictions which ... beset us" in essays III and IV. "Here is a universal which ... is no unreal form of the mind, but a living soul that penetrates and stands fast in the detail of actual existence" (163). "I am real in it" (163).

This is the theme we found in Hegel. *Sittlichkeit* overcomes the alienation of abstract right and *Moralität* and gives us something in and through which we and others can recognize ourselves and one another and so achieve collective self-actualization. Bradley identifies three besetting "defects" that make it impossible for the agent to "find self-realization in the morality of pure duty" (176): (1) the agent cannot recognize or "look upon himself as the realized moral law"; (2) they "can not look on the objective world as the realization of the moral law"; (3) they "can not realize the moral law at all, because it is defined as that which has no particular content, and therefore no reality" (176). All three defects are "mended by 'my station and its duties.'" "(1) the universal is concrete; (2) it is objective; and (3) it leaves nothing of us outside it" (176).

When we conceive of society as a living organic whole with each of us being defined by our respective functions, by our "station and its duties," subjective and objective, particular and universal, are synthesized in a way that overcomes these abstract dualities and allows us to realize and recognize ourselves in valuable social wholes: "The laws pronounce nothing but what everyone *is* and does. The individual recognizes the substance not only as his universal outward [objective] existence, but he recognizes also himself in it, particularized in his own individuality and in that of each of his fellow citizens" (186). Through this "the truth of individualism is saved, because, unless we have intense life and self-consciousness in the members of the state, the whole state is ossified" (187).

Like Green, Bradley holds that there are no natural rights. To be sure, there are social and legal rights of actual societies. But just as Bradley opposes abstract duty to actual duties, so also does he oppose (abstract) natural right to legal rights. There is, he says, "no such fixed code or rule of right" (189).

Bradley happily accepts that this commits him to a form of moral and rights relativism. To the worry that "if what is right here is wrong there, then all morality . . . becomes chance and convention, and so ceases," Bradley replies that "'my station and its duties' holds that *unless* morals varied, there could be no morality; that a morality which was *not* relative would be futile, and I should have to ask for something 'more relative than this'" (189).

In this, Bradley goes significantly farther in the direction of relativistic quietism than Green does. As we saw, Green fervently endorses the idea of moral progress and development in the direction of a universal community in which all who are capable of "communication" are mutually accountable as equals. This is no part of Bradley's view. Bradley does accept a version of the Hegelian/Greenian notion of "evolution" and "development," but he denies that any philosophical ideal like Green's can guide it (190–193). "It is not the business of philosophy" to give such guidance. "All philosophy has to do is 'to understand what is', and moral philosophy has to understand morals which exist" (193). The *phronimos*, Bradley says, "is the man who has identified his will with the moral spirit of the community, and judges accordingly" (196).

As Aristotle and Bradley consider things, the *phronimos* is definitely a man. If the "moral spirit" of the community supports, worse, demands, oppressive racial and gender hierarchy, then this will be reflected in the community's duties and in the judgment of those it deems practically wise.

Green's form of idealism does better here, since he understands self-realization in terms of an ideal community of mutually accountable equals. Even Green, however, recognizes no fundamental or natural *right* to such treatment; he is simply saying that a community where equal legal and social rights are recognized is best for the participants. Neither does Sidgwick provide any deontic or "jural" basis to resist oppressive hierarchy. The most his moral philosophy has the resources to afford is the thesis that such forms of injustice are bad "from the point of view of the universe" (Sidgwick 1962: xviii). And even there, Sidgwick's view is that any such reasons provided by rational benevolence are in irresolvable conflict with those provided by the agent's own good. What is lacking in all these writers is any defense of the thought that the fact that such oppression is *wrong* is sufficient reason *in itself* to override, defeat, or silence any reasons not to oppose it.

References

Albee, Ernest (1957). *A History of English Utilitarianism*. London: Allen & Unwin.

Allison, Henry (1990). *Kant's Theory of Freedom*. Cambridge: Cambridge University Press.

Allison, Henry (1991). "On a Presumed Gap in Kant's Derivation of the Categorical Imperative," *Philosophical Topics* 19: 1–15.

Anderson, Elizabeth (1999). "What Is the Point of Equality?" *Ethics* 109: 287–307.

Anderson, Elizabeth (2012). "The Fundamental Disagreement Between Luck Egalitarians and Relational Egalitarians," *Canadian Journal of Philosophy*, supp. vol. 36: 1–23.

Anderson, Elizabeth (2014). "Social Movements, Experiments in Living, and Moral Progress: Case Studies from Britain's Abolition of Slavery." The Lindley Lecture, The University of Kansas. https://kuscholarworks.ku.edu/entities/publication/80b87589-786a-442b-85f7-22af2ace63d7.

Anderson, Elizabeth (2023a). "John Dewey's Moral Philosophy," *Stanford Encyclopedia of Philosophy*. https://plato.stanford.edu/entries/dewey-moral/.

Anderson, Elizabeth (2023b). *Hijacked: How Neoliberalism Turned the Work Ethic against Workers and How Workers Can Take It Back*. Cambridge: Cambridge University Press.

Anscombe, G. E. M. (1958). "Modern Moral Philosophy," *Philosophy* 33: 1–19.

Apel, Karl-Otto (1988). *Diskurs und Verantwortung: Das Problem der Üntergangs zur postkonventionellen Moral*. Frankfurt: Suhrkamp Verlag.

Aquinas, Thomas (1997). *Summa Theologica*, in *Basic Writings of Thomas Aquinas*, vol. 2, ed. Anton C. Pegis. Indianapolis, IN: Hackett Publishing Co. Originally published in 1265–1273.

Aristotle (1998). *The Nicomachean Ethics*, trans. and intro., David Ross, rev., J. L. Ackrill and J. O. Urmson. Oxford: Oxford University Press.

Aristotle (2000). *Nicomachean Ethics*, ed. and trans. Roger Crisp. Cambridge: Cambridge University Press. References are to the standard Bekker numbers of passages.

Arpaly, Nomy (2004). *Unprincipled Virtue: An Inquiry into Moral Agency*. Oxford: Oxford University Press.

Austin, J. L. (1956–1957). "A Plea for Excuses," *Proceedings of the Aristotelian Society* 57: 1–30.

Austin, John (1832). *The Province of Jurisprudence Determined*. London: John Murray.

Ayer, A. J. (1952). *Language, Truth, and Logic*. New York, NY: Dover.

Baier, Annette (1993). "Moralism and Cruelty: Reflections on Hume and Kant," *Ethics* 103: 436–457.

Barry, C. (2014). "Against the Doctrine of Aristotle: Hutcheson on the Slave Trade," *Irish Philosophy*. www.irishphilosophy.com/2014/08/01/hutcheson-on-slavery/.

Batson, C. Daniel and Laura L. Shaw (1991). "Evidence for Altruism: Toward a Pluralism of Prosocial Motives," *Psychological Inquiry* 2: 107–122.

Beccaria, Cesare (1986). *On Crimes and Punishments*. Indianapolis, IN: Hackett Publishing Co.

Bentham, Jeremy (1838). *The Works of Jeremy Bentham*, ed. John Bowring. Edinburgh: William Tait.

Bentham, Jeremy (1977). *A Comment on the Commentaries and A Fragment on Government*, ed. J. H. Burns and H. L. A. Hart. London: Athlone Press of the University of London.

Bentham, Jeremy (1983). "Article on Utilitarianism," in *Deontology Together with A Table of the Springs of Action and the Article on Utilitarianism*, ed. A. Goldworth. Oxford: Clarendon Press.

Bentham, Jeremy (1996). *Introduction to the Principles of Morals and Legislation*, an authoritative edition, ed. J. H. Burns and H. L. A. Hart, with a new intro., F. Rosen, and interpretative essay, H. L. A. Hart. Oxford: Oxford University Press.

Bentham, Jeremy (2002). *Rights, Representation, and Reform: Nonsense upon Stilts and Other Writings on the French Revolution*, in *The Collected Works of Jeremy Bentham*, ed. Philip Schofield, Catherine Pease-Watkin, and Cyprian Blamires. Oxford: Oxford University Press.

Berkeley, George (1964a). *Alciphron, Or the Minute Philosopher*, in *The Works of George Berkeley, Bishop of Cloyne*, ed. A. A. Luce and T. E. Jessop. London: Thomas Nelson. Reference is to dialogue and numbered sections, followed by page number in volume 3 of the *Works*.

Berkeley, George (1964b). *Passive Obedience*, in *The Works of George Berkeley, Bishop of Cloyne*, ed. A. A. Luce and T. E. Jessop. London: Thomas Nelson. Reference is to numbered sections.

Berkeley, George (1964c). *An Essay towards a New Theory of Vision*, in *The Works of George Berkeley, Bishop of Cloyne*, ed. A. A. Luce and T. E. Jessop. London: Thomas Nelson. Reference is to numbered sections.

Berkeley, George (1964d). *Introduction to a Treatise Concerning the Principles of Human Knowledge*, in *The Works of George Berkeley, Bishop of Cloyne*, ed. A. A. Luce and T. E. Jessop. London: Thomas Nelson. Reference is to numbered sections.

Berkeley, George (1964e). *Philosophical Commentaries*, in *The Works of George Berkeley, Bishop of Cloyne*, ed. A. A. Luce and T. E. Jessop. London: Thomas Nelson. Reference is to entries, as numbered by Luce and Jessop.

Blackburn, Simon (1984). *Spreading the Word: Groundings in the Philosophy of Language*. Oxford: Oxford University Press.

Blight, David W. (2024). *Yale and Slavery: A History*. New Haven, CT: Yale University Press.

Boyer, Anne (2019). "An Interview with Anne Boyer," *The Believer*. www.thebeliever.net/an-interview-with-anne-boyer/.

Bradley, F. H. (1883). *The Principles of Logic*. London: K. Paul Trench.

Bradley, F. H. (1893). *Appearance and Reality*. London: S. Sonnenschein.

Bradley, F. H. (1877). *Mr. Sidgwick's Hedonism: An Examination of the Main Argument of The Methods of Ethics*. London: Henry S. King and Co.

Bradley, F. H. (1988). *Ethical Studies*, 2nd ed., rev., intro. Richard Wollheim. Oxford: Clarendon Press.

Brandom, Robert (1979). "Freedom and Constraint by Norms," *American Philosophical Quarterly* 16: 187–196.

Brandom, Robert (2019). *A Spirit of Trust: A Reading of Hegel's Phenomenology*. Cambridge, MA: Harvard University Press.

Brandt, Richard B. (1963). "Toward a Credible Form of Utilitarianism," in *Morality and the Language of Conduct*, ed. Hector Neri-Castañeda and George Nakhnikian. Detroit, MI: Wayne State University Press.

Brandt, Richard B. (1979). *A Theory of the Good and the Right*. Oxford: Oxford University Press.

Brink, David O. (1988). "Sidgwick's Dualism of Practical Reason," *Australasian Journal of Philosophy* 66: 291–307.

Broad, C. D. (1962). *Five Types of Ethical Theory*. London: Routledge & Kegan Paul.

Buchanan, Allen E. (1979). "Revolutionary Motivation and Rationality," *Philosophy & Public Affairs* 9: 59–82.

Buchanan, Allen E. (1982). *Marx and Justice: The Radical Critique of Liberalism*. Lanham, MD: Rowman & Littlefield.

Buchanan, Allen and Russell Powell (2018). *The Evolution of Moral Progress: A Biocultural Theory*. New York, NY: Oxford University Press.

Butler, Joseph (2017). *Fifteen Sermons and Other Writings on Ethics*, ed. David McNaughton. Oxford: Oxford University Press. Originally published in 1726. Reference to sermon and paragraph numbers.

Candlish, Stewart and Pierfrancesco Brasile (2021). "Francis Herbert Bradley," *Stanford Encyclopedia*. https://plato.stanford.edu/entries/bradley/.

Carlyle, Thomas (1853). *Occasional Thoughts on the N**ger Question*. London: Thomas Bosworth.

Carter, Matt (2003). *T. H. Green and the Development of Ethical Socialism*. Exeter, UK: Imprint Academic.

Case, Anne and Angus Deaton (2020). *Deaths of Despair and the Future of Capitalism*. Princeton, NJ: Princeton University Press.

Clarke, Samuel (1978a). *A Discourse Concerning the Being and Attributes of God*, in *Works*, vol. 2. New York, NY: Garland Publishing. Originally published in 1704.

Clarke, Samuel (1978b). *A Discourse Concerning the Unchangeable Obligations and the Truth and Certainty of the Christian Revelation*, in *Works*, vol. 2. New York, NY: Garland Publishing. Originally published in 1705.

Crawford, Neta C. (2002). *Argument and Change in World Politics: Ethics, Decolonization, and Humanitarian Intervention.* Cambridge: Cambridge University Press.

Crisp, Roger (2013). *The Cosmos of Duty: Henry Sidgwick's Methods of Ethics.* Oxford: Oxford University Press.

Csikszentmihalyi, Mihalyi (1997). *Finding Flow: The Psychology of Engagement with Everyday Life.* New York, NY: Basic Books.

Cudworth, Ralph (~1670). Manuscripts on freedom of the will. British Library, Additional Manuscripts, nos. 4978–4982.

Cudworth, Ralph (1678). *The True Intellectual System of the Universe.* London: Richard Royston.

Cudworth, Ralph (1996). *A Treatise Concerning Eternal and Immutable Morality*, ed. Sarah Hutton. Cambridge: Cambridge University Press.

Cumberland, Richard (1683). *De legibus naturae disquisitio philosophica*, 2nd ed. Lubeck. Originally published in 1672.

Cumberland, Richard (2005). *A Treatise of the Laws of Nature*, trans., with an intro. and appendix, ed. John Maxwell, with a foreword by John Parkin. Indianapolis, IN: Liberty Fund. Based on 1727 edition.

Cumhaill, Clare Mac and Rachael Wiseman (2022). *Metaphysical Animals: How Four Women Brought Philosophy Back to Life.* New York, NY: Doubleday.

Daly, James (2000). "Marx and Justice," *International Journal of Philosophical Studies* 8: 351–370.

Daniels, Norman (1979). "Wide Reflective Equilibrium and Theory Acceptance in Ethics," *Journal of Philosophy* 76: 256–282.

Dannenberg, Jorah (2017). "Promising By Right," *Philosophers' Imprint* 17: 1–18.

Darwall, Stephen (1974a). "Pleasure as Ultimate Good in Sidgwick's Ethics," *The Monist* 58: 475–489.

Darwall, Stephen (1974b). "Nagel's Argument for Altruism," *Philosophical Studies* 25: 125–130.

Darwall, Stephen (1977). "Two Kinds of Respect," *Ethics* 88: 36–49.

Darwall, Stephen (1980). "Is There a Kantian Foundation for Rawlsian Justice?" in *John Rawls' Theory of Social Justice*, ed. H. G. Blocker and E. Smith. Athens, OH: Ohio University Press.

Darwall, Stephen (1983). *Impartial Reason.* Ithaca, NY: Cornell University Press.

Darwall, Stephen (1986). "Agent-Centered Restrictions from the Inside Out," *Philosophical Studies* 50: 291–319.

Darwall, Stephen (1987). "Abolishing Morality," *Synthese* 72: 71–89.

Darwall, Stephen (1989). "Moore to Stevenson," in *Ethics in the History of Western Philosophy*, ed. Robert Cavalier, James Gouinlock, and James Sterba. London: MacMillan.

Darwall, Stephen (1994). "Hume and the Invention of Utilitarianism," in *Hume and Hume's Connexions*, ed. M. A. Stewart and J. Wright. Edinburgh: Edinburgh University Press.

Darwall, Stephen (1995). *The British Moralists and the Internal "Ought": 1640–1740.* Cambridge: Cambridge University Press.

Darwall, Stephen (1997). "Reasons, Motives, and the Demands of Morality: An Introduction," in, *Moral Discourse and Practice*, ed. Stephen Darwall, Allan Gibbard, and Peter Railton. New York, NY: Oxford University Press.
Darwall, Stephen (1998a). *Philosophical Ethics*. Boulder, CO: Westview Press.
Darwall, Stephen (1998b). "Under Moore's Spell," *Utilitas* 10: 286–291.
Darwall, Stephen (1999a). "The Inventions of Autonomy," *European Journal of Philosophy* 7: 339–350.
Darwall, Stephen (1999b). "Sympathetic Liberalism: Recent Work on Adam Smith," *Philosophy & Public Affairs* 28: 139–164.
Darwall, Stephen (2000a). "Normativity and Projection in Hobbes's *Leviathan*," *The Philosophical Review* 109: 313–347.
Darwall, Stephen (2000b). "Sidgwick, Concern, and the Good," *Utilitas* 12: 291–306.
Darwall, Stephen (2001). "Because I Want It," *Social Philosophy & Policy* 18: 129–153.
Darwall, Stephen (2002). *Welfare and Rational Care*. Princeton, NJ: Princeton University Press.
Darwall, Stephen (2003). "How Should Ethics Relate to the Rest of Philosophy? Moore's Legacy," *The Southern Journal of Philosophy* 41: 1–20.
Darwall, Stephen (2005). "Berkeley's Moral and Political Philosophy," in *The Cambridge Companion to Berkeley*, ed. Kenneth Winkler. Cambridge: Cambridge University Press.
Darwall, Stephen (2006). *The Second-Person Standpoint: Morality, Respect, and Accountability*. Cambridge, MA: Harvard University Press.
Darwall, Stephen (2008a). "How Is Moorean Value Related to Reasons for Attitudes," in *Themes from G. E. Moore: New Essays in Epistemology and Ethics*, ed. Susana Nuccetelli and Gary Seay. Oxford: Oxford University Press.
Darwall, Stephen (2008b). "Kant on Respect, Dignity, and the Duty of Respect," in *Kant's Virtue*, ed. Monika Betzler. Berlin: Walter de Gruyter. Reprinted in Darwall 2013c.
Darwall, Stephen (2010). Review of K. E. Løgstrup, *Beyond the Ethical Demand. Notre Dame Philosophical Reviews*. https://ndpr.nd.edu/reviews/beyond-the-ethical-demand-book-1-and-concern-for-the-other-perspectives-on-the-ethics-of-k-e-l-248-gstrup-book-2/.
Darwall, Stephen (2011b). "Demystifying Promises," in *Promises and Agreements: Philosophical Essays*, ed. Hanoch Sheinman. Oxford: Oxford University Press. Reprinted in Darwall 2013c.
Darwall, Stephen (2012a). "Grotius at the Creation of Modern Moral Philosophy," *Archiv für Geschichte der Philosophie* 94: 296–325. Reprinted in Darwall 2013c.
Darwall, Stephen (2012b). "Pufendorf on Morality, Sociability, and Moral Powers," *The Journal of the History of Philosophy* 50: 213–238. Reprinted in Darwall 2013c.
Darwall, Stephen (2013a). "Bipolar Obligation," in Stephen Darwall, *Morality, Authority, and Law: Essays in Second-Personal Ethics I*. Oxford: Oxford University Press.

Darwall, Stephen (2013b). *Morality, Authority, and Law: Essays in Second-Personal Ethics I*. Oxford: Oxford University Press.

Darwall, Stephen (2013c). *Honor, History, and Relationship: Essays in Second-Personal Ethics II*. Oxford: Oxford University Press.

Darwall, Stephen (2013d). "Respect as Honor and as Accountability," in *Honor, History, and Relationship: Essays in Second-Personal Ethics II*. Oxford: Oxford University Press.

Darwall, Stephen (2013e). "Kant on Respect, Dignity, and the Duty of Respect," in *Honor, History, and Relationship: Essays in Second-Personal Ethics II*. Oxford: Oxford University Press.

Darwall, Stephen (2013f). "Authority and Second-Personal Reasons for Acting," in *Morality, Authority, and Law: Essays in Second-Personal Ethics I*. Oxford: Oxford University Press.

Darwall, Stephen (2013g). "Fichte and the Second-Person Standpoint," in *Honor, History, and Relationship: Essays in Second-Personal Ethics II*. Oxford: Oxford University Press.

Darwall, Stephen (2013h). "'Forcing Freedom,' critical review of Arthur Ripstein's *Force and Freedom*," *Legal Theory* 19: 89–99.

Darwall, Stephen (2013i). "Justice and Retaliation," in *Honor, History, and Relationship: Essays in Second-Personal Ethics II*. Oxford: Oxford University Press.

Darwall, Stephen (2013j). "Morality and Principle," in *Honor, History, and Relationship: Essays in Second-Personal Ethics II*. Oxford: Oxford University Press.

Darwall, Stephen (2014a). "'Agreement Matters' (Critical Notice of Derek Parfit's *On What Matters*)", *The Philosophical Review* 123: 79–105.

Darwall, Stephen (2014b). Review of Richard Sorabji's *Moral Conscience, Its History through the Ages: 5th Century* BCE *to the Present*. *Notre Dame Philosophical Reviews*. https://ndpr.nd.edu/news/56313-moral-conscience-throu gh-the-ages-fifth-century-bce-to-the-present/.

Darwall, Stephen (2014c). "Why Fichte's Second-Personal Foundations Can Provide a More Adequate Account of the Relation of Right than Kant's," *Grazer Philosophische Studien* 90: 5–20.

Darwall, Stephen (2016). "Making the Hard Problem of Moral Normativity Easier." In *Weighing Reasons*, ed. Errol Lord and Barry Maguire. Oxford: Oxford University Press.

Darwall, Stephen (2017). "Trust as a Second-Personal Attitude (of the Heart)," in *The Philosophy of Trust*, ed. Paul Faulkner and Thomas Simpson. Oxford: Oxford University Press.

Darwall, Stephen (2018a). "Empathy and Reciprocating Attitudes," in *Forms of Fellow Feeling: Empathy, Sympathy, Concern, and Moral Agency*, ed. Neil Roughley and Thomas Schramme. Cambridge: Cambridge University Press.

Darwall, Stephen (2018b). "Contempt as an Other-Characterizing, 'Hierarchizing' Attitude," in *The Moral Psychology of Contempt*, ed. Michelle Mason. Lanham, MD: Rowman & Littlefield.

Darwall, Stephen (2021). "Doing Right by Wrong," in *Principles and Persons: The Legacy of Derek Parfit*, ed. Jeff McMahan, Tim Campbell, James Goodrich, and Ketan Ramakrishnan. Oxford: Oxford University Press.

Darwall, Stephen (2022a). "A Gibbardian Account of (Narrow) Moral Concepts," in *Meaning, Decision, and Norms: Themes From the Work of Allan Gibbard*, ed. Billy Dunaway and David Plunkett. Ann Arbor, MI: Maize Books.

Darwall, Stephen (2022b). "Williams, Kant, and Morality's 'Peculiarity,'" in *Morality and Agency*, ed. A. Szigeti and M. Talbert. Oxford: Oxford University Press.

Darwall, Stephen (2023a). *Modern Moral Philosophy: From Grotius to Kant*. Cambridge: Cambridge University Press.

Darwall, Stephen (2023b). "Review of *The Ethical Demand* and *Ethical Concepts and Problems*, by K. E. Løgstrup by K. E. Løgstrup." *Mind* 132: 558–567.

Darwall, Stephen (2023c). "I Owe You: Accountability in Finance and Morality," in *Value, Morality, and Social Reality*, ed. Andrés G. Garcia, Matthias Gunnemyr, and Jakob Werkmäster (2023). Lund: University of Lund Philosophy Department.

Darwall, Stephen (2023d). "On Being a "Self-Originating Source of Valid Claims," in *John Rawls's A Theory of Justice at 50*, ed. Paul Weithman. Cambridge: Cambridge University Press.

Darwall, Stephen (2024). *The Heart and Its Attitudes*. Oxford: Oxford University Press.

Darwall, Stephen (2025). *Modern Moral Philosophy in the Nineteenth Century*. Cambridge: Cambridge University Press.

Darwall, Stephen (in press). *Modern Moral Philosophy in the Twentieth Century*. Cambridge: Cambridge University Press.

Darwall, Stephen, Allan Gibbard, and Peter Railton (1997). "Toward *Fin de Siècle* Ethics: Some Trends," in *Moral Discourse and Practice*, ed. Stephen Darwall, Allan Gibbard, and Peter Railton. New York, NY: Oxford University Press.

Darwin, Charles (1872). *Expression of the Emotions in Man and Animals*. London: J. Murray.

Deigh, John (1992). "Sidgwick on Ethical Judgment," in *Essays on Henry Sidgwick*, ed. Bart Schultz. Cambridge: Cambridge University Press.

de Kenessey, Brendan (2017). "Joint Practical Deliberation." Diss., Massachusetts Institute of Technology.

Della Rocca, Michael (2020). *The Parmenidean Ascent*. Oxford: Oxford University Press.

Douglass, Frederick (2018). "What to the Slave is the Fourth of July?" in *The Speeches of Frederick Douglass: A Critical Edition*, ed. John McKivigan, Julie Husband, and Heather L. Kaufman. New Haven, CT: Yale University Press.

Du Bois, W. E. B. (1987). "The Souls of Black Folk," in *Writings*. New York, NY: The Library of America.

Elster, Jon (1986). *An Introduction to Karl Marx*. Cambridge: Cambridge University Press.

Engelmann, Jan and Michael Tomasello (2019). "Children's Sense of Fairness as Equal Respect," *Trends in Cognitive Science* 23: 454–463.

Engels, Friedrich (1975). *Socialism: Utopian and Scientific*, in Collected Works of Karl Marx and Friedrich Engels, vol. 24. New York, NY: International Publishers Co.

Feinberg, Joel (1980). "The Nature and Value of Rights," in *Rights, Justice, and the Bounds of Liberty*. Princeton, NJ: Princeton University Press.

Feuerbach, Ludwig (1989). *The Essence of Christianity*, trans. George Eliot. Buffalo, NY: Prometheus Books.

Fichte, Johann Gottlieb (1982). *The Science of Knowledge*, ed. and trans. John Lachs and Peter Heath. Cambridge: Cambridge University Press.

Fichte, Johann Gottlieb (1987). *The Vocation of Man*, ed. and trans. Peter Preuss. Indianapolis, IN: Hackett Publishing Co.

Fichte, Johann Gottlieb (1988). *Fichte: Early Philosophical Writings*, ed. and trans. Daniel Breazeale. Ithaca, NY: Cornell University Press.

Fichte, Johann Gottlieb (1992). *Foundations of Transcendental Philosophy (Wissenschaftslehre) novo methodo*, ed. and trans. Daniel Breazeale. Ithaca, NY: Cornell University Press.

Fichte, Johann Gottlieb (2000). *Foundations of Natural Right*, ed. Frederick Neuhouser, trans. Michael Bauer. Cambridge: Cambridge University Press.

Fichte, Johann Gottlieb (2005). *The System of Ethics*, trans. and ed. Daniel Breazeale and Günter Zöller. Cambridge: Cambridge University Press.

Fichte, Johann Gottlieb (2013). *Addresses to the German Nation*, trans. Isaac Nakhimovsky, Béla Kapossy, and Keith Tribe. Indianapolis, IN: Hackett Publishing Co.

Fishkin, James S. (1991). *Democracy and Deliberation: New Directions for Democratic Reform*. New Haven, CT: Yale University Press.

Fleischacker, Samuel (2004). *A Short History of Distributive Justice*. Cambridge, MA: Harvard University Press.

Foot, Philippa (1991). "Nietzsche's Immoralism," *The New York Review of Books* 38: 11.

Foucault, Michel (1995). *Discipline and Punish: The Birth of the Prison*. New York, NY: Vintage Books.

Frankena, William (1942). "Obligation and Value in the Ethics of G. E. Moore." *The Philosophy of G. E. Moore*, ed. Paul A. Schilpp. La Salle, IL: Open Court.

Frankena, William (1963). *Ethics*. Englewood Cliffs, NJ: Prentice Hall.

Frankena, William (1992). "Sidgwick and the History of Ethical Dualism," in *Essays on Henry Sidgwick*, ed. Bart Schultz. Cambridge: Cambridge University Press.

Frankfurt, Harry (1998). *The Importance of What We Care About*. Cambridge: Cambridge University Press.

Frankl, Viktor E. (1963). *Man's Search for Meaning: An Introduction to Logotherapy*. Boston, MA: Beacon Press.

Fromm, Erich (1941). *Escape From Freedom*. New York, NY: Holt, Rinehart, and Winston.

Furner, James (2019). *Marx on Capitalism: The Interaction-Recognition-Antinomy Thesis*. Leiden: Brill.

Ganesh, Akshay (2017). "Nietzsche on Honor and Empathy," *Journal of Nietzsche Studies* 48: 219–244.

Garrett, Aaron (2004). "Hume's 'Original Difference': Race, National Character and the Human Sciences," *Eighteenth-Century Thought* 2: 127–152.

Garrett, Aaron (2007). "Francis Hutcheson and the Origin of Animal Rights," *Journal of the History of Philosophy* 45: 243–265.

Gay, John (1731). *A Dissertation Concerning the Fundamental Principle and Immediate Criterion of Virtue. As Also, the Obligation to, and Approbation of It. With Some Account of the Origin of the Passions and Affection*. "Prefix'd" to William King, Essay on the Origin of Evil. London: R. Knaplock, J., J. Knapton, and W. Innis.

Gibbard, Allan (1990). *Wise Choices, Apt Feelings*. Cambridge, MA: Harvard University Press.

Godwin, William (2013). *An Enquiry Concerning Political Justice*, ed. Mark Philip. Oxford: Oxford University Press.

Gooding-Williams, Robert (2001). *Zarathustra's Dionysian Modernism*. Palo Alto, CA: Stanford University Press.

Graeber, David (2011). *Debt: The First 5,000 Years*. Brooklyn, NY: Melville House.

Green, T. H. (1881). *Liberal Legislation and the Freedom of Contract*. Oxford: Slatery and Rose.

Green, T. H. (1885–1888). *The Works of T. H. Green*, 3 vols., ed. R. L. Nettleship. London: Longmans Green.

Green, T. H. (1921). *Lectures on the Principles of Political Obligation*, in with a preface by Bernard Bosanquet. New York, NY: Longmans, Green and Co. References are to section number.

Green, T. H. (2003). *Prolegomena to Ethics*, ed. with an intro. David O. Brink. Oxford: Clarendon Press. References are to section number.

Grotius, Hugo (2005). *The Rights of War and Peace*, 3 vols., ed. Richard Tuck. From the 1738 English translation by John Morrice of Jean Barbeyrac's French translation, with Barbeyrac's notes. Indianapolis, IN: Liberty Fund. Originally published in 1625.

Habermas, Jürgen (1990a). *Moral Consciousness and Communicative Action*, trans. Christian Lenhardt and Shierry Weber Nicholsen. Cambridge, MA: MIT Press.

Habermas, Jürgen (1990b). *The Philosophical Discourse of Modernity*, trans. Frederick G. Laurence. Cambridge, MA: MIT Press.

Hannay, Alastair (2001). *Kierkegaard: A Biography*. Cambridge: Cambridge University Press.

Hardimon, Michael (1992). "The Project of Reconciliation: Hegel's Social Philosophy," *Philosophy & Public Affairs* 21: 165–195.

Hardimon, Michael (1994). *Hegel's Social Philosophy: The Project of Reconciliation*. Cambridge: Cambridge University Press.

Hare, R. M. (1952). *The Language of Morals*. Oxford: Clarendon Press.

Hare, R. M. (1980). *Moral Thinking: Its Levels, Methods, and Point*. Oxford: Oxford University Press.

Harrison, Ross (1983). *Bentham*. London: Routledge & Kegan Paul.

Harrison, Ross (1996). "Philosophers VI: Henry Sidgwick," *Philosophy* 71: 423–438.

Harsanyi, J. C. (1975). "Can the Maximin Principle Serve as a Basis for Morality? A Critique of John Rawls's Theory," *The American Political Science Review* 69: 594–606.

Harsanyi, J. C. (1977). "Morality and the Theory of Rational Behavior," *Social Research an International Quarterly* 44: 623–656.

Hart, H. L. A. (1961). *The Concept of Law*. Oxford: Clarendon Press.

Hart, H. L. A. (2012). *The Concept of Law*, 3rd ed., ed. Leslie Green. Oxford: Oxford University Press.

Harvey, David (2018). *A Companion to Marx's Capital: The Complete Edition*. London: Verso.

Hegel, Georg Wilhelm Friedrich (1975a). *Hegel's Logic*, trans. William Wallace. Oxford: Oxford University Press. References are to section numbers.

Hegel, Georg Wilhelm Friedrich Hegel (1975b). *Natural Law*, trans. T. M. Knox, intro. H. B. Acton, foreword John Silber. Philadelphia, PA: University of Pennsylvania Press.

Hegel, Georg Wilhelm Friedrich Hegel (1977). *Phenomenology of Spirit*, trans. A. V. Miller, analysis and foreword J. N. Findlay. Oxford: Oxford University Press. Originally published in 1807.

Hegel, Georg Wilhelm Friedrich (1991). *Elements of the Philosophy of Right*, ed. Allen W. Wood and Hugh B. Nisbett. Cambridge: Cambridge University Press. Originally published in 1821.

Heidegger, Martin (1962). *Being and Time*, trans. John Macquarrie and Edward Robinson. New York, NY: Harper & Row, Publishers.

Heinrich, Michael (2019). *Karl Marx and the Birth of Modern Society: The Life of Marx and the Development of His Work*, vol. 1: *1818–1841*, trans. Alexander Locascio. New York, NY: Monthly Review Press.

Helvétius, Claude (1759). *L'esprit or, Essays on the Mind: and its Several Faculties*. London: Dodsley and Co.

Hobbes, Thomas (1994). *Leviathan*, ed. Edwin Curley. Indianapolis, IN: Hackett Publishing Co., Inc. Originally published in 1651. References are to chapter and paragraph number.

Hochschild, Adam (2005). *Bury the Chains: Prophets and Rebels in the Fight to Free an Empire's Slaves*. Boston, MA: Houghton Mifflin Company.

Hockett, Robert and Aaron James (2020). *Money From Nothing: Or, Why We Should Stop Worrying About Debt and Love the Federal Reserve*. Brooklyn, NY: Melville House.

Hohfeld, Wesley Newcomb (1923). *Fundamental Legal Conceptions as Applied in Judicial Reasoning and Other Legal Essays*. New Haven, CT: Yale University Press.

Hollingdale, R. J. (1999). *Nietzsche: The Man and His Philosophy*. Cambridge: Cambridge University Press.

Honneth, Axel (1996). *The Struggle for Recognition*. Cambridge, MA: MIT Press.

Hudson, W. D. (1970). *Modern Moral Philosophy*. Garden City, NY: Anchor Books.

Hume, David (1978). *A Treatise of Human Nature*, ed. L. A. Selby-Bigge, 2nd ed., with rev. P. H. Nidditch. Oxford: Oxford University Press. Originally published in 1739, 1740.

Hume, David (1985a). *An Enquiry Concerning Human Understanding*, in Enquiries Concerning Human Understanding and Concerning the Principles of Morals, ed. L. A. Selby-Bigge, 3rd. ed., rev. P. H. Nidditch. Oxford: Clarendon Press. Originally published in 1748.

Hume, David (1985b). *An Enquiry Concerning the Principles of Morals*, in Enquiries Concerning Human Understanding and Concerning the Principles of Morals, ed. L. A. Selby-Bigge, 3rd. ed., rev. P. H. Nidditch. Oxford: Clarendon Press. Originally published in 1751.

Hurka, Thomas (2003). "Moore in the Middle," *Ethics* 113: 599–628.

Hurka, Thomas (2014). *British Ethical Theorists from Sidgwick to Ewing*. Oxford: Oxford University Press.

Hussain, Nadeem J. Z. (2013). "Nietzsche's Metaethical Stance," in *The Oxford Handbook of Nietzsche*, ed. Ken Gemes and John Richardson. Oxford: Oxford University Press.

Hutcheson, Francis (1755). *A System of Moral Philosophy*, 2 vols. Glasgow: R. A. Foulis. Facsimile edition in Collected Works, vols. 5 and 6. Hildesheim: Olms, 1969–1971.

Hutcheson, Francis (2002). *An Essay on the Nature and Conduct of the Passions and Affections, with Illustrations on the Moral Sense*, ed. with an intro., Aaron Garrett. Indianapolis, IN: Liberty Fund. Originally published in 1728, 2nd ed., 1730, 3rd ed., 1742. This edition is based on the first edition but also includes passages from later editions.

Hutcheson, Francis (2004). *An Inquiry into the Original of Our Ideas of Beauty and Virtue in Two Treatises*, ed., with an intro., Wolfgang Leidhold. Indianapolis, IN: Liberty Fund. Based on the second edition, 1726; originally published in 1725. This edition also includes passages from the revised fifth edition 1753.

Irwin, Terence (2007). *The Development of Ethics: A Historical and Critical Study*, vol. 1: *From Socrates to the Reformation*. Oxford: Oxford University Press.

Irwin, Terence (2008). *The Development of Ethics: A Historical and Critical Study*, vol. 2: *From Suarez to Rousseau*. Oxford: Oxford University Press.

Irwin, Terence (2009). *The Development of Ethics: A Historical and Critical Study*, vol. 3: *From Kant to Rawls*. Oxford: Oxford University Press.

Jackson, Frank (1998). *From Metaphysics to Ethics: A Defence of Conceptual Analysis*. Oxford: Oxford University Press.

Jacobson, Daniel (2003). "J. S. Mill and the Diversity of Utilitarianism," *Philosophers' Imprint* 3: 1–18.

Jacobson, Daniel (2011). "Fitting-Attitude Theories of Value," *Stanford Encyclopedia of Philosophy*. https://plato.stanford.edu/Archives/win2021/entries/fitting-attitude-theories/.

Kagan, Shelly (2009). "Well-being and Enjoying the Good," *Philosophical Perspectives* 23: 253–272.

Kain, Philip J. (1988). *Marx and Ethics*. Oxford: Clarendon Press.

Kant, Immanuel (1996a). *Groundwork of the Metaphysics of Morals*. In *Practical Philosophy*, trans. and ed. Mary J. Gregor. Cambridge: Cambridge University Press. References are to page numbers of the Preussische Akademie edition. Originally published in 1785.

Kant, Immanuel (1996b). *Critique of Practical Reason*, in *Practical Philosophy*, trans. and ed. Mary J. Gregor. Cambridge: Cambridge University Press. Page references are to page numbers of the Preussische Akademie edition.

Kant, Immanuel (1996c). *Metaphysics of Morals*, in Practical Philosophy, trans. and ed. Mary J. Gregor. Cambridge: Cambridge University Press. Page references are to page numbers of the Preussische Akademie edition.

Kant, Immanuel (2018). *Religion Within the Boundaries of Mere Reason*, ed. Allen W. Wood and George Di Giovanni, foreword Robert Merrihew Adams. Cambridge: Cambridge University Press.

Katsafanas, Paul (2013). *Agency and the Foundations of Ethics: Nietzschean Constitutivism*. Oxford: Oxford University Press.

Katsafanas, Paul (2016). *The Nietzschean Self: Moral Psychology, Agency, and the Subconscious*. Oxford: Oxford University Press.

Kierkegaard, Søren (1980). *The Concept of Anxiety*, ed. and trans., with notes, Reidar Thomte. Princeton, NJ: Princeton University Press.

Kierkegaard, Søren (1983). *Fear and Trembling* and *Repetition*, ed. and trans. Howard V. Hong and Edna H. Hong. Princeton, NJ: Princeton University Press.

Kierkegaard, Søren (1985). *Philosophical Fragments: Johannes Climacus*, ed. and trans. Howard V. Hong and Edna H. Hong. Princeton, NJ: Princeton University Press.

Kierkegaard, Søren (1987a). *Either/Or*, Part I. ed. and trans. Howard V. Hong and Edna H. Hong. Princeton, NJ: Princeton University Press.

Kierkegaard, Søren (1987b). *Either/Or*, Part II. ed. and trans. Howard V. Hong and Edna H. Hong. Princeton, NJ: Princeton University Press.

Kierkegaard, Søren (1989). *The Concept of Irony, with Continual Reference to Socrates*, ed. and trans., with intro. and notes, Howard V. Hong and Edna H. Hong. Princeton, NJ: Princeton University Press.

Kierkegaard, Søren (1995). *Works of Love*. ed. and trans. Howard V. Hong and Edna H. Hong. Princeton, NJ: Princeton University Press.

Kierkegaard, Søren (2006). *Fear and Trembling*, ed. C. Stephen Evans and Sylvia Walsh. Cambridge: Cambridge University Press.

Kierkegaard, Søren (2009a). *The Point of View*, in Kierkegaard's Writings, ed. and trans. Howard V. Hong and Edna H. Hong. Princeton, NJ: Princeton University Press.

Kierkegaard, Søren (2009b). *Concluding Unscientific Postscript to the Philosophical Crumbs*, ed. and trans. Alastair Hannay. Cambridge: Cambridge University Press.

Korsgaard, Christine (1996a). *The Sources of Normativity*. Cambridge: Cambridge University Press.

Korsgaard, Christine (1996b). *Creating the Kingdom of Ends*. Cambridge: Cambridge University Press.

Korsgaard, Christine (1996c). "Morality as Freedom," in *Creating the Kingdom of Ends*. Cambridge: Cambridge University Press.

Kosch, Michelle (2006). *Freedom and Reason in Kant, Schelling, and Kierkegaard*. Oxford: Clarendon Press.

Kosch, Michelle (2018). *Fichte's Ethics*. Oxford: Oxford University Press.

Kosch, Michelle (2021). "Fichtean Kantianism in Nineteenth-Century Ethics," *Journal of the History of Philosophy*, 53: 111–132.

Lamb, Robert (2014). "William Godwin," in *The Encyclopedia of Political Thought*. https://onlinelibrary.wiley.com/doi/10.1002/9781118474396.wbept0426.

Leiter, Brian (1995). "Morality in the Pejorative Sense: On the Logic of Nietzsche's Critique of Morality," *British Journal for the History of Philosophy* 3: 113–145.

Leiter, Brian (2000). "Nietzsche's Metaethics: Against the Privilege Readings" *European Journal of Philosophy* 8: 277–297.

Leiter, Brian (2015). *Nietzsche on Morality*. Abingdon: Routledge.

Levy, David M. (2002). *How the Dismal Science Got Its Name: Classical Economics and the Ur-Text of Racial Politics*. Ann Arbor, MI: University of Michigan Press.

Lipscomb, Benjamin J. B. (2021). *The Women Are Up to Something: How Elizbeth Anscombe, Philippa Foot, Mary Midgley, and Iris Murdoch Revolutionized Ethcs*. New York, NY: Oxford University Press.

Locke, John (1975). *An Essay Concerning Human Understanding*, ed. Peter H. Nidditch. Oxford: Oxford University Press. Originally published in 1690; final, 4th ed., 1700.

Løgstrup, Knud Ejler (2007). *Beyond the Ethical Demand*. Introduction by Kees van Kooten Niekerk. Notre Dame, IN: University of Notre Dame Press.

Løgstrup, Knud Ejler (2020a). *The Ethical Demand*, trans. with intro. and notes by Bjørn Rabjerg and Robert Stern. Oxford: Oxford University Press.

Løgstrup, Knud Ejler (2020b). *Ethical Concepts and Problems*, trans. Kees van Kooten Niekerk and Kristian-Alberto Lykke Cobos, intro. Hans Fink and Kees van Kooten Niekerk, and notes Bjørn Rabjerg and Robert Stern. Oxford: Oxford University Press.

Lukes, Steven (1985). *Marxism and Morality*. New York, NY: Oxford University Press.

Mackie, J. L. (1977). *Ethics: Inventing Right and Wrong*. London: Pelican Books.

Mandeville, Bernard (1988). *The Fable of the Bees or Private Vices, Publick Benefits*, 2 vols. With a Commentary Critical, Historical, and Explanatory by F. B. Kaye. Indianapolis: Liberty Fund, 1988. Originally published in 1714.

Marx, Karl (1970). *Critique of Hegel's Philosophy of Right*, ed. Joseph J. O'Malley. Cambridge: Cambridge University Press.

Marx, Karl (1975a). *Contribution to the Critique of Hegel's Philosophy of Right*, in *Collected Works of Karl Marx and Friedrich Engels*, vol. 3. New York, NY: International Publishers Co.

Marx, Karl (1975b). *Economic and Philosophic Manuscripts*, in *Collected Works of Karl Marx and Friedrich Engels*, vol. 3. New York, NY: International Publishers Co.

Marx, Karl (1975c). "The Future Results of British Rule in India," in *Collected Works of Karl Marx and Friedrich Engels*, vol. 12. New York, NY: International Publishers Co.

Marx, Karl l(1975d). "Comments on James Mill," in *Collected Works of Karl Marx and Friedrich Engels*, vol. 3. New York, NY: International Publishers Co.

Marx, Karl (1975e). "On the Jewish Question," in *Collected Works of Karl Marx and Friedrich Engels*, vol. 3. New York, NY: International Publishers Co.

Marx, Karl (1975f). *Capital*, vol. 1, in *Collected Works of Karl Marx and Friedrich Engels*, vol. 3. New York, NY: International Publishers Co.

Marx, Karl (1978a). "For a Ruthless Criticism of Everything Existing," in *The Marx-Engels Reader*, ed. Robert C. Tucker, 2nd ed. New York, NY: Norton.

Marx, Karl (1978b). "Theses on Feuerbach," in *The Marx-Engels Reader*, ed. Robert C. Tucker, 2nd ed. New York, NY: Norton.

Marx, Karl and Friedrich Engels (1975a). *Collected Works of Karl Marx and Friedrich Engels*. London: Lawrence & Wishart.

Marx, Karl and Friedrich Engels (1975b). Manifesto of the Communist Party, in *Collected Works of Karl Marx and Friedrich Engels*, vol. 6.

Marx, Karl and Friedrich Engels (1975c). The German Ideology, in *Collected Works of Karl Marx and Friedrich Engels*, vol. 5.

Marx, Karl and Friedrich Engels (1975d). Circular Against Kriege, in *Collected Works of Karl Marx and Friedrich Engels*, vol. 6.

McNulty, Jacob (2016). "Transcendental Philosophy and Intersubjectivity: Mutual Recognition as a Condition of the Possibility of Self-Consciousness in Sections 1–3 of Fichte's *Foundations of Natural Right*," *European Journal of Philosophy* 24: 788–810.

McNulty, Jacob (2023). *Hegel's Logic and Metaphysics*. Cambridge: Cambridge University Press.

Mill, John Stuart (1967). *Essays on Economics and Society (Collected Works of John Stuart Mill)*, ed. John M. Robson, intro. Lord Robbins. Toronto: University of Toronto Press.

Mill, John Stuart (1977). *On Liberty*, in *Essays on Politics and Society (Collected Works of John Stuart Mill)*, ed. John M. Robson, intro. Alexander Brady. Toronto: University of Toronto Press.

Mill, John Stuart (1981). *Autobiography and Literary Essays (Collected Works of John Stuart Mill)*, ed. John M. Robson and Jack Stillinger. Toronto: University of Toronto Press.

Mill, John Stuart (with the collaboration of Harriet Taylor) (1984). *The Subjection of Women*, in *Essays on Equality, Law, and Education (Collected Works of John Stuart Mill)*, ed. John M. Robson, intro. Stefan Collini. Toronto: University of Toronto Press.

Mill, John Stuart (1985). "Whewell on Moral Philosophy," in *Essays on Ethics, Religion and Society (Collected Works of John Stuart Mill)*, ed. John M. Robson, intro. F. E. L. Priestley. Toronto: University of Toronto Press.

Mill, John Stuart (2002). *Utilitarianism*, ed. George Sher. Indianapolis, IN: Hackett Publishing Co. References to chapter and paragraph numbers.

Mill, John Stuart (2004). *Principles of Political Economy: With Some of Their Applications to Social Philosophy*, abridged, ed., with an intro., Stephen Nathanson. Indianapolis, IN: Hackett Publishing Co.

Mill, J. S. and Jeremy Bentham (1987). *Utilitarianism and Other Essays*, ed. Alan Ryan. London: Penguin Books.

Mills, Charles W. (2005). "Ideal Theory as Ideology," *Hypatia* 20: 165–184.

Moore, G. E. (1993a). *Principia Ethica*, rev. ed. with the preface to the (projected) second ed and other papers, ed. with an intro. Thomas Baldwin. Cambridge: Cambridge University Press.

Moore, G. E. (1993b). "On the Concept of Intrinsic Value," in *Principia Ethica*, rev. ed. with the preface to the (projected) second ed and other papers, ed. with an intro. Thomas Baldwin. Cambridge: Cambridge University Press.

Muller, Jerry Z. (1995). *Adam Smith in His Time and Ours: Designing the Decent Society*. Princeton, NJ: Princeton University Press.

Murdoch, Iris (2001). *The Sovereignty of the Good*. London: Routledge Classics.

Nagel, Thomas (1970). *The Possibility of Altruism*. Oxford: Clarendon Press.

Nehamas, Alexander (1985). *Nietzsche: Life as Literature*. Cambridge, MA: Harvard University Press.

Neuhouser, Frederick (1990). *Fichte's Theory of Subjectivity*. Cambridge: Cambridge University Press.

Nietzsche, Friedrich (1967). *On the Genealogy of Morals and Ecce Homo*, ed., with commentary, Walter Kaufmann, trans. Walter Kaufmann and R. J. Hollingdale. New York, NY: Vintage Books.

Nietzsche, Friedrich (1982). *Daybreak: Thoughts on the Prejudices of Morality*, trans. R. J. Hollingdale, intro. Michael Tanner. Cambridge: Cambridge University Press.

Nietzsche, Friedrich (1989). *Beyond Good and Evil*, trans. and comment Walter Kaufmann. New York, NY: Vintage Books.

Nietzsche, Friedrich (1996). *Human, All Too Human*, trans. R. J. Hollingdale, intro. Richard Schacht. Cambridge: Cambridge University Press.

Nietzsche, Friedrich (1997). *Daybreak: Thoughts on the Prejudices of Morality*, ed. Maudemarie Clark and Brian Leiter. Cambridge: Cambridge University Press.

Nietzsche, Friedrich (1999). *The Birth of Tragedy and Other Writings*, ed. Raymond Geuss and Ronald Spiers, trans. Ronald Spiers. Cambridge: Cambridge University Press.

Nietzsche, Friedrich (2001). *The Gay Science: With a Prelude in German Rhymes and an Appendix of Songs*, trans. Josephine Nauckhoff and Adrian Del Caro. Cambridge: Cambridge University of Press.

Nietzsche, Friedrich (2002). *Beyond Good and Evil*, ed. Rolf-Peter Horstmann and Judith Norman, trans. Judith Norman. Cambridge: Cambridge University Press.

Nietzsche, Friedrich (2005). *The Anti-Christ, Ecce Homo, Twilight of the Idols*, ed. Aaron Ridley and Judith Norman, trans. Judith Norman. Cambridge: Cambridge University Press.

Nietzsche, Friedrich (2007). *On the Genealogy of Morality*, ed. Keith Ansell-Pearson, trans. Carol Diethe. Cambridge: Cambridge University Press.

Norcross, Alastair (2020). *Morality By Degrees: Reasons Without Demands*. Oxford: Oxford University Press.

Nozick, Robert (1974). *Anarchy, State, and Utopia*. New York, NY: Basic Books.

Overvold, Mark (1980). "Self-Interest and the Concept of Self-Sacrifice," *Canadian Journal of Philosophy* 10: 105–118.

Oxford English Dictionary (2024). Oxford: Oxford University Press.

Padover, Saul Kussiel (1979). *The Letters of Karl Marx*. Englewood Cliffs, NJ: Prentice-Hall.

Paley, William (2002). *Principles of Moral and Political Philosophy*. Indianapolis, IN: Liberty Fund.

Parfit, Derek (1984). *Reasons and Persons*. Oxford: Oxford University Press.

Parfit, Derek (2011). *On What Matters*, 2 vols. Oxford: Oxford University Press.

Perovic, Katarina (2017). "Bradley's Regress," *Stanford Encyclopedia of Philosophy*. https://plato.stanford.edu/entries/bradley-regress/.

Pettit, Philip and Michael Smith (1990). "Backgrounding Desire," *The Philosophical Review*, 99: 565–592.

Phillips, David (1998). "Sidgwick, Dualism, and Indeterminacy in Practical Reason," *History of Philosophy Quarterly* 15: 47–78.

Phillips, David (2011). *Sidgwickian Ethics*. Oxford: Oxford University Press.

Pinkard, Terry (1994). *Hegel's Phenomenology: The Sociality of Reason*. Cambridge: Cambridge University Press

Pinker, Steven (2011). *The Better Angels of Our Nature*. New York, NY: Viking Press.

Pippin, Robert (1997). *Idealism as Modernism: Hegelian Variations*. Cambridge: Cambridge University Press.

Plato (1997). *The Republic*, in *Plato: The Complete Works*, ed. John M. Cooper. Indianapolis, IN: Hackett Publishing Co.

Postema, Gerald (1986). *Bentham and the Common Law Tradition*. Oxford: Oxford University Press.

Prichard, H. A. (1912). "Does Moral Philosophy Rest on a Mistake?," *Mind* 21: 21–37.

Pufendorf, Samuel (1934). *On the Law of Nature and Nations*, trans. C. H. Oldfather and W. A. Oldfather. Oxford: Clarendon Press. Originally published in 1672.

Pufendorf, Samuel (2009). *Two Books of the Elements of Universal Jurisprudence*, ed. Thomas Behne, trans. W. A. Oldfather, with revisions by Thomas Behne. Indianapolis, IN: Liberty Fund. Originally published in 1660.

Quine, W. V. O. (1969). "Epistemology Naturalized," in *Ontological Relativity and Other Essays*. New York, NY: Columbia University Press.

Rawls, John (1955). "Two Concepts of Rules," *The Philosophical Review* 64: 3–32.

Rawls, John (1971). *A Theory of Justice*. Cambridge, MA: Harvard University Press.

Rawls, John (1980). "Kantian Constructivism in Moral Theory," *The Journal of Philosophy*, 77: 515–572.

Rawls, John (1985). "Justice as Fairness: Political, Not Metaphysical," *Philosophy & Public Affairs* 14: 223–251.

Rawls, John (1993). *Political Liberalism*. New York, NY: Columbia University Press.

Rawls, John (2000). *Lectures on the History of Moral Philosophy*, ed. Barbara Herman. Cambridge, MA: Harvard University Press.

Rawls, John (2007). *Lectures on the History of Moral Philosophy*, ed. Samuel Freeman. Cambridge, MA: Harvard University Press.

Rée, Paul (2003). *The Origin of the Moral Sensations*, ed. Robin Small. Chicago, IL: University of Illinois Press.

Regan, Donald H. (1980). *Utilitarianism and Cooperation*. Oxford: Clarendon Press.

Reginster, Bernard (2009). *The Affirmation of Life: Nietzsche on Overcoming Nihilism*. Cambridge, MA: Harvard University Press.

Ripstein, Arthur (2009). *Force and Freedom: Kant's Legal and Political Philosophy*. Cambridge, MA: Harvard University Press.

Ritchie, D.G. (1891). *The Principles of State Interference: Four Essays on the Political Philosophy of Mr. Herbert Spencer, J. S. Mill, and T. H. Green*. London: Swan Sonnenschein.

Rosen, Michael E. (1999). "Continental Philosophy from Hegel," in *Philosophy 2: Further Through the Subject*, vol. 2., ed. A. C. Grayling. Oxford: Oxford University Press.

Ross, W. D. (2002). *The Right and the Good*, ed. Philip Stratton-Lake. Oxford: Clarendon Press.

Rousseau, Jean Jacques (2011). *Discourse on the Origin of Inequality*, ed. Donald A. Cress. Indianapolis, IN: Hackett Publishing Co.

Rowe, David Emmanuel (2019). *A Nietzschean Metaethics: Criticism of Some Contemporary Themes in Metaethics*. Lanham, MD: Lexington Books.

Sartre, Jean-Paul (2020). *Being and Nothingness: An Essay in Phenomenological Ontology*, trans. and translator's introduction, Sarah Richmond, intro. Richard Moran. London: Routledge.

Scanlon, T. M. (1982). "Contractualism and Utilitarianism," in *Utilitarianism and Beyond*, ed. A. K. Sen and Bernard Williams. Cambridge: Cambridge University Press.

Scanlon, T. M. (1998). *What We Owe to Each Other*. Cambridge, MA: Harvard University Press.

Scanlon, T. M. (2014). *Being Realistic about Reasons*. Oxford: Oxford University Press.

Schacht, Richard (1983). *Nietzsche*. London: Routledge & Kegan Paul.

Schapiro, Tamar (2001). "Three Conceptions of Action in Moral Theory," *Noûs* 35: 93–117.

Schapiro, Tamar (2021). *Feeling Like It: A Theory of Inclination and Will.* Oxford: Oxford University Press.

Scheler, Max (1961). *Ressentiment.* Milwaukee, WI: Maquette University Press.

Scheler, Max (1994). *Ressentiment,* ed. Lewis A. Coser, trans. William W. Holdheim. New York, NY: Free Press of Glencoe.

Schneewind, J. B. (1977). *Sidgwick's Ethics and Victorian Moral Philosophy.* Oxford: Oxford University Press, 1977.

Schopenhauer, Arthur (1969). *The World as Will and Representation,* trans., E. F. J. Payne. New York, NY: Dover.

Schopenhauer, Arthur (1995). *On the Basis of Morality,* trans., E. F. J. Payne, intro. David E. Cartwright. Indianapolis, IN: Hackett Publishing Co.

Schultz, Bart (2004). *Sidgwick: The Eye of the Universe.* Cambridge: Cambridge University Press.

Sellars, Wilfrid (1963). "Empiricism and the Philosophy of Mind," in *Science, Perception, and Reality.* London: Routledge & Kegan Paul.

Sen, Amartya (1979). "Utilitarianism and Welfarism" *Journal of Philosophy* 76: 463–489,

Seth, Andrew (1901). "The Ethical System of Henry Sidgwick," *Mind* 38: 172–187.

Seth Pringle-Pattison, Andrew (1907). *Philosophical Radicals and Other Essays with Chapters Reprinted on the Philosophy of Religion in Kant and Hegel.* Edinburgh: W. Blackwood and Sons.

Shaver, Rob (2000). "Sidgwick's Minimal Metaethics," *Utilitas* 12: 26–277.

Shaver, Rob (2006). "Sidgwick on Moral Motivation," *Philosophers' Imprint* 6: 1–14.

Shaver, Rob (2014). "Sidgwick's Axioms and Consequentialism," *The Philosophical Review* 123: 173–204.

Sidgwick, Arthur, and Eleanor Sidgwick (1906). *Henry Sidgwick: A Memoir.* London: Macmillan and Co.

Sidgwick, Henry (1876). "*Ethical Studies*: Critical Notice," *Mind* 1: 545–549.

Sidgwick, Henry (1887). *Principles of Political Economy,* 2nd ed. London: Macmillan.

Sidgwick, Henry (1962). *The Methods of Ethics,* 7th ed. London: Macmillan.

Sidgwick, Henry (1964). *Outlines of the History of Ethics for English Readers,* 6th ed. Boston, MA: Beacon Press.

Sidgwick, Henry (1981). *The Methods of Ethics,* 7th ed., foreword, John Rawls. Indianapolis, IN: Hackett Publishing Company.

Sidgwick, Henry (2000). *Essays on Ethics and Method,* ed. Marcus G. Singer. Oxford: Oxford University Press.

Silk, Alex (2015). "Nietzschean Constructivism: Ethics and Metaethics for All and None," *Inquiry: An International Journal of Philosophy* 48: 244–280.

Singer, Peter (1974). "Sidgwick and Reflective Equilibrium," *The Monist* 58: 490–517.

Skelton, Anthony (2010). "Sidgwick's Moral Epistemology," *Journal of the History of Philosophy* 48: 491–519.

Skorupski, John (2006). "Green and the Idealist Conception of a Person's Good," in *T. H. Green: Ethics, Metaphysics, and Political Philosophy*, ed. Maria Dimova-Cookson and W. J. Mander. Oxford: Oxford University Press.

Smart, J. J. C. and Bernard Williams (1973). *Utilitarianism: For and Against*. Cambridge: Cambridge University Press.

Smith, Adam (1976). *An Inquiry into the Nature and Causes of the Wealth of Nations*, ed. R. H. Campbell and A. S. Skinner. Oxford: Clarendon Press. Originally published in 1776.

Smith, Adam (1982). *The Theory of Moral Sentiments*, ed. D. D. Raphael and A. L. MacFie. Indianapolis, IN: Liberty Classics. Originally published in 1759.

Smith, Michael (1994). *The Moral Problem*. Oxford: Blackwell.

Stern, Robert (2021). "Is Hegelian Recognition Second-Personal? Hegel Says 'No,'" *European Journal of Philosophy* 29: 608–623.

Stocker, Michael (1976). "The Schizophrenia of Modern Ethical Theories," *The Journal of Philosophy* 73: 453–466.

Strawson, P. F. (1968). "Freedom and Resentment," in *Studies in the Philosophy of Thought and Action*. London: Oxford University Press.

Suárez, Francisco (1944). *A Treatise on Laws and God the Lawgiver*, trans. Gwladys L. Williams, Ammi Brown, and John Waldron, rev. Henry Davis, S. J., intro. James Brown Scott, in *Selections from Three Works of Francisco Suarez, S. J.*, vol. 2. Oxford: Clarendon Press, 1944. Originally published in 1612.

Tilly, Charles (2005). *Identities, Boundaries, and Social Ties*. Boulder, CO: Paradigm Publishers.

Tilly, Charles and Sidney Tarrow (2006). *Contentious Politics*. New York, NY: Oxford University Press.

Tomasello, Michael (2016). *A Natural History of Human Morality*. Cambridge, MA: Harvard University Press.

Tucker, Robert C. (1969). *The Marxian Revolutionary Idea*. New York, NY: Norton.

Ullmann-Margalit, Edna and Sidney Morgenbesser (1977). "Picking and Choosing," *Social Research* 44: 757–785.

Wahrman, Dror (2006). *The Making of the Modern Self: Identity and Culture in Eighteenth-Century England*. New Haven, CT: Yale University Press.

Wallace, R. Jay (1994). *Responsibility and the Moral Sentiments*. Cambridge, MA: Harvard University Press.

Ware, Owen (2010). "Fichte's Voluntarism," *European Journal of Philosophy* 18: 262–282.

Watson, Gary (1975). "Free Agency," *Journal of Philosophy* 72: 205–220.

Watson, Gary (1987). "Responsibility and the Limits of Evil: Variations on a Strawsonian Theme," in *Responsibility, Character, and the Emotions: New Essays in Moral Psychology*, ed. F. D. Schoeman. Cambridge: Cambridge University Press.

Watson, Gary (1996). "Two Faces of Responsibility," *Philosophical Topics* 24: 227–248.

Weber, Max (2002). *The Protestant Ethic and the "Spirit" of Capitalism*, ed. Peter Baehr and Gordon C. Wells. New York, NY: Penguin Books.

Weil, Simone (2005). *Simone Weill: An Anthology*, ed. and intro. Siân Miles. London: Penguin Books.

Whewell, William (1852). *Lectures on the History of Moral Philosophy in England*. Cambridge: Deighton, Bell.

Williams, Bernard (1981a). *Moral Luck*. Cambridge: Cambridge University Press.

Williams, Bernard (1981b). "Internal and External Reasons," in *Moral Luck*. Cambridge: Cambridge University Press.

Williams, Bernard (1985). *Ethics and the Limits of Philosophy*. Cambridge, MA: Harvard University Press.

Williford, Miriam (1975). "Bentham on the Rights of Women," *Journal of the History of Ideas* 36: 167–176.

Wolf, Susan (1987). "Sanity and Moral Responsibility," *Responsibility, Character, and the Emotions: New Essays in Moral Psychology*, ed. F. D. Schoeman. Cambridge: Cambridge University Press.

Wolf, Susan (1997). "Meaning and Morality," *Proceedings of the Aristotelian Society* 97: 299–315.

Wolf, Susan (2014). "Lessons in Love from *The Philadelphia Story*," in *The Variety of Values: Essays on Morality, Meaning, and Love*. Oxford: Oxford University Press

Wollstonecraft, Mary (1995). *A Vindication of the Rights of Men and Women*. Cambridge: Cambridge University Press.

Wood, Allen W. (1990). *Hegel's Ethical Thought*. Cambridge: Cambridge University Press.

Wood, Allen W. (1999). *Kant's Ethical Thought*. Cambridge: Cambridge University Press.

Wood, Allen W. (2004). *Karl Marx*. New York, NY: Routledge.

Wood, Allen W. (2016). *Fichte's Ethical Thought*. Oxford: Oxford University Press.

Young, Julian (2010). *Friedrich Nietzsche: A Philosophical Biography*. Cambridge: Cambridge University Press.

Index